The Windows 2000 Professional Cram Sheet

This Cram Sheet contains the distilled, key facts about developing and implementing Windows 2000 Professional. Review this information as the last thing you do before you enter the testing center, paying special attention to those areas where you feel you need the most review. You can transfer any of these facts from your head onto a blank sheet of paper immediately before you begin the exam.

ADMINISTERING RESOURCES

1. Hidden or administrative shares are share names with a dollar sign ($) appended to their names. Administrative shares are created automatically for the root of each drive letter. Hidden shares do not display in the network browse list.

2. You can allow or deny share permissions of Full Control, Change, or Read for each shared folder. The default for new shares is Everyone, Allow, Full Control. If share permissions conflict with NTFS permissions, the *most restrictive* permissions take precedence.

3. NTFS permissions are cumulative for all permissions assigned to users and groups. When you combine NTFS permissions based on users and their group memberships, the *least restrictive* permissions take precedence. However, explicit Deny entries *always override* Allow entries.

4. By default, NTFS permissions are inherited from the parent folder. Permissions that are not inherited are referred to as *explicit*. Explicit permissions always override inherited permissions; explicit Allow will even override an inherited Deny permission.

5. To change NTFS permissions on a file or folder, you must be the owner or have the Change Permissions permission, which itself is part of Full Control. NTFS permissions are transferred when you move or copy files.

6. NTFS for Windows 2000 supports both file compression and data encryption. Encryption is implemented via Encrypting File System (EFS). You can compress or encrypt a file, but not both.

7. Windows 2000 print server computers automatically download the correct printer drivers for client computers running Windows as long as the correct drivers have been installed on the print server.

8. Windows 2000 Professional computers can connect to printers that are attached to Windows 2000 print servers through a Web browser. You can enter one of the following URLs into your Web browser:

   - http://print_server_name/printers
   - http://print_server_name/printer_share_name

9. To change NTFS permissions on a file or folder, you must be the owner or have the Change Permissions permission, which itself is part of Full Control. NTFS permissions are retained from the source folder whenever you move subfolders or files to another folder on the same NTFS volume. NTFS permissions are inherited from the destination folder for all other move and copy operations.

10. If the person who originally encrypted files using EFS moves or copies them to another NTFS folder, they remain encrypted. Encrypted files that are moved or copied to a FAT or FAT32 drive volume become decrypted. If users (other than the user who encrypted the file) attempt to move an encrypted file to a different NTFS volume or to a FAT or FAT32 drive volume, they receive an Access Is Denied error message. If users other than the user who encrypted the file attempt to move the encrypted file to a different folder located on the same NTFS volume, the file is moved.

USER AND GROUP ACCOUNTS

11. Local user and group accounts can be granted privileges and permissions to resources on the same system only. They cannot access resources on other systems.

58. Auto Private IP Addressing (APIPA) takes effect on Windows 2000 Professional computers if no DHCP server can be contacted. APIPA assigns the computer an IP address within the range of 169.254.0.0 through 169.254.255.254 with a subnet mask of 255.255.0.0.

59. IPSec negotiates encryption settings between the client and server to encrypt both passwords and data before an L2TP session is created.

60. EAP is an extension of Point-to-Point Protocol (PPP) for dial-up connections, and L2TP and PPTP clients. EAP supports several authentication protocols:

- Message Digest 5 Challenge Handshake Authentication Protocol (MD5-CHAP)
- Generic token cards
- Transport Layer Security (TLS) for use with smart cards

61. Bandwidth Allocation Protocol (BAP) works together with Bandwidth Allocation Control Protocol (BACP) as enhancements to Multilink to dynamically add or drop dial-up lines based on pre-defined usage levels. BAP is configured as a remote access policy.

62. Internet Connection Sharing (ICS) uses the DHCP Allocator service to assign dynamic IP addresses to clients on the LAN within the range of 192.168.0.2 through 192.168.0.254. In addition, the DNS Proxy service becomes enabled when you implement ICS.

TROUBLESHOOTING, MONITORING, AND OPTIMIZATION

63. You can back up and restore files and directories with Windows Backup. You can launch this from the Accessories Program group, the System applet, the ntbackup command, or the Properties sheet of any drive volume. Users can back up files to which they have at least the Read permission, and they can restore files to which they have at least the Write permission. To back up or restore other files, users must have the Backup Files and Directories, as well as Restore Files and Directories user rights.

64. Backing up the system state allows you to back up the registry, COM+ objects, and system startup files.

65. Know the following options for troubleshooting a system:

- The Recovery Console is a command-line interface you must boot to using the Windows 2000 CD-ROM, or startup floppies, or by running winnt32 /cmdcons *before* a failure. It is particularly useful for copying files from a CD-ROM or floppy disk to the system folder (WINNT) and for configuring services not to start up during the next boot. You can also run chkdsk (to scan the disk for file and sector errors), diskpart (to create or delete partitions), and fixboot (to replace the hard drive's boot sector).

- Safe Mode is generally the most useful troubleshooting mode because it starts the operating system with minimal services and drivers. It is best for removing services or drivers that are causing blue screens of death.

- Last Known Good Configuration starts the system with the ControlSet (a portion of the registry) that was used the last time the system booted successfully and instantiated the shell. If you install a driver or service that crashes *before you restart and log on again successfully*, you can restart the machine and select Last Known Good Configuration. Doing so effectively removes the driver or service from the active registry.

- The repair process allows you to recover system files, the startup environment, and the registry. To use it, boot a system with the Windows 2000 CD-ROM or start-up floppies and choose Repair. You can then select a Fast Repair or Manual Repair. Fast Repair is the only mode that restores the registry. Some options require the Emergency Repair Disk (ERD), which you create using Windows Backup. The Windows NT 4 command rdisk no longer works.

66. Task Manager allows you to monitor particular performance metrics and to set the priority of applications. You should not select Realtime priority, which can interfere with other applications.

67. Logical disk counters must be enabled using the diskperf -yv command.

36. Install hardware with the Add/Remove Hardware Wizard.

37. Update drivers with Device Manager.

38. Windows 2000 can control whether users can install signed or unsigned drivers, or both, for a chosen device. The selection for this is called Driver Signing and is made in a Group Policy Object (GPO) or Local Computer Policy Object. The three choices for Driver Signing are Ignore, Warn, and Block.

39. The Advanced Printer Properties sheet allows you to change the directory that contains the print spooler for a given printer.

40. To connect using both your own connection and your remote access server, you must have multi-link enabled. This is done in the network and dial-up connection properties.

41. Multiple displays have to use peripheral connection interface (PCI) or Accelerated Graphics Port (AGP) port devices to work properly with Windows 2000. Configure multiple displays in the Display properties.

42. Power Options in Control Panel lets you customize your power scheme settings. Standby does not save your desktop state to disk; if a power failure occurs while the computer is on standby, you can lose unsaved information. The hibernate feature saves everything in memory to disk, turns off your monitor and hard disk, and then turns off your computer.

43. Windows 2000 Professional supports a maximum of two CPUs, without OEM modifications.

DISKS AND FILE SYSTEMS

44. A Windows 2000 basic disk is a physical disk with primary and extended partitions. You can create up to three primary partitions and one extended partition with logical drives on a basic disk, or just four primary partitions. You cannot extend a basic disk.

45. A Windows 2000 dynamic disk is a physical disk that does not use partitions or logical drives. Instead, it has only dynamic volumes that you create using the Disk Management console. You can extend a volume on a dynamic disk. Dynamic disks can contain an unlimited number of volumes. Only Windows 2000 computers can directly access local dynamic volumes. However, computers that are not running Windows 2000 can access shared folders on dynamic volumes over the network.

46. You can convert a dynamic disk with volumes back to a basic disk, but you'll lose all your data. If you find yourself needing to do this, first save your data, convert the disk to basic, and then restore your data.

47. Mounted drives, also known as mount points or mounted volumes, are useful for increasing a drive's size without disturbing it. Drive paths are available only on empty folders on NTFS volumes. The NTFS volumes can be basic or dynamic.

48. Windows 2000 has FAT (also known as FAT16) and FAT32 file system support with the following conditions or specifications:

    - Pre-existing FAT32 partitions up to 127GB mount and are supported in Windows 2000.

    - Windows 2000 allows you to create new FAT32 volumes of only 32GB or less.

49. When you install Windows 2000, existing NTFS volumes are upgraded to NTFS 5 automatically.

50. Disk quotas track and control disk usage on a per-user, per-volume basis. You can apply disk quotas only to Windows 2000 NTFS volumes. Disk quotas do not use compression to measure disk space usage, so users cannot obtain or use more space simply by compressing their own data. To enable disk quotas, open the Properties dialog box for a disk, select the Quota tab, and configure the options.

51. If the uncompressed size of a compressed file is larger than the capacity of the floppy disk, you cannot copy or move the file to the disk. Use a third-party compression tool, such as WinZip, for this operation.

52. To convert a volume from FAT(32) to NTFS use convert d: /fs:ntfs. This command is one way and is not reversible. After the conversion, NTFS file permissions are set to Full Control for the Everyone group, whereas if you install Windows 2000 directly to NTFS, the default security settings for the WINNT and Program Files folders are more restrictive.

NETWORK PROTOCOLS AND SERVICES

53. TCP/IP is the default protocol suite. Its default setting is to obtain an IP address automatically. All IP addresses must have a subnet mask.

54. DHCP runs on Windows NT and Windows 2000 Server computers to automatically lease dynamic IP addresses to client computers.

55. DNS is required for Active Directory. DNS provides name resolution by mapping hostnames to IP addresses and vice versa.

56. WINS is not required for Active Directory. WINS offers name resolution by mapping NetBIOS computer names to IP addresses and vice versa.

57. To troubleshoot TCP/IP connectivity problems, use the ipconfig and ping command-line utilities. The ipconfig tool displays the local computer's IP configuration; ping tests connectivity to remote computers and can test the local configuration by pinging the loopback address of 127.0.0.1.

12. Local user accounts can belong to local groups on the same system only. They cannot belong to any other group type or to groups on any other system. A local group cannot be a member of any other group. Domain user accounts can belong to global groups in the domain, universal groups, domain local groups, and machine local groups.

13. Renaming an account maintains all group memberships, permissions, and privileges of the account. Copying a user account maintains group memberships, permissions, and privileges assigned to its groups, but doing so does not retain permissions associated with the original user account. Deleting and re-creating an account with the same name loses all group memberships and permissions.

14. The most powerful group on a system is its local Administrators group. Removing users from this group and putting them in groups such as Power Users and Backup Operators gives these users broad control of a system but less power.

15. Organizational Units (OUs) in Active Directory create a hierarchical structure of containers for other objects, such as users, groups, and computers. Objects inherit attributes of their parent objects.

16. You can remember the application of Group Policy as LSDOU (local, site, domain, OU). The closer a policy is to a user or computer, the more it wins over higher-level policies when a conflict occurs.

17. Incremental security templates for Windows 2000 can be applied to systems using the Security Configuration and Analysis snap-in.

INSTALLATION AND CONFIGURATION

18. Know all the following processes for unattended and Remote Installation Service (RIS) installations:

- winnt.sif—Used to automate CD-ROM–based installs.

- sysprep.inf—The answer file for System Preparation (Sysprep) installs.

- winnt.exe with the /u, /s, and /udf switches— Used for unattended installations.

- winnt32.exe and unattend.txt—Automate an upgrade to Windows 2000.

- Requirements for RIS—Active Directory, DNS, and DHCP.

19. winnt32.exe and checkupgradeonly are used to verify hardware and software compatibility.

20. Upgrade packs (or migration DLLs) are used during an upgrade to ensure that applications will run after the upgrade to Windows 2000 has been completed.

21. rbfg.exe is used to create remote boot disks for RIS clients if computers don't have network adapters with Pre-boot Execution Environment (PXE) boot ROM.

22. riprep.exe is used to create images of Windows 2000 Professional and applications for an RIS server.

23. risetup.exe is used to configure RIS.

24. update.exe /s is used to apply a service pack to a distribution share in slipstream mode.

CONFIGURING THE USER AND SYSTEM ENVIRONMENT

25. Know the purpose and configuration of all the accessibility features: StickyKeys, FilterKeys Narrator, Magnifier, and On-Screen Keyboard.

26. The Accessibility Wizard is an easy way to turn on accessibility features. The resulting settings can be saved with an .acw file extension. By default, this file is accessible only by the user who created the file and the administrator.

27. The Regional Options applet controls user and input locales. It can also be used to add new language groups. Also, you can use this applet to pair input locales with a specific keyboard layout when a user needs to type in different languages.

28. Use the Fax Service Management console to configure the fax modem to receive faxes. By default, only an administrator can configure the fax service options.

29. The Fax applet appears only if a fax device has been installed.

30. Applications can be deployed to users via a Group Policy. Applications can be either published or assigned. Install published applications via the Add/Remove Programs applet. Assigned applications have shortcuts in the Start menu, which will launch installation on first use.

31. Typically, only applications compiled as an MSI file can be deployed via a Group Policy. However, non-MSI applications can use a ZAP file to tell Group Policy how to install the application.

32. To enable roaming profiles, enter the UNC path to the user's profile in the user's account properties.

33. To configure mandatory profiles, rename ntuser.dat to ntuser.man.

34. Offline Files And Folders caches copies of network files locally. It is enabled by default on the client. On the server side, Manual Caching for Documents is the default setting for shared folders. Click the Caching button from the Sharing tab of a folder's Properties sheet to change the Offline Files settings.

35. Synchronization Manager is used to control which network device you can use to synchronize files that have changed and when synchronization will take place.

Windows® 2000 Professional

Dan Balter

Dan Holme

Todd Logan

Laurie Salmon

CERTIFICATION

MCSE Windows® 2000 Professional Exam Cram 2 (Exam 70-210)

International Standard Book Number: 0-7897-2872-9

Library of Congress Catalog Card Number: 2003100817

Printed in the United States of America

First Printing: April 2003

06   05   04   03   4   3

Trademarks

Warning and Disclaimer

Associate Publisher
Paul Boger

Executive Editor
Jeff Riley

Acquisitions Editor
Jeff Riley

Managing Editor
Charlotte Clapp

Project Editor
Tricia Liebig

Copy Editor
Kitty Jarrett

Indexer
Lisa Stumpf

Proofreader
Linda Seifert

Team Coordinator
Pamalee Nelson

Multimedia Developer
Dan Scherf

Interior Designer
Gary Adair

Page Layout
Michelle Mitchelll

Graphics
Tammy Graham

CERTIFICATION

Que Certification • 201 West 103rd Street • Indianapolis, Indiana 46290

A Note from Series Editor Ed Tittel

You know better than to trust your certification preparation to just anybody. That's why you, and more than two million others, have purchased an Exam Cram book. As Series Editor for the new and improved Exam Cram 2 series, I have worked with the staff at Que Certification to ensure you won't be disappointed. That's why we've taken the world's best-selling certification product—a finalist for "Best Study Guide" in a CertCities reader poll in 2002—and made it even better.

As a "Favorite Study Guide Author" finalist in a 2002 poll of CertCities readers, I know the value of good books. You'll be impressed with Que Certification's stringent review process, which ensures the books are high-quality, relevant, and technically accurate. Rest assured that at least a dozen industry experts—including the panel of certification experts at CramSession—have reviewed this material, helping us deliver an excellent solution to your exam preparation needs.

Best Study Guides

We've also added a preview edition of PrepLogic's powerful, full-featured test engine, which is trusted by certification students throughout the world.

As a 20-year-plus veteran of the computing industry and the original creator and editor of the Exam Cram series, I've brought my IT experience to bear on these books. During my tenure at Novell from 1989 to 1994, I worked with and around its excellent education and certification department. This experience helped push my writing and teaching activities heavily in the certification direction. Since then, I've worked on more than 70 certification-related books, and I write about certification topics for numerous Web sites and for *Certification* magazine.

In 1996, while studying for various MCP exams, I became frustrated with the huge, unwieldy study guides that were the only preparation tools available. As an experienced IT professional and former instructor, I wanted "nothing but the facts" necessary to prepare for the exams. From this impetus, Exam Cram emerged in 1997. It quickly became the best-selling computer book series since "...*For Dummies*," and the best-selling certification book series ever. By maintaining an intense focus on subject matter, tracking errata and updates quickly, and following the certification market closely, Exam Cram was able to establish the dominant position in cert prep books.

You will not be disappointed in your decision to purchase this book. If you are, please contact me at etittel@jump.net. All suggestions, ideas, input, or constructive criticism are welcome!

Ed Tittel

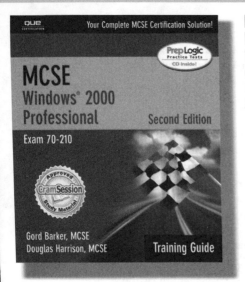

Contents at a Glance

Table of Contents

. . . .

About the Authors

. . . .

Dan Balter is the Chief Technology Officer for InfoTechnology Partners, Inc., a Microsoft Certified Partner company located in Camarillo, California. Dan works as an independent consultant and trainer for both corporate and government clients specializing in LANs, WANs, VPNs, firewalls, and remote access solutions. A graduate of University of Southern California's School of Business in 1983, Dan has authored more than 300 computer training courses on video and CD-ROM. Throughout his 18-year career, Dan has worked with numerous network operating systems, and achieved a long list of credentials and certifications. He regularly speaks at computer conferences throughout North America on Windows XP, Windows 2000, and other Microsoft BackOffice solutions. He is a contributing author for three books on the Windows NT 4.0 network operating system, in addition to coauthoring the *Exam Cram 2* series books on Windows 2000 Professional and Windows XP Professional. Dan Balter can be reached at dan@InfoTechnologyPartners.com.

Dan Holme is President and CEO of trainAbility, a global, integrated IT training company based in Scottsdale, Arizona. The company's independent, solutions-focused curricula and proprietary technologies allow it to deliver extremely customized solutions that bridge the gap between consulting and training. Dan spearheads the company's efforts to provide advanced, intensive ConsulTraining that meets twenty-first century clients' needs for cost- and time-efficient knowledge transfer.

Dan comes armed with a Bachelor's degree from Yale, a Master of International Management from Thunderbird, and 12 years of international training, public speaking, and management experience. If he's not buried in work or catching some big air on his snowboard, Dan can be reached at dan.holme@trainability.com.

Todd Logan has been training people how to actually use computers instead of throwing them out the window in frustration since 1992, back when the new thing was called email. Todd's wife took him away from his consulting business and the constant rain of Vancouver, British Columbia to sunny Phoenix, Arizona where he has been a technical trainer for ExecuTrain,

Mastering Computers, and now works as a ConsulTrainer at trainAbility, where he is known for his penchant for ferreting out extraordinary solutions for clients the likes of Compaq, Hewlett-Packard, Sprint, and Microsoft. In between his neverending quest for the truth of Windows and the pursuit of the ultimate tofu cookbook, you can reach Todd at todd.logan@ trainability.com.

Laurie Salmon is a full-time technical consultant with trainAbility, in Scottsdale, Arizona. Laurie has built a stellar eight-year track record in the computer business providing technical training and consulting services on Windows NT, Microsoft BackOffice, Internet Information Server, and Windows 2000. Microsoft asked Laurie to be a keynote speaker for the Windows 95 Launch series touring Texas in April of 1995. Courseware for Windows 95/98, NT, and Windows 2000 that Laurie has written or coauthored is in use at many companies around the world. Laurie has been an MCT and MCSE since 1994, and has taught fast-paced, entertaining technical workshops all over the United States. Laurie can be reached at laurie.salmon@trainability.com.

Acknowledgments

It was a thrill indeed to contribute to the continued success of the *Exam Cram 2* series and my thanks go to the whole team, especially Keith Weiskamp, Shari Jo Hehr, and Greg Balas, for their cooperation, support, and vision. The excellence required was more than met by my stellar colleagues on this project: Dan Balter, thank you, thank you! Todd and Laurie, I cannot begin to express how proud I am to count you as peers and friends at trainAbility—your professionalism, talent, and gusto are indeed the best in the training business! I hope that someday all of you reading these acknowledgements are honored by an opportunity to work with the likes of these folks, Hank, Thom, and the entire, extraordinary trainAbility team.

None of *my* work would be possible without the decades of support from my family. Mom, Dad, Bob, Joni, l love you with all my heart and I promise I will *try* to sleep when this page is submitted! Finally, to my beautiful Einstein, for bringing me lunch when I wouldn't have eaten and making the world a fabulous place to return to when the Shut Down command is finally clicked... thank you.

Dan Holme

Writing a book is never an easy task; writing a technical book for certification on a new software product is especially daunting and challenging. First of all, I want to express my gratitude to my awe-inspiring wife of over 10 years now, Alison Balter, for teaching me how to really be an effective trainer and author. I also appreciate her putting up with me during the time that I was writing the chapters for this book! I love you, honey—happy tenth anniversary! I also want to acknowledge my two darling kids—Alexis and Brendan, ages 6 and 3, respectively at the time of the Exam Cram 2 series, for just being so loving and fun to be around. Thanks for being so understanding of mom's and dad's long hours sometimes—I love you both very, very much!!!

An incredible amount of appreciation also goes to Sonia Aguilar, her husband Hugo, and their children Claudia, Gabby, and Little Hugo. Thank you all for your incessant love, support, and unparalleled care for our children when we're attending to business matters! Sonia, you're the best!

A big tip o' the hat goes to Dan Holme of Intelliem, Inc. (www.Intelliem.com), the finest team leader in the universe and one of the smartest men in the world (at least in my opinion). Congratulations on pulling all of us together and really making this project happen! Thanks for including me in this book and for hanging in there with me when deadlines were looming imminently overhead!

Huge thanks also go out to Greggory Peck of Blast Through Learning systems (www.BlastThroughLearning.com). Thank you for giving me the opportunity to become a trainer using video-based and CD-ROM–based technology. Jeremy Moskowitz, Derek Melber, and Alan Sugano are always there whenever I have a burning question—thank you both. A ton of gratitude goes out to Tim Leonard and Navin Jiawan for doing a tremendous job of supporting my clients when I have book deadlines imminently looming. Finally, to Charlotte and Bob Roman (my in-laws)—thank you both for everything that you do for us, all the time! To my Mom and Dad—thanks for emphasizing reading and writing, among other things. These skills sure come in handy for the IT industry!

Dan Balter

I would like to thank my coauthor Dan Holme for bringing me on board to help write this book. Dan, you are an inspiration to everyone at trainAbility and a true leader! A thanks also goes to Hank Carbeck for putting up with me while I have been working on this book. Hank, you've been a true friend to my family and me! I would also like to thank my coauthors Dan Balter and Laurie Salmon for their invaluable contributions to this book.

A special thanks goes to my wife Gladys and my son Seth for giving me the time and space to work on this book. I would not have been able to finish this book without your constant love and support. For this I thank you from the bottom of my heart and I promise we will go on vacation soon!

Todd Logan

Thanks to my loving husband, Scot, who patiently listens to my rants without laughing—I love you, and you are my rock. Chloe, Sasha, and Maggie would pursue certification if they had opposable thumbs—but I love them anyway! I would like to thank my family and friends for their unconditional, unwavering support. Dan—thanks for your constant support and for including me in this project! Hank—thanks for the flowers and for always making me smile! Cindy, Leslie, Gwen, Melany, and Holly—thanks for motivating and inspiring me and keeping me on track!

Laurie Salmon

We Want to Hear from You!

As the reader of this book, *you* are our most important critic and commentator. We value your opinion and want to know what we're doing right, what we could do better, what areas you'd like to see us publish in, and any other words of wisdom you're willing to pass our way.

As an executive editor for Que, I welcome your comments. You can email or write me directly to let me know what you did or didn't like about this book—as well as what we can do to make our books better.

Please note that I cannot help you with technical problems related to the *topic* of this book. We do have a User Services group, however, where I will forward specific technical questions related to the book.

When you write, please be sure to include this book's title and author as well as your name, email address, and phone number. I will carefully review your comments and share them with the author and editors who worked on the book.

Email: feedback@quepublishing.com

Mail: Jeff Riley
             Que Publishing
             201 West 103rd Street
             Indianapolis, IN 46290 USA

For more information about this book or another Que title, visit our Web site at www.quepublishing.com. Type the ISBN (excluding hyphens) or the title of a book in the Search field to find the page you're looking for. For information about the Exam Cram 2 Series, visit www.examcram2.com.

Introduction

Welcome to *MCSE Windows 2000 Professional Exam Cram 2*! Whether this is your first or your fifteenth *Exam Cram* series book, you'll find information here and in Chapter 1, "Microsoft Certification Exams," that will help ensure your success as you pursue knowledge, experience, and certification. This book aims to help you get ready to take—and pass—the Microsoft certification exam "Installing, Configuring, and Administering Microsoft Windows 2000 Professional" (Exam 70-210). This introduction explains Microsoft's certification programs in general and talks about how the *Exam Cram 2* series can help you prepare for Microsoft's Windows 2000 and Windows XP certification exams.

Exam Cram 2 books help you understand and appreciate the subjects and materials you need to pass Microsoft certification exams. *Exam Cram 2* books are aimed strictly at test preparation and review. They do not teach you everything you need to know about a topic. Instead, we authors present and dissect the questions and problems we've found that you're likely to encounter on a test. We've worked to bring together as much information as possible about Microsoft certification exams.

Nevertheless, to completely prepare yourself for any Microsoft test, we recommend that you begin by taking the self-assessment that is included in this book, immediately following this introduction. The self-assessment tool will help you evaluate your knowledge base against the requirements for a Microsoft Certified Systems Administrator (MCSA) or Microsoft Certified Systems Engineer (MCSE) under both ideal and real circumstances.

Based on what you learn from the self-assessment, you might decide to begin your studies with some classroom training or some background reading. On the other hand, you might decide to pick up and read one of the many study guides available from Microsoft or third-party vendors on certain topics, including the award-winning *MCSE Training Guide* series from Que Publishing. We also recommend that you supplement your study program with visits to www.examcram2.com to receive additional practice questions, get advice, and track the Windows 2000 MCSA and MCSE program.

We also strongly recommend that you install, configure, and play around with the software that you'll be tested on because nothing beats hands-on experience and familiarity when it comes to understanding the questions you're likely to encounter on a certification test. Book learning is essential, but without a doubt, hands-on experience is the best teacher of all!

The Microsoft Certified Professional (MCP) Program

The MCP program currently includes the following separate tracks, each of which boasts its own special abbreviation (as a certification candidate, you need to have a high tolerance for alphabet soup of all kinds):

➤ **MCP (Microsoft Certified Professional)**—This is the least prestigious of all the certification tracks from Microsoft. Passing one of the major Microsoft exams qualifies an individual for the MCP credential. Individuals can demonstrate proficiency with additional Microsoft products by passing additional certification exams.

➤ **MCP+SB (Microsoft Certified Professional + Site Building)**—This certification program is designed for individuals who are planning, building, managing, and maintaining Web sites. Individuals with the MCP+SB credential will have demonstrated the ability to develop Web sites that include multimedia and searchable content and Web sites that connect to and communicate with a back-end database. This certification requires one MCP exam, plus two of these three exams: 70-055, "Designing and Implementing Web Sites with Microsoft FrontPage 98," 70-057, "Designing and Implementing Commerce Solutions with Microsoft Site Server 3.0, Commerce Edition," and 70-152, "Designing and Implementing Web Solutions with Microsoft Visual InterDev 6.0." Microsoft retired Exam 70-055 on June 30, 2001, and it retired the MCP+SB certification on June 30, 2002.

➤ **MCSA (Microsoft Certified Systems Administrator)**—This exam is for anyone who has a Windows NT 4 MCSE and/or possesses a high level of networking expertise with Microsoft operating systems and products. This credential is designed to prepare individuals to plan, implement, maintain, and support information systems, networks, and internetworks built around Microsoft Windows 2000 and Windows XP.

To obtain MCSA certification, an individual must pass three core operating system exams and one elective exam. The operating system exams are designed to test competency over the server and client aspects of a network, as well as managing a Windows 2000 network.

If you have already passed the 70-240 exam, you only need to pass the 70-218 exam, "Managing a Microsoft Windows 2000 Network Environment," which is the Windows 2000 network management aspect of the MCSA certification. For more information on Exam 70-218, read the MCSE section that follows.

New MCSA candidates must pass four tests to meet the MCSA requirements. It's not uncommon for the entire process to take almost a year or so, and many individuals find that they must take a test more than once to pass. The primary goal of the *Exam Cram 2* test preparation books is to make it possible, given proper study and preparation, to pass all Microsoft certification tests on the first try.

Table 1 shows the required and elective exams for the Windows 2000 MCSA certification.

Microsoft had not yet published the MCSA certification requirements for the Windows Server 2003 track at the time that this book was published.

➤ **MCSE (Microsoft Certified Systems Engineer)**—Anyone who has a current MCSE is warranted to possess a high level of networking expertise with Microsoft operating systems and products. This credential is designed to recognize individuals who have the skills to plan, design, implement, maintain, and support information systems, networks, and internetworks built around Microsoft Windows 2000/XP, Windows Server 2003, and the Enterprise Servers family of products.

To obtain MCSE certification, an individual must pass four core operating system exams, one networking design core exam, and two elective exams. The operating system exams require individuals to prove their competence with desktop and server operating systems and networking/internetworking components.

For Windows NT 4 MCSEs, the accelerated exam, 70-240, "Microsoft Windows 2000 Accelerated Exam for MCPs Certified on Microsoft Windows NT 4.0," was an option. This free exam covered all the material tested in the four core exams. The hitch in this plan is that a candidate could take the test only once. If a candidate failed, he or she was required to take all four core exams to recertify. The four core exams are as follows: 70-210, or 70-270, "Installing, Configuring, and Administering Microsoft Windows XP Professional"; 70-215, "Installing, Configuring, and Administering Microsoft Windows 2000 Server"; 70-216, "Implementing and Administering a Microsoft Windows 2000 Network Infrastructure"; and 70-217, "Implementing and Administering a Microsoft Windows 2000 Directory Services Infrastructure."

 The 70-240 exam was no longer available after December 31, 2001. So if you received a voucher for this exam but were not able to take it in time, you need to take the four core exams to recertify.

To fulfill the networking design core exam requirement, a candidate can choose from four design exams: 70-219, "Designing a Microsoft Windows 2000 Directory Services Infrastructure," 70-220, "Designing Security for a Microsoft Windows 2000 Network," 70-221, "Designing a Microsoft Windows 2000 Network Infrastructure," or 70-226, "Designing Highly Available Web Solutions with Microsoft Windows 2000 Server Technologies." You are also required to take two elective exams. An elective exam can fall within any number of subject or product areas, primarily BackOffice Server 2000 components. The three design exams that a candidate doesn't select as core exams may also qualify as electives.

 If you are on your way to becoming an MCSE and have already taken some exams, you can visit **www.microsoft.com/traincert** for information about how to complete your MCSE certification.

New MCSE candidates must pass seven tests to meet the MCSE requirements. It's not uncommon for the entire process to take a year or so, and many individuals find that they must take a test more than once to pass. The primary goal of the *Exam Cram 2* test preparation guides is to make it possible, given proper study and preparation, to pass all Microsoft certification tests on the first try.

Table 2 shows the required and elective exams for the Windows 2000 MCSE certification.

 Microsoft had not yet published the MCSE certification requirements for the Windows Server 2003 track at the time that this book was published.

➤ **MCSD (Microsoft Certified Solution Developer)**—The MCSD credential reflects the skills required to create multitier, distributed, and Component Object Model (COM)-based solutions, in addition to desktop and Internet applications, using new technologies. To obtain MCSD certification, an individual must demonstrate the ability to analyze and interpret user requirements; select and integrate products, platforms, tools, and technologies; design and implement code; customize applications; and perform necessary software tests and quality assurance operations.

To obtain MCSD certification, an individual must pass a total of four exams: three core exams and one elective exam. A candidate must choose one of these three desktop application exams: 70-016, "Designing and Implementing Desktop Applications with Microsoft Visual C++ 6.0," 70-156, "Designing and Implementing Desktop Applications with Microsoft Visual FoxPro 6.0," or 70-176, "Designing and Implementing Desktop Applications with Microsoft Visual Basic 6.0." In addition, a candidate must choose one of these three distributed application exams: 70-015, "Designing and Implementing Distributed Applications with Microsoft Visual C++ 6.0," 70-155, "Designing and Implementing Distributed Applications with Microsoft Visual FoxPro 6.0," or 70-175, "Designing and Implementing Distributed Applications with Microsoft Visual Basic 6.0." The third core exam is 70-100, "Analyzing Requirements and Defining Solution Architectures." Elective exams cover specific Microsoft applications and languages, including Visual Basic, C++, the Microsoft Foundation Classes, Access, SQL Server, and Excel.

➤ **MCDBA (Microsoft Certified Database Administrator)**—The MCDBA credential reflects the skills required to implement and administer Microsoft SQL Server databases. To obtain MCDBA certification, an individual must demonstrate the ability to derive physical database designs, develop logical data models, create physical databases, create data services by using Transact-SQL, manage and maintain databases, configure and manage security, monitor and optimize databases, and install and configure Microsoft SQL Server.

To become an MCDBA, an individual must pass a total of three core exams and one elective exam. The required core exams are as follows: 70-028, "Administering Microsoft SQL Server 7.0" or 70-228, "Installing, Configuring, and Administering Microsoft SQL Server 2000 Enterprise Edition"; 70-029, "Designing and Implementing Databases with Microsoft SQL Server 7.0" or 70-229, "Designing and Implementing Databases with Microsoft SQL Server 2000 Enterprise Edition"; and 70-215, "Installing, Configuring, and Administering Microsoft Windows 2000 Server."

The elective exams that a candidate can choose from cover specific uses of SQL Server and include 70-015, "Designing and Implementing Distributed Applications with Microsoft Visual C++ 6.0," 70-019, "Designing and Implementing Data Warehouses with Microsoft SQL Server 7.0," 70-155, "Designing and Implementing Distributed Applications with Microsoft Visual FoxPro 6.0," 70-175, "Designing and Implementing Distributed Applications with Microsoft Visual Basic 6.0," and one exam that relate to Windows 2000, 70-216, "Implementing and Administering a Microsoft Windows 2000 Network Infrastructure."

➤ **MCT (Microsoft Certified Trainer)**—Those with MCT certification are deemed able to deliver elements of the official Microsoft curriculum, based on technical knowledge and instructional ability. Thus, it is necessary for an individual seeking MCT credentials (which are granted on a course-by-course basis) to pass the related certification exam for a course and complete the official Microsoft training in the subject area and to demonstrate an ability to teach.

A candidate can satisfy the teaching skills criterion by proving that he or she has already attained training certification from Novell, Banyan, Lotus, the Santa Cruz Operation, or Cisco, or by taking a Microsoft-sanctioned workshop on instruction. Microsoft makes it clear that MCTs are important cogs in the Microsoft training channels. Instructors must be MCTs before Microsoft will allow them to teach in any of its official training channels, including Microsoft's affiliated Certified Technical Education Centers (CTECs) and its online training partner network. An MCT candidate must also possess current MCSE, MCSD, or MCDBA certification before he or she can apply for MCT status.

NOTE

Microsoft has announced that the MCP+I and MCSE+I credentials will not be continued when the MCSE exams for Windows 2000/XP are in full swing because the skill set for the Internet portion of the program has been included in the new MCSE program. Therefore, details on these tracks are not provided here; you can go to **www.microsoft.com/traincert** if you need more information.

After a Microsoft product becomes obsolete, MCPs typically have to recertify on current versions. (If individuals do not recertify, their certifications become invalid.) Because technology keeps changing and new products continually supplant old ones, this should come as no surprise. It also explains why Microsoft announced that MCSEs had 12 months past the scheduled retirement date for the Windows NT 4 exams to recertify on Windows 2000 topics. (Note that this means taking at least two exams, if not more.)

The best place to keep tabs on the MCP program and its related certifications is on the Web. Currently the uniform resource locator (URL) for the MCP program is www.microsoft.com/traincert. But Microsoft's Web site changes often, so if this URL doesn't work, you should try using the Search tool on Microsoft's site with either MCP or the quoted phrase "Microsoft Certified Professional" as a search string. This will help you find the latest and most accurate information about Microsoft's certification programs.

Taking a Certification Exam

After you've prepared for your exam, you need to register with a testing center. Each computer-based MCP exam costs $125. If you don't pass, you can retest for $125 more for each additional try. In the United States and Canada, tests are administered by Prometric and by VUE. Here's how you can contact them:

➤ **Prometric**—You can sign up for a test through the company's Web site at www.prometric.com. Or, you can register by phone at 800-755-3926 (within the United States and Canada) or at 410-843-8000 (outside the United States and Canada).

➤ **Virtual University Enterprises (VUE)**—You can sign up for a test or get the phone numbers for local testing centers through the Web page at www.vue.com/ms/.

To sign up for a test, you must possess a valid credit card or contact either Prometric or VUE for mailing instructions to send a check (in the United States). Only when payment is verified, or a check has cleared, can you actually register for a test.

To schedule an exam, you need to call the number or visit either of the Web pages at least one day in advance. To cancel or reschedule an exam, you must call before 7 p.m. Pacific standard time the day before the scheduled test time (or you might be charged, even if you don't show up to take the test). When you want to schedule a test, you should have the following information ready:

➤ Your name, organization, and mailing address.

➤ Your Microsoft test ID. (Inside the United States, this means your Social Security number; citizens of other nations should call ahead to find out what type of identification number is required to register for a test.)

➤ The name and number of the exam you want to take.

➤ A method of payment. (As mentioned previously, a credit card is the most convenient method, but alternate means can be arranged in advance, if necessary.)

After you sign up for a test, you are told when and where the test is scheduled. You should try to arrive at least 15 minutes early. You must supply two forms of identification—one of which must be a photo ID—to be admitted into the testing room.

All exams are completely closed book. In fact, you are not permitted to take anything with you into the testing area, but you are given a blank sheet of paper and a pen or, in some cases, an erasable plastic sheet and an erasable pen. We suggest that you immediately write down on that sheet of paper all the information you've memorized for the test. In *Exam Cram 2* books, this information appears on a tear-out sheet inside the front cover of each book. You are given some time to compose yourself, record this information, and take a sample orientation exam before you begin the real thing. We suggest that you take the orientation test before taking your first exam, but because all the certification exams are more or less identical in layout, behavior, and controls, you probably don't need to do this more than once.

When you complete a Microsoft certification exam, the software tells you whether you've passed or failed. If you need to retake an exam, you have to schedule a new test with Prometric or VUE and pay another $125.

 The first time you fail a test, you can retake the test the next day. However, if you fail a second time, you must wait 14 days before retaking that test. The 14-day waiting period remains in effect for all retakes after the second failure.

Tracking MCP Status

As soon as you pass any Microsoft exam, you attain MCP status. Microsoft generates transcripts that indicate which exams you have passed. You can view a copy of your transcript at any time by going to the MCP secured site and selecting Transcript Tool. This tool enables you to print a copy of your current transcript and confirm your certification status.

After you pass the necessary set of exams, you are certified. Official certification is normally granted after six to eight weeks, so you shouldn't expect to get your credentials overnight. The package for official certification that arrives includes a Welcome Kit that contains a number of elements (see Microsoft's Web site for other benefits of specific certifications):

➤ A certificate that is suitable for framing, along with a wallet card and lapel pin.

➤ A license to use the MCP logo, which means you can use the logo in advertisements, promotions, and documents, and on letterhead, business cards, and so on. Along with the license comes an MCP logo sheet, which includes camera-ready artwork. (Note that before you use any of the artwork, you must sign and return a licensing agreement that indicates you'll abide by its terms and conditions.)

➤ A subscription to *Microsoft Certified Professional Magazine*, which provides ongoing data about testing and certification activities, requirements, and changes to the program.

Many people believe that the benefits of MCP certification go well beyond the perks that Microsoft provides to newly anointed members of this elite group. We're starting to see more job listings that request or require applicants to have MCP, MCSE, and other certifications, and many individuals who complete Microsoft certification programs can qualify for increases in pay and/or responsibility. As an official recognition of hard work and broad knowledge, one of the MCP credentials is a badge of honor in many IT organizations.

How to Prepare for an Exam

Preparing for any Windows 2000– or Windows XP–related test (including Exam 70-210) requires that you obtain and study materials designed to provide comprehensive information about the product and its capabilities that will appear on the specific exam for which you are preparing. The following list of materials can help you study and prepare:

➤ The Windows 2000 Professional product CD. This CD includes comprehensive online documentation and related materials; it should be a primary resource when you are preparing for the test.

➤ The exam preparation materials, practice tests, and self-assessment exams on the Microsoft Training & Services page, at www.microsoft.com/traincert. The Exam Resources link offers samples of the new question types found on the Windows 2000 MCSA and MCSE exams. You should find the materials, download them, and use them!

➤ The exam preparation advice, practice tests, questions of the day, and discussion groups on www.examcram2.com.

In addition, you'll probably find any or all of the following materials useful in your quest for Windows 2000 Professional expertise:

➤ **Microsoft training kits**—Microsoft Press offers a training kit that specifically targets Exam 70-210. For more information, visit http://mspress. microsoft.com/findabook/list/series_ak.htm. This training kit contains information that you will find useful in preparing for the test.

➤ **Microsoft TechNet CD**—This monthly CD-based publication delivers numerous electronic titles that include coverage of Directory Services Infrastructure and related topics on the Technical Information (TechNet) CD. Its offerings include product facts, technical notes, tools and utilities, and information on how to access the Seminars Online training materials for Windows 2000 Professional. A subscription to TechNet costs $299 per year, but it is well worth the price. Visit www.microsoft.com/technet/ and check out the information under the "TechNet Subscription" menu entry for more details.

➤ **Study guides**—Several publishers—including Que—offer Windows 2000 titles. Que Certification includes the following:

➤The *Exam Cram 2* series—These books give you information about the material you need to know to pass the tests.

➤The *Training Guide* series—These books provide a greater level of detail than the *Exam Cram 2* books and are designed to teach you everything you need to know from an exam perspective. Each book comes with a CD that contains interactive practice exams in a variety of testing formats.

Together, the two series make a perfect pair.

➤ **Multimedia**—The *PrepLogic Practice Tests* CD that comes with each Exam Cram and Training Guide features a powerful, state-of-the-art test engine that prepares you for the actual exam. *PrepLogic Practice Tests* are developed by certified IT professionals and are trusted by certification students around the world. For more information, visit www.preplogic.com.

➤ **Classroom training**—CTECs, online partners, and third-party training companies (such as Wave Technologies, Learning Tree, Data-Tech, and others) all offer classroom training on Windows 2000. These companies aim to help you prepare to pass Exam 70-210. Although such training runs upwards of $350 per day in class, most of the individuals lucky enough to partake find it to be quite worthwhile.

➤ **Other publications**—There's no shortage of materials available about Windows 2000 Professional. The resource sections at the end of each chapter should give you an idea of where we think you should look for further discussion.

By far, this set of required and recommended materials represents a nonpareil collection of sources and resources for Windows 2000 Professional and related topics. We anticipate you'll find that this book belongs in this company.

About This Book

Each topical *Exam Cram 2* chapter follows a regular structure and contains graphical cues about important or useful information. Here's the structure of a typical chapter:

➤ **Opening hotlists**—Each chapter begins with a list of the terms, tools, and techniques that you must learn and understand before you can be fully conversant with that chapter's subject matter. The hotlists are followed by one or two introductory paragraphs to set the stage for the rest of the chapter.

➤ **Topical coverage**—After the opening hotlists and introductory text, each chapter covers a series of topics related to the chapter's subject. Throughout that section, we highlight topics or concepts that are likely to appear on a test, using a special element called an alert:

 This is what an alert looks like. Normally, an alert stresses concepts, terms, software, or activities that are likely to relate to one or more certification test questions. For that reason, we think any information found in an alert is worthy of unusual attentiveness on your part. Indeed, most of the information that appears on the Cram Sheet appears as alerts within the text.

You should pay close attention to material flagged in Exam Alerts; although all the information in this book pertains to what you need to know to pass the exam, Exam Alerts contain information that is really important. You'll find what appears in the meat of each chapter to be worth knowing, too, when preparing for the test. Because this book's material is very condensed, we recommend that you use this book along with other resources to achieve the maximum benefit.

In addition to the alerts, we provide tips that will help you build a better foundation for Windows 2000 Professional knowledge. Although the tip information might not be on the exam, it is certainly related and will help you become a better test-taker.

> This is how tips are formatted. Keep your eyes open for these, and you'll become a Windows 2000 Professional guru in no time!
>
> This is how notes are formatted. Notes direct your attention to important pieces of information that relate to Windows 2000 and Microsoft certification.

➤ **Practice questions**—Although we talk about test questions and topics throughout the book, a section at the end of each chapter presents a series of mock test questions and explanations of both correct and incorrect answers.

➤ **Details and resources**—Every chapter ends with a section titled "Need to Know More?" That section provides direct pointers to Microsoft and third-party resources that offer more details on the chapter's subject. In addition, that section tries to rank or at least rate the quality and thoroughness of the topic's coverage by each resource. If you find a resource you like in that collection, you should use it, but you shouldn't feel compelled to use all the resources. On the other hand, we recommend only resources that we use on a regular basis, so none of our recommendations will be a waste of your time or money (but purchasing them all at once probably represents an expense that many network administrators and would-be MCPs and MCSEs might find hard to justify).

The bulk of the book follows this chapter structure slavishly, but we'd like to point out a few other elements. Chapter 11, "Sample Test," provides a good review of the material presented throughout the book, to ensure that you're ready for the exam. Chapter 12, "Sample Test Answer Key," offers the correct answers to the questions on the sample test in Chapter 11. In addition, you'll find a handy glossary and an index.

Finally, the tear-out Cram Sheet attached next to the inside front cover of this *Exam Cram 2* book represents a condensed and compiled collection of facts and tips that we think you should memorize before taking the test. Because you can dump this information out of your head onto a piece of paper before taking the exam, you can master this information by brute force—you need to remember it only long enough to write it down when you walk into the test room. You might even want to look at it in the car or in the lobby of the testing center just before you walk in to take the test.

How to Use This Book

We've structured the topics in this book to build on one another. Therefore, some topics in later chapters make the most sense after you've read earlier chapters. That's why we suggest that you read this book from front to back for your initial test preparation. If you need to brush up on a topic or if you have to bone up for a second try, you can use the index or table of contents to go straight to the topics and questions that you need to study. Beyond helping you prepare for the test, we think you'll find this book useful as a tightly focused reference to some of the most important aspects of Windows 2000 Professional.

The book uses the following typographical conventions:

➤ Command-line strings that are meant to be typed into the computer are displayed in monospace text, as in the following example:

```
net use lpt1: \\print_server_name\printer_share_name
```

➤ New terms are introduced in *italics*.

Given all the book's elements and its specialized focus, we've tried to create a tool that will help you prepare for—and pass—Microsoft Exam 70-210. Please share with us your feedback on the book, especially if you have ideas about how we can improve it for future test-takers. Send your questions or comments about this book via email to feedback@quepublishing.com. We'll consider everything you say carefully, and we'll respond to all suggestions. For more information on this book and other Que Certification titles, visit our Web site at www.quepublishing.com. You should also check out the new *Exam Cram 2* Web site, at www.examcram2.com, where you'll find information updates, commentary, and certification information.

Thanks, and enjoy the book!

Self-Assessment

The reason we include a self-assessment in this *Exam Cram 2* book is to help you evaluate your readiness to tackle MCSE certification. It should also help you understand what you need to know to master the topic of this book—namely, Exam 70-210 "Installing, Configuring, and Administering Microsoft Windows 2000 Professional." But before you tackle this self-assessment, let's talk about concerns you might face when pursuing an MCSE for Windows 2000 Server or Windows Server 2003, and what an ideal MCSE candidate might look like.

MCSEs in the Real World

In the next section, we describe an ideal MCSE candidate, knowing full well that only a few real candidates will meet that ideal. In fact, our description of that ideal candidate might seem downright scary, especially with the changes that have been made to the MCSE program to support Windows 2000 and Windows XP. But take heart: Although the requirements to obtain MCSE certification might seem formidable, they are by no means impossible to meet. However, you need to be keenly aware that getting through the process takes time, involves some expense, and requires real effort.

Increasing numbers of people are attaining Microsoft certifications. You can get all the real-world motivation you need from knowing that many others have gone before, so you will be able to follow in their footsteps. If you're willing to tackle the process seriously and do what it takes to obtain the necessary experience and knowledge, you can take—and pass—all the certification tests involved in obtaining MCSE certification. In fact, at Que Publishing, we've designed the *Exam Cram 2* series and the *MCSE Training Guide* series to make it as easy for you as possible to prepare for these exams. We've also greatly expanded our Web site, www.examcram2.com, to provide a host of resources to help you prepare for the complexities of Windows 2000 and Windows XP.

Besides MCSE, other Microsoft certifications include the following:

➤ *MCSA (Microsoft Certified Systems Administrator)*—This is the brand-new certification that Microsoft has provided for Microsoft professionals who are not going to design networks but are going to administer networks. This certification includes three core exams (70-210 or 70-270, "Installing, Configuring, and Administering Windows XP Professional," 70-215, "Installing, Configuring, and Administering Windows 2000 Server," and 70-218, "Managing a Microsoft Windows 2000 Network Environment") and a single elective.

➤ *MCSD (Microsoft Certified Solution Developer)*—This certification is aimed at software developers and requires one specific exam, two more exams on client and distributed topics, plus a fourth, elective, exam drawn from a different, but limited, pool of options.

➤ *Other Microsoft certifications*—The requirements for these certifications range from one test, to attain the Microsoft Certified Professional (MCP) designation, to several exams, to obtain Microsoft Certified Systems Engineer (MCSE), Microsoft Certified Database Administrator (MCDBA), and several other certifications.

The Ideal Windows 2000 MCSE Candidate

To give you an idea of what an ideal MCSE candidate is like, here are some relevant statistics about the background and experience such an individual might have:

Don't worry if you don't meet these qualifications or even come very close—this is a far-from-ideal world, and where you fall short is simply where you'll have more work to do.

➤ Academic or professional training in network theory, concepts, and operations. This includes everything from networking media and transmission techniques through network operating systems, services, and applications.

➤ Three or more years of professional networking experience, including experience with ethernet, token ring, modems, and other networking media. This must include installation, configuration, upgrade, and troubleshooting experience.

The Windows 2000 MCSE program is much more rigorous than the Windows NT 4.0 MCSE program; therefore, you really need some hands-on experience if you want to obtain this certification. Some of the exams require you to solve real-world case studies and network design issues, so the more hands-on experience you have, the better.

➤ Two or more years in a networked environment that includes hands-on experience with Windows 2000 Server, Windows 2000/XP Professional, Windows NT 4.0 Server, Windows NT 4.0 Workstation, and Windows 98 or Windows 95. A solid understanding of each system's architecture, installation, configuration, maintenance, and troubleshooting is also essential.

➤ Knowledge of the various methods for installing Windows 2000, including manual and unattended installations.

➤ A thorough understanding of key networking protocols, addressing, and name resolution, including Transmission Control Protocol/Internet Protocol (TCP/IP), Novell NetWare's Internetwork Packet Exchange/Sequenced Packet Exchange (IPX/SPX), and Microsoft's NetBIOS Extended User Interface (NetBEUI).

➤ A thorough understanding of NetBIOS naming, browsing, and file and print services.

➤ Familiarity with key Windows 2000–based TCP/IP–based services, including Hypertext Transfer Protocol (HTTP; used for Web servers), Dynamic Host Configuration Protocol (DHCP), Windows Internet Name Service (WINS), and Domain Name System (DNS), plus familiarity with one or more of the following: Internet Information Server (IIS), Index Server, and Proxy Server or Internet Security and Acceleration (ISA) Server.

➤ An understanding of how to implement security for key network data in a Windows 2000 or a Windows XP environment.

➤ Working knowledge of NetWare 3.x and 4.x, including IPX/SPX frame formats; NetWare file, print, and directory services; and both Novell and Microsoft client software. Working knowledge of Microsoft's Client Service for NetWare (CSNW), the Gateway Service for NetWare (GSNW), the NetWare Migration Tool (NWCONV), and the NetWare Client for Windows (NT, 95, and 98) is essential.

➤ A good working understanding of Active Directory. The more you work with Windows 2000 or Windows Server 2003, the more you'll realize that it is quite different from Windows NT. New technologies such as Active Directory have really changed the way Windows is configured and used.

We recommend that you find out as much as you can about Active Directory and acquire as much experience using this technology as possible. The time you take learning about Active Directory will be time very well spent!

To meet all these qualifications, you'd need a bachelor's degree in computer science plus three years of work experience in PC networking design, installation, administration, and troubleshooting. Don't be concerned if you don't have all these qualifications. Fewer than half of all Microsoft certification candidates meet these requirements. This self-assessment chapter is designed to show you what you already know and to prepare you for the topics that you need to learn.

Put Yourself to the Test

The following series of questions and observations is designed to help you figure out how much work you must do to pursue Microsoft certification and what kinds of resources you may consult on your quest. Be absolutely honest in your answers, or you'll end up wasting money on exams you're not yet ready to take. There are no right or wrong answers—only steps along the path to certification. Only you can decide where you really belong in the broad spectrum of aspiring candidates. Two things should be clear from the outset, however:

➤ Even a modest background in computer science will be helpful.

➤ Hands-on experience with Microsoft products and technologies is an essential ingredient in certification success.

Educational Background

The following questions concern your level of technical computer experience and training. Depending on your answers to these questions, you might need to review some additional resources to get your knowledge up to speed for the types of questions that you will encounter on Microsoft certifications exams.

1. Have you ever taken any computer-related classes? [Yes or No]

If Yes, proceed to Question 2; if No, proceed to Question 4.

2. Have you taken any classes on computer operating systems? [Yes or No]

If Yes, you will probably be able to handle Microsoft's architecture and system component discussions. If you're rusty, you should brush up on basic operating system concepts, especially virtual memory, multitasking regimes, user-mode versus kernel-mode operation, and general computer security topics.

If No, you should consider doing some basic reading in this area. We strongly recommend a good general operating systems book, such as *Operating System Concepts* by Abraham Silberschatz and Peter Baer Galvin (John Wiley & Sons). If this book doesn't appeal to you, check out reviews for other, similar, books at your favorite online bookstore.

3. Have you taken any networking concepts or technologies classes? [Yes or No]

If Yes, you will probably be able to handle Microsoft's networking terminology, concepts, and technologies (brace yourself for frequent departures from normal usage). If you're rusty, you should brush up on basic networking concepts and terminology, especially networking media, transmission types, the OSI reference model, and networking technologies such as ethernet, token ring, Fiber Distributed Data Interface (FDDI), and wide area network (WAN) links.

If No, you might want to read one or two books in this topic area. The two best books that we know of are *Computer Networks* by Andrew S. Tanenbaum (Prentice Hall) and *Computer Networks and Internets* by Douglas E. Comer and Ralph E. Droms (Prentice Hall).

Hands-On Experience

The most important key to success on all the Microsoft tests is hands-on experience, especially with Windows 2000 Server and Windows 2000 Professional, plus the many add-on services and BackOffice components around which so many of the Microsoft certification exams revolve. If we leave you with only one realization after you take this self-assessment, it should be that there's no substitute for time spent installing, configuring, and using the various Microsoft products on which you'll be tested repeatedly and in depth:

1. Have you installed, configured, and worked with the following:

➤ Windows 2000 Server? [Yes or No]

If Yes, make sure you understand basic concepts as covered in Exam 70-215. You should also study the TCP/IP interfaces, utilities, and services for Exam 70-216, and you should implement security features for Exam 70-220.

 You can download objectives, practice exams, and other data about Microsoft exams from the Training and Certification page at **www.microsoft.com/traincert**. You can use the "Exam Resources" link to obtain specific exam information.

If No, you must obtain one or two machines and a copy of Windows 2000 Server. Then, you should learn about the operating system and any other software components on which you'll also be tested. In fact, we recommend that you obtain two computers, each with a network interface, and set up a two-node network on which to practice. With decent Windows 2000–capable computers selling for about $500 to $600 apiece these days, this shouldn't be too much of a financial hardship. You might have to scrounge to come up with the necessary software, but if you scour the Microsoft Web site, you can usually find low-cost options to obtain evaluation copies of most of the software that you'll need.

➤ Windows 2000 Professional? [Yes or No]

If Yes, make sure you understand the concepts covered in Exam 70-210.

If No, you should obtain a copy of Windows 2000 Professional and learn how to install, configure, and maintain it. You can use this book to guide your activities and studies, or you can work straight from Microsoft's test objectives if you prefer.

 For any and all of these Microsoft exams, the Resource Kits for the topics involved are good study resources. You can purchase softcover Resource Kits from Microsoft Press (you can search for them at **http://mspress. microsoft.com**), but they also appear on the TechNet CDs (**www.microsoft.com/technet**). Along with the *Exam Cram 2* books, we believe that Resource Kits are among the best tools you can use to prepare for Microsoft exams.

2. For any specific Microsoft product that is not itself an operating system (for example, SQL Server), have you installed, configured, used, and upgraded this software? [Yes or No]

If Yes, skip to the next section, "Testing Your Exam-Readiness." If No, you must get some experience. Read on for suggestions about how to do this.

Experience is a must with any Microsoft product exam, be it something as simple as FrontPage 2002 or as challenging as SQL Server 2000. For trial copies of other software, you can search Microsoft's Web site, using the name of the product as your search term. Also, you can search for bundles such as "BackOffice," "Enterprise Servers," or "Small Business Server."

If you have the funds, or if your employer will pay your way, you should consider taking a class at a Certified Training and Education Center (CTEC) or at an Authorized Academic Training Partner (AATP). In addition to classroom exposure to the topic of your choice, you get a copy of the software that is the focus of your course, along with a trial version of whatever operating system it needs, as part of the training materials for that class.

Before you even think about taking any Microsoft exam, you should make sure you've spent enough time with the related software to understand how it can be installed and configured, how to maintain such an installation, and how to troubleshoot the software when things go wrong. This will help you in the exam—and in real life!

Testing Your Exam-Readiness

Whether you attend a formal class on a specific topic to get ready for an exam or use written materials to study on your own, some preparation for the Microsoft certification exams is essential. At $125 a pop—whether you pass or fail—you'll want to do everything you can to pass on your first try. That's where studying comes in.

We have included a practice exam in this book, so if you don't score very well on the test, you can study the practice exam more and then tackle the test again. We also have exams that you can take online through www.examcram2.com. If you still don't hit a score of at least 70% after practicing with these tests, you should investigate the other practice test resources that are mentioned in this section.

For any given subject, you should consider taking a class if you've tackled self-study materials, taken the test, and failed anyway. The opportunity to interact with an instructor and fellow students can make all the difference in the world, if you can afford that privilege. For information about Microsoft classes, visit the Training and Certification page at www.microsoft.com/education/?ID=ctec for Microsoft CTECs or www.microsoft.com/education/?ID=aatp for Microsoft AATPs.

If you can't afford to take a class, you can visit the Training and Certification pages anyway because they include pointers to free practice exams and to MCP Approved Study Guides and other self-study tools. And even if you can't afford to spend much money at all, you should still invest in some low-cost practice exams from commercial vendors.

The next question deals with your personal testing experience. Microsoft certification exams have their own style and idiosyncrasies. The more acclimated you become to the Microsoft testing environment, the better your chances will be to score well on the exams:

1. Have you taken a practice exam on your chosen test subject? [Yes or No]

   If Yes, and if you scored 70% or better, you're probably ready to tackle the real thing. If your score isn't above that threshold, you should keep at it until you break that barrier.

   If No, you should obtain all the free and low-budget practice tests you can find and get to work. You should keep at it until you can break the passing threshold comfortably.

 When it comes to assessing your test-readiness, there is no better way than to take a good-quality practice exam and pass with a score of 70% or better. When we're preparing, we shoot for 80% or higher, just to leave room for the "weirdness factor" that sometimes shows up on Microsoft exams.

Assessing Readiness for Exam 70-210

In addition to the general exam-readiness information in the previous section, there are several things you can do to prepare for the Exam 70-210. As you're getting ready for Exam 70-210, you should visit the *Exam Cram 2* Windows 2000 Resource Center at www.examcram2.com. We also suggest that you join an active MCSE mailing list. One of the best ones is managed by Sunbelt Software. You can sign up at www.sunbelt-software.com (look for the Subscribe button).

You can also cruise the Web, looking for "brain dumps" (recollections of test topics and experiences recorded by others) to help you anticipate topics you're likely to encounter on the test. The MCSE mailing list is a good place to ask where the useful brain dumps are.

You can't be sure that a brain dump's author can provide correct answers. Thus, you should use the questions to guide your studies, but you shouldn't rely on the answers in a brain dump to lead you to the truth. You should double-check everything you find in any brain dump.

Microsoft exam mavens also recommend that you check the Microsoft Knowledge Base (available on its own CD as part of the TechNet collection, and on the Microsoft Web site, at `http://support.microsoft.com`) for "meaningful technical support issues" that relate to your exam's topics. Although we're not sure exactly what the quoted phrase means, we have also noticed some overlap between technical support questions on particular products and troubleshooting questions on the exams for those products.

Onward, Through the Fog!

After you've assessed your readiness, undertaken the right background studies, obtained the hands-on experience that will help you understand the products and technologies at work, and reviewed the many sources of information to help you prepare for a test, you'll be ready to take a round of practice tests. When your scores come back positive enough to get you through the exam, you're ready to go after the real thing. If you follow our assessment regime, you'll not only know what you need to study, but you'll know when you're ready to set a test date. Good luck!

Microsoft Certification Exams

Terms you'll need to understand:

✓ Case study
✓ Multiple-choice question format
✓ Build-list-and-reorder question format
✓ Create-a-tree question format
✓ Drag-and-connect question format
✓ Select-and-place question format
✓ Fixed-length test
✓ Simulation
✓ Adaptive test
✓ Short-form test

Techniques you'll need to master:

✓ Assessing your exam-readiness
✓ Answering Microsoft's various question types
✓ Altering your test strategy depending on the exam format
✓ Practicing to make perfect
✓ Making the best use of the testing software
✓ Budgeting your time
✓ Guessing as a last resort

Exam taking is not something that most people anticipate eagerly, no matter how well prepared they may be. In most cases, familiarity helps offset test anxiety. In plain English, this means you probably won't be as nervous when you take your fourth or fifth Microsoft certification exam as you'll be when you take your first one.

Whether it's your first exam or your tenth, understanding the details of taking the new exams (how much time to spend on questions, the environment you'll be in, and so on) and the new exam software will help you concentrate on the material rather than on the setting. Likewise, mastering a few basic exam-taking skills should help you recognize—and perhaps even outfox—some of the tricks and snares you're bound to find in some exam questions.

This chapter, besides explaining the exam environment and software, describes some proven exam-taking strategies that you should be able to use to your advantage.

Assessing Exam-Readiness

We strongly recommend that you read through and take the self-assessment included with this book (it appears just before this chapter). This will help you compare your knowledge base to the requirements for obtaining MCSE certification, and it will also help you identify parts of your background or experience that may be in need of improvement, enhancement, or further learning. If you get the right set of basics under your belt, obtaining Microsoft certification will be that much easier.

After you've gone through the self-assessment, you can remedy those topical areas where your background or experience may not measure up to those of an ideal certification candidate. But you can also tackle subject matter for individual tests at the same time, so you can continue making progress while you're catching up in some areas.

After you've worked through an *Exam Cram 2* series book, have read the supplementary materials, and have taken the practice test, you'll have a pretty clear idea of when you should be ready to take the real exam. Although we strongly recommend that you keep practicing until your scores top the 75% mark, 80% would be a good goal, to give yourself some margin for error in a real exam situation (where stress will play more of a role than when you practice). After you hit that point, you should be ready to go. But if you get through the practice exam in this book without attaining that score, you should keep taking practice tests and studying the materials until you get there. You'll find more pointers on how to study and prepare in the self-assessment. At this point, let's talk about the exam itself.

The Exam Situation

When you arrive at the testing center where you scheduled your exam, you need to sign in with an exam coordinator. He or she asks you to show two forms of identification, one of which must be a photo ID. After you sign in and your time slot arrives, you are asked to deposit any books, bags, or other items you brought with you. Then you are escorted into a closed room.

All exams are completely closed book. In fact, you are not permitted to take anything with you into the testing area, but you are furnished with a blank sheet of paper and a pen or, in some cases, an erasable plastic sheet and an erasable pen. Before the exam, be sure to carefully review this book's Cram Sheet, located in the very front of the book. You should memorize as much of the important material as you can so that you can write that information on the blank sheet as soon as you are seated in front of the computer. You can refer to that piece of paper anytime you like during the test, but you have to surrender the sheet when you leave the room.

You are given some time to compose yourself, to record important information, and to take a sample exam before you begin the real thing. We suggest that you take the sample test before taking your first exam, but because all exams are more or less identical in layout, behavior, and controls, you probably don't need to do this more than once.

Typically, the testing room is furnished with anywhere from one to six computers, and each workstation is separated from the others by dividers designed to keep you from seeing what's happening on someone else's computer. Most testing rooms feature a wall with a large picture window. This permits the exam coordinator to monitor the room, to prevent exam-takers from talking to one another, and to observe anything out of the ordinary that might go on. The exam coordinator will have preloaded the appropriate Microsoft certification exam—for this book, that's Exam 70-210, "Installing, Configuring, and Administering Microsoft Windows 2000 Professional"—and you are permitted to start as soon as you're seated in front of the computer.

All Microsoft certification exams allow a certain maximum amount of testing time (this time is indicated on the exam by an onscreen counter/clock, so you can check the time remaining whenever you like). All Microsoft certification exams are computer generated. In addition to multiple choice, most exams contain select–and-place (drag-and-drop), create-a-tree (categorization and prioritization), drag-and-connect, and build-list-and-reorder (list prioritization) types of questions. Although this might sound quite simple, the questions are constructed not only to check your mastery of basic facts and figures about Windows 2000 Professional but also to require you to evaluate one or more sets of circumstances or requirements. Often, you are asked to give more than one answer to a question. Likewise, you might be asked to select the best or most effective solution to a problem from a range of choices, all of which are technically correct. Taking the exam is quite an adventure, and it involves real thinking. This book shows you what to expect and how to deal with the potential problems, puzzles, and predicaments.

In the next section, you'll learn more about how Microsoft test questions look and how you must answer them.

Exam Layout and Design

The format of Microsoft's Windows 2000 exams is different from that of its previous exams. For the design exams (70-219, "Designing a Microsoft Windows 2000 Directory Services Infrastructure," 70-220, "Designing Security for a Microsoft Windows 2000 Network," 70-221, "Designing a Microsoft Windows 2000 Network Infrastructure," and 70-226, "Designing Highly Available Web Solutions with Microsoft Windows 2000 Server Technologies"), each exam consists entirely of a series of case studies, and the questions can be of six types. For the four core exams (70-210 or 70-270, "Installing, Configuring, and Administering Microsoft Windows XP Professional"; 70-215, "Installing, Configuring, and Administering Microsoft Windows 2000 Server"; 70-216, "Implementing and Administering a Microsoft Windows 2000 Network Infrastructure"; and 70-217, "Implementing and Administering a Microsoft Windows 2000 Directory Services Infrastructure"), the same six types of questions may appear, but you are not likely to encounter complex multiquestion case studies.

NOTE

The Windows 2000 MCSE certification requirements include the Windows 2000 Professional exam as one of the required four core exams. You can either take Exam 70-270 (for Windows XP Professional) or Exam 70-210 (for Windows 2000 Professional) to meet the client operating system exam requirement. So when someone refers to one of the four core exams, he or she actually means the four core out of the available pool of five possible exams. In addition to choosing between the Windows 2000 Professional exam and the Windows XP Professional exam, in the near future you will be able to choose between the MCSE track for Windows 2000 Server and the MCSE track for Windows Server 2003.

For design exams, each case study, or "testlet," presents a detailed problem that you must read and analyze. Figure 1.1 shows an example of what a case study looks like. You must select the different tabs in the case study to view the entire case.

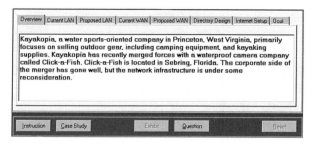

Figure 1.1 The format for case studies.

Following each case study is a set of questions related to the case study; these questions can be one of six types (which are discussed in the following sections). Careful attention to details provided in the case study is the key to success. You should be prepared to frequently toggle between the case study and the questions as you work. Some of the case studies include diagrams, which are called *exhibits*, that you'll need to examine closely to understand how to answer the questions.

After you complete a case study, you can review all the questions and your answers. However, after you move on to the next case study, you might not be able to return to the previous case study and make any changes.

These six types of question formats appear on Microsoft certification exams, and they are discussed in the following sections:

➤ Multiple-choice, single answer

➤ Multiple-choice, multiple answers

➤ Build-list-and-reorder (list prioritization)

➤ Create-a-tree

➤ Drag-and-connect

➤ Select-and-place (drag-and-drop)

The Single-Answer and Multiple-Answer Multiple-Choice Question Formats

Some exam questions require you to select a single answer, whereas others ask you to select multiple correct answers. The following multiple-choice question requires you to select a single correct answer. Following the question is a brief summary of each potential answer and why it is either right or wrong.

Question 1

> You have three domains connected to an empty root domain under one con-
> tiguous domain name: **tutu.com**. This organization is formed into a forest
> arrangement, with a secondary domain called **frog.com**. How many schema
> masters exist for this arrangement?
>
> ○ a. 1
> ○ b. 2
> ○ c. 3
> ○ d. 4

The correct answer is Answer a. Only one schema master is necessary for a
forest arrangement. The other answers (Answers b, c, and d) are misleading
because they try to make you believe that schema masters might be in each
domain, or perhaps that you should have one for each contiguous namespace
domain.

This sample question format corresponds closely to the Microsoft certification exam format. The only difference is that on the exam, the questions are
not followed by answers and their explanations. To select an answer, you
position the cursor over the radio button next to the answer you want to
select. Then you click the mouse button to select the answer.

Let's examine a question where one or more answers are possible. This type
of question provides check boxes rather than radio buttons for marking all
appropriate selections.

Question 2

> What can you use to seize FSMO roles? (Select all the correct answers.)
>
> ❑ a. The **ntdsutil.exe** utility
> ❑ b. The Replication Monitor
> ❑ c. The **secedit.exe** utility
> ❑ d. Active Directory domains and trusts

Answers a and b are correct. You can seize roles from a server that is still running through the Replication Monitor or, in the case of a server failure, you
can seize roles with the ntdsutil.exe utility. The secedit.exe utility is used to
force group policies into play; therefore, Answer c is incorrect. Active
Directory domains and trusts are a combination of truth and fiction; therefore, Answer d is incorrect.

For this particular question, two answers are required. Microsoft sometimes gives partial credit for partially correct answers. For Question 2, you have to check the boxes next to Answers a and b to obtain credit for a correct answer. Notice that choosing the right answers also means knowing why the other answers are wrong!

The Build-List-and-Reorder Question Format

Questions in the build-list-and-reorder format present two lists of items—one on the left and one on the right. To answer the question, you must move items from the list on the right to the list on the left. The final list must then be reordered into a specific order.

These questions generally sound like this: "From the following list of choices, pick the choices that answer the question. Arrange the list in a certain order." To give you practice with this type of question, some questions of this type are included in this book. Question 3 shows an example of how they appear in this book; for an example of how they appear on the test, see Figure 1.2.

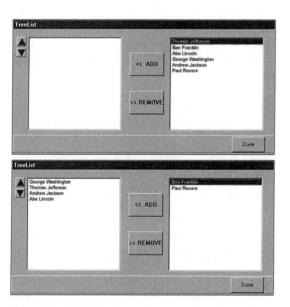

Figure 1.2   Build-list-and-reorder question format.

Question 3

> From the following list of famous people, choose those that have been elected
> president of the United States. Arrange the list in the order in which the presi-
> dents served.
>
> Thomas Jefferson
>
> Ben Franklin
>
> Abe Lincoln
>
> George Washington
>
> Andrew Jackson
>
> Paul Revere

The correct answer is:

George Washington

Thomas Jefferson

Andrew Jackson

Abe Lincoln

On an actual exam, the entire list of famous people would initially appear in
the list on the right. You would move the four correct answers to the list on
the left and then reorder the list on the left. Notice that the answer to
Question 3 does not include all items from the initial list. However, that
might not always be the case.

To move an item from the right list to the left list on the exam, you first select
the item by clicking it, and then you click the Add button (left arrow). After
you move an item from one list to the other, you can move the item back by
first selecting the item and then clicking the appropriate button (either the
Add button or the Remove button). After items have been moved to the left
list, you can move an item by selecting the item and clicking the up or down
button.

The Create-a-Tree Question Format

Questions in the create-a-tree format also present two lists—one on the left
side of the screen and one on the right side of the screen. The list on the
right consists of individual items, and the list on the left consists of nodes in
a tree. To answer the question, you must move items from the list on the
right to the appropriate node in the tree.

These questions can best be characterized as simply a matching exercise.
Items from the list on the right are placed under the appropriate category in

the list on the left. Question 4 shows an example of how they appear in this book; for a sample of how they appear on the test, see Figure 1.3.

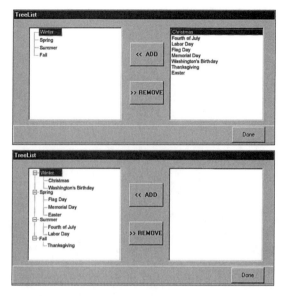

Figure 1.3   Create-a-tree question format.

Question 4

The calendar year is divided into four seasons:

Winter

Spring

Summer

Fall

Identify the season during which each of the following holidays occurs:

Christmas

Fourth of July

Labor Day

Flag Day

Memorial Day

Washington's Birthday

Thanksgiving

Easter

The correct answer is:

➤ Winter

　Christmas

　Washington's Birthday

➤ Spring

　Flag Day

　Memorial Day

　Easter

➤ Summer

　Fourth of July

　Labor Day

➤ Fall

　Thanksgiving

In this case, all the items in the list are used. However, that might not always be the case.

To move an item from the right list to its appropriate location in the tree, you must first select the appropriate tree node by clicking it. Then you select the item to be moved and click the Add button. If one or more items have been added to a tree node, the node is displayed with a + icon to the left of the node name. You can click this icon to expand the node and view the item(s) that has been added. If any item has been added to the wrong tree node, you can remove it by selecting it and clicking the Remove button.

The Drag-and-Connect Question Format

Questions in the drag-and-connect format present a group of objects and a list of "connections." To answer the question, you must move the appropriate connections between the objects.

This type of question is best described using graphics. Question 5 shows an example.

Question 5

The following objects represent the different states of water:

| Ice | Water Vapor | Water | Steam |

Use items from the following list to connect the objects so that they are scientifically correct:

Sublimates to form

Freezes to form

Evaporates to form

Boils to form

Condenses to form

Melts to form

The correct answer is:

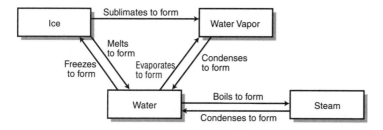

For this type of question, it's not necessary to use every object, and each connection can be used multiple times.

The Select-and-Place Question Format

Questions in the select-and-place (drag-and-drop) format present a diagram with blank boxes and a list of labels that need to be dragged to correctly fill in the blank boxes. To answer such a question, you must move the labels to their appropriate positions on the diagram.

This type of question is best described using graphics. Question 6 shows an example.

Question 6

Place the items in their proper order, by number, on the following flowchart. Some items may be used more than once, and some items may not be used at all:

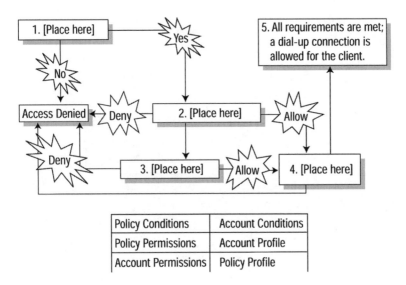

Policy Conditions	Account Conditions
Policy Permissions	Account Profile
Account Permissions	Policy Profile

The correct answer is:

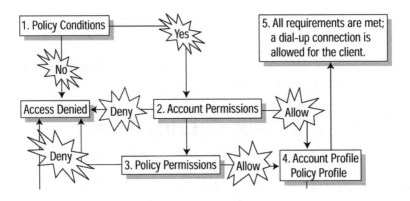

Figure 1.4 shows an example of a select-and-place question.

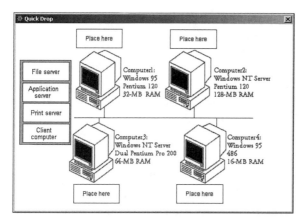

Figure 1.4   A sample select-and-place question.

Microsoft's Testing Formats

Currently, Microsoft uses four different testing formats:

➤ Case study

➤ Fixed length

➤ Adaptive

➤ Short form

As mentioned earlier, the case study approach is used with Microsoft's design exams. These exams consist of a set of case studies that you must analyze so that you can answer questions related to the case studies. Such exams include one or more case studies (tabbed topic areas), each of which is followed by 4 to 10 questions. The question types for design exams and for the four core Windows 2000 exams are multiple-choice, build-list-and-reorder, create-a-tree, drag-and-connect, and select-and-place. Depending on the test topic, some exams are totally case based, whereas others are not.

Other Microsoft exams employ advanced testing capabilities that might not be immediately apparent. Although the questions that appear are primarily multiple-choice, the logic that drives them is more complex than that in older Microsoft tests, which use a fixed sequence of questions, called a *fixed-length test*. Some questions employ a sophisticated user interface, which Microsoft calls a *simulation*, to test your knowledge of the software and systems under consideration in a more-or-less "live" environment that behaves just like the real thing. You should review the Microsoft Training and Certification Web pages at www.microsoft.com/traincert for more information.

 Exam formats may vary by test provider (VUE or Prometric). You might want to call the test center or visit **www.examcram2.com** to inquire about which type of test you might encounter.

For some exams, Microsoft has turned to a well-known technique called *adaptive testing* to establish a test-taker's level of knowledge and product competence. Adaptive exams look the same as fixed-length exams, but they discover the level of difficulty at which an individual test-taker can correctly answer questions. Test-takers with differing levels of knowledge or ability therefore see different sets of questions; individuals with high levels of knowledge or ability are presented with a smaller set of more difficult questions, whereas individuals with lower levels of knowledge are presented with a larger set of easier questions. Two individuals may answer the same percentage of questions correctly, but the test-taker with a higher knowledge or ability level will score higher because his or her questions are worth more. Also, the lower-level test-taker will probably answer more questions than his or her more-knowledgeable colleague. This explains why adaptive tests use ranges of values to define the number of questions and the amount of time it takes to complete the test.

Adaptive tests work by evaluating the test-taker's most recent answer. A correct answer leads to a more difficult question, and the test software's estimate of the test-taker's knowledge and ability level is raised. An incorrect answer leads to a less difficult question, and the test software's estimate of the test-taker's knowledge and ability level is lowered. This process continues until the test targets the test-taker's true ability level. The exam ends when the test-taker's level of accuracy meets a statistically acceptable value (in other words, when his or her performance demonstrates an acceptable level of knowledge and ability) or when the maximum number of items has been presented (in which case the test-taker is almost certain to fail).

Microsoft has also introduced a short-form test for its most popular tests. This test delivers 25 to 30 questions to its takers, giving them exactly 60 minutes to complete the exam. This type of exam is similar to a fixed-length test, in that it allows readers to jump ahead or return to earlier questions and to cycle through the questions until the test is done. Microsoft does not use adaptive logic in short-form tests, but it claims that statistical analysis of the question pool is such that the 25 to 30 questions delivered during a short-form exam conclusively measure a test-taker's knowledge of the subject matter in much the same way as an adaptive test. You can think of the short-form test as a kind of "greatest hits exam" (that is, the most important questions are covered) version of an adaptive exam on the same topic.

NOTE Microsoft certification exams may use either the adaptive-question format or the more traditional fixed-length question format. Historically, Microsoft tests have been primarily fixed-length format; however, the company seems to be moving in the direction of publishing more adaptive-question format exams in the near future.

Microsoft tests can come in any one of these forms. Whatever you encounter, you must take the test in whichever form it appears; you can't choose one form over another. If anything, it pays more to prepare thoroughly for an adaptive exam than for a fixed-length or a short-form exam: The penalties for answering incorrectly are built in to the test itself on an adaptive exam, whereas the layout remains the same for a fixed-length or short-form test, no matter how many questions you answer incorrectly.

TIP The biggest difference between an adaptive test and a fixed-length or short-form test is that on a fixed-length or short-form test, you can review any or all of the questions after you've answered them. On an adaptive test, you must answer each question when it's presented and you have no opportunity to revisit a question thereafter.

Strategies for Different Testing Formats

Before you choose a test-taking strategy, you must know if your test is a case-study based, fixed-length, short-form, or adaptive exam. When you begin your exam, you know right away if the test is based on case studies because the interface consists of a tabbed window that allows you to easily navigate through the sections of the case.

If you are taking a test that is not based on case studies, and if in fact the version you're taking is an adaptive test, the software tells you that the test is adaptive. If your introductory materials fail to mention this, you're probably taking a fixed-length test (50 to 70 questions). If the total number of questions involved is 25 to 30, you're taking a short-form test.

You can tell for sure if you are taking an adaptive, fixed-length, or short-form test when you see the first question. If it includes a check box that lets you mark the question for later review, you're taking a fixed-length or short-form test. If the total number of questions is 25 to 30, it's a short-form test; if the number of questions is greater than 30, it's a fixed-length test. Adaptive test questions can be visited (and answered) only once, and they do not include a check box that lets you mark a question for later review.

The Case Study Exam Strategy

Most test-takers find that the case study type of test used for the design exams (Exams 70-219, 70-220, 70-221, and 70-226) is the most difficult to master. When it comes to studying for a case study test, your best bet is to approach each case study as a standalone test. The biggest challenge you're likely to encounter with this type of test is that you might feel that you won't have enough time to get through all the cases that are presented.

Each case study provides a lot of material that you need to read and study before you can effectively answer the questions that follow. The trick to taking a case study exam is to first scan the case study to get the highlights. You should make sure you read the overview section of the case so that you understand the context of the problem at hand. Then, you should quickly move on to scanning the questions.

As you are scanning the questions, you should make mental notes to yourself so that you'll remember which sections of the case study you should focus on. Some case studies may provide a fair amount of extra information that you don't really need in order to answer the questions. The goal with this scanning approach is to avoid having to study and analyze material that is not completely relevant.

When studying a case study, you should carefully read the information on each tab. It is important that you answer each and every question. You can toggle back and forth between the case study and questions and between questions within a case study. However, after you leave a case study to move on to the next one, you may not be able to return to it. You might want to take notes while reading useful information so you can refer to them when you tackle the test questions. It's hard to go wrong with this strategy when taking any kind of Microsoft certification test.

The Fixed-Length and Short-Form Exam Strategy

A well-known strategy is that when you're taking fixed-length or short-form exams, you should first read over the entire exam from start to finish, while answering only those questions you feel absolutely sure of. On subsequent passes, you can dive in to more complex questions more deeply, knowing how many such questions you have left.

Fortunately, the Microsoft exam software for fixed-length and short-form tests makes the multiple-visit approach easy to implement. At the top-left corner of each question is a check box that permits you to mark that question so that it is available for later visits.

NOTE   Marking questions makes review easier, but you can return to any question—even those for which you did not mark the check box—by clicking the Forward or Back button repeatedly.

As you read each question, if you answer only those questions that you're sure of and mark for review those that you're not sure of, you can keep working through a decreasing list of questions as you answer the trickier ones.

TIP   Reading over an exam completely before answering the trickier questions has at least one potential benefit: Sometimes, information supplied in later questions sheds more light on earlier questions. Or information you read in later questions might jog your memory about Windows 2000 Professional facts, figures, or behavior that helps you answer earlier questions. Either way, you'll come out ahead if you defer answering those questions about which you're not absolutely sure.

The following are some question-handling strategies that apply to fixed-length and short-form tests:

➤ When you return to a question after your initial read-through, you should read every word again; otherwise, your mind can quickly fall into a rut. Sometimes, revisiting a question after turning your attention elsewhere lets you see something you missed, but the strong tendency is to see what you've seen before. You should try to avoid that tendency at all costs.

➤ If you return to a question more than twice, you should try to articulate to yourself what you don't understand about the question, why answers don't appear to make sense, or what appears to be missing. If you chew on the subject awhile, your subconscious might provide the details you lack, or you might notice something that points to the right answer.

As you work your way through the exam, another counter that Microsoft provides will come in handy—the number of questions completed and questions outstanding. For fixed-length and short-form tests, it's wise to budget your time by making sure that you've completed one-quarter of the questions one-quarter of the way through the exam period and three-quarters of the questions three-quarters of the way through.

If you're not finished when only five minutes remain, you should use that time to guess your way through any remaining questions. Remember that guessing is potentially more valuable than not answering because blank answers are always counted as wrong, but a guess might turn out to be right. If you don't have a clue about any of the remaining questions, you should pick answers at random, or choose all a's, b's, and so on. The important thing is to submit for scoring an exam that has an answer for every question.

 At the very end of your exam period, you're better off guessing than leaving questions unanswered.

The Adaptive Exam Strategy

If there's one principle that applies to taking an adaptive test, it could be summed up as "Get it right the first time." You cannot elect to skip a question and move on to the next one when taking an adaptive test because the testing software uses your answer to the current question to select the question it presents next. You also cannot return to a question after you've moved on because the software gives you only one chance to answer the question. You can, however, take notes, and sometimes information supplied in earlier questions sheds more light on later questions.

Also, when you answer a question correctly, you are presented with a more difficult question next, to help the software gauge your level of skill and ability. When you answer a question incorrectly, you are presented with a less difficult question, and the software lowers its current estimate of your skill and ability. This continues until the program settles into a reasonably accurate estimate of what you know and can do, and it takes you, on average, through somewhere between 15 and 30 questions to complete the test.

The good news is that if you know your stuff, you are likely to finish most adaptive tests in 30 minutes or so. The bad news is that you must really, really know your stuff in order to do your best on an adaptive test. That's because some questions are so convoluted, complex, or hard to follow that you're bound to miss one or two, at a minimum, even if you do know your stuff. So the more you know, the better you'll do on an adaptive test, even accounting for the occasionally weird or unfathomable questions that appear on these exams.

Because you can't always tell in advance if a test is a fixed-length, short-form, or adaptive exam, you should prepare for the exam as if it were adaptive. That way, you should be prepared to pass, no matter what kind of test you take. But if you do take a fixed-length or short-form test, you need to remember the tips from the preceding sections. These tips should help you perform even better on a fixed-length or short-form exam than on an adaptive test.

If you encounter a question on an adaptive test that you can't answer, you must guess an answer immediately. Because of how the software works, however, you might suffer for your guess on the next question if you guess right because you get a more difficult question next!

Question-Handling Strategies

For a question that takes only a single answer, usually two or three of the answers are obviously incorrect, and two of the answers are plausible—but of course, only one can be correct. Unless the answer leaps out at you (if it does, you should reread the question to look for a trick; sometimes those are the ones you're likely to get wrong), you should begin the process of answering by eliminating the answers that are most obviously wrong.

Almost always, at least one answer out of the possible choices for a question can be eliminated immediately because it matches one of these conditions:

➤ The answer does not apply to the situation.

➤ The answer describes a nonexistent issue, an invalid option, or an imaginary state.

After you eliminate all answers that are obviously wrong, you can apply your retained knowledge to eliminate further answers. You should look for items that sound correct but refer to actions, commands, or features that are not present or not available in the situation that the question describes.

If you're still faced with making a blind guess among two or more potentially correct answers, you should reread the question. You should try to picture how each of the possible remaining answers would alter the situation. You need to be especially sensitive to terminology; sometimes the choice of words (*remove* instead of *disable*) can make the difference between a right answer and a wrong one.

Only when you've exhausted your ability to eliminate answers but you remain unclear about which of the remaining possibilities is correct should you guess at an answer. An unanswered question offers you no points, but guessing gives you at least some chance of getting a question right; you just shouldn't be too hasty when making a blind guess.

> If you're taking a fixed-length or a short-form test, you can wait until the last round of reviewing marked questions (just as you're about to run out of time or out of unanswered questions) before you start making guesses. You have this same option within each case study on a case study exam, but when you leave a case study, you may not be allowed to return to it. If you're taking an adaptive test, you have to guess in order to move on to the next question if you can't figure out an answer some other way. In any case, guessing should be your technique of last resort!

Numerous questions assume that the default behavior of a particular utility is in effect. If you know the defaults and understand what they mean, this knowledge will help you cut through many of the trickiest questions.

Mastering the Inner Game

In the final analysis, knowledge breeds confidence, and confidence breeds success. If you study the materials in this book carefully and review all the practice questions at the end of each chapter, you should become aware of the areas where you need additional learning and study.

After you've worked your way through the book, you should take the practice exam in Chapter 11, "Sample Test." Taking this test will provide a reality check and help you identify areas to study further. You should make sure you follow up and review materials that are related to the questions you miss on the practice exam before you schedule a real exam. Only when you've covered that ground and feel comfortable with the whole scope of the practice exam should you set an exam appointment. Only if you score 90% or better should you proceed to the real thing; otherwise, you should obtain some additional practice tests so you can keep trying until you hit this magic number.

> If you take a practice exam and don't score at least 90% correct, you should practice further. Microsoft provides links to practice exam providers and also offers self-assessment exams at **www.microsoft.com/traincert**. You should also check out **www.examcram2.com** for downloadable practice questions.

Armed with the information in this book and with the determination to augment your knowledge, you should be able to pass the certification exam. However, you need to work at it, or you'll spend the exam fee more than once before you finally pass. If you prepare seriously, you should do well. We are confident that you can do it!

The next section covers other sources you can use to prepare for Microsoft certification exams.

Additional Resources

A good source of information about Microsoft certification exams is Microsoft itself. Because Microsoft's products and technologies—and the exams that go with them—change frequently, the best place to go for exam-related information is online.

If you haven't already visited the Microsoft Training & Certification Web site, you should do so right now. Microsoft's Training & Certification home page resides at www.microsoft.com/traincert (see Figure 1.5).

Figure 1.5   The Microsoft Training & Certification home page.

NOTE

This page might not be there by the time you read this, or might be replaced by something new and different, because things change regularly on the Microsoft site. Should this happen, please read the sidebar titled "Coping with Change on the Web."

Coping with Change on the Web

Sooner or later, all the information we've shared with you about the Microsoft Certified Professional pages and the other Web-based resources mentioned throughout this book will go stale or be replaced by newer information. In some cases, the uniform resource locators (URLs) you find here might lead you to their replacements; in other cases, the URLs will go nowhere, leaving you with the dreaded **404 File not found** error message. When that happens, you shouldn't give up.

There's always a way to find what you want on the Web if you're willing to invest some time and energy. Most large or complex Web sites—and Microsoft's qualifies on both counts—offer search engines. On all of Microsoft's Web pages, a Search button appears at the top edge of the page. As long as you can get to Microsoft's site (it should stay at **www.microsoft.com** for a long time), you can use the Search button to find what you need.

The more focused you can make a search request, the more likely the results will include information you can use. For example, you can search for the string:

```
"training and certification"
```

to produce a lot of data about the subject in general, but if you're looking for the preparation guide for Exam 70-058, "Networking Essentials," you'll be more likely to get there quickly if you use a search string similar to the following:

```
"Exam 70-058" AND "preparation guide"
```

Likewise, if you want to find the Training and Certification downloads, you should try a search string such as this:

```
"training and certification" AND "download page"
```

Finally, you should feel free to use general search tools—such as **www.search.com**, **www.google.com**, and **www.excite.com**—to look for related information. Although Microsoft offers great information about its certification exams online, there are plenty of third-party sources of information and assistance that need not follow Microsoft's party line. Therefore, if you can't find something where the book says it lives, you should intensify your search.

2

Implementing and Administering Resources

. . . .

Terms you'll need to understand:

✓ Shared folders

✓ Hidden shares

✓ Offline files and client-side caching

✓ Share permissions

✓ NT File System (NTFS)

✓ NTFS permissions

✓ User rights

✓ Access control list (ACL)

✓ NTFS compression

✓ Object ownership

✓ Auditing

✓ NTFS Encrypting File System (EFS)

✓ Printer port

✓ Internet Printing Protocol (IPP)

Techniques you'll need to master:

✓ Creating network shares

✓ Configuring share permissions

✓ Configuring options for offline files

✓ Setting basic and advanced NTFS permissions

✓ Enabling/disabling NTFS data compression

Why do we have computer networks, anyway? Networks empower us to collaborate on projects and share information with others. If you're working on a Windows 2000 Professional system that is connected to a network, you can share one or more of that system's folders with other computers and users on that network. Drive volumes and folders are not automatically shared for all users in Windows 2000 Professional. Members of the Administrators and the Power Users groups, as discussed later in this chapter, retain the rights to create shared network folders.

Managing Access to Shared Folders

In Windows 2000 Professional, if you want to share various folders on a computer with other users on the network, you need to specify those folders as shared. If you do not specifically share any folders on the computer, users do not have network access to the files that are stored on your workstation. As a general rule, you should not share an entire drive volume at the root level (for example, the c: drive) because when you share an entire drive this way, anyone with network access to the computer can try to read, modify, or delete all the files stored on that drive. By selectively sharing only the necessary folders with the network, you can eliminate unwanted snooping into personal or confidential data.

To share a folder with the network, follow these steps:

1. Open either My Computer or Windows Explorer.

2. Right-click the folder that you want to share and then select Sharing from the pop-up menu.

3. Click the Share This Folder radio button, as shown in Figure 2.1.

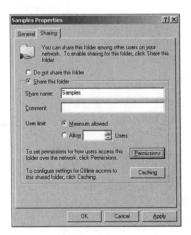

Figure 2.1   Creating a network share by accessing the Sharing tab of a folder's properties sheet.

4. Enter a share name or accept the default one. Windows 2000 uses the actual folder name as the default share name.

5. (Optional) Enter a comment. Comments appear in the Browse list when users search for network resources. Comments can help users locate the proper network shares.

6. Specify the user limit by selecting either Maximum Allowed or Allow [fill in number] Users. Windows 2000 Professional permits a maximum of 10 concurrent network connections per share. You should specify the Allow x [fill in number] Users option only if you need to limit the number of concurrent users for the share to fewer than 10 users.

7. Click OK to create the shared folder. The folder becomes available to others on the network.

 NOTE

To remove a network share, you right-click the shared folder and choose the Sharing option. Then you click the Do Not Share This Folder radio button and click OK. The folder is then no longer shared with the network.

Connecting to Shared Resources on a Windows Network

Users and network administrators have several options available to them for connecting to shared network resources. These options include the following:

➤ Typing in a uniform naming convention (UNC) path from the Run dialog box in the format *servername**sharename*.

➤ Navigating to the share from the My Network Places window.

➤ Using the net use command from a command prompt window.

Connecting to Network Resources by Using a UNC

You can connect to network resources by using a UNC path from the Run dialog box. For example, if you want to connect to a shared folder named samples that resides on a Windows computer named 7800pro, you should click Start, Run. Next, you type \\7800pro\samples and then click OK. At this point, you are connected to that shared resource, provided that you possess the security permissions needed to access the shared folder.

Connecting to Network Resources by Using the My Network Places Window

You can connect to a network share from My Network Places. To do so, you need to double-click the My Network Places icon on the Windows 2000 desktop. Then you double-click the Add Network Place icon, which opens the Add Network Place Wizard, as shown in Figure 2.2. Next, you need to enter the location of the network place or click Browse to locate the network share by viewing the available network resources. Finally, you click Next to enter a name for the network place or accept the default name and then click Finish to establish the connection to the shared folder, provided that you have the proper permissions. A list of network resources to which you have already connected is then displayed within the My Network Places window.

Figure 2.2   Connecting to a shared network folder with the Add Network Place Wizard.

Connecting to Network Resources by Using the net use Command

You have the option of connecting to network shares via the net use command. For help with the various options and syntax of the net use command, you can type net use /? at the command prompt. To connect to a remote resource from the command line, you need to follow these steps:

1. Open a command prompt window by selecting Start, Programs, Accessories, Command Prompt.

2. At the command prompt, type net use *drive_letter*: \\7800pro\samples and press Enter, where *drive_letter* is a drive letter that you designate. If you have the appropriate permissions for that network share, you should see the message The Command Completed Successfully displayed in the command prompt window.

Using Automatically Generated Hidden Shares

Windows 2000 Professional automatically creates shared folders by default each and every time the computer is started. These default shares are often referred to as *hidden* or *administrative* because a dollar sign ($) is appended to each share name. The dollar sign at the end of a share name prevents the shared folder from being displayed on the network Browse list; users cannot easily discover that these shares exist. When users browse through the My Network Places window, for example, they cannot see that such hidden shares even exist; Microsoft Windows Networking does not allow hidden shares to be displayed. These hidden network shares include the following:

➤ *C$, D$, E$, and so on*—One share gets created for the root of each available hard drive volume on the system.

➤ *ADMIN$*—This share shares the system root folder (for example, C:\WINNT) with the network.

➤ *IPC$*—This share is used for interprocess communications (IPC). IPC supports communications between objects on different computers over a network by manipulating the low-level details of network transport protocols. IPC enables the use of distributed application programs that enable multiple processes to work together to accomplish a single task.

Although you can temporarily disable hidden shares, you cannot delete them without modifying the registry (which is not recommended) because they are re-created on each restart. You can connect to a hidden share only if you provide a user account with administrative privileges along with the appropriate password for that user account. Administrators can create their own custom administrative (hidden) shares simply by adding a dollar sign to the share name of any shared folder. Administrators can view all the hidden shares that exist on a Windows 2000 Professional system by accessing the Shares folder within the System Tools/Shared Folders container of the Computer Management console.

Controlling Access to Shared Folders

When a network administrator grants access to shared resources over the network, the shared data files become very vulnerable to unintentional as well as intentional destruction or deletion by others. This is why network administrators must be vigilant in controlling data access security permissions. If access permissions to shared folders are too lenient, shared data may become compromised. On the other hand, if access permissions are set too stringently, the users who need to access and manipulate the data may not be able to do their jobs. Managing access control for shared resources can be quite challenging.

Using Offline Files and Client-Side Caching

By right-clicking a shared folder and selecting Sharing, you can modify some of the shared folder's properties. For example, you can specify whether network users can cache shared data files on their local workstations. To configure offline access settings for the shared folder, you click the Caching button. If you allow caching of files for a shared folder, you must choose one of three options in the Caching Settings dialog box:

➤ *Automatic Caching for Documents*—This option relies on the workstation and server computers to automatically download and make available offline any opened files from the shared folder. Older copies of files are automatically updated.

➤ *Automatic Caching for Programs*—This setting is recommended for folders that contain read-only data and for application programs that have been configured to be run from the network. This option is not designed for sharing data files, and file sharing in this mode may or may not work.

➤ *Manual Caching for Documents*—This is the default caching setting. This setting requires network users to manually specify any files they want to have available when working offline. This setting is recommended for folders that contain user documents.

You need to click OK in the Caching Settings dialog box after making any configuration changes for offline access to the shared folder.

If you do not want files within the shared folder to be cached locally on workstations, you must deselect the Allow Caching of Files in This Shared Folder check box (see Figure 2.3).

The default cache size is configured as 10% of the client computer's available disk space. You can change this setting by selecting Tools, Folder Options from the menu bar from any My Computer or Windows Explorer window. The Offline Files tab of the Folder Options dialog box displays the system's offline files settings, as shown in Figure 2.4.

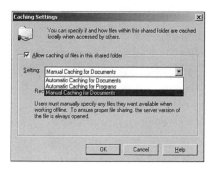

Figure 2.3   The Caching Settings dialog box, with Manual Caching for Documents selected.

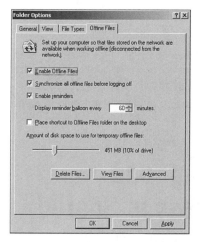

Figure 2.4   The Offline Files tab of the Folder Options dialog box.

The offline files feature is also known as client-side caching (CSC). The default location on Windows 2000 computers for storage of offline files is *SystemRoot*\CSC (for example, **C:\WINNT\CSC**). You can use the **Cachemov.exe** tool from the *Windows 2000 Professional Resource Kit* and the *Windows 2000 Server Resource Kit* to relocate the **CSC** folder onto a different drive volume. The **Cachemov.exe** utility moves the **CSC** folder to the root of the drive volume that is specified. After the **CSC** folder has been moved from its default location, all subsequent moves place it in the root of the drive volume. **Cachemov.exe** never returns the folder to its original default location.

Network Share Permissions

In addition to the Caching button located at the bottom of the Sharing tab of a shared folder's properties sheet is the Permissions button. The caption next to this button reads To Set Permissions for How Users Access This Folder over the Network, Click Permissions. However, these share permissions are intended solely for backward-compatibility purposes; you should

actually avoid setting such permissions unless a share resides on a file allocation table (FAT) or FAT32 drive volume, which provide no file system security. In most circumstances, you should store all data and applications on
NTFS drive volumes. In fact, as a general rule, you should configure all system drive volumes in NTFS. With the availability of third-party tools as well
as the native Windows 2000 Recovery Console, which permit command-line
access to NTFS drives (even if the system won't boot), it's difficult to argue
against using NTFS for all drives in Windows 2000.

Network share permissions have their roots back in the days of Windows for
Workgroups 3.1x, before Windows NT and NTFS. Share permissions provided a way for administrators to control access to files for network users.
Only three permissions are available: Full Control, Change, and Read. These
three permissions can be explicitly allowed or denied. The default is Allow
Full Control for the Everyone group. For shared folders that reside on FAT
or FAT32 drives, share permissions offer some degree of access control for
network users. However, they provide no security for local access! Share permissions apply only to access over the network; they have absolutely nothing
to do with the underlying file system.

Monitoring, Managing, and Troubleshooting Access to Shared Files and Folders Under NTFS

Although you can somewhat control access to shared network folders by
managing share permissions, Windows 2000 NTFS provides a very robust
access control solution. In addition to offering administrators more granu-
larity of security access control over files and folders than network share permissions, NTFS permissions reside at the file system level, which allows
administrators to manage only one set of access control settings for both network users and local users.

NTFS Security: Users and Groups

You can apply NTFS security permissions to resources such as files, folders,
and printers for specific users or groups of users. Windows 2000 Professional
installs two local user accounts by default: Administrator and Guest. The
Guest user account is disabled by default. The Administrator user account is
all-powerful on the local machine and cannot be deleted, although it can be
renamed. Six local groups are installed automatically: Administrators,

Backup Operators, Guests, Power Users, Replicator, and Users. The Power Users group is not present in any edition of Windows 2000 Server; it exists only as a local group in Windows 2000 Professional. The Administrators account is all-powerful because it is a member of the Administrators group, and you cannot remove the Administrator user account from membership in the Administrators group. Table 2.1 outlines the local groups that are installed by default when you first install Windows 2000 Professional.

Table 2.1 Local Groups Installed by Default in Windows 2000 Professional	
Local Group	**Role**
Administrators	Group members possess full administrative control for managing the local system, local users, and local groups.
Backup Operators	Group members have the rights to back up and restore files and folders on the local system.
Guests	Group members can't make permanent alterations to their desktop settings. The default Guest account is automatically a member of this group. By default, group members possess no specific rights or permissions on objects. If the local computer joins a Windows NT Server or Windows 2000 Server domain, the global domain Guests group automatically becomes a member of the local Guests group.
Power Users	Group members can add new local user accounts and change existing local user accounts. Members can also create shared folders and shared printers on the network.
Replicator	This group supports file replication within a Windows 2000 domain context.
Users	Group members can perform tasks only after an administrator has specifically granted them rights to do so. They can access resources for only those objects that an administrator has granted them permissions. When user accounts are created, each new user automatically becomes a member of the local Users group. If the local computer becomes a member of a Windows NT Server or Windows 2000 Server domain, the global domain Users group automatically becomes a member of the local Users group.

Table 2.2 displays the special built-in system groups that are present in the Windows 2000 Professional network operating system (NOS). The primary purpose of the groups listed in Tables 2.1 and 2.2 is to facilitate managing access control settings (especially for NTFS) by allowing administrators to assign security permissions to groups of users rather than having to assign and maintain security permissions on resources to hundreds or thousands of individual users. Special built-in system groups also exist in Windows 2000

Professional. Built-in system groups are also known as special identity groups—they identify different roles that users play, depending on how the users are accessing the system. These built-in system groups include the groups that appear in Table 2.2.

Table 2.2 Built-in System Groups Installed by Default in Windows 2000 Professional	
Built-in Group	**Role**
Everyone	Group members include all users who access the computer. The best practice is to avoid using this group. If you enable the Guest account, any user can become authorized to access the system, and the user inherits the rights and permissions assigned to the Everyone group.
Authenticated Users	Group members have valid user accounts on the local system, or they possess a valid user account within the domain of which the system is a member. It is better to use this group than to use the Everyone group in order to prevent anonymous access to resources.
Creator Owner	A user becomes a member of this built-in group by creating or taking ownership of a resource. Whenever a member of the Administrators group creates an object, the Administrators group—rather than the actual name of the user who created the resource—is listed as the owner of that resource.
Network	Group members include any user accounts from a remote computer that access the local computer via a current network connection.
Interactive	This group includes the user account for the locally logged on user.
Anonymous Logon	Group members include any user accounts that Windows 2000 did not validate or authorize.
Dialup	Group members include any user accounts that are currently connected via Dial-up Networking.

Setting NTFS Security Permissions

Because share permissions apply to network access only, they can serve only to complicate and possibly confuse access control settings when you apply them on top of NTFS security permissions, which take effect at the file system level. If share permissions and NTFS permissions conflict, the most restrictive permissions apply. For example, let's say that you set share permissions on the shared folder named c:\Samples. Suppose you have set the share permissions for the Users group to Read. At the same time, let's suppose that you also have NTFS permissions set on that folder; let's say that you've applied the Change permission for the Users group on that folder in

NTFS. So you have conflicting permissions: Read at the share level and Change at the NTFS level. The net result is that members of the Users group are granted only the ability to read the files within that folder; they cannot make any changes to those files because the most restrictive permissions always win.

As you can see, conflicting permissions may make it difficult to decipher which permissions users are granted when they are accessing files over a network. Therefore, the best practice is to place all shared network data and applications on NTFS drive volumes and set the appropriate security permissions for users and groups at the NTFS level. You should not change the default shared folder permissions; you should leave them at Full Control for the Everyone group. The most restrictive permissions apply, so all NTFS permissions flow through the network share. NTFS security settings can then apply equally to both local users and network users, and administrators have to manage only one set of permissions.

Local Accounts Versus Domain Accounts

In Windows NT and Windows 2000 environments, user accounts and group accounts always participate in one of two security contexts: workgroup security (also known as *peer-to-peer networking*) and domain security. Workgroup security is the default security context for individual and networked Windows NT Workstation 4 and Windows 2000 Professional computers that are not members of Windows NT Server or Windows 2000 Server domains. *Workgroups* are logical groupings of computers that do not share a centrally managed user and group database. Local users and groups are managed from each computer's Local Users and Groups folder within the Computer Management console. Users and groups must be maintained separately on each computer. No centralized management scheme exists within a workgroup environment; duplicate user and group accounts must exist on each computer in order to grant and control access permissions on each workstation's individual resources. User and group accounts are stored within a local database on each Windows 2000 Professional computer.

In a Windows NT Server/Windows 2000 Server domain network environment, on the other hand, the domain acts as a central administration point for managing users, groups, and security permissions. A *domain* is simply a logical grouping of computers that share a centrally managed database. Duplicate user and group accounts are unnecessary and unwarranted within the domain security context. Users simply log on to the domain from any domain member computer, and their domain group memberships, along with their user rights, follow them wherever they travel throughout the domain.

A Windows 2000 Server Active Directory domain maintains a domainwide database of users and groups that is referred to as the *directory*. The Active Directory database is physically stored on domain controller (DC) computers. The Active Directory can contain a lot of detailed information about its users. The Active Directory database is replicated and synchronized with all the other DCs within a domain. For Windows NT Server domains, domain group memberships can travel with users across domains, provided that the proper trust relationships have been established among domains. For Windows 2000 Server Active Directory domains, group memberships can travel with users throughout the entire forest.

The Windows 2000 Logon Process

When a Windows 2000 Professional computer initially boots, the boot process ends with the system displaying the Welcome to Windows dialog box. The Ctrl+Alt+Delete keystroke sequence invokes the Winlogon process, which runs as a service in the background on Windows 2000 machines, unless you, as an administrator, have set up an automatic logon procedure or you have removed the Windows 2000 Professional requirement for users to press Ctrl+Alt+Delete to log on to the system. This keystroke combination advances you to the Log on to Windows dialog box, where you are prompted for a valid user name and password. By clicking the Options button, you can log on by using a Dial-Up Networking connection. Another option, if the computer is a member of a domain, is that you can select to log on to a domain or to log on to the local system by using the Log on To drop-down list.

After you enter your logon credentials and click OK, the Winlogon process passes the information to the Windows 2000 local security authority (LSA) subsystem, which compares the information you entered with the user information stored within the local security database for the system. When you are logging on to a domain, the Winlogon process forwards the user logon information that was entered to the LSA, which then forwards the information to the Netlogon process. The Netlogon process locates a DC computer, where the information is compared to the domain's directory database of valid users and passwords. After the user and password information is processed and the results are returned, if the Winlogon process can confirm that the user's logon credentials are valid, an *access token* is generated for the user, and the user is permitted to log on.

After the user has been allowed to log on to the system, the Windows 2000 operating system shell (that is, Windows Explorer) launches to provide the user's desktop. The user's access token that is generated is like a passport with various admission tickets attached. The access token is similar to a passport in that users carry it with them wherever they go. The admission tickets that come with the passport consist of a list of objects and resources that users can access. In Windows 2000, users are granted two types of access control settings:

➤ *Rights*—Windows 2000 user rights determine what privileges the user has to interact with the operating system (for example, shut down the system, install software, log on locally, log on over the network). Administrators for Windows 2000 Professional computers can modify the default rights for users through the Local Security Settings snap-in of the Microsoft Management Console (MMC), shown in Figure 2.5.

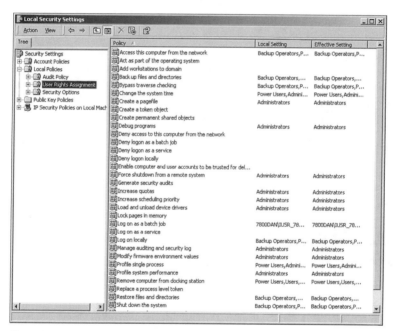

Figure 2.5   User Rights Assignment in the Local Security Settings snap-in.

➤ *Permissions*—Windows 2000 permissions pertain to what the user can do to objects (for example, permissions for reading, creating, modifying, or deleting files, folders, or printers). Windows 2000 objects include a wide variety of items in addition to files, folders, and printers, including processes, threads, ports, and devices.

ACLs

Every object within Windows 2000 Professional has various properties associated with it. One of those properties is the ACL. The ACL for an object delineates the specific users and groups that have been granted access to the object, along with the particular security permissions that have been granted to each one of those listed users and groups. To view the ACL for an object, such as a folder or a file, you right-click the object, click Properties, and then click the Security tab (see Figure 2.6). NTFS uses the information stored within ACLs to allow or deny users access permissions on files and folders.

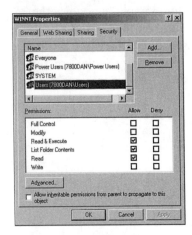

Figure 2.6 The Security tab of the WINNT Properties dialog box.

Another way to view and modify the ACL for a file or folder is to use the command-line tool CACLS.exe, as shown in Figure 2.7.

Figure 2.7 Viewing an object's ACL by using **CACLS.exe**.

Here's the CACLS.exe command syntax, which is explained in Table 2.3:

```
CACLS filename [/T] [/E] [/C] [/G user:perm] [/R user [...]]
[/P user:perm [...]] [/D user [...]]
```

Table 2.3 Command-Line Options for the CACLS.exe Utility	
Option	**Description**
filename	Displays ACLs for the specified file or folder.
/t	Changes ACLs of specified files in the current directory and all subdirectories.
/e	Edits the ACL instead of replacing it.
/c	Continues to change ACLs and ignores errors.
/g *user.perm*	Grants specified user access rights. The permission can be Read (**R**), Write (**W**), Change (**C**), or Full Control (**F**).
/r *user*	Revokes a specified user's access rights (valid only with /e).
/p *user.perm*	Replaces a specified user's access rights. The permission can be None (**N**), Read (**R**), Write (**W**), Change (**C**), or Full Control (**F**).
/d *user*	Denies access to the specified user.

You can use wildcard characters (* or ?) to specify more than one file or folder for a given command as well as to specify more than one user in a command. ACLs are broken down into basic and advanced security permission entries, as described in the following sections.

Basic Permissions

Basic permissions are actually comprised of predefined advanced NTFS permissions and are applied per user and per group. Individual file permissions differ slightly from the permissions that apply to folders. Table 2.4 describes the basic permissions available for files, and Table 2.5 outlines the basic permissions available for folders.

Table 2.4 Basic NTFS Security Permissions for Files for Specified Users and Groups	
Permission	**Description**
Full Control	Allows/denies full access to the file. Includes the ability to read, write, delete, modify, change permissions for, and take ownership of the file.
Modify	Allows/denies the ability to read, write, delete, modify, and read permissions for the file.
Read & Execute	Allows/denies specified users and groups the ability to execute the file and read its contents, read the file's attributes and extended attributes, and read the file's permissions.
Read	Allows/denies specified users and groups the ability to read the file's attributes and extended attributes and read the file's permissions.
Write	Allows/denies the ability to write data to the file, create files and append data, and write attributes and extended attributes.

Table 2.5 Basic NTFS Security Permissions for Folders for Specified Users and Groups	
Permission	**Description**
Full Control	Allows/denies full access to objects within the folder. Includes the ability to read, write, delete, modify, change permissions for, and take ownership of the folder.
Modify	Allows/denies the ability to read, write, delete, modify, and read permissions for the folder.
Read & Execute	Allows/denies specified users and groups the ability to traverse the folder, execute files within the folder, list the folder's contents, read the folder's contents, read the folder's attributes and extended attributes, and read the folder's permissions.
List Folder Contents	Allows/denies specified users and groups the ability to traverse the folder, list the folder's contents, read the folder's contents, read the folder's attributes and extended attributes, and read the folder's permissions. This permission does not affect a user's ability to run (execute) an application program as does the Read & Execute permission.
Read	Allows/denies specified users and groups the ability to list the folder's contents, read the folder's contents, read the folder's attributes and extended attributes, and read the folder's permissions.
Write	Allows/denies the ability to create files and write data, create folders and append data, and write attributes and extended attributes.

 The List Folder Contents permission is inherited by folders but not by files, and it should appear only when you view folder permissions. Read & Execute is inherited by both files and folders and is always present when you view file or folder permissions.

By default, NTFS security permissions are inherited from an object's parent. An administrator can manually override the default inheritance and can explicitly configure ACL settings. To disable permission inheritance, you need to deselect the Allow Inheritable Permissions from Parent to Propagate to This Object check box on the Security tab of the folder's properties sheet. As soon as you uncheck this box, the Security message box shown in Figure 2.8 appears. It prompts you to either copy the existing permissions or remove them entirely.

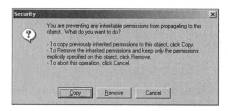

Figure 2.8 A Security message box that prompts you to either copy the existing permissions or remove them entirely.

Advanced Permissions

NTFS advanced permissions are the building blocks for basic permissions. In Windows 2000 advanced permissions allow administrators to have very granular control over exactly what types of access users can have to files and folders. Advanced permissions are somewhat hidden from view. They allow administrators to fine-tune ACL settings. The Security tab in a file or folder's properties sheet notifies you when advanced permissions are present. You can click the Advanced button on a properties sheet to view, add, modify, or remove advanced permissions. Figure 2.9 shows how Windows 2000 notifies you that more than just basic permissions exist for an object: At the bottom of the Security tab, the system displays a text message notification just to the right of the Advanced button that says Additional Permissions Are Present But Not Viewable Here. Press Advanced to See Them.

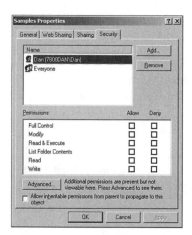

Figure 2.9 The Security tab of the Samples Properties dialog box.

After you click Advanced, you see the Access Control Settings dialog box, which shows each access control setting that has been applied per user and per group. To view individual advanced permission entries, you can click one of the users or groups listed and then click the View/Edit button. The Permission Entry dialog box, shown in Figure 2.10, appears. It gives administrators very fine control over individual users' and groups' abilities to manipulate data and program files that are stored on NTFS drive volumes.

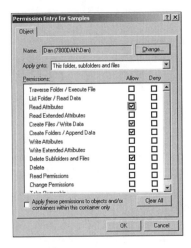

Figure 2.10   The Object tab of the Permission Entry for Samples dialog box.

From this dialog box, you can do the following:

➤ Change the name so that this permission entry applies to some other user or group.

➤ Modify the Apply Onto drop-down list to specify exactly where these advanced permissions should apply.

➤ Alter the actual permission entries themselves by marking or clearing the Allow or Deny check box for each permission that you want to affect.

 To change NTFS security permissions, you must be the owner of the file or folder whose permissions you want to modify, or the owner must grant you permission to make modifications to the object's security settings. Groups or users who are granted Full Control for a folder can delete files and subfolders within that folder regardless of the permissions protecting those files and subfolders. If the check boxes for the Security tab under Permissions are shaded, the file or folder has inherited the permissions from the parent folder. By clearing the Allow Inheritable Permissions from Parent to Propagate to This Object check box, you can copy those inherited permissions and turn them into explicit permissions or you can remove them entirely and manually establish new explicit permissions.

Table 2.6 defines Windows 2000 advanced permissions.

Table 2.6   Advanced NTFS Security Permission Entries for Files and Folders

Permission	Description
Traverse Folder/Execute File	Allows/denies moving through folders to reach other files or folders, even if the user has no permissions for the traversed folders (applies to folders only). Traverse Folder takes effect only when the group or user is not granted the Bypass Traverse Checking user right in the Group Policy snap-in. (By default, the Everyone group is given the Bypass Traverse Checking user right.) Also allows/denies the ability to execute files.
Execute File	Allows/denies running application program files. Setting the Traverse Folder permission on a folder does not automatically set the Execute File permission on all files within that folder.
List Folder/Read Data	Allows/denies viewing filenames and subfolder names within the folder. Also allows/denies viewing data in folders and files.
Read Data	Allows/denies viewing data in files.
Read Attributes	Allows/denies viewing the attributes—such as read-only, hidden, and archive—of a file or folder.
Read Extended Attributes	Allows/denies viewing the extended attributes of a file or folder. Some extended attributes are defined by application programs and can vary by application. The NTFS compression and encryption attributes are considered extended (or advanced) attributes.
Create Files/Write Data	Allows/denies creating files within a folder. Allows/denies writing data to files (applies to folders only).
Write Data	Allows/denies making changes to a file and overwriting the existing data (applies to files only).
Write Attributes	Allows/denies changing the attributes—such as read-only or hidden—of a file or folder.
Write Extended Attributes	Allows/denies changing the extended attributes of a file or folder. Extended attributes are defined by programs and may vary by program. Some extended attributes are defined by application programs and can vary by application. The NTFS compression and encryption attributes are considered extended (or advanced) attributes.
Delete Subfolders and Files	Allows/denies deleting subfolders and files, even if the Delete permission has not been granted on the subfolder or file.

(continued)

Table 2.6   Advanced NTFS Security Permission Entries for Files and Folders *(continued)*

Permission	Description
Delete	Allows/denies deleting the file or folder. If you don't have the Delete permission on a file or folder, you can still delete it if you have been granted Delete Subfolders and Files permission on the parent folder.
Read Permissions	Allows/denies reading permissions of the file or folder.
Change Permissions	Allows/denies changing permissions—such as Full Control, Read, and Modify—of the file or folder.
Take Ownership	Allows/denies taking ownership of a file or folder. The owner of a file or folder can always change permissions on it, regardless of any other permissions that have been assigned to protect the file or folder.
Create Folders/Append Data	Allows/denies creating folders within a folder. Also allows/denies making changes to the end of a file, but not changing, deleting, or overwriting existing data.
Append Data	Allows/denies making changes to the end of a file, but not changing, deleting, or overwriting existing data. (This permission applies to files only.)

 NTFS security permissions are *cumulative*. That is, users obtain permissions by having them assigned directly to their user accounts in addition to attaining permissions via group memberships. Users retain all permissions as they are assigned. If a user named Dan has the Allow Read permission for the **Graphics** folder and if Dan is a member of the Users group, which has been assigned Allow Write for the same folder, Dan has both the Allow Read and Allow Write permissions. Permissions continue to accumulate. However, Deny entries always override Allow entries for the same permission type (Read, Modify, Write, and so on).

Default NTFS Security Permissions

By default, all NTFS-formatted drive volumes are assigned the Allow Full Control permission for the Everyone group for the root of each drive. Folders and subfolders within each drive volume automatically inherit this default permission setting. Unfortunately, this setting leaves Windows 2000 systems very vulnerable. By default, any user who can log on to the system, either locally or over a network, can modify or delete some or all of the files and folders that reside on the system. As a best practice, you should remove the Everyone group's permissions entry from all drive volumes, except from the system root drive where the Windows 2000 system files are stored. When you install Windows 2000 Professional on an NTFS volume, the system root folder (for example, C:\WINNT) is automatically assigned special default security permissions for the groups Administrators, Creator Owner, Everyone, Power Users, System, and Users.

By default, the Everyone group's permissions are not assigned any permissions (no Allows and no Denies) for the system root folder. Users must be granted permission to access a file or a folder with the type of access specified (Read, Modify, Full Control, and so on). If the user's account, or one of the groups that the user is a member of, is not specifically granted or denied permission, the user cannot access the file or folder. This is known as an *implied* or *implicit Deny*.

 You should not change the default security settings for the system root folder and its subfolders. Modifying the default permissions for the Windows 2000 Professional system files can have very adverse effects on the system. In addition to not changing its default permissions, you should never attempt to compress or encrypt the system root folder or any of its subfolders. Compression or encryption placed on the system folders can render Windows 2000 Professional unstable and possibly unbootable.

NTFS Permission Conflicts

Obviously, a user may be a member of several different groups. You can apply NTFS permissions to both users and groups for access control on resources such as files and folders. For security permissions assigned to a user that conflict with other security permissions that have been granted to groups of which the user is also a member, the most liberal permissions take precedence for that user. The one overriding exception is any explicit Deny permission entry. Deny permissions always take precedence over Allow permissions.

 Just as Deny permissions always take precedence over Allow permissions, explicit permissions always override inherited permissions.

Monitoring, Managing, and Troubleshooting Access to Files and Folders

NTFS for Windows 2000 Professional offers several accessibility features that help administrators maintain and safeguard applications and data. In addition to providing local and network access control permissions, NTFS offers native data compression to save disk space. Folders that do not implement NTFS data compression can take advantage of native data encryption to help protect the confidentiality of data. For access to troubleshooting resources, you can enable auditing for folders and files housed on NTFS volumes.

Configuring, Managing, and Troubleshooting NTFS File and Folder Compression

Unlike previous data compression schemes, such as DoubleSpace and DriveSpace for the Windows 9x platform (with which you have to compress entire drive volumes), Windows 2000 NTFS data compression works folder by folder—or even file by file. NTFS compression is simply an advanced (or extended) file system attribute that you can apply to files and folders. NTFS data compression enables you to compress individual files or folders. You can compress individual files within uncompressed folders; compressed files and folders are displayed in blue.

NTFS Compression for Files

To enable compression for a specific file, you need to follow these steps:

1. Right-click the file in Windows Explorer or My Computer.

2. Click Properties.

3. Click the Advanced button in the Compress or Encrypt Attributes section of the Advanced Attributes dialog box, which is shown in Figure 2.11. This dialog box gives you mutually exclusive options to either compress contents to save disk space or encrypt contents to secure data.

Figure 2.11   The Advanced Attributes dialog box.

4. Click the Compress Contents to Save Disk Space check box.

5. Click OK in the Advanced Attributes dialog box.

6. Click OK in the file's properties sheet.

The name of the files that is compressed is displayed in blue, indicating that it is now a compressed file. Figure 2.12 shows uncompressed files along with one compressed file.

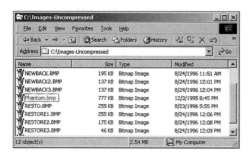

Figure 2.12   Several uncompressed files along with one compressed file.

To uncompress a specific file, you need to be sure that sufficient disk space exists for the uncompressed file, and then you need to follow these steps:

1. Right-click the file in Windows Explorer or My Computer.

2. Click Properties.

3. Click the Advanced button in the Attributes section.

4. Deselect the Compress Contents to Save Disk Space check box.

5. Click OK in the Advanced Attributes dialog box.

6. Click OK in the file's properties sheet.

NTFS Compression for Folders

You turn on compression for NTFS folders the same way you do for files:

1. Right-click the folder in Windows Explorer or My Computer.

2. Click Properties.

3. Click the Advanced button in the Attributes section.

4. Select the Compress Contents to Save Disk Space check box.

5. Click OK in the Advanced Attributes dialog box.

6. You are attempting to compress an entire folder, not just a single file, so the Confirm Attribute Changes dialog box, shown in Figure 2.13, appears. It prompts you to specify which files and/or folders compression is applied to. If you click Cancel, you can abort the data compression process. In this case, however, you don't want to do this. Therefore, click one of the two available options—either Apply Changes to This Folder Only or Apply Changes to This Folder, Subfolders and Files.

Figure 2.13 The Confirm Attribute Changes dialog box.

7. Click OK after you have chosen an option. The Confirm Attribute Changes dialog box closes, and the compression attributes are applied to the files and any subfolders you specified.

Figure 2.14 illustrates the significant difference that compression can make on saving valuable disk storage space. By right-clicking a folder and selecting Properties, you can determine the folder's actual physical size on the disk, as shown next to Size on Disk in Figure 2.14. By comparing folders with identical contents, one compressed and the other uncompressed, you can readily assess the impact that compression can make.

To uncompress a folder, you first need to make sure that enough disk space is available to accommodate the uncompressed folder. Next, you simply reverse procedure for compressing a folder.

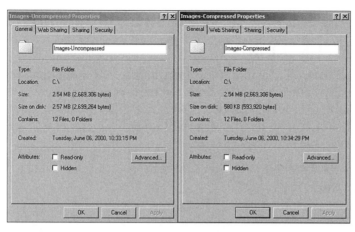

Figure 2.14   Comparing sizes of uncompressed (left) and compressed (right) files and folders.

Moving and Copying Compressed Files and Folders

Moving or copying compressed files and folders to non-NTFS drive volumes results in those objects being stored in their uncompressed state for the destination drive volume. If you move a compressed file or folder into an uncompressed folder, the object retains its compressed attribute: It remains compressed. If you copy a compressed file or folder into an uncompressed folder, the object inherits its attribute from the destination folder: It loses its compression attribute and becomes uncompressed within the target folder. Of course, the original file or folder that is copied remains unchanged; it stays compressed.

If you move an uncompressed file or folder into a compressed folder located on the same drive volume, the object retains its uncompressed attribute: It remains uncompressed. If you move an uncompressed file or folder into a compressed folder located on a different drive volume, or from a non-NTFS volume, the object inherits the compression. If you copy an uncompressed file or folder into a compressed folder, the object inherits its attribute from the destination folder: It gains the compression attribute and becomes compressed within the target folder. Of course, the original file or folder that is copied remains unchanged; it stays uncompressed.

 Compressed files and folders need NTFS security permission settings to ensure data privacy and safety.

Controlling Access to Files and Folders by Using Permissions

Users attain access to NTFS files and folders by virtue of being granted explicit or implicit (inherited) permissions for those resources directly to their user accounts or through access permissions granted to groups to which they belong. To assign Read Only security permissions to a user or a group for a specific folder, you need to follow these steps:

1. Right-click the folder on which you want to apply permissions and then select Properties.

2. Click the Security tab.

3. If permissions are being inherited for the user and/or group that you want to work with, deselect the Allow Inheritable Permissions from Parent to Propagate to This Object check box.

4. If the user(s) or group(s) to which you want to assign permissions does not currently appear, click the Add button.

5. From the Select Users, Computers, or Groups dialog box, shown in Figure 2.15, select the group or user to which you want to assign permissions. This dialog box lets you choose from available users and groups for assigning NTFS security permissions onto files and folders.

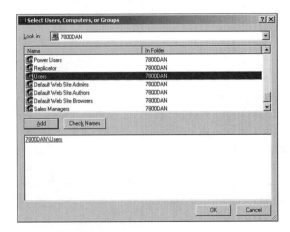

Figure 2.15 The Select Computers, Users, or Groups dialog box.

6. Click the Add button.

7. Click OK to return to the Security tab of the folder's properties sheet.

8. Verify that the Allow check boxes are marked for the Read and Execute, List Folder Contents, and Read permissions.

9. Click OK to accept your settings.

Denying Access to a Resource

Deny permissions always override Allow permissions, so you can be assured that after you establish Deny permissions for a particular user or group on a resource, no other combination of Allow permissions through group memberships can circumvent the Deny. To assign Deny security permissions to a user or a group for a specific folder, you need to follow these steps:

1. Right-click the folder for which you wish to apply permissions and then select Properties.

2. Click the Security tab.

3. If permissions are being inherited for the user and/or group that you want to work with, deselect the Allow Inheritable Permissions from Parent to Propagate to This Object check box.

4. If the user(s) or group(s) to which you want to assign permissions does not currently appear, click the Add button.

5. From the Select Users, Computers, or Groups dialog box select the group or user to which you want to assign permissions.

6. Click the Add button.

7. Click OK to be returned to the Security tab of the folder's properties sheet.

8. Click the Deny check box for each permission that you want to explicitly deny.

9. Click OK to accept the settings.

If you deny the Read permission for a group on a particular folder, any member of that group is denied the ability to read the contents of that folder. When you assign to a file or folder Deny permissions for a user or a group, as soon as you click OK in the properties sheet, the Security message box shown in Figure 2.16 appears. This message box reminds you that Deny permissions take precedence over Allow permissions.

Figure 2.16 A Security message box that reminds you that Deny permissions take precedence over Allow permissions.

You should click Yes in the Security message box to have the new Deny permissions take effect. When users who are members of the group that was assigned Deny permissions for reading the folder attempt to gain access to that folder, they are greeted by an Access Is Denied message box, as shown in Figure 2.17.

Figure 2.17 An Access Is Denied message box.

Optimizing Access to Files and Folders

It is a good idea to always assign NTFS security permissions to groups rather than to individual users. You should place users into appropriate groups and set NTFS permissions on those groups. Doing this makes permissions easier to assign and maintain.

Moving and Copying Files and Folders

Moving or copying files and folders from an NTFS drive volume to network drives or other media that are non-NTFS volumes results in the loss of all NTFS security permission settings for the objects that are moved or copied. The result of moving or copying NTFS files and folders to different NTFS folders varies, depending on whether the objects are being moved or copied and depending on the destination drive volume. Table 2.7 shows the different effects on NTFS permissions of copying files and folders and moving files and folders.

Table 2.7   NTFS Permissions That Are Retained or Inherited When You Move and Copy Files and Folders

Type of Transfer	Effective Permissions After Move or Copy
Moving within the same NTFS volume	Files and folders that are moved retain their permissions from the source folder.
Moving to a different NTFS volume	Files and folders that are moved inherit their permissions from the destination folder.
Copying within the same NTFS volume	Files and folders that are copied inherit their permissions from the destination folder.
Copying to a different NTFS volume	Files and folders that are copied inherit their permissions from the destination folder.

The standard Windows 2000 xcopy.exe command-line utility offers -o and -x options that retain an object's NTFS permissions in addition to inheriting the destination folder's permissions. The -x switch also retains any auditing settings (which are discussed later in this chapter, in the "Auditing System Access" section). To retain only an object's source permissions, without inheriting any permissions from the destination folder, you can use the scopy.exe tool or the robocopy.exe tool from the *Windows 2000 Professional Resource Kit* or the *Windows 2000 Server Resource Kit*.

Taking Ownership of Files and Folders

A user who has ownership of a file or folder can transfer ownership of it to a different user or to a group. Administrators can grant users the ability to take ownership of specified files and folders. In addition, administrators have the authority to take ownership of any file or folder for themselves. Object ownership cannot be assigned to others; a user must have permission to take ownership of an object.

Changing ownership of files and folders can become necessary when someone who is responsible for certain files and folders leaves an organization without granting any other users permissions to them. To take ownership of a folder as an administrator, you need to follow these steps:

1. Log on to the system as the administrator or an equivalent user.

2. In Windows Explorer or My Computer right-click the folder for which you need to take permissions and then select Properties.

3. Click the Security tab.

4. Click the Advanced button.

5. Click the Owner tab in the Access Control Settings dialog box.

6. Click the name of the person in the Change Owner To section to change the folder's ownership, as shown in Figure 2.18.

Figure 2.18   Changing the ownership of a file or folder.

7. If you want the ownership to change for the subfolders and files, click the Replace Owner on Subcontainers and Objects check box.

8. Click OK in the Access Control Settings dialog box.

9. Click OK in the properties sheet.

Auditing System Access

Windows 2000 Professional allows administrators to audit both user and system events by using the auditing feature. When auditing is enabled for specific events, the occurrence of any of the events triggers a log entry in the Windows 2000 Professional security log. You can view the security log with the Event Viewer snap-in of the MMC. By default, auditing is turned off. Before you enable auditing, you should formulate an audit policy to determine which workstations will be audited and which events will be audited on them. When planning the events to audit, you also need to decide whether you will audit successes and/or failures for each event.

Auditing for the local Windows 2000 system is enabled through the Local Security Settings console of the MMC, which is shown in Figure 2.19. You must initially turn on auditing from the Local Security Settings console for each type of event that you want to monitor.

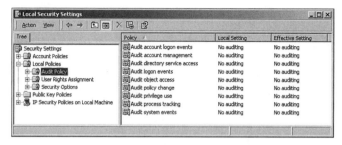

Figure 2.19   The Local Security Settings console.

You can audit several types of events, including the following:

➤ File and folder access

➤ Logons and logoffs

➤ System shutdowns and restarts

➤ Changes to user and group accounts

➤ Changes attempted on Active Directory objects if the Windows 2000 Professional computer is a member of a Windows 2000 Server domain

When you track successful events, you can gauge how often different resources are used. This information can be useful when you are planning for future resource allocation. By tracking failed events, you can become aware of possible security intrusions. Unsuccessful logon attempts, attempts to change security permissions, and efforts to take ownership of files or folders can all indicate that someone is trying to gain unauthorized access to the system or the network. If such attempts occur at odd hours, these events take on an even more suspicious tone. To enable auditing on a Windows 2000 Professional system, you need to follow these steps:

1. Launch the Local Security Policy MMC snap-in from the Start, Programs, Administrative Tools folder.

2. At the Local Security Settings console, expand the Local Policies folder and then click Audit Policy.

3. Double-click the event policy that you want to enable; the Local Security Policy Setting dialog box, shown in Figure 2.20, appears. To enable object access auditing, double-click Audit Object Access Policy (refer to Figure 2.19).

Figure 2.20 The Local Security Policy Setting dialog box for the Audit Object Access event.

4. Click the Success check box, the Failure check box, or both check boxes.

5. Click OK.

6. Close the Local Security Settings console and restart the computer.

After you have turned on audit tracking for object access events, you need to specify which files and folders you want to audit. You should be fairly selective about which ones you choose to audit. If you have enabled auditing for successes as well as failures, the system's security event log may become filled very quickly if you are auditing heavily used files and folders.

To enable audit logging for specific files and folders, you need to follow these steps:

1. Log on to the system as the administrator or as a user who has administrator privileges.

2. In Windows Explorer or My Computer right-click the file or folder on which you want to enable audit logging and then select Properties.

3. Click the Security tab.

4. Click the Advanced button.

5. Click the Auditing tab in the Access Control Settings dialog box.

6. Click the Add button.

7. Click the user or group that you want to track for access to the file or folder and click OK. The Auditing Entry dialog box, shown in Figure 2.21, appears.

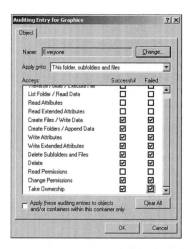

Figure 2.21   The Auditing Entry dialog box.

8. Select each access event that you want to track by marking each event's associated Successful check box, Failed check box, or both.

9. By default, audit settings apply to the current folder, subfolders, and files. You can change this behavior by clicking the Apply Onto drop-down list.

10. Click OK in the Auditing Entry dialog box.

11. Click OK in the Access Control Settings dialog box.

12. Click OK in the properties sheet.

After you have properly set up auditing, all events that meet your auditing criteria are logged in the system's event viewer security log. You access the Event Viewer console by selecting Start, Administrative Tools, Event Viewer or by right-clicking the My Computer desktop icon and then selecting Manage. You should see the Event Viewer beneath the System Tools folder in the Computer Management console. By selecting the security log, you can view all the auditing events that the system has recorded, based on the parameters you have set. If a user deletes an object, for example, that event is listed with all the pertinent information in the security log, as shown in Figure 2.22. Double-clicking an event in the log displays the detailed information.

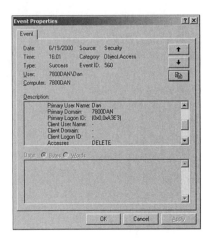

Figure 2.22 An Event Properties window from the event viewer security log.

Keeping Data Private with EFS

Microsoft designed the new EFS for Windows 2000 to ensure the confidentiality of sensitive data. EFS employs public key/private key-based cryptography. EFS works only under Windows 2000, Windows XP, and Windows Server 2003 on NTFS-formatted drive volumes. Its use is transparent to users. You can either compress or encrypt files and folders, but you can't do both. Files that are encrypted using EFS remain encrypted even if you move or rename them. Encrypted files that are backed up or copied also retain their encryption attributes, as long as they reside on NTFS-formatted drive volumes. EFS leaves no file remnants behind when it modifies an encrypted file, nor does it leave any traces of decrypted data from encrypted files in temporary files or in the Windows 2000 pagefile. You can encrypt and decrypt files and folders from a graphical user interface (GUI), by using Windows Explorer, as well as from the command line, by using the cipher.exe tool.

The best practice for using encryption is to first encrypt a folder and then move files into the encrypted folder. Folders do not actually become encrypted; folders are marked with the encryption attribute. The files contained within an encrypted folder are the objects that actually become encrypted. You can also individually encrypt files without having then reside within a folder that is marked for encryption. To encrypt and decrypt files that are physically located on a Windows 2000 server over the network, the server must be trusted for delegation. By definition, DCs are already trusted for delegation. Member servers require this Trust for Delegation security option if you want to enable users to encrypt and decrypt files remotely on those member servers.

To encrypt a file or folder from Windows Explorer, you need to follow these steps:

1. Right-click the file or folder and select Properties.

2. Click the Advanced button in the Compress or Encrypt Attributes section of the General tab of the folder's properties sheet.

3. Click the Encrypt Contents to Secure Data check box in the Advanced Attributes dialog box.

4. Click OK.

5. Click OK in the properties sheet. An empty folder is then encrypted, and any files and folders that are placed within it are encrypted. If subfolders or files exist within the folder, the Confirm Attribute Changes dialog box, shown in Figure 2.23, appears.

Figure 2.23   The Confirm Attribute Changes dialog box.

6. Click either Apply Changes to This Folder Only or Apply Changes to This Folder, Subfolders and Files for the object(s) that you want encryption to affect.

7. Click OK. The encryption attribute is applied to the appropriate objects.

Accessing Encrypted Files and Data Recovery Agents (DRAs)

Encryption is just an extended (or advanced) attribute of a file or folder. If you set NTFS permissions to deny the Write Extended Attributes permission on a file or folder, the users to whom you have assigned that Deny permission cannot use encryption. When a file has the encryption attribute, only the user who encrypted it or the DRA can access it. *DRAs* are users who are designated as recovery agents for encrypted files. Only these users have the ability to decrypt any encrypted file, no matter who has encrypted it. Other users who attempt to access an encrypted file receive an Access Is Denied message. The following are the default DRAs:

➤ The local Administrator account for Windows 2000 Professional nondomain member computers

➤ The local Administrator account for Windows 2000 Server nondomain member computers

➤ The domain Administrator account for Windows 2000 Server DCs, Windows 2000 domain member servers, and Windows 2000 Professional domain member computers

A DRA can log on to a system and decrypt files and folders so that they are once again accessible to other users. In fact, if you remove the DRA from a standalone Windows 2000 computer or from a Windows 2000 Server domain, no data recovery policy is in place, and EFS prohibits users from encrypting files and folders.

Moving and Copying Encrypted Files

Encrypted files that are moved or copied to another NTFS folder remain encrypted. Encrypted files that are moved or copied to a FAT or FAT32 drive volume become unencrypted because EFS is supported only on NTFS 5 volumes. Files also become unencrypted if they are moved or copied to floppy disk. Users who did not originally encrypt a file or folder receive an Access Is Denied message if they try to copy an encrypted file or folder. If users other than the one who encrypted the file attempt to move it to a different NTFS volume or to a FAT or FAT32 drive volume, they receive an Access Is Denied error message. If users other than the one who encrypted the file attempt to move the encrypted file to a different folder located on the *same* NTFS volume, the file is moved.

Managing and Troubleshooting Web Server Resources

Unlike its big brother, Windows 2000 Server, Windows 2000 Professional does not install Internet Information Services (IIS) by default. You must manually install IIS by going to the Control Panel, double-clicking the Add/Remove Programs icon, and clicking the Add/Remove Windows

Components button. You need to select the Internet Information Services (IIS) check box and click Next to have the Windows Components Wizard install the Web server resources for you. If you upgrade your computer from Windows NT 4 Workstation to Windows 2000 Professional and if you installed Peer Web Services on your previous version of Windows, IIS 5 is installed automatically.

Before you can install IIS, your computer must already have the Transmission Control Protocol/Internet Protocol (TCP/IP) network protocol and its related connectivity utilities installed. In addition, Microsoft recommends that you have a Domain Name System (DNS) server available on the network for hostname-to-IP address resolution. For very small networks, you can use a HOSTS file or an LMHOSTS file in lieu of a DNS server. A HOSTS file maps DNS host computer names to IP addresses. An LMHOSTS file maps NetBIOS computer names to IP addresses. Windows 2000 Professional looks for these two text files in the SystemRoot\system32\drivers\etc folder. Sample HOSTS and LMHOSTS files are also installed by default into this folder.

After you have installed IIS, you can manage the services from the IIS snap-in of the MMC. You can launch the IIS console by selecting Start, Programs, Administrative Tools, Internet Service Manager. From the IIS console, you can administer the default File Transfer Protocol (FTP) site, default Web site, and default Simple Mail Transfer Protocol (SMTP) virtual server for the Windows 2000 Professional computer, as shown in Figure 2.24.

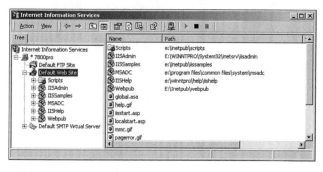

Figure 2.24   The IIS console.

You can find Web-based documentation about IIS administration by pointing to http://localhost/iisHelp/iis/misc/default.asp in your Web browser, as shown in Figure 2.25.

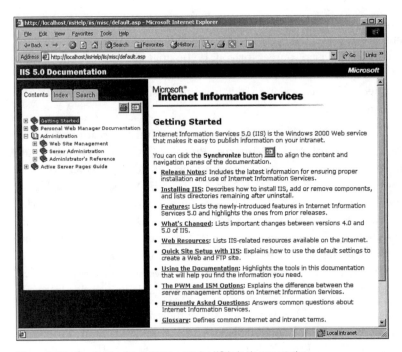

Figure 2.25 The Getting Started Web page for IIS help documentation.

Administering the Default Web and FTP Sites for IIS

You can view and modify the settings for IIS through the IIS console by right-clicking the computer name container in the left pane of the console window and selecting Properties. From the computer name properties sheet, you can view the system's overall master properties for both the World Wide Web (WWW) service and the FTP service for all sites created on the computer. The WWW service master properties that you can modify include the following:

➤ Web site identification, connections, and logging settings

➤ Performance tuning settings

➤ Internet Server API (ISAPI) filters

➤ Home directory settings

➤ Default document names

➤ Directory security

➤ Hypertext Transfer Protocol (HTTP) header information

➤ Custom HTTP error messages

➤ IIS 3 administration options

You can work with the properties for the default FTP site by right-clicking the Default FTP Site folder and selecting Properties. Similarly, you can right-click the Default Web Site folder and choose Properties to configure many of the same settings that apply to the WWW master service properties at the individual Web site level. You can create a new virtual directory for the default Web site by right-clicking Default Web Site and selecting New, Virtual Directory. When the Virtual Directory Creation Wizard launches, you need to assign a name to the new virtual directory. You must also designate the path for the physical folder where the Web files are stored for the new virtual directory. After you have entered that information, you can complete the wizard and you will have set up a new virtual directory that users can access via the `http://computer_name/virtual_directory_name` uniform resource locator (URL), also known simply as a *Web address*.

Troubleshooting IIS

If users are experiencing problems connecting to the default Web site, to the default FTP site, or to a new virtual directory that you have created, you can follow the steps listed in the next two sections to rectify the problems.

Troubleshooting an Internet Web Site

To isolate problems that are preventing users from connecting to the Internet Web site, you should try the following:

1. Check whether the Web server contains Hypertext Markup Language (HTML) files in the `drive_letter:\inetpub\wwwroot` folder.

2. Attempt to connect to the Web server's home directory by using a browser on a computer that has a live connection to the Internet. The Web site must have a public IP address that is registered with the InterNIC, and that public IP address must be registered with the Internet's DNS servers. For example, if your registered domain name is `examcram.com` and you want to view on that Web site a virtual directory named `aboutus`, you should enter `www.examcram.com/aboutus` in the Address line of your Web browser. The Web page that you request should then appear in your Web browser's window.

Troubleshooting an Intranet Web Site

To isolate problems that may be preventing users from connecting to an intranet Web site, you should try the following:

1. Check whether the Web server and the client computers have active network connections.

2. Verify that a Windows Internet Naming Service (WINS) and/or DNS server is available and functioning on the network for computer name-to-IP address name resolution.

3. Go to a client computer, launch a Web browser, and enter a valid URL for the Web server computer. Intranet URLs take the form `http://computer_name/home_page_name.htm` or `http://computer_name/virtual_directory_alias_name` (for example, `http://computer1/myhomepage.htm` and `http://computer1/myvirtualdirectory`).

Managing Local and Network Print Devices

You manage print devices in Windows 2000 Professional from the `Printers` folder, which is accessible from the Control Panel or by selecting Start, Settings, Printers. When you're working with printing in Windows 2000, you need to fully understand the following printing terminology:

➤ *Printer*—A software interface between the operating system and a print device. A printer defines ports through where print jobs are routed. Printer names direct print jobs to one or more print devices.

➤ *Print device*—A piece of equipment (hardware) that physically produces printed documents. A print device may be attached to a local computer or connected via a network interface.

➤ *Printer port*—A software interface through which print jobs are directed to either a locally attached print device or a network-connected print device. Windows 2000 supports local line printer terminal (LPT), COM (serial), and universal serial bus (USB) ports. It also supports network-connected printer port devices such as Intel NetPort and Hewlett-Packard (HP) JetDirect.

➤ *Print server*—A computer that serves as a host for printers that are associated with print devices.

➤ *Printer driver*—Software that is specific to each print device and is designed to run in Windows 2000 that translates printing commands into printer language codes for each print device. PCL5 and PostScript are examples of printer languages.

➤ *Print job*—The actual document to be printed, along with the necessary print processing command.

➤ *Print resolution*—A specification that determines the quality and smoothness of the text or images that the print device will render. Print resolution is expressed in dots per inch (DPI). Higher DPI numbers generally result in better print quality than lower numbers.

➤ *Print spooler*—The process (service) that runs in the background of Windows 2000 that initiates, processes, and distributes print jobs. The print spooler saves print jobs into a temporary physical file on disk. Print jobs are then despooled and transferred to the appropriate print devices.

➤ *Print queue*—A waiting area on the print server computer that uses the print spooler service. This waiting area is where print jobs are temporarily stored until the print device is available and ready to process each job, according to the job's priority level and according to its order within the queue.

Connecting to Local and Network Printers

After you add a local printer to a Windows 2000 Professional computer, you have the option of sharing it with other users on the network. To add a local printer to a system, you need to follow these steps:

1. Log on as an administrator.

2. Select Start, Settings, Printers.

3. Double-click the Add Printer icon from the Printers folder. The Add Printer Wizard appears. Click Next to continue.

4. Click the Local Printer button. If the printer you are adding is not Plug and Play–compatible, you should clear the Automatically Detect and Install My Plug and Play Printer check box. If the printer is Plug and Play–compliant, Windows 2000 Professional automatically installs and properly configures it for you.

5. If you clear the Automatically Detect and Install My Plug and Play Printer check box and click Next, the Select Printer Port dialog box

appears. Click the port you want to use, or click the Create New Port button and choose the type of port to create from the drop-down list.

6. Click Next.

7. Select the printer manufacturer and model. Click the Have Disk button if you have a CD-ROM or floppy disk with the proper printer drivers from the manufacturer.

8. Click Next.

9. Enter a name for the printer. The name should not exceed 31 characters, and best practice dictates that the printer name should not contain any spaces. Specify whether this printer will be designated as the system's default printer.

10. Click Next.

11. In the Printer Sharing dialog box, click the Share As button if you want to share this printer with the network. Enter a share name for the printer; it's good to limit the share name to 14 or fewer characters and to use no spaces within the share name.

12. Click Next.

13. (Optional) Enter a location and a comment.

14. Click Next.

15. Click Next when you are prompted to print a test page; it's always a good idea to make sure that the printer has been set up and is working properly.

16. Click Finish to exit the Add Printer Wizard.

To connect to a network printer, you also use the Add Printer Wizard from the Printers folder. To connect to a network printer, you simply follow these steps:

1. Log on as an administrator.

2. Select Start, Settings, Printers.

3. Double-click the Add Printer icon from the Printers folder. The Add Printer Wizard appears. Click Next to continue.

4. Click the Network Printer button.

5. Click Next.

6. Enter the network printer name or leave the Name box blank and click Next to browse for the printer on the network.

7. Locate the network printer in the Browse for Printer dialog box, which is shown in Figure 2.26.

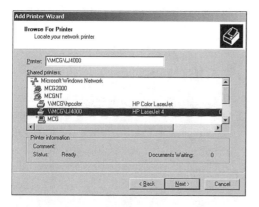

Figure 2.26   The Browse for Printer dialog box.

8. Click Next.

9. If the print server for the printer that you are connecting to does not have the correct printer driver installed, you are prompted to install the correct version on the local Windows 2000 computer, as shown in Figure 2.27. Click OK to install the correct printer driver.

Figure 2.27   The Connect to Printer message box.

10. Click Yes or No to indicate whether this printer should be the default printer for this computer.

11. Click Next.

12. Click Finish to exit the Add Printer Wizard.

Connecting to Network Printers via the Command Line

As mentioned earlier in this chapter, you can use the net use command to connect to network drive shares. You can also use this command to connect to remote printers from a command prompt window. The syntax for the net use command is as follows:

```
net use lptx: \\print_server_name\printer_share_name
```

Printer ports lpt1, lpt2, and lpt3 are represented by lptx. The net use command is the only way to connect client computers that are running MS-DOS to network printers.

Configuring Printer Properties

You can easily configure Windows 2000 Professional print server settings by selecting the File menu from the Printers window and selecting Properties. You can configure many print server settings—such as changing the location of the Spool Folder—from the Print Server Properties dialog box, which is shown in Figure 2.28. Using this dialog box means that you don't have to edit the registry directly.

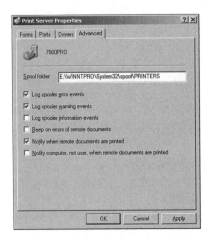

Figure 2.28   The Print Server Properties dialog box.

By right-clicking one of the available printer icons in the Printers folder and choosing Properties, you can configure that printer's settings and options. The printer properties sheet contains six tabs—General, Sharing, Ports, Advanced, Security, and Device Settings—as described in the following sections.

The General Tab

On the General tab, you can do the following:

➤ Add or modify printer location and comment information

➤ Set printing preferences, such as portrait or landscape orientation

➤ Select paper source and quality

➤ Print a test page

The Sharing Tab

The Sharing tab lets you do the following:

➤ Share the printer, change the network share name, or stop sharing the printer

➤ Set printing preferences, such as portrait or landscape orientation

➤ Install additional printer drivers for client computers that use different operating systems or different Windows NT central processing unit (CPU) platforms

 Windows 2000 print server computers automatically download the correct printer drivers for client computers running Windows 95, Windows 98, Windows NT, and Windows 2000 that connect to the print server, as long as the correct drivers have been installed on the print server.

The Ports Tab

On the Ports tab, you can do the following:

➤ Select a port to print to

➤ Add, configure, and delete ports

➤ Enable bidirectional printing support

➤ Enable printer pooling, which allows you to select two or more identical print devices that are configured as one logical printer; print jobs are directed to the first available print device

The Advanced Tab

On the Advanced tab, you work with scheduling and spooling settings. For example, you can do the following:

➤ Set time availability limits

➤ Set print job priority

➤ Change the printer driver or add a new driver

➤ Spool print jobs and start printing immediately or start printing after the last page has spooled

➤ Print directly to the printer; do not spool print jobs

➤ Hold mismatched documents

➤ Print spooled documents first

➤ Retain documents after they have been printed

➤ Enable advanced printing features (such as metafile spooling) and enable advanced options (such as page order, booklet printing, and pages per sheet); advanced options vary depending on printer capabilities

➤ Set printing defaults

➤ Select a different print processor: RAW, EMF, or Text

➤ Specify a separator page

The Security Tab

You can do the following on the Security tab:

➤ Set permissions for users and groups (similar to NTFS file and folder permissions): Allow Print or Deny Print, Manage Printers, and Manage Documents

➤ Set up printer auditing (similar to NTFS file and folder access auditing) via the Auditing tab by clicking the Advanced button

➤ Take ownership of the printer (similar to taking ownership of NTFS files and folders) via the Owner tab by clicking the Advanced button

The Device Settings Tab

The Device Settings tab allows you to configure printer-specific settings. The available settings on this tab vary depending on the manufacturer and the model of the printer you are working with.

Managing Printers and Print Jobs

Members of the Printer Owners, Print Operators, and Print Job Owners groups have permissions to manage print jobs that are listed in the print queue. From the Printers folder, you manage print jobs by double-clicking the icon for the printer that you want to work with. After you have opened the printer's print queue window, you can pause printing or cancel all documents from the Printer menu. You can also take the printer offline from the Printer menu. If you select an individual print job that is listed, you can pause, resume, start, or cancel that job by selecting one of those options from the Documents menu. The print queue window displays the document name, the status, the document owner, the number of pages for each print job, the size of the job, the time and date that the job was submitted, and the port used.

Users can manage only their own print jobs unless they are members of the Administrators group, the Power Users group, or the Print Operators group (if the print server is a member of a domain). Users who have been granted the Allow Manage Documents permission can also manage other users' print jobs.

Using IPP

Windows 2000 Professional computers can connect through a Web browser to printers that are attached to Windows 2000 print servers. IPP works over a corporate intranet or through an Internet connection. IPP gives users the ability to print over an Internet connection. You can enter one of two URLs into a Web browser:

➤ *http://print_server_name/printers*—This address connects you to the Web page for the `Printers` folder on the Windows 2000 print server computer.

➤ *http://print_server_name/printer_share_name*—This address connects you to the Web page for the print queue folder for the printer you specify, as shown in Figure 2.29.

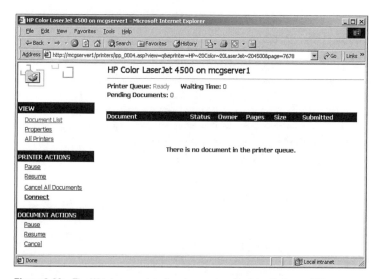

Figure 2.29   The Web browser interface for a network printer that uses IPP.

Practice Questions

Question 1

John Smith of XYZ Corporation has used EFS to encrypt all the files stored within the **\\Server1\Projects\JohnS** folder. John subsequently leaves XYZ Corporation. John's boss has permissions to fully access the **\\Server1\Projects\JohnS** folder; however, he cannot work with any of the files because he receives an Access Is Denied message whenever he attempts to open any of the encrypted files. What needs to be done in order for John's files to become accessible to other users?

- O a. Log on to the domain as a member of the Backup Operators group and decrypt the files.
- O b. Log on to the domain as the DRA and decrypt the files.
- O c. Restore the files from a recent backup.
- O d. Have John's boss take ownership of the files.

Answer b is correct. Only a DRA can unencrypt files that someone else encrypted. Answer a is incorrect because members of the Backup Operators group do not have the ability to decrypt files encrypted by other users. Answer c is incorrect because backup copies retain the original encryption attribute. Answer d is incorrect because taking ownership of files does not allow the owner to decrypt them.

Question 2

Stuart Scott of ABC Company encrypts a folder named **Spreadsheets** and applies the encryption attribute to the subfolders and files within this folder. Two days later, Stuart's co-worker Lisa attempts to copy one of the encrypted files to a different NTFS folder located on the same drive volume on the same server. Neither Stuart nor Lisa is a member of the Administrators group, and neither user is a DRA. What happens when Lisa attempts to copy the encrypted file?

- O a. The encrypted file is copied successfully.
- O b. The encrypted file is not copied successfully.
- O c. Lisa is prompted for the password for the DRA before the copy process can be completed.
- O d. The encrypted file is copied successfully, but an entry is logged in the Event Viewer about the encrypted file being copied.

Answer b is correct. Only the person who encrypted the files or the DRA can copy encrypted files. Answer a is incorrect because only the person who encrypted the files or the DRA can copy encrypted files. Answer c is incorrect because EFS never prompts a user for a password for decryption or for copying encrypted files. Answer d is incorrect because the encrypted file cannot be copied by anyone other than the person who encrypted the file or the DRA—no entry is logged in the Event Viewer.

Question 3

Where can members of the Administrators group view all the shared folders for a Windows 2000 Professional computer?

○ a. In the **Shared Folders** folder within the My Computer window.

○ b. From the Control Panel Folder Options icon.

○ c. From the **System Tools** folder of the Computer Management console.

○ d. In the **usrmgr.exe** utility.

Answer c is correct. The Computer Management console is an MMC snap-in. Shared folders for the local computer are listed for administrators if they select System Tools, Shared Folders, Shares. Answer a is incorrect because there is no Shared Folders folder within the My Computer window. Answer b is incorrect because the Folder Options applet in the Control Panel does not display the system's shared folders. Answer d is incorrect because the usrmgr.exe program is a legacy utility that is not available under Windows 2000 Professional; it is the User Manager for Domains tool used for Windows NT 4.0 domain controllers.

Question 4

Jeff is an administrator who creates a network share named **Docs** on Server7. He sets the share permissions on the shared folder by leaving the default Everyone group, but he clears the Allow check boxes for Full Control, Change, and Read. Jeff sets NTFS permissions on the folder as well: He sets NTFS permissions to Allow Read for the Everyone group. What happens when users attempt to connect to the **Docs** share over the network?

○ a. Users inherit the Allow Read permission for the folder.

○ b. Users inherit Allow Full Control permissions for the folder.

○ c. Members of the Administrators group are allowed access to the folder over the network.

○ d. Users are denied access to the shared folder over the network.

Answer d is correct. Whenever share permissions and NTFS permissions conflict, the most restrictive permissions take precedence. Clearing all the Allow check boxes establishes an implicit Deny for those permissions. Answers a and b are incorrect because the share permissions are being denied for the Everyone group. Answer c is incorrect because the Everyone group is being denied share permissions, and no other user or group is assigned permissions on that share.

Question 5

Amy moves a file from a FAT32 drive volume over to an NTFS drive volume folder named **Compressed**. The **Compressed** folder and its subfolders and files have been marked for NTFS compression. What happens when the file is moved into the **Compressed** folder?

○ a. The file remains uncompressed within the **Compressed** folder.

○ b. The file becomes compressed because it inherits the compression attribute from the destination folder.

○ c. Amy receives an error message, informing her that encrypted files cannot be compressed.

○ d. Amy receives an error message, informing her that files from FAT32 volumes do not support compression.

Answer b is correct. Files that are moved to an NTFS compressed folder from a non-NTFS drive volume inherit the compression attribute from the destination folder. Answer a is incorrect because files that are moved into an NTFS compressed folder become compressed. Answer c is incorrect because files stored on FAT32 volumes cannot be encrypted by using EFS; Amy would not receive such an error message. Answer d is incorrect because although FAT32 volumes do not support NTFS compression, any file of any type of volume moved to an NTFS compressed folder inherits the NTFS compression attribute from the destination folder.

Question 6

Robert is using the network to print to **\\wkstn4\printer11**. All of a sudden, the print device for **printer11** stops functioning. Fortunately, a similar print device is available on **\\wkstn5\printer22**. How can you, as an administrator, allow users to continue to print to the same network printer name without having to reconfigure any of the users' computers?

○ a. Add a new port for **\\wkstn4\printer11**, and have the new port point to **\\wkstn5\printer22**.

○ b. Change the share name for **printer11** to **printer22**.

○ c. Change the print server properties for **printer11** so that the Print Spool folder points to **\\wkstn5\admin$\system32\spool\printers**.

○ d. Enable printer pooling on **\\wkstn5\printer22**.

Answer a is correct. By adding a new port with a UNC path for a similar printer on another computer, you effectively redirect the print jobs to another functioning printer. Answer b is incorrect because changing the printer's share name would require you to reconfigure the user's computers to use the new share name. Answer c is incorrect because you cannot change the print spool folder to a network drive; even if you could make this change, it would not resolve the problem. Answer d is incorrect because enabling printer pooling on the functioning printer would not solve this problem.

Question 7

Gregory is member of the Administrators group. Some executives in his company feel that he may be reading or even altering confidential company documents. What can you, as the head of IT, do for the company to track which users are accessing sensitive files? (Select all the correct answers.)

❑ a. Enable auditing for success and failure of process tracking in the Local Security Settings console.

❑ b. Enable auditing for failure of object access in the Local Security Settings console.

❑ c. Enable auditing for success of object access in the Local Security Settings console.

❑ d. Enable auditing for the folder that contains the confidential files. Audit activities such as successful list contents/read data and successful create files/write data.

❑ e. Turn on auditing for privilege use.

Answers c and d are correct. You should enable auditing for success, failure, or both for object access from the Local Security Settings console. Then you can audit the success of object access events. Answer a is incorrect because auditing process tracking does not record object access events. Answer b is incorrect because auditing for failure only of object access events does not detect when someone successfully changes or deletes an object (such as a file). Answer e is incorrect because auditing for privilege use does not detect object access events.

Question 8

As the network administrator, you are concerned about several encrypted folders on Server A that contain very important data. You want to back up those folders while maintaining all security permission settings and having all the files retain their encryption attributes. What is the best way to accomplish this?

- ○ a. Copy the files and folders onto a network share on Server B that resides on a FAT32 drive volume by using the **scopy.exe** utility from the *Windows 2000 Resource Kit.*
- ○ b. Copy the files and folders onto a Novell NetWare server.
- ○ c. Copy the files and folders onto a network share on Server B that is formatted as NTFS.
- ○ d. Copy the files and folders onto CD-recordable media.

Answer c is correct. Only NTFS-formatted drive volumes in Windows 2000 support NTFS security permissions and EFS. Only DRAs and the person who originally encrypted each file can copy EFS-encrypted files, and the administrator is the default DRA. Answer a is incorrect because FAT32 drive volumes do not support EFS. Answer b is incorrect because Novell NetWare volumes do not support EFS. Answer d is incorrect because CD-ROM, CD-R, CD/RW, DVD-ROM, DVD recordable, and DVD rewritable media do not support EFS.

Question 9

> The office administrative personnel in your company are members of a group
> called Staff. The members of the Staff group are responsible for managing print
> jobs in the office. The Staff group has been assigned the Allow Manage
> Documents permission for all the printers in the office. Kimberly joins the com-
> pany as a new Staff group member, and she is going to be responsible for man-
> aging the printers and the print jobs. What is the best way to assign permissions
> to Kimberly so that she can manage printers and print jobs?
>
> ○ a. Create a new group named Printer Admins and add Kimberly to that
>   group. Assign the Allow Manage Printers permission to the Printer
>   Admins group for each printer in the office.
>
> ○ b. Place Kimberly in the Print Operators group. Remove her from the
>   Staff group.
>
> ○ c. Keep her as a member of the Staff group and add her to the
>   Administrators group.
>
> ○ d. Change the printer permissions for all the printers in the office to Allow
>   Manage Printers for the Staff group. Assign the Deny Manage Printers
>   permission individually for each member of the Staff group except for
>   Kimberly. Assign the Allow Manage Documents permission to the
>   Everyone group for all the printers in the office.

Answer a is correct. It is best to assign permissions only to groups. The Print
Operators group is a domain group. Membership in that group would give
Kimberly authority to manage printers within the entire domain, and such a
wide scope of authority is unnecessary; therefore, Answer b is incorrect.
Answer c is incorrect because making Kimberly a member of the
Administrators group would grant her too much authority for her job assignment. Answer d is incorrect because it denies Kimberly the Manage Printers
permission and it grants too much authority for all users to manage other
users' documents.

Question 10

IIS is installed and running on your Windows 2000 Professional computer. Your users want to utilize IPP to print from their Web browsers over the corporate intranet. When users type in the URL **http://server1/printers**, they receive a Cannot Find Server message. However, you notice that if you type **http://192.168.1.103/printers**, you are connected to the printer's Web page for that server. What's the most probable cause of this problem?

○ a. Dynamic Host Configuration Protocol (DHCP) is not functioning.

○ b. DNS or WINS—or both—is not set up properly on the network.

○ c. The default gateway IP address information is missing on the computer.

○ d. APIPA is turned on by default. You need to make a change in the registry to turn off this feature.

Answer b is correct. If you can access a TCP/IP network resource by its IP address but not by its computer name (that is, hostname), it is most likely a name resolution problem. You can solve this problem by installing either a DNS server or by manually adding a HOSTS file on each computer on the network. Answer a is incorrect because you cannot determine whether DHCP is functioning from the information given, and DHCP is not the cause of nor the remedy for this problem. Answer c is incorrect because the default gateway IP address is not the cause nor the remedy for a name resolution issue. Answer d is incorrect because APIPA assigns IP addresses to computers that are configured to obtain IP addresses automatically; it has nothing to do with mapping IP addresses to computer hostnames and vice versa.

Need to Know More?

 Microsoft Corporation. *Microsoft Windows 2000 Professional Resource Kit*. Redmond, Washington: Microsoft Press, 2000. This book provides invaluable information on administering resources and setting NTFS security permissions.

 Stinson, Craig, and Siechert, Carl. *Running Microsoft Windows 2000 Professional*. Redmond, Washington: Microsoft Press, 2000. This book is a good source for information on administering resources.

 Hudson, James, and Fullerton, Sean. *Special Edition Using Microsoft Active Directory*. Indianapolis: Que Publishing, 2001. This book provides complete, in-depth coverage of the newest directory service from Microsoft. Authors Fullerton and Hudson use their previous training and administration experiences to explain how to design, implement, and troubleshoot by using Active Directory.

 To find more information, search the TechNet CD-ROM (or its online version, through www.microsoft.com) and/or the *Windows 2000 Professional Resource Kit* CD-ROM, using the keywords NTFS, offline file, EFS, compression, auditing, shared folder, and Internet Printing Protocol.

3

Implementing, Monitoring, and Troubleshooting Security Accounts and Policies

. . . .

Terms you'll need to understand:

✓ Local users and groups
✓ Workgroup
✓ Domain
✓ Domain users and groups
✓ Active Directory
✓ Organizational unit (OU)
✓ Policy
✓ Privilege or user right

Techniques you'll need to master:

✓ Creating local users and groups
✓ Creating domain users and groups
✓ Managing user and group properties
✓ Dealing with changes in your user population, such as renaming and copying accounts
✓ Securing a system
✓ Creating a local and group policy

Networks' *raison d'être*—their reason for being—is to allow users to access resources such as files, printers, and applications on computers other than the ones at which they are sitting. In an ideal world, we would trust every user with every file we create, and all we'd have to do is connect our computers to a network and share it all. Unfortunately, we don't trust every user with every file we create. In the real world, certain users need access to resources that others should be restricted from accessing. Therefore, we need user accounts to identify and authenticate users when they attempt to access resources. But imagine trying to define who can access a resource and at what level if you had to worry about each individual user! Using groups significantly eases the process of defining resource access; you can assign permissions and privileges to groups and thereby define access for their members, and groups may contain one, dozens, hundreds, or thousands of users.

This chapter highlights critical skills and concepts related to user, group, and computer accounts, and the process of creating security configurations and policies for a Windows 2000 Professional system.

User and Group Accounts

Windows 2000 Professional creates several default local users and groups when you first install the operating system. When you join a Windows 2000 Professional computer to a Windows domain (within a Windows NT Server, Windows 2000 Server, or a Windows Server 2003 network), several additional user and group accounts come into play from the domain. Understanding the functions of the various local users and groups and knowing the differences between local user and group accounts and domain user and group accounts is key to being an effective network administrator and important for success on the Windows 2000 Professional certification exam.

Local and Domain Accounts

User and group accounts are stored in one of two locations: the *local security database* or the domain's *Active Directory* database. When an account is created in the local security database, that account is called a *local user* or *local group*.

Each Windows 2000 Professional system has two default local user accounts—Administrator and Guest (which is disabled by default)—and several built-in group accounts, which are discussed shortly. Local user and group accounts provide privileges and permissions to resources of the system on which they are defined. For example, the Users group has the privilege to log on locally. As you create local user accounts, they are members of the Users group by default; those users are then given the privilege to log on to that system.

Local user and group accounts cannot be given privileges or permissions to resources on any other system because the security database of the system where they are created is truly local: No other system can "see" it. If a user has logged on to a computer by using a local account, the only way that user can gain access to resources of a remote system is through an account for that user on the remote system. That account must be given privileges and permissions or must be placed into appropriate groups on the remote system. When a duplicate or redundant account is created with the same username and password on the remote system as on the local system, the user "seamlessly" accesses resources on the remote system; such users cannot tell that the remote system is authenticating them. However, if the username or password on the remote system is different from that on the local system, the user is prompted with an authentication dialog box when he or she first attempts to connect to the remote system.

Two or more systems that use only their own local accounts being on a network creates what is called a *workgroup*, a kind of peer-to-peer network. You can imagine how difficult managing redundant accounts for a single user on two different systems might become. If a user changes his or her password on one machine, he or she must remember to change it on the other; otherwise, the user is prompted for authentication at each connection. Such challenges would become multiplied many times over in a large workgroup with multiple users and multiple machines.

Thus, networks of any size turn to a *domain* model, in which one or more servers, called *domain controllers*, maintain a centralized database of users and groups. Security accounts in a domain are stored in the domain's Active Directory database. When a user is created in a domain, that single user account can be given privileges and permissions to resources and systems throughout the domain and in other domains within the enterprise's Active Directory database. Active Directory is covered in more detail in the "Understanding Active Directory" section later in this chapter.

Domain user and group accounts are stored within the Active Directory database for Windows 2000 Server and Windows Server 2003 domains only. The user and group domain accounts for Windows NT Server and Windows NT Server 4.0 domains are stored within the legacy Security Accounts Manager (SAM) database, which is a less robust user and group directory than Active Directory.

In a domain, it is unusual (and not a best practice) to create or use local user accounts. Most computers that are members of a domain have only the local Administrator and Guest user accounts in their security databases.

Managing Local User and Group Accounts

The Local Users and Groups snap-in allows you to manage—surprise!—local users and groups. You can get to the snap-in by choosing Start, Settings, Control Panel, Administrative Tools, Computer Management and then by expanding the tree pane of the Computer Management console until you see snap-in. In this snap-in, you can create, modify, duplicate, and delete users (in the Users folder) and groups (in the Groups folder).

Using Built-in User and Group Accounts

As mentioned earlier in this chapter, there are two built-in user accounts: Administrator and Guest. The Administrator account

➤ Cannot be disabled, locked out, or deleted.

➤ Cannot be removed from the Administrators group.

➤ Has, through its membership in the Administrators group, all privileges required to perform system administration duties.

➤ Can be renamed.

The Guest account

➤ Is disabled by default. Only a member of the Administrators group can enable the account. If the Guest account is enabled, it should be given a password, and User Cannot Change Password should be set if multiple users will log on with the account.

➤ Cannot be deleted.

➤ Can be locked out.

➤ Can be renamed.

➤ Does not save user preferences or settings.

Built-in local groups have assigned to them specific privileges (also called *user rights*) that allow them to perform specific sets of tasks on a system. The following are the default local group accounts on a Windows 2000 Professional system:

➤ *Administrators*—Members of this group have all built-in system privileges assigned. They can create and modify user and group accounts, manage security policies, create printers, and manage permissions to resources on the system. The local Administrator account is the default member and cannot be removed. Other accounts can be added and removed. When a system joins a domain, the Domain Admins group is added, but it can be removed.

➤ *Backup Operators*—Members of this group can back up and restore files and folders, regardless of security permissions assigned to those resources. They can log on and shut down a system but cannot change security settings.

➤ *Power Users*—Members of this group can share resources and create user and group accounts. They cannot modify user accounts they did not create, nor can they modify the Administrators or Backup Operators groups. Members of the Power Users group cannot take ownership of files, back up or restore directories, load or unload device drivers, or manage the security and auditing logs. Members of the Power Users group can run all Windows 2000–compatible applications as well as legacy applications, some of which members of the Users group cannot execute.

 If you want certain users to have broad system administration capabilities but do not want them to be able to access all system resources, you should consider putting them in the Backup Operators and Power Users groups rather than in the Administrators group.

➤ *Users*—Members of this group can log on to a system, shut down a system, use local and network printers, create local groups, and manage the groups they create. They cannot create local printers or share folders. Some older (legacy) applications do not run for members of the Users group because security settings are tighter for the Users group in Windows 2000 than in Windows NT 4. By default, all local user accounts you create are added to the Users group. In addition, when a system joins a domain, the Domain Users group is made a member of that system's local Users group.

➤ *Guests*—Members of this group have limited privileges but can log on to a system and shut it down. Members of the Guests group cannot make permanent changes to their desktops or profiles. By default, the built-in local Guest account is a member of this group. When a system joins a domain, the Domain Guests group is added to the local Guests group.

➤ *Replicator*—This group is used to support file replication services in a domain.

A Windows 2000 Professional system also has built-in *system* groups, which you do not see in the user interface while managing other group accounts. Membership of system groups changes based on how the computer is being accessed or utilized, not based on who is accessing the computer. Built-in system groups are also referred to as special identity groups and include the following:

➤ *Everyone*—This group includes all users who access the computer, including the Guest account.

➤ *Authenticated Users*—This group includes all users who have valid user accounts in the local security database or (in the case of domain members) in Active Directory's directory services. You should use the Authenticated Users group rather than the Everyone group to assign privileges and group permissions because doing so prevents anonymous access to resources.

➤ *Creator Owner*—This group contains the user account that created or took ownership of a resource. If the user is a member of the Administrators group, the Creator Owner group is the owner of the resource.

➤ *Network*—This group contains any user who currently has a connection from a remote system.

➤ *Interactive*—This group contains the user account for the user who is logged on to the system locally.

➤ *System*—This group includes any operating system services that are configured to run within the security context of the operating system itself.

➤ *Terminal Server User*—This group includes all users who are currently connected to the computer via a remote desktop (that is, terminal services client) connection.

➤ *Anonymous Logon*—This group includes any user account that Windows 2000 has not authenticated.

➤ *Dial-up*—This group contains all users that currently use dial-up connections.

Creating Local User and Group Accounts

To create a local user or group account, you right-click the appropriate folder (Users or Groups) and choose New User (or New Group), enter the appropriate attributes, and then click Create.

The following guidelines apply to user account names:

➤ They must be unique.

➤ They are recognized only up to the twentieth character, although the name itself can be longer.

➤ They cannot contain the following characters: " / \ [ ] ; : , = + * ? < >.

➤ They are not case sensitive, although the user account's name property displays the case as entered.

You should determine a policy for accommodating users who have the same name. For example, you can add a number after the username (for example, JohnD1, JohnD2). Some organizations also identify certain types of users by their usernames (for example, JohnDoe-Temp for a temporary employee).

The following guidelines apply to user account passwords:

➤ They are recommended.

➤ They are case sensitive.

➤ They can contain up to 127 characters, although down-level operating systems such as Windows NT 4 and Windows 9x support only 14-character passwords.

➤ They should be a minimum of 7 to 8 characters.

➤ They should be difficult to guess and, preferably, should mix uppercase and lowercase letters, numerals, and nonalphanumeric characters (other than those listed previously as being prohibited).

➤ They can be set by the administrator (who can then determine whether users must, can, or cannot change their passwords) or the user (if the administrator has not specified otherwise).

From the Local Users and Groups node of the Computer Management console, or from the Active Directory Users and Computers console on a domain controller, you can select User Must Change Password at Next Logon to ensure that the user is the only one who knows the account's password. You can select User Cannot Change Password when more than one person (such as the Guest user account) uses the account.

NOTE

The User Cannot Change Password option is not available when User Must Change Password at Next Logon is selected.

The Password Never Expires option is helpful when a program or a service uses an account. To avoid having to reconfigure the service with a new password, you can simply set the service's account to retain its password indefinitely.

Configuring Account Properties

The information you can specify when creating an account is limited in Windows 2000. Therefore, after you create an account, you often need to go to the account's properties sheet, which you can access by right-clicking the account and choosing Properties. Figure 3.1 shows the properties sheets of two accounts.

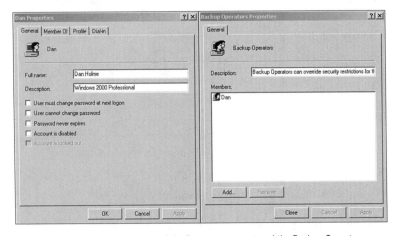

Figure 3.1   The properties sheets of the Dan user account and the Backup Operators group account.

Managing Local Group Membership

To manage the membership of a local group, you right-click the group and choose Properties. To remove a member, you select the account and click Remove. To add a member, you click Add and select or enter the name of the account.

In a workgroup, local groups can contain only accounts defined in the same machine's local security database. When a system belongs to a domain, its local groups can also include domain accounts, including user accounts, universal groups, and global groups from the enterprise's Active Directory database, as well as domain local groups from within the system's domain.

 Universal groups and domain local groups can be added as members only when the domain is in native mode, meaning that it contains only Windows 2000 domain controllers and no legacy (that is, Windows NT 4.0) backup domain controllers.

Renaming Accounts

To rename an account, you right-click the account and choose Rename. Then you type the new name and press Enter. Each user and group account is represented in the local security database by a long, unique string called a *security identifier* (SID), which is generated when the account is created. The SID is what is actually assigned permissions and privileges. The user or group name is just a user-friendly "face" on that process. Therefore, when you rename an account, the account's SID remains the same, so the account retains all its group memberships, permissions, and privileges.

Two situations mandate renaming an account. The first occurs when one user stops using a system and a new user requires the same access as the first. Rather than create a new local user account for the new user, you can simply rename the old user account. The account's SID remains the same, so its group memberships, privileges, and permissions are retained. You should also specify a new password in the account's properties sheet and select the User Must Change Password at Next Logon option.

 The easiest way to "replace" a user is to rename the account. Therefore, when one user leaves and another requires the same group memberships, rights, and resource access permissions as the first, you can simply rename the former user's account. You should not forget to reset the account's password because the new user won't otherwise know the old user's password.

The second situation that warrants renaming a user account is the security practice of renaming the built-in Administrator and Guest accounts. You cannot delete these accounts, nor can you disable or remove the Administrator account from the Local Administrators group, so renaming the accounts is a recommended practice for hindering malicious access to a system.

Disabling or Enabling User Accounts

To disable or enable a user account, you open its properties sheet and select or clear the Account Is Disabled check box. If an account is disabled, a user cannot log on to the system by using that account. The Administrator account cannot be disabled, and only administrators can enable the Guest account.

Deleting Accounts

You can delete a local user or group account (but not built-in accounts such as Administrator, Guest, or Backup Operators) by right-clicking the account and choosing Delete. When you delete a group, you delete the group account only, not the accounts of its members. A group is a membership list, not a container.

 When you delete an account, you are deleting its SID. Therefore, if you delete an account by accident and then re-create the account, even with the same name, the account does not have the same permissions, privileges, or group memberships as before—you have to regenerate them. For that reason, and to facilitate auditing, it is recommended that you disable, not delete, any user who leaves an organization.

Using the Users and Passwords Applet

A different tool for administering local user accounts is the Users and Passwords applet in the Control Panel. This utility allows you to create and remove user accounts as well as specify group membership for those users. The Users and Passwords applet is wizard driven and is useful for novice administrators and home users. You double-click the Users and Passwords icon in the Control Panel to run this utility. To launch the Local Users and Groups snap-in from the Users and Passwords applet, you click the Advanced tab and then click the Advanced button (in the Advanced User Management section).

 The Users and Passwords applet provides an opportunity to override the logon requirement for a system. This feature is discussed later in this chapter, in the "Authentication" section.

Managing Domain User Accounts

You manage domain user accounts with the Active Directory Users and Computers snap-in. To access it, you choose Start, Settings, Control Panel, Administrative Tools, Active Directory Users and Computers. Note that unlike in Windows NT 4, in Windows 2000 all domain controllers can make changes to the Active Directory database. When you open the Active Directory Users and Computers snap-in, you connect to an available domain controller. If you want to specify which domain controller or which domain you want to connect to, you right-click the Active Directory Users and

Computers node and choose Connect to Domain or Connect to Domain Controller.

Unlike the local security database, which is a flat list of users and groups, Active Directory has containers such as domains and organizational units (OUs), which collect database objects such as users that are administered similarly to one another. *OUs* are simply containers that allow administrators to logically group Active Directory objects, such as users, groups, and computers. All the objects that are contained within an OU can be administered together. Administration tasks may also be delegated to other administrators for each OU. Therefore, when you manage domain user accounts in Windows 2000, you need to start in the container or OU where the objects reside that you want to work with.

Creating Domain User Accounts

You create a domain user account by right-clicking the OU or container in which you want the user account and then choosing New User. A wizard prompts you for basic account properties, including the following:

➤ First name

➤ Initials

➤ Last name

➤ Full name (by default, the combination of the first name and last name)

➤ User logon name and user principal name (UPN) suffix

➤ User logon name (pre-Windows 2000)

➤ Password and confirmed password

Windows 2000 user accounts have two logon names. The UPN is used for logon to a Windows 2000 system and consists of a logon name followed by the @ symbol and a suffix, which by default is the Domain Name System (DNS) name of the domain. Each user must have a unique UPN in the domain. The pre-Windows 2000 logon name is used for logging on to pre-Windows 2000 systems such as Windows NT 4, and Windows 95, 98, and Me. Each user's pre-Windows 2000 logon name must be unique in the domain and by default is the same as the logon name portion of the UPN.

Modifying User Account Properties

After an account is created, Active Directory provides dozens of attributes to further define that user. You can right-click a user and choose Properties to open a tabbed dialog box full of attributes that can be defined for that user.

The only properties you can specify when creating the user are those on the Account tab. You must set the remainder of the properties after the account has been instantiated.

Copying User Accounts

A user object in Active Directory may have numerous attributes defined, including work location, group membership, and superiors within the organization. Often, a new user object shares many of its attributes with one or more other user objects. In that case, it is faster to copy an existing user object than to create a new object and define each and every property for the object. To copy a user, you right-click the object and choose Copy. You are asked to enter some of the basic account properties, such as name and password.

You can copy a user only with domain user accounts, not with local user accounts.

Creating Template User Accounts

When you expect to create multiple user objects with highly similar properties, you can create a "template" account that, when copied, initiates the new accounts with its defined attributes. The only trick to working with templates is to disable the template account. Then, when you copy the account to create a new user with predefined attributes, you need to make sure to enable the new account.

When you copy a user account—whether it's a "real" user account or a template—the new copy belongs to all the same groups as the original and therefore has the same resource access that is assigned to the groups of the original account. However, the new copy does *not* have access to resources for which permissions are assigned directly to the original user account.

Disabling and Deleting User Accounts

The process for disabling and deleting domain user accounts is the same as for local user accounts, except that you use the Active Directory Users and Computers snap-in to perform the tasks. The check box for disabling an account is on the user's Account properties sheet.

Adding Domain User Accounts to Local Groups

In Windows 2000 you can add a user to a group with either the group's Members properties sheet or the user's Member Of properties sheet, except when adding *domain* user accounts to *local* groups, in which case you must use the group's Members properties sheet. A domain user's Member Of properties sheet displays only memberships in global, domain, local, and universal groups.

Authentication

When a user wants to access resources on a machine, that user's identity must first be verified through a process called *authentication*. For example, when a user logs on, the security subsystem evaluates the user's username and password. If there is a match, the user is authenticated. The process of logging on to a machine where you are physically sitting is called *interactive logon*. Authentication also happens when you access resources on a remote system. For example, when you open a shared folder on a server, you are being authenticated, but the process is called *remote* or *network logon* because you are not physically at the server.

The Security Dialog Box

The *security dialog box* allows for interactive logon to a Windows 2000 system. You can access the Security dialog box shortly after a system has started, and at any time after logon, by pressing Ctrl+Alt+Delete. If you are not currently logged on, you can enter a username and password. If the system belongs to a domain, you need to be certain that the domain in which your account exists is authenticating you. You can either select the domain from the drop-down list or enter your UPN. The UPN is an attribute of an Active Directory user object and, by default, has the form *username@dnsdomain.name*. The suffix, following the @ symbol, indicates the domain against which to authenticate the user.

If you are currently logged on to a system, pressing Ctrl+Alt+Delete takes you to the Windows 2000 Security dialog box, at which point you can do one of the following:

➤ Log off the system, which closes all programs and ends the instance of the shell.

➤ Lock the system, which allows programs to continue running but prevents access to the system. When a system is locked, you can unlock it by pressing Ctrl+Alt+Delete and entering the username and password of the user who locked the system or an administrator's username and password.

To lock a workstation automatically after a period of idle time, you use a screen-saver password.

➤ Shut down the system.

➤ Change your password.

➤ Open Task Manager.

Automating Logon

You can configure Windows 2000 Professional systems so that you are not required to enter a username and password; in this case, your system automatically logs on as a specified user account. From the Users and Passwords applet in the Control Panel, you click the Advanced tab and clear the Require Users to Press Ctrl+Alt+Delete Before Logging On check box. The same setting is available through a group policy object (GPO) setting. GPOs are configured via Active Directory under Windows 2000 Server and Windows Server 2003; they are discussed later in this chapter.

Understanding Active Directory

Windows 2000's Active Directory goes far beyond what the Security Accounts Manager (SAM) database does for Windows NT 4. SAM and Active Directory both store security account information for users, groups, computers, and user rights, but that's where the similarity ends. Active Directory's database stores *objects* that represent enterprise resources, including users, groups, computers, printers, folders, applications, connections, security and configuration settings, and network topology. For each of these types, or *classes*, of objects, Active Directory can store numerous properties, or *attributes*. So a user account is far more than a username and password; it is information about the user's mailbox, the user's address and phone number, the role of the user within the organization (including the user's manager and location), and far, far more.

As a central store of information related to the enterprise network, Active Directory allows administrators to create a virtual representation or model of the enterprise—linking various objects together, grouping objects based on how they are administered, and structuring the enterprise information technology (IT) to best support the organization's goals. In addition, Active

Directory's database is *extensible*, which means you can customize and append it with additional attributes and object classes. So if an organization wants to keep track of salary information for each employee, it can simply extend the information that Active Directory stores about employees to include salary or, better yet, purchase a payroll application that is Active Directory aware and can automatically extend the directory appropriately.

A database is of no use if it simply stores information. One must be able to somehow access and manipulate that information in the database, and Active Directory includes numerous services, most based on Internet standard, that allow you to do just that. To provide the functionality required to search or query a database for a particular enterprise resource, locate that resource out on the network, manage that resource's record in Active Directory, and ensure that the record is consistent throughout the network.

Active Directory's database and services reside on servers that have been designated domain controllers. Unlike with Windows NT 4, Windows 2000 domain controllers are not created while the operating system is installed. Rather, a functioning server is *promoted* to act as a domain controller, at which time it obtains a copy of Active Directory and launches the required services. Also unlike with NT 4, there is no "primary" domain controller. All domain controllers can write to the directory. Therefore, a change to the domain is replicated to all domain controllers, making Active Directory a *multimaster* replication model.

For the Windows 2000 Professional exam, it is important that you have a basic understanding of Active Directory's structure, which, like that of Windows NT 4, begins with a domain. The *domain* is the fundamental administrative, security, and replication unit of Active Directory. The domain is specified by two names: its down-level Network Basic Input/Output System (NetBIOS) name—such as CONOSCO, which was also used in NT 4—and its DNS name, such as conosco.com. DNS is the primary name resolution methodology in Windows 2000.

When an enterprise decides to implement a multidomain model within its Active Directory database, it creates what are called domain *trees* or *forests*. Multidomain models, however, fall outside the scope of the Windows 2000 Professional exam, so this chapter focuses on what you need to know in a single-domain environment.

In a single domain, Active Directory can contain millions of objects. To increase the manageability of those objects, you can place them in containers called OUs. OUs can contain other OUs, allowing a nested, hierarchical structure to be created within a domain (see Figure 3.2).

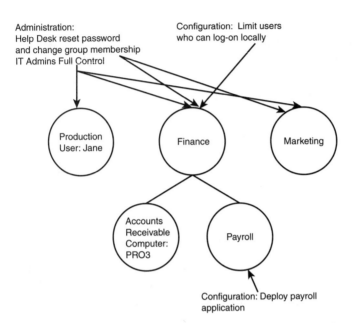

Figure 3.2 An example of an Active Directory domain that contains several OUs.

An enterprise uses its OU structure to control the administration and configuration of objects in the enterprise. For example, the organization depicted in Figure 3.2 might give an IT Admins group full control over the OUs displayed, which would allow that group to create, delete, and fully manage all the objects within those OUs. A Help Desk group might be given permission to reset passwords for user objects in the Finance and Marketing OUs and to put users in those OUs into groups based on the resource access they require. Workstations in the Finance OU could be configured to limit which users are allowed to log on locally. And users in the Payroll OU might have the payroll application installed on their machines, all through properties of the OU.

The OUs' virtual model of administration and configuration offers enormous flexibility and simplifies the effort it takes to manage large and small networks. As objects are moved between OUs, they are administered and configured differently. For example, referring to Figure 3.2, if a user named Jane is moved from the Production OU to the Payroll OU, the payroll application is deployed automatically. In addition, the Help Desk can reset Jane's password because, by default, properties of OUs (including delegated administrative permissions) are inherited from their parent OUs. If the computer PRO3 is moved from the Accounts Receivable OU to the Marketing OU, the limitation on which users can log on locally (which it was inheriting from the Finance OU) is removed.

The complexities and mechanics of designing and implementing Active Directory are not among the objectives of the Windows 2000 Professional exam. However, it is important that you realize that within a domain, you can use OUs to control administration and configuration of all objects, including users and computers, and that OUs by default inherit the administrative and configuration properties of OUs higher up in the OU structure. You will see these concepts in action in the section "Group Policy," later in this chapter.

Understanding and Implementing Policy

Configuring a particular system and the environment for a particular user begins with its defaults—the settings determined by Microsoft during the development of Windows 2000. Of course, there are numerous settings for which Microsoft's defaults are not appropriate for one or more computers or users. Therefore, users and administrators often find themselves modifying the defaults.

In the past, if several settings needed to be changed, you often had to use several tools, including User Manager, Server Manager, System Policy Editor, and even Registry Editor. If settings needed to be changed on multiple computers, it was often necessary to make those changes on each system individually. And if a setting you specified was later changed inappropriately, there was often no way to set it back to the desired setting except by manually making the change again.

Managing changes and configuration has been significantly improved in Windows 2000, thanks to the introduction into the Windows environment of *policy-based administration*. Policies provide administrators with a single list of configuration settings in one tool, rather than many tools, and allow administrators to apply those configuration settings to one machine, many machines, or every machine.

Local Policy

On a Windows 2000 Professional system, you can configure security-related settings by using the Local Security Settings console, which contains the Security Settings Microsoft Management Console (MMC) snap-in. To open this snap-in, you simply choose Start, Settings, Control Panel, Administrative Tools, Local Security Settings. Each of the nodes in the Local

Security Settings console is a security area or scope within which you will find dozens of security related settings (also called *attributes*).

The Local Setting column of the details pane displays the settings as specified by the local policy. The Effective Settings column shows what is currently in effect. The two columns may differ if the local policy has not been implemented; changes to security settings take effect when the system is restarted or following a refresh interval, which is by default 90 minutes. The columns may also differ because local policy settings are overridden by group policy settings, which is discussed later in this chapter.

Local policy settings include user rights assignments such as the ability of certain users to log on locally to the computer. You can use local policy to enable auditing for various types of events, such as which users are successfully or unsuccessfully logging on to the computer. You can use local policy to configure several different security options, such as whether to have Windows 2000 display the username of the last logged-on user in the Log On to Windows dialog box. Local policy also provides account policy settings for users that allow you to specify password requirements, among other things.

Account Policies

Account policies control the password requirements and how the system responds to invalid logon attempts. The policies you can specify include the following:

➤ *Maximum password age*—This is the period of time after which a password must be changed.

➤ *Minimum password length*—This is the number of characters in a password. Passwords can contain up to 127 characters; however, most passwords should not exceed 14.

➤ *Passwords must meet complexity requirements*—This policy, if in effect, does not allow a password change unless the new password contains at least three of four character types: uppercase (A through Z), lowercase (a through z), numeric (0 through 9), and nonalphanumeric (such as !).

➤ *Enforce password history*—This policy specifies the number of previous passwords that the system can remember. When a user attempts to change his or her password, the new password is compared against the history; if the new password is unique, the change is allowed.

➤ *Minimum password age*—This specifies the number of days that a new password must be used before it can be changed again.

➤ *Account lockout threshold*—This is the number of denied logon attempts after which an account is locked out. For example, if this policy is set to three, a lockout occurs if a user enters the wrong password three times; any further logon attempts are denied. If this policy is set to zero, there is no lockout threshold.

➤ *Reset account lockout counter after*—This is the number of minutes after which the counter, which applies to the lockout threshold, is reset. For example, if the counter is reset after five minutes and the account lockout threshold is three, a user can log on twice with the incorrect password. After five minutes, the counter is reset, so the user can log on twice more. A third invalid logon during a five-minute period locks out the account.

➤ *Account lockout duration*—This specifies how long logon attempts are denied after a lockout. During this period, a logon with the locked out username is not authenticated.

Audit Policies

Audit policies specify what types of events are entered into the security log. The following are the most important policies to understand:

➤ *Logon events*—This policy deals with authentication of users logging on or off locally and making connections to the computer from remote systems.

➤ *Account management*—This policy deals with any change to account properties, including password changes and the addition, deletion, or modification of users or groups.

➤ *Object access*—This policy deals with access to objects on which auditing has been specified. Auditing object access, for example, enables auditing of files and folders on an NT File System (NTFS) volume, but you must also configure auditing on those files and folders. See Chapter 2, "Implementing and Administering Resources," for a detailed discussion of auditing.

➤ *Privilege use*—This policy deals with use of any user right, called a *privilege*. For example, this policy audits a user who changes the system time because changing system time is a privilege.

For each policy, you can specify to audit successes, failures, or both. As events are logged, they appear in the security log, which can be viewed, by default, only by administrators. Other logs can be viewed by anyone.

User Rights Assignment

User rights, also called *privileges*, allow a user or group to perform system functions such as change the system time, back up or restore files, and format a disk volume. Some rights are assigned to built-in groups. For example, the Administrators group can format a disk volume. You cannot deny that right to members of the Administrators group, nor can you assign that right to a user or group you create. Other rights are assignable. For example, the right to back up files and folders is given by default to the Administrators group and the Backup Operators group, but you can remove the right for those groups or assign the right to other users or groups. You can modify the rights that are displayed in the Local Security Settings console. Other built-in rights that are not displayed in this console are not modifiable.

User rights, because they are system oriented, override object permissions when the two are in conflict with each other. For example, a user may be denied permission to read a folder on a disk volume. However, if the user has been given the privilege to back up files and folders, a backup of the folder succeeds, even though the user cannot actually read the folder.

Security Options

The Security Options node contains a number of useful security settings. This node highlights one of the advantages of using (local or group) policy settings: Although many of these settings are accessible elsewhere in the user interface (for example, you can specify driver signing in the System applet), policy settings allow you to compile all those settings, from all those tools and applets, into a unified configuration tool.

Some particularly useful options to be familiar with are the following:

> *Disable Ctrl+Alt+Delete requirement for logon*—If this policy is enabled, the logon dialog box does not appear at startup, and the system boots directly to the desktop. This policy is enabled by default on standalone systems and disabled by default when a machine joins a domain, due to the obvious security implications of bypassing a secure logon.

> *Clear the Virtual Memory Pagefile when the system shuts down*—With this policy, by default, the pagefile is not cleared and could allow unauthorized access to sensitive information that remains in the pagefile.

> *Do not display last username in logon screen*—This policy forces users to enter both usernames and passwords at logon. By default, this policy is disabled, which means the name of the previously logged-on user is displayed.

Managing Local Policies

The Local Security Settings console is most helpful on standalone systems. The local policy sets the configuration of the computer, and if a setting is changed through tools other than the Local Security Settings console, the change is reverted to the policy-specified setting when the system is restarted or following the policy refresh interval.

It is possible, however, to transfer security policies between systems. If you right-click the Security Settings node, you can export and import policies. This allows you to copy a policy you have created on one machine to other machines. However, you can imagine the complexity of trying to maintain consistent local policies across multiple systems. That complexity is addressed by group policy, which is discussed in the following section.

The Security Configuration and Analysis snap-in allows you to capture the security configuration of a system as a database and to use that database as a baseline against which you can gauge changes to security settings. When modifications are made that deviate from the database setting, you can reapply the original setting. You can also save the database as a template, which you can then apply to other systems to duplicate security settings. There are also preconfigured security templates that you can apply to Windows 2000 systems to implement a variety of security environments.

Group Policy

Group policy (technically referred to as GPOs)applies the concept of policy-enforced configuration to one or more computers with one or more users. Similar to local policy, group policy provides Active Directory administrators with a centralized group of configuration settings that get inherited from a parent container, such as a domain, to child containers, such as OUs, that are stored within the domain. You can apply, or *link*, a group policy to the following:

➤ *A domain*—This causes the configuration specified by the policy to be applied to every user or computer within the domain.

➤ *An OU*—This applies group policy settings to users or computers within the OU.

➤ *A site*—This is an Active Directory object that represents a portion of your network topology with good connectivity (such as a local area network [LAN]).

To access group policy, you must go to the properties of a site, domain, or OU (SDOU) and click the Group Policy tab. Therefore, to work with group policy for a site, you use the Active Directory Sites and Services console, right-click on a site, and choose Properties. To work with group policy for a domain or an OU, you use the Active Directory Users and Computers console, right-click a domain or an OU, and choose Properties.

Whereas an individual machine can have only one local policy, an SDOU can have multiple policies. On the Group Policy properties sheet, you can create a new GPO by clicking New or you can link an existing group policy to the SDOU by clicking Add. If you select a group policy and click Edit, you expose the GPO in the Group Policy Editor.

> The terms *group policy* and *GPOs* are routinely used interchangeably. Whenever you hear or see references made to group policy in relation to Active Directory, rest assured that, technically, GPOs are being discussed.

Application of Group Policy

Group policy (or GPOs) are divided into the Computer Settings and User Settings nodes. The computer settings apply to every computer in the SDOU to which the policy is linked and, by default, to all child OUs. Computer settings take effect at startup and every refresh interval (which is by default 90 minutes). User settings affect every user in the SDOU and its children at logon, and after each refresh interval.

When a computer starts up, its current settings are modified first by any configuration specified by the local policy. Then, the configuration in group policies is applied: first, the policies linked to the computer's site, then the policies for its domain, and finally the policies for each OU in the branch that leads to the computer's OU. If there is ever a conflict in a particular configuration setting, the last setting applied takes effect. Therefore, the policies that are "closest" to the computer—for example, the policies linked to its OU—take precedence if a conflict arises. The same application of policies applies to a user at logon: local policy, site policy, domain policy, and OU policy.

> You can remember the order of policy application as LSDOU, or "el-stew." Policies are applied in the order local, site, domain, and OU.

The process of applying group policy settings is an intuitive process, at first. But applying group policy can get extremely complex when multiple policy settings are applied to a single container (SDOU), when inheritance is blocked or No Override is specified, and when policies are modified by access control lists (ACLs). Luckily, the enterprise scale application of group policy is not an objective of the Windows 2000 Professional exam. You need to simply understand the basic order of policy application—local, site, domain, and OU (LSDOU).

Group Policy and OU Design

Group policy is a major factor in determining an enterprise's OU structure. If an OU contains users or computers that require different configurations and settings, the best practice is to create separate OUs, each of which contains objects that are configured similarly. By doing so, you can then manage the configuration by applying an appropriate group policy to each OU.

For example, think about the organization depicted in Figure 3.2. If within the Marketing OU a group of salespeople needed a sales application, and that sales application was not appropriate for all users in the Marketing OU, the best practice would be to create an OU, perhaps called Sales, within the Marketing OU (see Figure 3.3). If you place the Sales OU within the Marketing OU, the Sales OU inherits all the existing administration and configuration of the Marketing OU. But you can create a policy linked only to the Sales OU, and you can use that policy to deploy the sales application. As users are moved into the Sales OU, the sales application is deployed to them. See Chapter 4, "Configuring and Troubleshooting the User Experience," for more information about deploying applications through group policy.

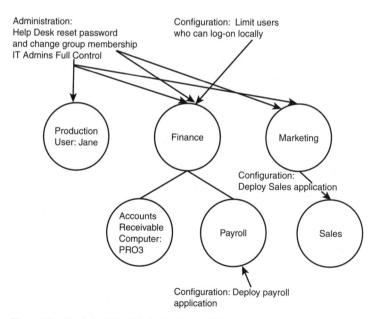

Figure 3.3 The Sales OU within the Marketing OU.

Practice Questions

Question 1

> **Computer1** is a member of the SAFTA domain. A local user account, **John**, is in the Administrators group. When John logs on to the SAFTA domain, he is unable to perform all administrative functions on his system. What should you do to enable John to have full administrative control over his computer?
>
> ○ a. Delete the local user account **John**.
>
> ○ b. Add John's domain user account to the Administrators group.
>
> ○ c. Add John's domain user account to the Administrators group on the domain.
>
> ○ d. Give John Full Control permission to the **C:\WINNT** directory.

Answer B is correct. John is logging on to the domain, and even if his domain username is John, it is still a different account than the local user account. Therefore, John is not actually a member of the Administrators group when he is logging on to the domain.

Question 2

> Susan is an administrator of **Computer5**. Other users who log on to **Computer5** complain that Susan occasionally formats the **D:** drive to get rid of old files and folders and that she is destroying their data in the process. You want Susan to be able to manage basic user and group accounts as well as restore files, but you want to prevent her from unnecessarily harming the system. What should you do? (Select all the correct answers.)
>
> ❏ a. Add Susan to the Backup Operators group.
>
> ❏ b. Add Susan to the Power Users group.
>
> ❏ c. Deny Susan Full Control permission to the **System32** folder.
>
> ❏ d. Remove Susan from the Administrators group.

Answers a, b, and d are correct. The Backup Operators group can restore files and folders, and the Power Users group can manage basic user and group accounts. By removing Susan from the Administrators group, you deny her many privileges that are built in to that group, including the privilege to format disk volumes.

Question 3

You want to enable a colleague to access files on your Windows 2000 Professional system from her system, which is part of a Novell network. You have shared the folder in which the files are stored, and both share and NTFS permissions indicate that Everyone has Full Control. However, your colleague calls you and indicates that she still cannot access the files. What can you do to grant her access? (Select all the correct answers.)

❑ a. Give the Authenticated Users group Full Control of the folder.

❑ b. Create a user account for your colleague and tell her the password.

❑ c. Enable the Guest account and tell your colleague the password.

❑ d. Stop the **WINLOGON** service.

Answers b and c are correct. In order to access a resource, one must first have a valid user account. Because the system is part of a Novell network, it is not in a domain and is a standalone or workgroup system. Therefore, all accounts must be created locally. You can either create an account for your colleague or enable the Guest account.

Question 4

You have just installed Windows 2000 Professional, and when it starts up, it goes directly to the desktop, without asking for a username and password. You want to improve the security of the system by enforcing logon. What tools could you use? (Select all the correct answers.)

❑ a. Local security policy

❑ b. Domain security policy

❑ c. Group policy

❑ d. The Users and Passwords applet

❑ e. The System applet

❑ f. The Computer Management console

Answers a, c, and d are correct. All three of these tools expose the security setting to automate logon or require logon. The System applet and the Computer Management console do not expose the setting to require logon. Therefore, Answers e and f are incorrect.

Question 5

You are deploying a mobile computer called **Laptop3** for Maria. **Laptop3** is in the Sales OU. Maria is in the Outside Sales OU, which is contained within the Sales OU. You want to ensure that the sales application is deployed to Maria and all others who take **Laptop3** on the road. Which of the following is the best-practice solution for deploying the sales application?

○ a. Configure the User Settings node of a GPO to deploy the application's Windows Installer Package (MSI) file to the Outside Sales OU.

○ b. Use local policy to deploy the application's MSI file to **Laptop3**.

○ c. Configure the User Settings node of a GPO to deploy the application's MSI file to the Sales OU.

○ d. Configure the Computer Settings node of a GPO to deploy the application's MSI file to the Outside Sales OU.

○ e. Configure the Computer Settings node of a GPO to deploy the application's MSI file to the Sales OU.

Answer e is correct. You want all users to have the application when they are on Laptop 3, so you want to use the Computer Settings node of group policy. Laptop3 belongs to the Sales OU. Applying the policy to the Outside Sales OU would not affect Laptop3, which is above the Outside Sales OU in the OU structure.

Question 6

Lou has an account in the domain that is a member of the Sales, Trainers, and Managers groups. You are hiring Beth, who will be a member of the same groups as Lou. You want to create Beth's account with the least administrative effort. What should you do?

○ a. Create an account for Beth and add the account to the Sales, Trainers, and Managers groups.

○ b. Rename Lou's account as Beth.

○ c. Copy Lou's account and call the new account Beth.

○ d. Rename the Guest account Beth.

Answer c is correct. If you copy Lou's account, the new account will be a member of the same groups as Lou's.

Question 7

Lou has a local user account that is a member of the Sales, Trainers, and Managers groups. You are hiring Beth, who will also be a member of the same groups. You want to create Beth's account with the least administrative effort. What should you do?

○ a. Create an account for Beth and add the account to the Sales, Trainers, and Managers groups.

○ b. Rename Lou's account as Beth.

○ c. Copy Lou's account and call the new account Beth.

○ d. Rename the Guest account Beth.

Answer a is correct. You cannot copy a local user account.

Question 8

Lou has an account in the domain that is a member of the Sales, Trainers, and Managers groups. The Sales group has access to the Sales Reports folder, the Trainers group can read the Curricula folder, and the Managers can read the Financials folder. Lou can also modify the Curricula folder. You hire Beth, who will be performing the same job function as Lou. You copy Lou's account and name the new account **Beth**. Which of the following statements are true? (Select all the correct answers.)

❑ a. Beth is a member of the Sales, Trainers, and Managers groups.

❑ b. Beth can read the Curricula folder.

❑ c. Beth can modify the Curricula folder.

❑ d. Beth's password is the same as Lou's.

Answers a and b are correct. The access Beth enjoys is because her account is a member of the same groups as Lou's, but access permissions assigned to a user account are not changed when you copy the account. Similarly, user passwords are not copied when an account is copied. Beth cannot modify the Curricula folder because that permission was assigned directly to Lou. Therefore, Answer c is incorrect.

Question 9

You bring your system from your home network into the office and connect it to the enterprise network. When you log on, the settings and applications that normally affect you at the office do not apply. What can you do to correct the situation?

○ a. Renew your system's DHCP address.

○ b. Log on with the Administrator account.

○ c. Join your system to the domain and log on with your domain account.

○ d. Log on as with the Guest account.

Answer c is correct. The system is not part of the domain, so it does not apply policies that are part of your domain's Active Directory database.

Question 10

You have configured the local policy of your domain workstation, a Windows 2000 Professional machine, to disable the requirement to press Ctrl+Alt+Delete and log on. However, when you start the computer, it still requires you to press Ctrl+Alt+Delete. What tool should you use to locate the source of the problem?

○ a. Computer Management

○ b. System Information

○ c. Event Viewer

○ d. Local security policy

○ e. Group policy

Answer e is correct. Your system's local policy is being overridden by a site, a domain, or an OU group policy. Group policy allows you to examine the policies applied to your system's SDOUs. Although local security policy shows you that there is a discrepancy between the local policy and the effective policy, it does not help you locate the source of the discrepancy. Therefore, Answer d is incorrect.

Need to Know More?

 Microsoft Corporation. *Microsoft Windows 2000 Professional Resource Kit*. Redmond, Washington: Microsoft Press, 2000. This book has invaluable information on implementing security accounts and policy.

 Stinson, Craig, and Carl Siechert. *Running Microsoft Windows 2000 Professional*. Redmond, Washington: Microsoft Press, 2000. This guidebook to Windows 2000 Professional is a good source for information on user and group account management.

 Hudson, James, and Fullerton, Sean. *Special Edition Using Microsoft Active Directory*. (ISBN: 0789724340), Indianapolis. Que Publishing, 2001. This book provides complete, in-depth coverage of the newest directory service from Microsoft. Authors Fullerton and Hudson use their previous training and administration experiences to explain how to design, implement, and troubleshoot using Active Directory.

 To find more information, you can search the TechNet CD (or its online version, through www.microsoft.com) and/or the Windows 2000 Professional Resource Kit CD using the keywords account, policy, SAM, authentication, group, user rights, and group policy.

4

Configuring and Troubleshooting the User Experience

. . . .

Terms you'll need to understand:

✓ User profiles
✓ Offline files and folders
✓ Windows Installer Service
✓ MSI files
✓ ZAP files

Techniques you'll need to master:

✓ Configuring offline file and folder options
✓ Implementing Windows Installer Service packages
✓ Understanding the functionality of various Control Panel applets
✓ Implementing software deployment group policy

With Windows 2000 Professional, Microsoft has answered various complaints that many users had about Windows NT Workstation. Mobile users of Windows NT Workstation had a difficult time keeping files on a network file server synchronized with copies they kept on their laptops. Windows 2000 Professional goes a long way toward fixing this age-old problem and other problems such as dynamic link library (DLL) conflicts, application repair, and software updates. This chapter discusses how Windows 2000 Professional addresses these problems. This chapter also discusses how the user environment has been configured and enhanced in Windows 2000 Professional through the availability of various control applets.

Configuring and Managing User Profiles

A *user profile* controls the look and feel of the user's desktop environment. A profile is a combination of folders, data, shortcuts, application settings, and personal data. For example, a user can configure his or her computer with a specific screen saver and particular desktop wallpaper. These settings are independent of other users' settings. When a user logs on to his or her computer for the very first time, a new profile is created for that user from a default user profile. So, for example, when Joe logs on, a profile is created just for Joe. This type of profile is known as a *local profile*, and it is stored on the computer on which it was created. If Joe logs on to a different computer, his profile does not follow him to the computer he logs on to. However, you can have a user's profile follow a user around the network if you so choose. This type of profile is called a *roaming user profile*. These profiles are stored on a network server. A local copy of the roaming profile is also found on the client computer.

User Profiles

User profiles in Windows 2000 contain a different folder structure from that in Windows NT. A new Local Settings folder in a profile is local to the machine it resides on, and it doesn't roam. Also, a new folder called My Documents is contained in a profile. This folder is the default location to which files are saved, and it does roam.

Local Profiles

Windows 2000 Professional local profiles are found in a different location than those in Windows NT 4 Workstation—maybe. If you perform a clean installation of Windows 2000 Professional, a user profile is stored in a system partition called `%SystemDrive%\Documents` and `Settings\user_logon_name` (for example, `C:\Documents and Settings\Joe`). If, however, you upgrade a Windows NT 4 Workstation to Windows 2000 Professional, the local profile is stored in the same location as it always was: `%SystemRoot%\Profiles\user_logon_name` (for example, `C:\Winnt\Profiles\Joe`).

Logon Scripts and Home Folders

When a user logs on, a *logon script* might execute, and a *home folder* might be assigned to the user. Logon scripts are stored on a network server called a *domain controller* (DC) and are often used to map network drives or to execute some type of batch file.

To configure a logon script for a user, you perform the following steps on a Windows 2000 Server DC computer:

1. Place the logon script in `%SystemRoot%\SYSVOL\sysvol\domain_name\scripts` (this is a new location for logon scripts in Windows 2000).

2. Next, open the Active Directory Users and Computers MMC snap-in and double-click a username to display its properties sheet. On the Profile tab type the name of the logon script in the Logon Script field.

A *home folder* is a central location on a network server where users can store their files. Each user has his or her own home folder in which to store data. This way, if users' computers fail, they don't lose all their data. Home folders also provide one central location in which users can back up all their data.

To create a home folder, you perform the following steps:

1. Create a share on a network server to enable home folders.

2. Open the Active Directory Users and Computers snap-in and double-click a username to display its properties sheet. On the Profile tab select the Connect radio button.

3. Select the drop-down arrow and choose an available drive letter.

4. Type in the uniform naming convention (UNC) path to the user's home folder (for example, `\\server1\homedir\Todd`).

Microsoft suggests that users store their data in **My Documents** instead of in home directories. When they do so, you can enable a group policy to redirect **My Documents** files from the local computer to a network file server. The group policy can also activate offline caching of **My Documents** files to the user's local computer. Group policy as well as offline files and folders are covered later in this chapter, in the section "Using Offline Files and Folders."

Roaming User Profiles

For users who move from computer to computer, you can configure their profiles to move with them. A roaming profile is stored on a network server so that the profile is accessible regardless of which computer a user logs on to in the domain. You can put the profile on the server in two ways:

➤ You can copy a profile that is stored locally on a client computer to the profile server the next time the user logs on to the computer.

➤ You can create on a client computer a profile that you will use as a company standard and then manually copy it to the profile server.

 Roaming user profiles behave differently in Windows 2000 and Windows XP than in Windows NT 4 Workstation. When a user logs on to a computer for the first time in Windows 2000 and Windows XP, the roaming profile is copied to the client computer. From that point forward, whenever a user logs on to a computer, the locally cached copy of the profile is compared to the roaming user profile. If the local profile and the roaming profile are the same, the local copy is used. Windows 2000 and XP copy only files that have changed, not the entire profile, as is the case in Windows NT.

You follow these steps to configure a roaming profile:

1. Create a shared folder on a server to store the roaming user profiles (for example, \\server1\profiles).

2. On a Windows 2000 Professional computer, go to the Control Panel and launch the System applet.

3. From the User Profile tab, select the profile that you want to use as a roaming profile and click Copy To.

4. Type in the UNC path to the shared folder that you created on the server and append the username to the UNC path (for example, \\server1\profiles\Todd).

5. On a DC, run the Active Directory Users and Computers snap-in and double-click a username to display its properties sheet.

6. Select the Profile tab and enter in the Profile Path text box the UNC path to the user profile that has now been copied to a server.

In Windows 2000, new permissions are assigned to the roaming profile directory. If you create a roaming profile on an NTFS volume by using the **%*username*%** variable, the user and the built-in local Administrators group are assigned Full Control permission for that directory.

You can protect local and roaming profiles against permanent change by renaming **NTUSER.DAT** to **NTUSER.MAN**. By renaming the file, you effectively make the profile read-only, meaning that Windows 2000 does not save any changes made to the profile when the user logs off. **NTUSER.DAT** is found in the root of a profile and is hidden by default. This file is responsible for the user portion of the Registry and contains all the user settings.

Using Offline Files and Folders

Windows 2000 offers a new feature called *offline files*. This feature addresses several file access problems that plague Windows NT, such as the file server being down and users needing to access files on the file server and users not being connected to the network and being unable to access the files they need. By using offline files and folders, users can mark files on a network file server for offline usage. This means that users can have cached copies of files on their local computers and can work on the files just as if they were connected to the network. Any offline files that have been changed on a local computer are synchronized with the network file server when the users connect to the network.

Setting Up Offline Files and Folders

Two steps are involved in configuring offline files. The first is to configure the share point for offline usage. The second is to cache the files to the client computer.

Configuring Share Points

You use the following steps to configure the share point:

1. For each folder that you want to make available to users offline, right-click the folder and select Sharing to make it available to network users.

2. From the Sharing tab, click the Caching button.

3. Select the Allow Caching of Files in This Shared Folder check box (which is selected by default).

4. Select one of the following three options from the Settings drop-down list and then click OK:

> ➤ *Manual Caching for Documents*—This option is the default setting. With this option selected, users must select the files they want to be available for offline usage.

> ➤ *Automatic Caching for Documents*—This option caches for offline usage all files that users have opened to their local disks. Any older files that are out of synchronization are automatically deleted and replaced by newer versions of the same files.

> ➤ *Automatic Caching for Programs*—This option provides the same capabilities as Automatic Caching for Documents and also caches applications that are run from the network.

5. Click OK to close the Share Point dialog box and to accept the options that you selected.

By default, Windows 2000 does not allow you to cache files with the **.slm**, **.ldb**, **.mdw**, **.mdb**, **.pst**, and **.db** extensions. However, you can override this setting by using a group policy. To do so, you create a computer policy for Administrative templates, Network, Offline Files, Files not cached.

The policy excludes files with specific file extensions from being cached. However, if the policy is enabled and no file extensions are added, all file types are made available offline. This group policy setting overrides the default configuration; it allows files with the **.slm**, **.ldb**, **.mdw**, **.mdb**, **.pst**, and **.db** extensions to be cached.

Making Files and Folders Available Offline

By default, a Windows 2000 Professional computer is configured for offline file and folder usage. You use the following steps to make a file or folder available offline:

1. Connect to a share point on a domain or workgroup file server. Right-click a file that you want. Select Make Available Offline. A wizard appears if you are using this feature for the first time. The wizard asks if offline files should be synchronized during logon and logoff.

2. Click the Next button to accept the default. (Additional options are available after the wizard is finished.)

3. If you want the operating system to remind you that you are not connected to the network, click the Finish button to accept the default option, Enable Reminders. If you accept this option, a computer icon

appears in the system tray. Whenever you are disconnected from the network, a balloon appears to notify you that offline files are available.

When you have completed these steps, a double arrow icon, as shown in Figure 4.1, appears on the file or folder that you have selected for offline usage. This is a graphic indicator to inform the user that the file is located on the network and that a local cached copy of the file is located on the user's computer.

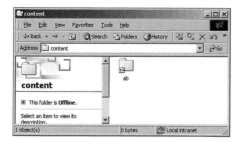

Figure 4.1 The offline file indicator.

 Windows NT 4.0 and Windows 9x clients cannot use the offline files feature of Windows 2000 servers and Windows Server 2003 computers. However, a Windows 2000 Professional or Windows XP client can make files available for offline usage from a Windows NT 4.0 server share.

To view offline files when you are disconnected from the network, you open My Network Places. Yes, that is correct. Offline files maintain their original location, even though the computer is offline. You go to My Network Places and select the file server that contains the files. You can see only the files that were previously designated to be available offline. Users don't see the network while they are offline.

Synchronizing Offline Files and Folders

To synchronize your offline files with the network, you must reconnect and log on to the network. Any changes you made to the offline file(s) while you were offline are synchronized with the original file(s) on the network. Keep in mind that if you log on to the network from a slow dial-up connection, it could take a long time to synchronize the offline files.

Several options are available to customize the synchronization process to deal with problems such as slow connections. To customize the process that occurs when offline files are synchronized, you open a Windows Explorer window and then select Tools, Synchronize. The first dialog box that appears displays the files and folders that are available offline. To configure synchronization, you click the Setup button. This brings up the Synchronization Settings dialog box, which is shown in Figure 4.2. This dialog box, also known as the Synchronization Manager, offers three tabs that help you determine when you should synchronize offline files: Logon/Logoff, On Idle, and Scheduled. However, you can also select over what network connection synchronization takes place. For example, to have synchronization occur only when you are connected to the network (versus when you have a slow dial-up connection), you can select LAN Connection in the When I Am Using This Network Connection drop-down list.

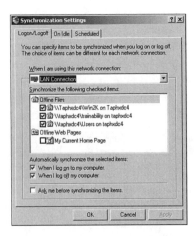

Figure 4.2 The Synchronization Settings dialog box.

Synchronization Details

Now that you know how to configure synchronization, you are probably wondering what actually happens during this process. Well, it depends. The following are several synchronization scenarios:

➤ *An offline file has been deleted, and the original network version of the file has not changed*—If this happens, Windows 2000 Professional removes the file from the network file server during synchronization.

➤ *A network file has been deleted, and the offline version of the file has not changed*—If this happens, Windows 2000 Professional presents a dialog box that gives you the option to either remove the file from the local computer during synchronization or keep the local version.

➤ *The offline file has changed, and the network version has changed*—If this happens, you are presented with a dialog box during the synchronization; it asks you what should be done. The options are keep the network version, keep the local version, and keep both and rename the local version.

➤ *Only files that have changed are synchronized*—If no changes have occurred, the locally cached copy is used before the network version of the offline file is used.

Accessing Offline Files and Folders

To access offline files, you use My Network Places; however, that is not where the files are actually stored. Offline files are kept in %SystemRoot%\CSC. (csc is hidden by default.) This directory contains a database of offline files. You cannot view or edit individual files from this location. However, if the csc directory gets quite large and if you use offline files frequently, it is advisable to move this directory from the system partition to a different partition or drive. However, you can't move this directory by using Windows Explorer. To move the csc directory from one partition to another, you use the Windows 2000 Resource Kit utility named cachemov.exe.

Managing Offline Files and Folders

To manage offline files, you open a Windows Explorer window and then select Tools, Folder Options and then select the Offline Files tab. The key options for managing offline folders are Enable Offline Files, Delete Files, and View Files (to view all the Offline files within one window). You can also use a sliding bar to control the amount of disk space made available for files that have automatically been cached to the local drive. The default disk space made available for automatically cached files is 10%.

Configuring and Troubleshooting Desktop Settings

The Windows 2000 desktop is a combination of Windows NT options, Windows 98 options, and some new options. In general, a regular local or domain user account can configure very few changes on a Windows 2000 Professional computer. Users can configure the following Control Panel applets and customization options to customize their desktops:

> ➤ The Keyboard applet

> ➤ The Display applet

> ➤ The Mouse applet

> ➤ The Sound applet

> ➤ The personalized Start menu

> ➤ Quick Launch Pad

> ➤ Toolbars

The following sections describe each of these applets and options.

The Keyboard Applet

The Keyboard applet adjusts the cursor blink rate, the speed at which a character repeats when you hold down a key, the time lapse before a character repeats, and the input locale for different language groups of keyboard hardware. For example, you can use several language locales with a U.S. keyboard layout so that you can add foreign accent marks to documents that are written in French, Spanish, Italian, and so on. You can also use the Regional applet to configure input locales. Chapter 5, "Configuring and Troubleshooting System Services and the Desktop Environment," provides more information on this topic.

The Display Applet

The Display applet in Windows 2000 has changed a little from that in Windows NT. You can now use six tabs to affect various aspects of the display:

> ➤ *Background*—Selects and adds a desktop wallpaper or pattern.

> ➤ *Screen Saver*—Selects a screen saver and is also a shortcut to the Power Options applet. The Power button on the Screen Saver tab allows you to adjust power schemes and configure Standby and Hibernate modes.

> ➤ *Appearance*—Adjusts the color and font schemes that are displayed in all dialog boxes and windows.

> ➤ *Web*—Displays an HTML page on the desktop. This is a new tab in Windows 2000.

➤ *Effects*—Adjusts how menus appear, changes the default icons, and makes other visual enhancements.

➤ *Settings*—Assigns default color depths and resolutions if Windows 2000 doesn't detect a Plug and Play monitor. This is probably the most important of the tabs.

Often, these parameters need to be changed to suit the users' needs.

The Mouse Applet

The Mouse applet adjusts for left-handed or right-handed use. It also adjusts the double-click speed and the rate at which the cursor moves across the screen.

The Sound Applet

The Sound applet controls the startup and logoff sounds. It also controls what .wav files are used for critical error alerts and general alerts.

The Personalized Start Menu

Windows 2000 makes it much easier than Windows NT to arrange and customize Start menu items. In Windows 2000 you can very easily sort menu items by dragging and dropping them. You can drag a menu item from one submenu to another. Also, you can open the menu folders by right-clicking them. Windows 2000 automatically adjusts menu items as well. Windows 2000 attempts to clean up the Start menu by displaying only the items that are used most frequently. Items that are not used often are hidden.

Windows 2000 Professional displays a Screen Tip to click on a double down arrow so that you can access the infrequently used or hidden items on the Start menu. You can turn off this feature quite easily: by right-clicking the taskbar and selecting the Properties option. Doing so displays the General tab of the Taskbar and Start Menu Properties dialog box. You need to deselect the option Use Personalized Menus.

You can find even more customization options on the Advanced tab of the Taskbar and Start Menu Properties dialog box, as shown in Figure 4.3. You can add cascading menus for typical Start menu items such as the Control Panel. Some Start menu items, such as Administrative Tools, are hidden by default.

Figure 4.3 Customizing Start menu settings.

The following is a list of the configuration items on the Advanced tab:

➤ Display Administrative Tools

➤ Display Favorites

➤ Display Logoff

➤ Expand Control Panel

➤ Expand My Documents

➤ Expand Network and Dial-up Connections

➤ Expand Printers

➤ Scroll the Programs Menu

Quick Launch Pad

The taskbar can serve as a multipurpose tool to help make navigating the interface more efficient. The taskbar in Windows 2000, similar to that in Windows 98, contains a Quick Launch Pad, which is a location that contains shortcuts to programs that are used most frequently. By default, Windows 2000 places the Show Desktop, Internet Explorer, and Outlook Express shortcuts on the Quick Launch Pad. You can add or remove shortcuts simply by dragging and dropping them on or off the Quick Launch Pad.

Toolbars

The taskbar can display toolbars that allow you to access frequently used files and folders. A default toolbar called the Address toolbar, for example, provides space on the taskbar to allow you to go directly to a Web site or a file path by simply typing the uniform resource locator (URL) or the path to the file that you want to reach. For example, instead of opening a Web browser and then typing the URL, you can simply type the URL (such as www.microsoft.com) in the Address toolbar and press Enter. The Web browser starts automatically and goes to www.microsoft.com.

To configure an Address toolbar, you right-click the taskbar and select the Toolbars submenu and then select Address. A field called Address is then added to the taskbar.

Windows Installer Service Packages

Microsoft has created a new method, called *Windows Installer Service*, for installing applications in Windows 2000. The Windows Installer Service actually installs packages on a computer.

The Windows Installer Service has two essential functions:

➤ It is an operating system service that is responsible for installing, removing, and updating software by asking the Windows Installer Service package for instructions on how the application should be installed, removed, or modified.

➤ To create a standard for installing, removing, or modifying applications, you use an application programming interface (API) to communicate with the Windows Installer Service about how a package should be modified after an application is installed.

After an application has been installed, the Windows Installer Service checks the state of the application while it is being launched. This service provides self-healing capabilities to applications that were installed as Windows Installer Service packages. The service is always checking to see if applications need to be repaired.

The service also helps to resolve DLL conflicts. Windows 2000 has devised a way to allow an application to alter the location from which DLLs are loaded, instead of having all DLLs located in the system32 directory. This helps protect DLLs from being overwritten and protects them against other conflicts.

Key parts of an application have protected tags on them. A Windows Installer Service package lists critical files that you would need to replace if they were deleted or missing. For example, executables are listed as critical files. If, for example, Todd.exe were deleted, the Windows Installer Service would locate Todd.exe from a network server or ask the user to insert the CD-ROM that contains Todd.exe. When Todd.exe was located, it would be installed, and the application would launch.

The Windows Installer Service does a much better job of removing applications than do previous versions of Windows. During the installation of an application, the Windows Installer Service sits in the background, looking at everything that is installed, where everything is installed, and what has been changed during the installation. When it is time to uninstall an application, the Windows Installer Service knows exactly where every component of the application is, and it can therefore successfully uninstall the application.

If during the installation of an application something happens and the installation fails, the Windows Installer Service can restart the installation from the point of failure. That might not always be the best solution, though, and the Windows Installer Service can also roll back everything that was installed up to the point of failure, allowing the user to start the installation from scratch.

Installing Packages

A Windows Installer Service package (.msi file) contains all the information necessary to tell the Windows Installer Service how the application should be installed. To take advantage of the features that Windows Installer Service offers, you must install an application as an .msi file. Applications such as Office 2000 have their own .msi files. Software developers must design their applications to use this new service. However, existing applications can still gain some of the functionality that .msi files have to offer.

An application can repackage existing applications by using third-party tools such as WinInstall LE. WinInstall is available on the Windows 2000 Professional CD-ROM. This application tracks the installation process and notes all the files that were installed, their locations, and modifications they made to the Registry. You can then customize this information and turn it into an .msi file.

You might be wondering what you should do if you don't have an .msi file or if you can't repackage the file. Non-Windows Installer–based applications such as setup.exe must use a ZAP file in order to be published as packages. A *ZAP file* is a text file with a .zap extension. Such a file provides information about how to install a program and the application properties. The following is a basic example of how to create a ZAP file:

```
[application]
FriendlyName= "WinZip Version 7.0"
SetupCommand= \\server1\apps\winzip\WinZip70.EXE
DisplayVersion = 7.0
[ext]
ZIP =
```

Publishing MSI Packages

You typically install .msi files over a network or locally on a client computer. A common method for installing .msi files in a Windows 2000 domain environment is to publish or assign applications to users through Active Directory. Users in Active Directory can be grouped into containers called organizational units (OUs). You can create a group policy object (GPO) for an OU that either publishes or assigns Windows Installer Service packages (that is, .msi files). Any users in the OU then receive the software when they log on to their Windows 2000 Professional computers. The software they receive when they log on can be either published to them or assigned to them.

Using Group Policy to Publish or Assign Windows Installer Service Packages

Windows Installer Service packages are published or assigned to users through an Active Directory–based group policy. You perform the following steps to create a software group policy:

1. Open the Active Directory Users and Computers snap-in.

2. Select the domain from which to deploy the software to all users in the domain, or select a specific OU from which to deploy software to users just in that OU.

3. Right-click the domain or OU selected in step 2 and choose Properties from the context menu.

4. Select the Group Policy tab.

5. Click the New button to create a new group policy. Type a name for the group policy and press Enter.

6. Select the policy and then click Edit.

7. Under User Configuration, expand Software Settings. Next, right-click Software Installation and then select New, Package from the context menu.

8. Type the UNC path to the `.msi` package on the network (for example, `\\server1\office2000\data1..msi`).

9. Select either Published or Assigned from the Deploy Software dialog box and then click OK.

 If you are using a transform, you must select Advanced Published or Assigned. (You can create a transform to install only specific applications from a software suite of applications.) You can find more information on using transform files in the *Microsoft Office 2000 Resource Kit* or by visiting **www.microsoft.com/office/ork/2000/two/30t3_2.htm**.

10. Close the Group Policy console and click the Close button for the OU properties.

The software group policy takes effect when the users of the domain or OU log on to the network. The users can then install the software.

Publishing Applications

A software package is typically published to users when it is not mandatory that they have a particular application installed on their computer. This is a way to make the applications available for users if they decide they want to use them. After you have created a GPO to publish a software package, you can log on to your computer and find any applications that were published from Add/Remove Programs, as shown in Figure 4.4.

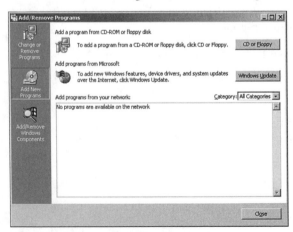

Figure 4.4 The Add/Remove Programs applet.

You can select Add New Programs to see which applications have been published. Users can install a published application if they have user credentials. The Windows Installer Service installs a published application with elevated credentials on behalf of users. Users therefore have a central location for installing applications. This prevents users from having to search for network share points that contain applications they want to install.

Assigning Applications

Assigning an application is very similar to publishing one. When an application has been assigned, you can install it from Add/Remove Programs. In addition, a shortcut for the application that has been assigned is placed on the Start, Programs menu when users log on to their computers. The software is not installed on a machine until a user selects the shortcut for the first time.

Software that has been published or assigned is installed if a user double-clicks a file that has an extension that is supported by the published or assigned application.

Practice Questions

Question 1

A salesperson for your company has selected files from the network file server to be made available offline to her laptop computer. She needs access to the files for a sales presentation in another city. When she connects to the corporate office from her hotel room over a dial-up connection, the synchronization process is unacceptably slow. What can be done to resolve this problem without disabling offline files?

- ○ a. Verify that the share point on the network file server is set to Automatic Caching for Documents.
- ○ b. Use the Synchronization Manager to synchronize files only during a scheduled interval.
- ○ c. Use the Synchronization Manager to synchronize files only while the computer is connected to the local area network (LAN) connection.
- ○ d. Select the Never Allow My Computer to Go Offline option from the Offline Files tab in the Folder Options dialog box.

Answer c is correct. When the Synchronization Manager is set to synchronize only while the computer is connected to the LAN, the offline files aren't synchronized via the dial-up connection. Therefore, Answer a is incorrect. Automatic caching has nothing to do with controlling when synchronizing of offline files will occur; rather, it has to do with making files available while a user is offline. Scheduling an interval for synchronization while the computer is connected via a dial-up connection might simply delay the process of synchronization, but it won't prevent synchronizing of files while a user is connected to a modem. Therefore, Answer b is incorrect. If the Never Allow My Computer to Go Offline option is selected, the salesperson will not have access to the files she made available offline. Therefore, Answer d is incorrect.

Question 2

A user who works for a global organization needs to add foreign accent characters to memos that are sent to its employees in France. How can this be accomplished? (Select all the correct answers.)

- ❏ a. Use the Regional Control Panel and select the language in which the user needs to communicate.
- ❏ b. Install the Multilanguage edition of Windows 2000.
- ❏ c. Use the Keyboard applet and select Input Locales Properties for United States—International.
- ❏ d. Use the Regional Control Panel and select Input Locales Properties for United States—International.

Answers c and d are correct. Both the Keyboard applet and the Regional Control Panel allow users to select a keyboard layout that they can use to add foreign accents to documents. It is not necessary to use the Regional Control Panel to select a separate language, nor is it necessary to install the separate Multilanguage edition of Windows 2000. Therefore, Answers a and b are incorrect.

Question 3

While at work, you add data to an Access database that is located on a Windows 2000 network file server. You want to finish adding the data to the database from home. You select the database and make it available to your laptop computer offline. When you log off the network, the synchronization process begins, but it stops due to an error. The error message states that files with an **.mdb** extension cannot be made available for offline usage. How do you resolve this problem?

- ○ a. Verify that Access is installed on the laptop and manually synchronize the database.
- ○ b. Ensure that the **.mdb** file extension is associated with the correct application.
- ○ c. Enable a group policy to allow for files with the **.mdb** extension to be cached offline.
- ○ d. View the Synchronization Manager options to ensure that the database is selected for offline usage.

Answer c is correct. By default, files with the .mdb extension cannot be cached for offline usage. To override this default, you must configure the Files Not

Cached policy by not listing .mdb files for Access databases to be made available for offline usage. The error you receive is not related to whether Access is installed. Therefore, Answer a is incorrect. Synchronization proceeds normally whether or not a file extension is registered correctly to an application. Therefore, Answer b is incorrect. An error is not displayed if the file isn't selected to be synchronized via the Synchronization Manager. Therefore, Answer d is incorrect.

Question 4

A public library has asked you to create a common desktop for all Windows 2000 Professional machines that the library patrons use. You need to ensure that if a library patron makes a change to the desktop, the change cannot be saved. Currently the library has a mixed environment of Windows 95, 98, and 2000 computers. The following is a list of user account configurations. You need to create a list of required settings and configurations to implement a common desktop for all Windows 2000 Professional machines, placing the items in the list in the correct order:

User Account Configurations

Logon scripts for all clients

Home directories for all clients

Ntuser.man

User.man

UNC path to profile

Common Windows 2000 profile

Common Windows 95 and 98 profile

Required Settings

Common Windows 2000 profile

Ntuser.man

UNC path to profile user **Ntuser**

User.dat is the profile settings file that Windows 95 and Window 98—not Windows 2000—use. To lock down the patron's desktop, a mandatory profile needs to be implemented. You create a mandatory profile for Windows 2000 by renaming ntuser.dat to ntuser.man and then pointing users to the profile via the UNC path. User.dat is the wrong file.

Question 5

A user at a Windows NT 4 workstation is logged on to a Windows 2000 domain and is accessing a Windows 2000 file server. The user reports that he cannot make files available for offline usage. What is the problem?

○ a. The file server is not configured to allow caching of files in the shared folder.

○ b. The user has not enabled offline files from the Offline tab in the Folder Options dialog box.

○ c. The offline files and folders feature is not available on the Windows NT 4 operating system.

○ d. The Active Directory client needs to be installed on the Windows NT 4 workstation.

Answer c is correct. Windows NT 4 (Server and Workstation) cannot cache files for offline use; therefore, Answer b is incorrect. Also, a Windows NT server lacks the capability for configuring caching options; therefore, Answer a is incorrect. However, a Windows 2000 computer can make files available for offline use from a Windows NT 4 server or workstation. Adding the Active Directory client does not enable its functionality on a Windows NT 4 workstation; therefore, Answer d is incorrect.

Question 6

You create a group policy for users at the domain level to publish a Windows Installer Service package. When users log on to their computers, they report that the software has not been installed. What needs to be done to install the software?

○ a. Users should select the shortcut for the application from the Programs menu. This installs the application.

○ b. Users should use Add/Remove Programs to install the software.

○ c. Users should configure a logon script to execute the Windows Installer Service package when they log on.

○ d. Users should configure the group policy to publish the software for computers.

Answer b is correct. When an application has been published to users, you can install the application in two ways: Users can use Add/Remove Programs or they can double-click a file that is associated with the application that needs to be installed. Answer a is incorrect because the application was published, which does not create a shortcut from the Programs menu. Answers c and d are not related to the problem; the application has been published and is ready to install via the Add/Remove Programs applet.

Question 7

> Nurses need to log on to nursing stations equipped with Windows 2000 Professional in a Windows 2000 domain. A nurse might need to log on to three or four different stations. You need to ensure that each nurse's desktop environment is available, no matter which station the nurse logs on to. What do you need to do to implement this?
>
> ○ a. Configure each nurse's account profile on each workstation with the UNC path to the nurse's profile.
>
> ○ b. Configure each nurse's domain account with the UNC path to the nurse's home directory.
>
> ○ c. Configure each nurse's domain account with the UNC path to the **Profile** directory.
>
> ○ d. Configure a logon script to map the **Profile** directory.

Answer c is correct. To make each nurse's desktop available on any workstation, you must create a roaming user profile. The workstations are in a domain environment, so the domain user account must have the UNC path for the profile configured. Answer a is incorrect because the question states that the nurses are in a domain; configuring each workstation would be correct for a workgroup environment. Answer b is incorrect because the home directory is not used for roaming profiles. Answer d won't make a user profile roam.

Question 8

> You have implemented roaming user profiles and home directories for all users. However, users report that their files are being saved to their local hard disks instead of to the network server. What must be done to ensure that users' files are being saved to the network server? (Select all the correct answers.)
>
> ❑ a. Redirect the **My Documents** folder to a network file server by using a group policy.
>
> ❑ b. Redirect the **My Documents** folder to a network file server by providing the UNC path to the user's home directory on the Target tab of the My Documents properties sheet.
>
> ❑ c. Verify that the UNC path to the home directory is correct.
>
> ❑ d. Verify that the UNC path to the **Profile** directory is correct.

Answers a and b are correct. The default location to which applications save their files is the My Documents directory. The default location for the My Documents directory is in the user's profile. However, this portion of the profile is not included in the roaming user profile. The My Documents directory needs to be redirected via a group policy or through the My Documents properties sheet. Therefore, Answers c and d are incorrect.

Question 9

You create a group policy for users at the domain level to assign a Windows Installer Service package. When users log on to their computers, they select the shortcut for the assigned application. The installation of the application fails. What needs to be done to ensure that the assigned application will install?

○ a. The users must install the application from Add/Remove Programs.

○ b. The users must verify that the correct UNC path to the software distribution point was configured for the group policy.

○ c. The users must double-click a file that has a file extension that is supported by the assigned application in order to trigger the installation process.

○ d. The users must create a logon script that maps the software distribution point for the domain user accounts.

Answer b is correct. You must use a UNC path to point to the location of the Windows Installer Service package to assign or publish a Windows Installer Service package via a group policy. If the UNC path is incorrect or if a local path is used, the group policy points to the wrong location for the software distribution point, so the installation fails.

Question 10

You want to deploy a legacy application to all Windows 2000 Professional clients in the Windows 2000 domain via group policy. The legacy application is not a Windows Installer Service package. What do you need to do to deploy this application by using a group policy?

○ a. Non-Windows Installer applications cannot be deployed with a group policy.

○ b. Create a .**zap** file for the legacy application.

○ c. Add to the package a transform that executes a batch file to install the legacy application.

○ d. Choose Advanced Published or Assigned when you create the software package to select the Allow Legacy Application Environment variable.

Answer b is correct. Applications that install by using a `setup.exe` command require a `.zap` file or a third-party utility in order to use a group policy to deploy the application. If a `.zap` file is used, non-Windows applications can be deployed with a group policy. Therefore, Answer a is incorrect. You cannot use a transform with a `setup.exe` command to install the application; therefore, Answer c is incorrect. The Advanced Published or Assigned option doesn't include any options to install legacy applications; therefore, Answer d is incorrect.

Need to Know More?

 Finnel, Lynn. *MCSE Training Kit: Microsoft Windows 2000 Server*. Redmond, Washington: Microsoft Press, 2000. Chapter 7 discusses roaming user profiles. Chapter 15 provides information on deploying applications through group policy.

 Wallace, Rick. *MCSE Training Kit: Microsoft Windows 2000 Professional*. Redmond, Washington: Microsoft Press, 2000. Chapter 4 discusses user account properties. Chapter 15 provides information on offline files and folders.

 `www.microsoft.com/windows2000/techinfo/planning/management/` `swinstall.asp.` This Web site provides information regarding ZAP files.

Configuring and Troubleshooting System Services and the Desktop Environment

. . . .

Terms you'll need to understand:

✓ User locale
✓ Input locale
✓ StickyKeys
✓ FilterKeys
✓ ToggleKeys
✓ MouseKeys
✓ Narrator
✓ Utility Manager
✓ Fax Service Management console
✓ Scheduled Task Wizard

Techniques you'll need to master:

✓ Configuring support for multiple languages
✓ Configuring accessibility options
✓ Implementing and configuring the Fax service
✓ Configuring and managing tasks by using Task Scheduler

Windows 2000 offers many new services and options that can accommodate people's special needs. You can configure Windows 2000 very easily to adjust for different locales and languages. You can also customize Windows 2000 Accessibility options to adjust the interface and keyboard responses for people who have disabilities. In this chapter you will learn about these topics, and you will also learn how to configure and troubleshoot the Fax service and Task Scheduler.

Multiple-Location and Multiple-Language Support

The Windows 2000 operating system jumps ahead of previous versions of Windows in terms of support of multiple languages. It allows you to support people and companies that need to communicate in different languages by using locales. In addition, the Multilanguage edition of Windows 2000 allows users to easily switch between different language user interfaces to suit their needs.

Language Configuration Options

There are essentially two key areas of language configuration options within Windows 2000: locales and language groups.

Locales

A *locale* is a collection of information that Windows 2000 maintains about a user's language. A locale contains information such as the following:

➤ Currency symbol

➤ Format of date, time, and numbers

➤ Localized calendar settings

➤ Character encoding

➤ Country abbreviation

Applications use the locale information to input the correct symbols and characters. There are two types of locales:

➤ *User locale*—A separate user locale is maintained for each user. This locale controls the settings for date, time, and numbers on a per-user basis. When a locale is changed, Windows 2000 adjusts all the regional settings (such as the currency symbol) to reflect the selected locale.

➤ *Input locale*—With an input locale, a language is associated with an input method. For example, you could add the Spanish input locale to combine the Spanish keyboard with the English and French languages. This configuration would allow a user to use the Spanish keyboard layout to input data in both English and French. Input locales allow users who need to converse in multiple languages to use one keyboard layout that can be switched on-the-fly and that maps to other languages as needed.

You configure all locales and language settings through the Regional Options applet in the Control Panel folder. You perform the following steps to select a different user locale:

1. Open the Regional Options applet.

2. Select the General tab.

3. Select the locale required in the Your Locale (Location) drop-down list.

4. Click OK.

No reboot is required after you choose a new locale; the change of locale takes effect immediately. In addition, applications that depend on these settings reflect the new locale immediately. When you change the locale, the Numbers, Currency, Time, and Date tabs reflect the new configurations that are related to the new locale. Another way to configure these settings is to type a new entry for the desired option. For example, a user could select the Currency tab and enter a new currency symbol to be used.

If a keyboard needs multiple layouts, you must add input locales. Doing so allows a user to switch between locales when he or she is working in different languages. To add an input locale, you need to follow these steps:

1. Open the Regional Options applet.

2. Select the Input Locales tab.

3. Click Add and choose an input locale from the drop-down list.

4. Click OK.

5. Select one of the following methods for switching between input locales:

   ➤ Cycle through input locales by pressing left Alt+Shift.

   ➤ Assign a hotkey sequence to specific input locales.

6. Click OK to close the Regional Options applet.

When you have completed these steps, an icon appears in the system tray; it indicates what input locale is currently being used. Another way to select input locales (besides assigning hotkeys) is to click the Input Locale icon and then select the specific input locale that you need.

Additional input locales are available for each new language that is installed. For example, if a user needs an input locale for Estonia, you can install the Baltic language setting.

Language Groups

You know that you can use locales to adjust keyboard layouts for entering text. However, what if a user needs to read text that is in a different language than the current default language? In this situation, you can install additional language groups in Windows 2000. For example, if the English-language version of Windows 2000 is installed and a user needs to read documents written in French, you can add the French-language group to Windows 2000. In this instance, the application that is being used to read the French text must also support the ability to use Windows 2000 language groups.

To install additional language groups, you need to follow these steps:

1. Log on as an administrator. (Users can't install language settings.)

2. Open the Regional Options applet.

3. Select the General tab.

4. Click the check box for the language settings to be installed.

5. Insert the Windows 2000 Professional CD-ROM to copy the files. After the files have been copied, reboot the computer so that the changes take effect.

After the computer has been rebooted, the additional language settings and locales are available.

The Multilanguage Edition of Windows 2000

A company that has a global presence might need different language versions of its operating systems. Versions of Windows prior to Windows 2000 require that you install a separate version of the operating system for each language that you are using. This procedure goes a step further than input locales and language settings. The separate language edition of Windows 95, 98, or NT displays the user interface of the language edition that was installed. For instance, if the French edition of Windows 98 is installed, the user interface is displayed in French characters and symbols. This, however, adds a tremendous amount of administrative overhead. Other-language operating systems are distinctly different from the English versions, so they require separate service packs (SPs) and hotfixes. In such an environment, an administrator might have to support three or four different versions of Windows 98.

Windows 2000 changes all this. You can install a separate Multilanguage edition of Windows 2000, which allows you to install additional languages to the existing English version of the operating system. After you have completed the basic installation of Windows 2000, you can install additional user interfaces that support other languages. The end result is a single version of Windows 2000 that supports multiple languages. The same SPs, hotfixes, and upgrades that you apply to the standard English version of Windows 2000 also apply to the Multilanguage edition of Windows 2000.

After you have installed a language user interface, a user can easily switch between interfaces via the Regional Options applet. A new tab that can be used to select the desired interface is added to the applet. After the user selects the interface, he or she must log off and log back on in order for the change to take effect. The user interface selection is established on a per-user basis. Several people can use the same computer but have completely different interfaces. Each user's profile contains the settings for which user interface should be used. The user interface provides the local language characters and symbols for the operating system and for the installed applications.

Accessibility Options

Windows 2000 provides several options that make navigating and using the operating system easier. You can enhance the interface and keyboard settings for users who have limited vision, hearing, and manual dexterity.

The Windows 2000 Professional Control Panel contains the Accessibility Options applet which allows users to specify special settings for usage of the keyboard, system sounds, the video display, mouse input via the keyboard, and other general accessibility features. By clicking Start, Programs, Accessories, Accessibility, you can work with several more Accessibility tools: Magnifier, Narrator, On-Screen Keyboard, Utility Manager, and the Accessibility Wizard.

Accessibility Options Applet

The Accessibility Options applet contains several useful tabs—Keyboard, Sound, Display, and Mouse—as described in the following sections.

The Keyboard Tab

The Keyboard tab of the Accessibility Options applet provides several options for controlling repeat rate and key combinations:

➤ *StickyKeys*—This option allows a user to press multiple keystrokes, such as Ctrl+Alt+Delete, by using one key at a time. To enable this feature, you select the StickyKeys option on the Keyboard tab of the Accessibility Options applet. You can also enable it by pressing the Shift key five times; in this case, a dialog box appears, asking if this feature should be turned on. You can click OK to enable the feature and close the dialog box. In addition, a StickyKeys icon appears in the system tray. Double-clicking this icon opens the Accessibility Options applet.

➤ *FilterKeys*—This option lets you control the keyboard repeat rate, ignore repeated keystrokes, and control the rate at which a key repeats the key-stroke if a user holds down a key. You can apply granular settings to configure the repeat delay in number of seconds. If, for example, a user presses the L key and holds it down, the letter L will repeat every x seconds (where x represents the number of seconds for which the repeat key delay is set). When FilterKeys is enabled, an icon with the shape of a stopwatch appears in the system tray. You can also enable FilterKeys via the Keyboard tab of the Accessibility Options applet. When you mark the Use Shortcut checkbox, a user can invoke Filterkeys at any time by holding down the right Shift key for eight seconds.

 If a user has enabled FilterKeys but finds that the keystrokes repeat with no delay, either someone has selected the No Keyboard Repeat settings or the repeat time delay has been configured to its lowest setting.

➤ *ToggleKeys*—When this option is enabled, a high-pitched sound is played when the Num Lock, Caps Lock, or Scroll Lock key is pressed. You can enable this feature via the Keyboard tab of the Accessibility Options applet or by holding down the Num Lock key for five seconds.

The Sound Tab

On the Sound tab of Accessibility Options applet, you can enable the following two sound features to help notify users of warnings and other events:

➤ *SoundSentry*—When this option is enabled, visual warnings display when Windows 2000 generates audible alerts. This feature is helpful for users who have hearing impairments. A user can specify which part of the screen actually flashes when a sound is generated. The options are Flash Active Window, Flash Active Caption Bar, and Flash Desktop. To enable this feature, you select the SoundSentry check box on the Sound tab of the Accessibility Options applet. No shortcut is available for enabling this feature.

➤ *ShowSounds*—If applications use sounds to convey messages and information, this feature displays text captions that represent those sounds. Selecting the ShowSounds check box on the Sound tab of the Accessibility Options applet enables this feature. No shortcut is available for setting ShowSounds.

The Display Tab

The Display tab of Accessibility Options applet allows you to set color schemes. When the High Contrast option is enabled, applications are informed to change the color scheme to a high-contrast scheme to allow for easier reading. For example, you can enable a white-on-black scheme, a black-on-white scheme, or a custom color scheme. Enabling a custom scheme allows users to adjust colors and font sizes for Windows 2000 and all applications. To enable this feature, you select the Use High Contrast check box on the Display tab of the Accessibility Options applet. You can also enable this feature by pressing left Alt+left Shift+Print Screen. When you press these three keys at the same time, a dialog box appears, asking if the feature should be turned on.

The Mouse Tab

The Mouse tab of the Accessibility Options applet allows you to use the keyboard as a mouse by using these two features:

➤ *MouseKeys*—When this feature is enabled, users can use use the numeric keypad to move the mouse pointer and to perform single-click, double-click, and drag-mouse actions. In addition, you can assign settings that control the pointer speed. To enable this feature, you select the MouseKeys check box on the Mouse tab of the Accessibility Options applet. You can also enable this option by pressing left Alt+left Shift+Num Lock; if you do, a dialog box appears, asking if the MouseKeys feature should be enabled. If you click the OK button, an icon appears in the system tray to graphically indicate that the feature has been enabled.

You can turn off StickyKeys, FilterKeys, ToggleKeys, SoundSentry, High Contrast, and MouseKeys after a specified idle period has passed. For example, you could assign a five-minute idle period. These six features would then all be turned off if the computer were idle for five or more minutes. To assign an idle period, you select the General tab in the Accessibility Options applet and then mark the Turn Off Accessibility Features After Idle For checkbox.

➤ *SerialKey*—You can enable this option for users who cannot use a standard keyboard and must install an alternative input device into a serial port. This option is located on the General tab.

The Accessibility Wizard

You can configure most of Windows 2000's accessibility options quite easily through the Accessibility Wizard. This wizard asks a series of questions to determine whether you need to configure keyboard, sound, display, and mouse accessibility features. For example, the wizard displays a sentence in varying font sizes so that the user can select the sentence with the font size that is easiest to read. After the user has answered all the questions, the interface immediately changes to reflect large fonts and any other options that have been configured.

The Accessibility Wizard allows users to save the settings they have selected. These settings are saved in a file with an **.acw** extension. These settings can be used on another computer or can serve as a backup. If many users require the same accessibility configuration, an administrator can save some time by saving the settings and using them on other computers that need the same configuration. However, there is a gotcha here: The default permissions assigned to the **.acw** file are for the user who is logged on and for the administrator. Before you can share the settings, you need to make sure that you have added to the access control list (ACL) any global groups or individual user accounts that need access to this file.

Additional Accessibility Features

Windows 2000 provides three additional accessibility tools that are not available in the Accessibility Options applet (you can locate by selecting Start, Programs, Accessories, Accessibility):

➤ *Narrator*—This tool is for people who have low vision or are blind. When it is enabled, Narrator uses a synthesized voice to read what is displayed (such as menu options, text, dialog boxes, and alerts).

➤ *Magnifier*—This tool splits the screen into two portions: magnified and nonmagnified. The magnified portion of the screen magnifies the size of anything that the mouse pointer is hovering over. The nonmagnified area selects what needs to be magnified. You can increase or decrease the magnification level and the size of the magnification.

➤ *On-Screen Keyboard*—This tool displays a virtual keyboard on the Windows 2000 desktop. Users can use the mouse pointer to press the virtual keys. They can also use a joystick with the On-Screen Keyboard to select keys.

Utility Manager

Utility Manager allows users to access the Narrator, Magnifier, and On-Screen Keyboard tools from one interface. You can also use Utility Manager to check the status of and start or stop the tools. In addition, an administrator can configure these tools to start when Windows 2000 starts.

Fax Features

Windows 2000 provides support for sending and receiving faxes via an internal or external modem. The Fax applet appears in the Control Panel folder after a modem has been installed. You use this applet to configure the Fax service and to access the Fax Service Management console. By default, the Fax service is configured to allow users to send faxes but not receive them.

The Send Fax Wizard

To fax a document via the Send Fax Wizard, you follow these steps:

1. Select the Print command within the Windows application in which the document resides (Word, Excel, WordPerfect, and so on).

2. Select the fax printer and then click the Print option to submit a fax. The Send Fax Wizard opens. (Figure 5.1 shows the Send Fax Wizard.)

3. Enter the recipient's name and fax number, cover page information, and any other configuration information that is needed.

The Fax Applet

The Send Fax Wizard gathers some information, such as the sender's name and fax number, from settings contained in the Fax applet. You can use this applet to troubleshoot and monitor fax transmissions. The following tabs appear in the Fax applet:

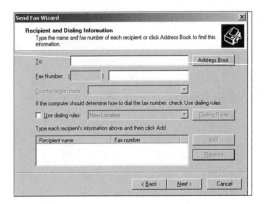

Figure 5.1 The Send Fax Wizard.

➤ *User Information*—This tab contains information such as fax number, email address, name, mailing address, and phone numbers. The Send Fax Wizard and the Fax Cover Page Editor use this information.

➤ *Cover Pages*—This tab contains options to add existing cover pages or to create new ones by using the Fax Cover Page Editor.

➤ *Status Monitor*—This tab contains options to display the send/receive status monitor, stop fax transmissions, display a status icon on the taskbar, and manually answer incoming fax calls.

➤ *Advanced Options*—This tab is visible only if the user logs on as an administrator. This is a key area of fax administration. You can configure the Fax service and add fax printers via this tab. Of particular importance is the Fax Service Management option; when this option is selected, the Fax Service Management console opens.

Managing the Fax Service Management Console

You can do the following with the Fax Service Management console:

➤ Configure the modem(s) to send or receive faxes. If more than one modem is installed, the first modem is used by default to send or receive faxes.

➤ Change or apply fax-related security permissions for users or groups. By default, the Everyone group can submit faxes and view fax jobs. However, only members of the Administrators and Power Users groups can manage fax jobs, services, and devices.

➤ Configure the number of rings before a fax device answers a fax call. The default is two.

➤ Configure the number of retries that are allowed before the fax device aborts sending the fax job.

➤ Choose where to store faxes that have been sent or received. The default location for both options is %SystemDrive%\Documents and Settings\All Users\Documents\My Faxes.

➤ Adjust the priority for sending faxes.

➤ Change the detail of the fax logs.

➤ Print faxes upon reception.

➤ Prevent the use of personal cover pages.

➤ Configure the transmitting station identifier (TSID), which is typically the sender's fax number.

➤ Configure the called station identifier (CSID), which is typically the recipient's fax number.

As mentioned earlier, you can open the Fax Service Management console by selecting the Fax Service Management option. You can also open it by selecting Start, Programs, Accessories, Communications, Fax, Fax Service Management. Any user can open the console by using this method. However, a user is denied access to making any configurations in the console. Only members of the Administrators and Power Users groups can actually configure this service.

 One of the main reasons for having a computer network is to share resources, but unfortunately, the Windows 2000 fax printer cannot be shared.

If faxes aren't being sent or received, you should verify that a user has permission to use the fax printer and make sure that the fax printer is configured to send and receive faxes. If these settings are correct and faxes are still not being sent or received, you should stop and then restart the Fax service.

Task Scheduler

In Windows NT 4 Workstation you use the at command to schedule when batch files, scripts, or backups should run. Windows 2000 provides a graphical user interface (GUI) utility called Task Scheduler to run these same tasks. This utility is almost a carbon copy of the Windows 98 Task Scheduler.

You can open Task Scheduler from the Scheduled Tasks folder (located in the Control Panel folder) or by selecting Start, Programs, Accessories, System Tools, Scheduled Tasks. The Scheduled Tasks folder is shared by default. You can create a task on one computer and then copy it to another one. This is helpful if a similar task needs to run on many computers. If you copy the task from one computer to another, you don't have to re-create it multiple times.

Creating a Task

To create a new task, you open the Scheduled Tasks folder and double-click the Add Scheduled Task icon to launch the Scheduled Task Wizard. This wizard steps you through the process of selecting a program, batch file, or script to run automatically at a scheduled time. You need to perform the following steps to create a task:

1. Select the program to be scheduled and then click Next.

2. Choose how often the task should run and then click Next. The options are as follows:

   ➤ Daily

   ➤ Weekly

   ➤ Monthly

   ➤ One Time Only

   ➤ When My Computer Starts

   ➤ When I Log On

3. Depending on your selection in Step 2, you might have to set up what time of the day, what days of the week, or what months of the year the task should run. Choose the appropriate options and then click Next.

4. Enter a username and password. The username must have the right to run the selected application. Click Next.

5. The last dialog box of the wizard asks whether to open the Advanced properties sheet after the task has been created. This properties sheet allows the user to edit the schedule, delete the task if it is not scheduled to run again, stop the task, start the task during idle periods, and not start the task if the computer is running on batteries. Also, you can

assign Security permissions to the task to control which users can modify the task options. After you have made your selections, click Finish.

After you close the Scheduled Task Wizard and the Advanced properties sheet, an icon that represents the task is created. After you have created a task, you can double-click a task to view and configure its advanced properties.

Troubleshooting Tasks

The Scheduled Task Wizard makes it very easy to create tasks. However, sometimes tasks fail to run. The most common reason for this is that the wrong username or password was entered for the task. If a task fails, you should verify that you entered the correct username and password for the task.

Another area where an incorrect account can cause problems is if a task has been created for old 16-bit applications. Such a task might fail to run if the system account is used on the Task Scheduler service. If an error related to the Task Scheduler service is generated, you should change the account used to run the service. Open the Task service by selecting Start, Programs, Administrative Tools, Services. Then select the Log On tab to change the account. Figure 5.2 shows the Task Scheduler properties sheet. If the task still won't run, you should stop and restart the Task service. You can configure it to restart automatically if it fails. To do so, you go to the Recovery tab of the Task Scheduler properties sheet.

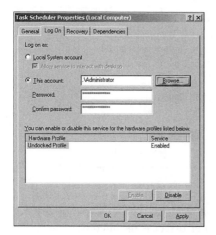

Figure 5.2   The Task Scheduler properties sheet.

Practice Questions

Question 1

> A user has the Fax service configured to send faxes, but when a fax is sent to this user, the computer cannot receive any faxes. What must you do in order to allow the client computer to receive faxes?
>
> ○ a. Install a new fax printer and select Receive Faxes when you install the printer.
>
> ○ b. Reinstall the fax service and select Receive Faxes during the installation.
>
> ○ c. Use the Fax Service Management console to redirect faxes to the **My Faxes** folder.
>
> ○ d. Use the Fax Service Management console to configure the fax modem to receive faxes.

Answer d is correct. You can configure the fax modem to receive faxes after installation. You do not have to reinstall any fax-related services in order to configure the modem to receive faxes. Therefore, Answer b is incorrect. You can configure the fax modem to receive faxes via the Fax Service Management console by selecting Devices, selecting the properties of the device, and choosing Receive.

Question 2

> A user has completed a document that needs to be faxed. The user wants to fax the document by using the Windows 2000 Fax service, but there is no fax printer to print the document to. What do you need to do so that the user can fax the document?
>
> ○ a. Restart the Fax service so the user can print to the fax printer.
>
> ○ b. Install a modem device.
>
> ○ c. Select the Advanced Options tab in the Fax applet to add a fax printer.
>
> ○ d. Use the Add Printer Wizard to add a fax printer.

Answer b is correct: The Fax service won't install unless a modem has been detected. When Windows 2000 detects a modem, the Fax applet is present in the Control Panel folder, and a fax printer driver is installed so a client can send and receive faxes. Answers a, c, and d are not viable options until a fax modem has been installed.

Question 3

A user has limited dexterity. You want to configure his Windows 2000 Professional computer to ignore brief or repeated keystrokes. What must be enabled to configure the computer for this user?

○ a. FilterKeys

○ b. StickyKeys

○ c. ToggleKeys

○ d. MouseKeys

Answer a is correct. You should enable FilterKeys if you want Windows 2000 to ignore repeated keystrokes. StickyKeys allows keystrokes such as Ctrl+Alt+Delete to be selected individually; therefore, Answer b is incorrect. ToggleKeys plays a high-pitched sound when the Num Lock, Caps Lock, or Scroll Lock key is pressed; therefore, Answer c is incorrect. The MouseKeys option is used to control the mouse pointer with the numeric keypad. The other options do not allow for this functionality; therefore, Answer d is incorrect.

Question 4

You are the administrator of a small network of 50 Windows 2000 Professional clients and 4 Windows 2000 servers. You want to use one of the Windows 2000 Professional clients as a fax server. How do you configure that client to function as a fax server?

○ a. Enable sharing of the fax printer driver.

○ b. Use the Fax Service Management console to select the properties of the modem and enable sharing.

○ c. The Windows 2000 fax print driver cannot be shared.

○ d. Open the Fax applet in the Control Panel and enable sharing from the Advanced tab.

Answer c is correct. The current release of Windows 2000 Professional does not support the sharing of the fax printer; therefore, Answer c is correct. Because Windows 2000 doesn't support fax sharing natively, Answers a, b, and d are incorrect. Third-party fax software is required to configure Windows 2000 as a fax server.

Question 5

> You require users to log on to your Windows 2000 domain to gain access to their computers and network resources. Several users in your organization have limited dexterity. You need to configure computers for these users to allow the Ctrl+Alt+Delete sequence to be pressed one key at a time. What must be enabled to allow for this functionality?
>
> ○ a. FilterKeys
> ○ b. StickyKeys
> ○ c. ToggleKeys
> ○ d. MouseKeys

Answer b is correct. You should enable StickyKeys to allow multiple keystroke combinations, such as Ctrl+Alt+Delete, to be pressed one key at a time. You should enable FilterKeys if you want Windows 2000 to ignore repeated keystrokes; therefore, Answer a is incorrect. ToggleKeys plays a high-pitched sound when the Num Lock, Caps Lock, or Scroll Lock key is pressed; therefore, Answer c is incorrect. The MouseKeys option is used to control the mouse pointer with the numeric keypad. The other options do not allow for this functionality; therefore, Answer d is incorrect.

Question 6

> You need to enable Windows 2000 Professional to read text from all dialog boxes and applications to visually impaired users. What must you configure to allow for this functionality?
>
> ○ a. SoundSentry
> ○ b. ShowSounds
> ○ c. Narrator
> ○ d. Windows Media Player Captions

Answer c is correct. The Narrator accessibility option is used to read aloud onscreen text, dialog boxes, menus, and buttons that are selected in Windows 2000 Professional. SoundSentry generates visual warnings when the computer generates sound alerts, and ShowSounds tells applications to display captions for sounds the application may make; therefore, Answers a and b are incorrect. Windows Media Player cannot speak aloud written text, but it can display text in closed captioning; therefore, Answer d is incorrect.

Question 7

> You have been asked to help plan the deployment of Windows 2000 Professional for a company that has offices in New York, France, and Germany. The offices in Europe frequently send documents in their native languages to the office in New York. The office in New York sends documents in English to the offices in Europe. Users in all offices need to quickly switch between their native language and the language in which they need to correspond. Also, it is required that ongoing administration of this environment be kept to a minimum. How can you deploy Windows 2000 to facilitate this?
>
> ○ a. Deploy the Multilanguage edition of Windows 2000 Professional to the offices in New York, France, and Germany.
>
> ○ b. Include the input locales for each language, and deploy them by using a Remote Installation Service (RIS) image.
>
> ○ c. Deploy the English-language edition and manually add input locales for each language needed.
>
> ○ d. Add the keyboard layout/Input Method Editor (IME) for each language.

Answer a is correct. To allow users to regularly work in multiple languages and to reduce the administration of a computer with different language requirements, you should deploy the Multilanguage edition of Windows 2000 Professional because it uses the same SPs and hotfixes as the English-language edition of Windows 2000. Installing a separate edition of Windows 2000 Professional for each language that is used would add to the ongoing administration of the environment because separate SPs and hotfixes would be required for these systems. Answers b, c, and d would add to the administrative overhead to maintain the required environment and would not achieve all the goals. Answers b, c, and d don't allow a user to change user interfaces on-the-fly. Only the Multilanguage edition of Windows 2000 provides that functionality.

Question 8

You have used Task Scheduler to configure a 16-bit application to run every night at 11 p.m. However, when you log on the next day, you see an error stating that the application could not run due to a service error. How do you resolve this problem?

- ○ a. Enter the correct password for the domain account on the scheduled task.
- ○ b. Configure the Task Scheduler service to log on with a domain username and password.
- ○ c. Verify that the task is set to run daily.
- ○ d. Verify that the local administrator username and password were used to run the task.

Answer b is correct. By default, the Task Scheduler service runs under the security context of the local system account. Some older applications might try to start the service with a different account; thus, a service-related error is displayed. You need to enter a domain username and password for the service to resolve this problem. The error that is displayed is not related to the user account that was entered for the task to run. Two accounts are used: one for the task and the other for the service. The problem here is the account for the Task Scheduler service; therefore, Answers a and d are incorrect because they are concerned with the account being used to run the task. The problem is with the account used to run the service and not with the task. Answer c has nothing to do with the problem because if the service won't run, then the task won't run either. Verifying whether the task is set to run daily doesn't affect the underlying problem with the service account.

Question 9

You have configured Task Scheduler to run a disk defragmentation tool at 11 p.m. each night. You want five other Windows 2000 Professional computers to use the same task. How can you configure the five computers to use the same task without re-creating the task?

- ○ a. Configure a group policy for the five computers to run a logon script that executes the task.
- ○ b. Go to each computer and copy the task that was created from its shared **Scheduled Tasks** folder to each client's **Scheduled Tasks** folder.
- ○ c. Import the scheduled task by using the **at** command.
- ○ d. Import the scheduled task by using the Task Scheduler service properties sheet.

Answer b is correct. Tasks are placed in the Scheduled Tasks folder, which is shared to everyone by default. Users can access any Scheduled Tasks folder on the network and either move or copy a task that has already been created to their Scheduled Tasks folders. You cannot use a group policy to copy tasks that were created on one computer to another computer; therefore, Answer a is incorrect. The at command is a command-line scheduler that does not allow for the importation of tasks that were created by using the Scheduled Task Wizard; therefore, Answer c is incorrect. The Task Scheduler properties sheet does not provide any options for importing a task; therefore, Answer d is incorrect.

Question 10

> You need to configure a Windows 2000 Professional computer to use Danish configurations (such as Danish usage of numbers and Danish currency) for an employee who is visiting the head office of your company in the United States. You want to allow the user to quickly switch from one locale to another by using a keystroke sequence or the system tray. Currently, the computer is using only the Western European and United States settings. How do you configure the computer to also use Danish settings?
>
> O a. Open the Regional Options applet and select the General tab. Add the Danish locale.
>
> O b. Open the Regional Options applet and select the General tab. Add the Danish language group for the system.
>
> O c. Open the Regional Options applet and select the Input Locales tab. Add Danish as a new locale and assign a hotkey to that locale.
>
> O d. Open the Regional Options applet and manually enter the Danish configurations on the Numbers, Currency, Time, and Date tabs.

Answer c is correct. The Input Locales tab allows you to assign which input languages are loaded into memory every time the computer is started. It also allows you to assign hotkeys that let you switch between input locales, and it places a small icon in the system tray to also allow a user to switch between input locales on-the-fly. Answer a would change the user locale to Danish and would then be used as the default locale. The goal is to allow users using an English keyboard to switch on-the-fly to Danish when needed, which is not achieved by making Danish the default locale; therefore, Answer a is incorrect. Adding the Danish group simply makes the keyboard layout available as an input locale, which it is as the default. This option doesn't add the Danish keyboard layout to the system tray—only input locales provide that functionality; therefore, Answer b is incorrect. Answer d simply hard-codes these options as default configurations. It does not allow a user to select the Danish keyboard layout from the system tray or via a keystroke; therefore, Answer d is incorrect.

Need to Know More?

 Microsoft Corporation. *Microsoft Windows 2000 Professional Resource Kit*. Redmond, Washington: Microsoft Press, 2000. The book provides invaluable information on Windows 2000 Professional.

 Stinson, Craig, and Carl Siechert. *Running Microsoft Windows 2000 Professional*. Redmond, Washington: Microsoft Press, 2000. This book is a good source for information on administering and configuring Windows 2000 Professional.

 To find more information, search the TechNet CD-ROM (or its online version, through www.microsoft.com) and/or the *Windows 2000 Professional Resource Kit* CD-ROM, using the keywords fax, accessibility, and regional options.

Installing Windows 2000 Professional

. . . .

Terms you'll need to understand:

✓ **winnt.exe**

✓ **winnt32.exe**

✓ **unattend.txt**

✓ **sysprep** folder

✓ Remote Installation Service (RIS)

✓ **winnt32.exe /checkupgradeonly**

✓ Migration dynamic link library (DLL)

✓ Slipstreaming

Techniques you'll need to master:

✓ Understanding the different options available for installing Windows 2000 Professional

✓ Installing Windows 2000 Professional

✓ Performing upgrades

✓ Applying service packs (SPs)

✓ Understanding RIS configurations

Microsoft has made available several ways to install Windows 2000 Professional. This chapter looks at the key areas involved in deploying a manual installation or an automated installation of Windows 2000 Professional. In addition, this chapter explains how to use all the utilities that are required for installing, upgrading, and verifying compatibility with Windows 2000.

Performing Attended Installations of Windows 2000 Professional

An attended installation of Windows 2000 Professional requires that someone sit in front of the target computer and answer all the installation prompts, such as the end user license agreement (EULA) prompt. Before you start the installation process, you need to ensure that the computer meets the minimum hardware requirements for Windows 2000 Professional. Unlike Windows NT, Windows 2000 supports only Intel-based computers. The following are the minimum hardware requirements for installing Windows 2000 Professional:

➤ 133MHz Pentium or higher central processing unit (CPU)

➤ 32MB of memory (Microsoft recommends 64MB)

➤ A 2GB hard drive with a minimum of 650MB of free space

➤ VGA, or higher-resolution, monitor

➤ Keyboard

➤ Mouse

➤ 10X CD-ROM for CD-ROM installations

After you've verified that the computer meets these minimum hardware requirements, you should check to see if devices such as the video adapter and the network adapter are compatible. To do this, you check Microsoft's Hardware Compatibility List (HCL), which every Windows 2000 CD-ROM contains. However, that file is out of date. To view the most current HCL, you can visit `www.microsoft.com/hcl`.

You can perform an attended install of Windows 2000 in three ways: by using a CD-ROM, by using the setup disks, or by using the network.

CD-ROM Installation

One of the easiest methods for installing Windows 2000 Professional is to put the Windows 2000 Professional CD-ROM in the computer and boot the computer. The computer boots from the CD-ROM, starts the first phase of the installation, and copies the installation files to the local hard drive. Then the computer reboots (remember to remove the CD-ROM) and starts the graphical user interface (GUI) phase of the installation. You can install Windows 2000 Professional in this fashion if your computer's basic input/output system (BIOS) supports the option to boot from a CD-ROM drive and the CD-ROM is El-Torito compatible.

Setup Disks Installation

If you can't configure a computer to boot from a CD-ROM, you can install Windows 2000 Professional by using the four floppy setup disks that come with the Windows 2000 Professional CD-ROM. To do so, you simply place Setup Disk 1 in the computer to start the installation.

 If the four setup disks are lost or become corrupted, you can create them by using the Windows 2000 Professional CD-ROM. To do so, you open the **Bootdisk** folder on the CD-ROM and execute either **makeboot.exe** or **makebt32.exe**. A command prompt window opens, asking you to insert a floppy disk into drive **A:**. You should continue the process until you have created all four disks. You should use **makeboot.exe** if you are running in a DOS environment or in Windows for Workgroup. You should use **makebt32.exe** if you are running in Windows 95, 98, NT, or 2000. This method of creating a boot disk replaces the Windows NT 4 method of executing the **winnt32.exe** **/ox** switch, which does not create Windows 2000 setup disks.

Network Installation

You can place the contents of the Windows 2000 Professional CD-ROM in a folder on a network server and then share the folder. This network server is referred to as a *distribution server*. You need to establish a network connection to the distribution server in order to start the installation. If Windows 9x or NT is on the target computer, you should connect to the share point and execute winnt32.exe to start the installation process. If no operating system is on the target computer, you should use a network boot disk to connect to the source files. You use winnt.exe to start the installation in a 16-bit/DOS environment, and you use winnt32.exe in a 32-bit environment.

Automating the Installation of Windows 2000 Professional

When you use any of the three attended installation options, someone must be in front of the computer to answer all the installation prompts. This is a very inefficient means of installing Windows 2000 Professional when you need to install the operating system on many computers. The following sections discuss how to use Setup Manager, the System Preparation tool, and RIS to automate the installation process.

Using Setup Manager to Create an Unattended Installation

The Setup Manager utility answers the installation prompts and saves the answer results in an answer file called unattend.txt. Windows 2000 can then use unattend.txt during the installation to configure the screen resolution and other typical hardware and operating system settings. This tool is much improved in Windows 2000 and adds more options and greater flexibility than its predecessor. Setup Manager can now do the following:

➤ Agree to the EULA

➤ Create a distribution share point

➤ Create a listing of unique computer names for a uniqueness database file (UDF)

➤ Add third-party Plug and Play drivers and other resources

➤ Add printers, scripts, batch files, and other commands to the distribution share

You must extract Setup Manager from a .cab file on the Windows 2000 Professional CD-ROM. Setup Manager enables you to create an unattended installation answer file that is named unattend.txt by default. You can also create an answer file manually, without using Setup Manager, but Setup Manager makes the process easier. To extract Setup Manager, you perform the following steps:

1. Insert the Windows 2000 Professional CD-ROM into the computer and select the deploy.cab file, which is located in the Support\Tools folder.

2. Double-click the deploy.cab file to view the contents.

3. Right-click `setupmgr.exe` and select Extract. From the Explorer menu choose a location to which to extract the file. Right-click `setupmgx.dll` and extract this file to the same location as `setupmgr.exe`.

You can now create the answer file. To do so, you double-click the `setupmgr.exe` icon to launch the wizard. The `setupmgr.exe` utility is a multipurpose tool because you can use it to create answer files for several types of unattended installations. This chapter concentrates on a Windows 2000 unattended installation. You need to perform the following steps to create an answer file:

1. Double-click the `setupmgr.exe` icon to start the utility.

2. Click Next to pass the welcome page.

3. Select the Create a New Answer File radio button (which is selected by default) and click Next.

4. The next page displays which product the answer file installs. There are three choices: Windows 2000 Unattended Installation, Sysprep Install, and RIS. Select the Windows 2000 Unattended Installation radio button and click Next.

5. Choose the Windows 2000 Professional radio button and click Next.

6. The next page displays several options regarding user interaction. Typically, no user interaction is required. If, however, you want the installation to stop so you can enter the computer name, select Hide Pages. This option hides all pages in which answers were provided but stops at any areas that you have left blank. Select the Fully Automated radio button and click Next.

7. Select the check box to agree to the EULA and click Next.

8. Enter a name and an organization and then click Next.

9. Enter the computer names or import a comma-delimited file that contains all computer names that should be used for the installation of new computers. Optionally, you can select the Automatically Generate Computer Names Based on Organization Name check box. Checking this results in a combination of the organization name that you entered in the dialog box and a unique alphanumeric combination (for example, `que-1AD2RT`). Use either method and then click the Next button.

10. Enter a password that the local administrator of the computer will use and then click Next.

The password can be up to 127 characters long.

11. Select display settings such as color, screen area, and refresh frequency. Unless all computers have identical video cards with identical monitors, you should set these fields to Use Windows Default. Click Next to continue.

12. This page provides two options for network settings—Typical and Custom. If you select Typical, Microsoft Client, File and Print Sharing, and Transmission Control Protocol/Internet Protocol (TCP/IP) are installed. In addition, the client is configured as a Dynamic Host Configuration Protocol (DHCP) client. If you need to enter a static IP address or add or subtract network services, use the Custom option; select Typical or Custom and click Next.

13. The Workgroup or a Domain page appears next. If the computer is to join a domain during the installation, you must enter the name of the domain as well as a username and password of a user who has the right to add workstations to a domain. Fill in the appropriate fields and click Next.

14. The Time Zone page appears next. Choose the time zone in which the computer is located and click Next.

15. You've reached the end of creating a basic answer file. If you need to add other drivers or scripts, select the Yes, Edit the Additional Settings radio button. For the purposes of our discussion, select No, Do Not Edit the Additional Settings and click Next.

16. Use the next page to create a distribution share for the Windows 2000 Professional files or to create an answer file that you will use in conjunction with the CD-ROM distribution. For demonstration purposes, select Yes, Create or Modify a Distribution Folder and then click Next to continue.

If you choose to create a distribution share, you must name the answer file **winnt.sif**, and you must place it on a floppy disk. A CD-ROM–based installation looks for the presence of this file on a floppy disk and uses it to provide an unattended installation via the CD-ROM distribution.

17. The next page offers suggested locations and folder names for the distribution share point. If you have already created the distribution share, select Modify an Existing Distribution Folder. If you select this option, just the answer file is created. Accept the default by clicking the Next button.

18. If you need drivers for a hardware Redundant Array of Independent Disks (RAID) controller card, add them here. Click Next to continue.

19. If you need a third-party Hardware Abstraction Layer (HAL) for multiple-processor support or other configurations, add that now and click Next.

20. If you need to run a batch file after the installation is done, add those files in the Additional Commands page and click Next.

21. The OEM Branding page appears next. It allows you to replace the default bitmaps that are displayed during the installation process with custom bitmaps and logos. Click Next to continue.

22. The Additional Files or Folders page appears. Use this page to specify where to place files on the computer and install any third-party Plug and Play drivers that don't come with Windows 2000. Click Next.

23. You're almost finished. Enter a name for the answer file and the location of the distribution share. The default name for the answer file is `unattend.txt`. In a working environment, you should change this name because `setupmgr.exe` takes a basic answer file from the Windows 2000 CD-ROM that overwrites the one you create. Click Next.

24. Copy the distribution files from the Windows 2000 Professional CD-ROM to the distribution share. Put the CD-ROM in the computer and click Next. The files are copied to the distribution share.

25. The last page displayed is a summary page of the files that you created. Click Finish.

Now that you have created the answer file and the distribution share, let's put it all together to see how to launch an unattended installation of Windows 2000 Professional. To master this task, you must understand a few switches that are involved. `winnt.exe` has multiple switches to control its functionality. The following is a list of switches that relate to unattended installations:

➤ `/u:answer file`—This switch is used for an unattended installation. `file` contains answers to the installation prompts.

➤ `/s:sourcepath`—This switch points to the location of the Windows 2000 installation files.

➤ /udf:id—This switch is used in conjunction with a UDF file, which overrides the values of the answer file. You typically use this file to provide unique configuration parameters during the installation process. id designates which settings contained in the UDF file should be used.

➤ /unattend—This switch is used with winnt32.exe to create an unattended upgrade to Windows 2000.

You use these switches in combination with one another to launch an unattended installation of Windows 2000 Professional via Setup Manager. To launch an unattended installation, you need to follow these steps:

1. Use a network boot disk to connect the target computer to the network.

2. Use the net use command to map to the distribution share point, using an available drive letter.

3. Switch the command prompt to the mapped drive letter (such as I:) and launch the installation by using winnt.exe. The following example launches an unattended installation for a computer called machine1:

```
I:\WINNT.EXE /s:I:\i386 /u:unattend.txt /udf:machine1,unattend.udf
```

You should practice using Setup Manager several times, choosing different options each time, to see how the results vary. You should also remember that you can use Setup Manager to create answer files for System Preparation tool installations, which are described in the following section, and RIS installations, which are discussed a bit later in this chapter, in the section "Using RIS."

Using the System Preparation Tool

The *System Preparation tool* prepares a master image of a computer that contains Windows 2000 Professional and any software applications that users might need. You can use this tool in conjunction with third-party disk imaging software. *Disk imaging software* makes an exact mirror image of whatever is on the computer, including all the unique parameters of Windows 2000. Each Windows 2000 computer has its own unique security identifier (SID) and its own unique computer name. Other computers can't use these settings. If you applied to several computers an image that contained these unique settings, the computers would all have the same computer name and the same SID. The System Preparation tool removes all the unique parameters from a Windows 2000 computer before the computer is imaged. The tool is very easy to use, but you must follow several specific steps to use it.

The first step is to create a folder called `sysprep` in `%SystemRoot%` (for example, `c:\sysprep`).

To use the System Preparation tool, you must extract it from the `deploy.cab` file and place it in the `sysprep` folder. You need to perform the following steps to extract `sysprep.exe` and a helper file called `setupcl.exe`:

1. Insert the Windows 2000 Professional CD-ROM into the computer and select the `deploy.cab` file, which is located in the `Support\Tools` folder.

2. Double-click the `deploy.cab` file to view the contents.

3. Right-click `sysprep.exe` and select Extract. Use the Explorer menu to extract the file to the `sysprep` folder that you created. Right-click `setupcl.exe` and extract it to the `sysprep` folder.

The next step is to install and configure all applications that must be in the disk image. When you have accomplished that, you can run `sysprep.exe` in the `sysprep` folder. `sysprep.exe` removes all unique parameters from the computer and then shuts down the computer. You need to reboot the computer with a disk image boot disk and create an image of the computer.

After you have applied an image to a computer, the Mini-Setup Wizard runs. It prompts you to put back the unique parameters that you took out. The SID is generated automatically at this point. However, you have to set the following:

➤ Computer Name

➤ User Name

➤ Product ID

➤ Regional Settings

➤ Company Name

➤ Network Settings

➤ Time Zone

➤ Place Computer in a Workgroup or Join a Domain

As you can see, you need to enter a fair amount of information for every computer to which you apply the image. You can use Setup Manager to create an answer file that must be named `sysprep.inf` (a renamed version of the `unattend.txt` answer file) and is used for automating disk imaging installations. This file provides these settings to the Mini-Setup Wizard to answer all the installation prompts. The end result is an unattended install of the image.

> You must place **sysprep.inf** in the **sysprep** folder or on a floppy disk, which are the default locations where the Mini-Setup Wizard looks for the answer file (it checks the **sysprep** folder first) after you have applied the image.
>
> Also, you should apply the image to computers with similar hardware. When you apply the image, **sysprep.exe** triggers Plug and Play into action. Plug and Play can resolve some differences in hardware. However, if the hard disk controller and the HAL on the image are different than those on the computer to which you are applying the image, the image installation fails. For example, if you create the image on a computer that contains an HAL for a computer with multiple processors but you are applying the image to a single-processor computer, the installation fails.

Using RIS

You can use RIS to deploy Windows 2000 Professional over a network from a remote installation server. RIS integrates a few of the installation methods discussed so far in this chapter into one tight bundle. You can use it to install Windows 2000 Professional to a computer with a blank hard drive or to reinstall Windows 2000 Professional to repair a corrupted installation.

The main goal of RIS is to reduce total cost of ownership (TCO) by having one central location for either the end users or administrators to install Windows 2000 Professional. To install Windows 2000 Professional using RIS, a user presses the F12 key during the boot process to find RIS and start the installation. Four steps are involved in making RIS work: configuring the clients, configuring network servers, installing and configuring an RIS server, and creating Windows 2000 Professional images. The next few sections uncover the details of these areas.

Configuring Clients

You can have a client computer connect to an RIS server in two ways. The first method is to install a peripheral connection interface (PCI) network adapter that contains an onboard preboot execution (PXE) ROM chip. You then have to configure the computer's BIOS to boot from the PXE network adapter. When the computer boots from the PXE network adapter, it attempts to get an IP address from a DHCP server. When the network adapter has an IP address, the user is prompted to press the F12 key to locate an RIS server.

In the second method for connecting a client computer to an RIS server, if the network adapter is not PXE compliant, you can use an RIS boot disk with some network adapter manufacturers such as 3Com and Intel. You can use the rbfg.exe utility to create an RIS boot disk. After you have installed RIS, you can find the utility at RemoteInstall\Admin\i386\rbfg.exe.

Configuring Network Servers

Before you can install and configure RIS, several prerequisites must be in place on the network. The following is a list of the requirements the network must meet before you install RIS:

➤ *DHCP server*—The client needs to obtain an IP address from a DHCP server during the boot process. You cannot configure RIS until a DHCP server is available. A Windows 2000 DHCP server cannot give IP addresses to clients unless it is authorized to do so. You need to perform the following steps to authorize the DHCP server:

   1. Open the DHCP Manager Microsoft Management Console (MMC) by selecting Start, Programs, Administrative Tools, DHCP.

   2. Select the DHCP node and choose Action, Manage Authorized Servers from the menu.

   3. Click the Authorize button and enter the hostname or IP address of the DHCP server. Click OK to close the dialog box.

➤ *Active Directory and Domain Name System (DNS)*—When the network adapter has an IP address, it needs to find an RIS server. The client finds an RIS server by querying a DNS server to find where an Active Directory server (domain controller[DC]) is located. Active Directory then tells the client where an RIS server can be found.

➤ *A separate disk partition for RIS images*—RIS demands its own partition. You cannot install RIS on a system or a boot partition, which usually the means that you cannot use the c: drive partition. RIS stores its system images using single instance storage (SIS). SIS technology stores only one copy of each file; duplicate copies are not stored on disk but are referenced using pointers to the single copy that is already stored on the hard drive, to save disk space. This is why RIS needs its own partition.

When you have met these three conditions for an RIS installation, you need to make sure a separate partition is available (or will be created) for RIS. It is recommended that you reserve at least 2GB for an RIS partition.

Installing and Configuring an RIS Server

You can install RIS on a Windows 2000 DC or on a Windows 2000 member server if you have met all the prerequisites. After you have installed the service, you must configure it. You need to perform the following steps to install RIS:

1. Log on to the server as an administrator.

2. Open the Control Panel (by selecting Start, Settings, Control Panel) and double-click Add/Remove Programs.

3. Click the Add/Remove Windows Components button and select the Remote Installation Services check box.

4. Insert the Windows 2000 Server CD-ROM. The service is copied to the server, and you are prompted to reboot the server after the service has been installed.

After you have installed RIS, you must run `risetup.exe` to respond to clients' requests for an RIS server and to put the initial image of Windows 2000 Professional on the RIS server. The initial image is simply a copy of the `I386` folder found on the Windows 2000 Professional CD-ROM.

You need to perform the following steps to configure RIS:

1. Select Start, Run. Type `risetup.exe` and then click the OK button.

2. The Remote Installation Services Setup Wizard presents a welcome page that reminds you of some of the prerequisites for RIS. Click the Next button.

3. By default, the wizard offers to create the RIS folder structure and files on the `c:` partition (even though the wizard itself reminds you that this can't be done). Choose a drive letter for a nonsystem partition into which the files can be placed and click the Next button.

4. The next dialog box asks if the RIS server should respond immediately to client requests before you have even finished the configuration. Leave the check box unselected. You can select it when you further configure the RIS server's properties, using the Active Directory Users and Computers console.

5. The next dialog box asks where the system should look for the Windows 2000 Professional installation files. Type the drive letter for the CD-ROM drive and the path to the installation files (for example, `D:\I386`). Click Next.

6. The next dialog box suggests a folder name for the initial image. Each image that is created has its own folder. Use the default name provided or enter a different name and then click Next.

7. The next dialog box asks you to provide a descriptive name for the image. Use the default or enter a different name. Click the Next button to get to the finish line.

8. You're at the end. The final dialog box summarizes the parameters that you selected. Click the Finish button. `risetup.exe` copies the contents of the `I386` folder to the folder structure that you just created and completes the installation process.

When the installation is finished, you need to configure the RIS server to respond to RIS clients. You have to log on as a domain administrator to complete this step. You need to launch the Active Directory Users and Computers console by selecting Start, Programs, Administrative Tools, Active Directory Users and Computers. Next, you need to double-click the Domain Controllers container if RIS was installed on a DC; otherwise, you need to double-click the Computers container to locate the RIS computer. Next, you right-click the RIS Server Computer object and select Properties. You then select the Remote Install tab from the Properties page. On this tab, you select the Respond to Client Computers Requesting Service option, as shown in Figure 6.1.

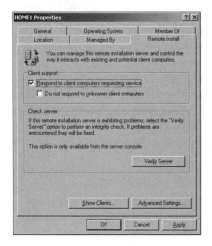

Figure 6.1   The Remote Install tab of an RIS server's properties sheet.

Creating Windows 2000 Professional Images

The Remote Installation Services Setup Wizard creates the first image of Windows 2000 Professional for you. However, that image provides only an attended installation of the operating system. You can create additional images that contain the operating system as well as any necessary applications and configuration. RIS installs a utility called `riprep.exe` that you can use to create images of the operating system and any installed applications. The functionality of `riprep.exe` is similar to that of a third-party disk imaging application. However, `riprep.exe` has some limitations. It can only make an image of the c: partition of a computer. If a computer contains a c: partition and a d: partition, only the c: partition is part of the image. Also, when you apply the image to a computer via RIS, any existing partitions are deleted. The entire hard drive is repartitioned as a single partition and is then formatted with NT File System (NTFS). If you can work within those limits, you can easily configure and deploy riprep.exe images.

You need to perform the following steps to create a riprep.exe image:

1. Connect the computer that you are imaging to the network.

2. Install Windows 2000 Professional and any applications that users may need. Connect to the REMINST share point on the RIS server. Run riprep.exe from \RIS Server\REMINST\Admin\I386\riprep.exe.

3. The Remote Installation Preparation Wizard is launched. when it asks you on which RIS server the image should be placed and the name of the folder to which the image should be copied, provide the appropriate information.

4. Provide a user-friendly name for the image (such as Marketing or Sales).

After you complete these steps, riprep.exe copies the image to the designated RIS server. However, riprep.exe acts a lot like sysprep.exe. In addition to creating an image, riprep.exe removes the unique attributes, such as the SIDs and the computer name. When the RIS client downloads the image, the Mini-Setup Wizard asks you to put back what was taken out.

You can use Setup Manager to create answer files for RIS images.

Downloading an RIS Image to a Client

After you have configured an RIS server with several images, users can boot their computers from the network adapter and press F12 to find an RIS server. The server then displays a welcome screen; a user simply presses Enter to bypass this screen. Next, the user must log on to the domain. When he or she is logged on, the user sees a list of images to choose from. The user selects an image from the list, and RIS reformats the entire drive and downloads the image to the target computer. After about 30 to 40 minutes, the user has a clean installation of the operating system and applications.

Upgrading to Windows 2000 Professional

Windows NT 4 supports only upgrades from previous Windows NT operating systems. Windows 2000, on the other hand, allows for many upgrade paths. The following is a list of Windows operating systems that you can directly upgrade to Windows 2000 Professional:

➤ Windows NT 4 and 3.51

➤ Windows 95 (all editions)

➤ Windows 98 (all editions)

 You can directly upgrade Windows NT 4 or 3.51 with or without SPs. Installing a specific SP before installation of Windows 2000 is not required when you are upgrading. SPs are discussed in the section "Deploying SPs," later in the chapter.

The easiest operating system to upgrade from is Windows NT because it shares a lot of features with Windows 2000, including its registry. You can upgrade Windows 95 and 98 quite smoothly as well, but you need to take some precautions, which are detailed in the next section.

Pre-Upgrade Checklist

Before you upgrade to Windows 2000 Professional, you need to check the current operating system configuration for any of the following areas that could cause conflicts during and after the upgrade process:

➤ *Hardware and software compatibility*—The Windows 2000 Professional CD-ROM contains a utility called chkupgrd.exe, which scans the current operating system and hardware to see if there are any known items that are incompatible with Windows 2000 Professional. You can run the utility using various methods. One of the most common methods is to place the Windows 2000 CD-ROM in the computer and click the Upgrade option. The utility runs before the upgrade to alert you about any incompatibilities. However, if you are not prepared to perform an upgrade on the computer, you can run the utility by placing the Windows 2000 Professional CD-ROM in the computer, selecting Start, Run, and then typing *drive_letter*:\I386\winnt32.exe /checkupgradeonly (where *drive_letter*: is the drive letter your CD-ROM drive uses). The utility scans the system and creates a text file of the results, which you can save to the computer or print. chkupgrd.exe is also referred to as the Readiness Analyzer.

➤ *Update packs*—Due to the major differences between the Windows 2000 registry and the registries of Windows 95 and 98, some applications may not work after the upgrade. Software vendors may supply an update pack (also called a *migration DLL*) that you can use during the upgrade process. You obtain an upgrade pack and place it on the local hard drive. During the upgrade process, the installer asks if any upgrade packs should be used. You need to select Yes and then enter the file path to the upgrade pack to continue the installation process.

➤ *Disk utilities*—Windows 2000 Professional uses a new version of NTFS that causes conflicts with antivirus software and disk defragmenting software. You should remove such applications before you upgrade. After the upgrade, you should install only updated versions of applications that are known to be compatible with Windows 2000.

➤ *Drive compression*—Before you upgrade, you should uncompress any drives that you have compressed by using DriveSpace or DoubleSpace. These Windows 95 and 98 drive compression utilities are incompatible with Windows 2000.

Deploying SPs

Installing SPs in Windows NT is a very time-consuming process. First, you have to install the operating system, and then you must apply the SP. Windows 2000 allows you to incorporate an SP with the installation files. Combining the latest SP with the Windows 2000 installation files allows you to install them as one. In Windows NT, however, if you install a new service after applying an SP, you have to reapply the SP for the new service in order to gain any benefits the SP might have to offer. In addition, you have to reinstall some services after you apply an SP. Thankfully, you don't have to contend with these situations in Windows 2000.

Slipstreaming SPs

The process of combining the Windows 2000 installation files with an SP is called *slipstreaming*. You apply an SP to a distribution share of the installation files by executing update.exe /s:[path] (or update.exe -s:[path]), where *path* must be replaced with the location of the Windows 2000 installation files that you want updated (that is, the distribution share). You should not include the 1386 folder name as part of the path; the SP assumes this, and it looks for the 1386 folder by default. In fact, you must place a folder named 1386 that contains the installation files within the UNC or drive letter path to prevent the slipstream process from failing.

If you install Windows 2000 by using the slipstreamed distribution, the installations contain the SP. Using this method can save you a ton of time and helps you avoid having to apply an SP after each installation.

Applying SPs After Installing Windows 2000

If you didn't have the opportunity or ability to create a slipstreamed distribution share, you can apply an SP simply by running update.exe on the local machine. If you install any new services after applying the SP, Windows 2000 gets any files it needs for those services from the installation files or the SP. This process updates a service or an application without requiring you to continually reapply the SP whenever you add something new.

Troubleshooting Failed Installations

Windows 2000 Professional should install on most new computers without too much difficulty. However, there are some common reasons it may not install properly. The following is a list of typical installation problems:

➤ *Media errors*—These are problems you encounter with the distribution CD-ROM. You should make sure the problem exists with the media itself, not with access to the media. If you place the Windows 2000 Professional CD-ROM in a shared drive for installation, too many people could be using the drive at one time. This could generate some errors. However, if only one person is connected to the shared drive and errors persist, you should get a replacement for the distribution CD-ROM. In addition, you should always restart failed installations that are due to media errors.

➤ *Incompatible CD-ROM drive*—There are many specifications for CD-ROM drives. You can install Windows 2000 from most drives, but there are some exceptions. If the CD-ROM drive is not compliant, you need to replace it or place the distribution files on the network. Also, as mentioned earlier in this chapter, the Windows 2000 CD-ROM is bootable and can be installed from El-Torito–compatible drives. If the CD-ROM can't boot, you need to ensure that the drive is compliant and that the boot order in the BIOS has been set to the CD-ROM drive. Also, the controller card for the CD-ROM drive could be failing, or the drive itself could be failing.

➤ *Installation halts or errors*—If a stop error occurs during the installation, it is typically the result of incorrect or incompatible drivers. You need to obtain the correct and current drivers and restart the installation process. Also, the installation may stop just after the copy or text phase due to a warning that the master boot record has a virus. This warning typically results when the BIOS has enabled the virus warning option. You should turn off this option and restart the installation. As a final measure, you need to ensure that all devices are on the HCL.

➤ *Lack of drive space*—Windows 2000 needs much more free space than its predecessors. You should ensure that at least 650MB of free space is available.

➤ *Dependency failures*—For the installation to be completed successfully, all services must be able to start when needed. Some services depend on others in order to complete tasks. For example, if the drivers for the network adapter cannot load, that affects all services that depend on the network adapter's successful installation. As a result, the computer can't be join the domain.

➤ *Problems joining the domain*—If the network adapter has initialized but the computer still can't join the domain, you should verify that the DNS server is online and that you are using the correct IP address of the DNS. You also need to verify that you typed the domain name correctly. If problems persist, you should install the computer to a workgroup to complete the installation.

Practice Questions

Question 1

> You want to use an RIS server to install Windows 2000 Professional on 200
> client computers. To use RIS, what other network services must you install and
> configure? Choose from the following list the network services that must be
> installed in order to implement an RIS server.
>
> Active Directory
>
> Remote Access Services (RAS) server
>
> DHCP server
>
> Windows Internet Naming Service (WINS) server
>
> Proxy server
>
> DNS server

This is the answer:

Active Directory

DHCP server

DNS server

Active Directory contains information about the RIS servers, DHCP gives
IP addresses to the RIS clients during the boot process, and DNS locates the
RIS server. You cannot configure RIS for use until Active Directory, the
DHCP server, and the DNS server are installed. RAS, WINS, and proxy
servers are not used by RIS, and they cannot be used for the installation and
configuration of RIS. They can be in place, but they do not provide any roles
for an RIS server.

Question 2

> You want to install Windows 2000 Professional on 500 client workstations by
> using an RIS server. The workstations do not have a PXE-compliant network
> card. How can these clients boot to the network to locate an RIS server?
>
> ○ a. You can't use RIS without a PXE-compliant network card.
>
> ○ b. Boot the client workstation with an **rbfg.exe** boot floppy disk.
>
> ○ c. Use Network Client Administrator to create a network boot floppy disk.
>
> ○ d. Configure the BIOS to boot from the network card.

Answer b is correct. If the computer doesn't have a PXE-compliant network card, you can use `rbfg.exe` to create an RIS boot disk. Answer a is incorrect because a remote boot disk can be used. Network Client Administrator does not create remote boot disk floppy disks—just network boot disks. Answer d is incorrect because the computers don't have a PXE-compliant network card.

Question 3

You want to use an **unattend.txt** file to automate the installation of Windows 2000 Professional from a CD-ROM. You place **unattend.txt** on a floppy disk and boot from the Windows 2000 Professional CD-ROM. However, the installation proceeds without using the **unattend.txt** file. What do you need to do to automate the installation?

- ○ a. You can't automate a CD-ROM–based installation.
- ○ b. Change the name of **unattend.txt** to **winnt.sif**.
- ○ c. During the text phase of the installation, press F3 to locate **unattend.txt** on a network server.
- ○ d. During the text phase of the installation, press F3 to locate **unattend.txt** on the floppy disk.

Answer b is correct. You can automate a CD-ROM–based installation if an answer file named `winnt.sif` is located on a floppy disk during the installation. The default `unattended.txt` answer file must be renamed `winnt.sif` and used for a CD-ROM–based installation. Answer a is incorrect because a CD-ROM–based installation can be automated with `winnt.sif`. Answers c and d are incorrect because pressing F3 doesn't allow a user to locate these files from a network server or from a floppy disk.

Question 4

You use **sysprep.exe** to prepare a model computer to be imaged by using third-party imaging software. You create the **sysprep** folder at the root of **C:**, and you place **sysprep.exe** and **setupcl.exe** in that directory. You use Setup Manager to create an answer file for the **sysprep** image. However, when you apply the image to a workstation, the Mini-Setup Wizard prompts you for every installation parameter. Why does this happen?

- ○ a. You did not place **sysprep.sif** in the **sysprep** folder.
- ○ b. You did not place **unattend.txt** in the **sysprep** folder.
- ○ c. You did not place **winnt.inf** in the **sysprep** folder.
- ○ d. You did not place **sysprep.inf** in the **sysprep** folder.

Answer d is correct. For the Mini-Setup Wizard to use the `sysprep` answer file, `sysprep.inf` must be located in the `sysprep` folder. Answer a is incorrect because the wrong file extension is used. Answers b and c are incorrect because the wrong file is used; the correct file is `sysprep.inf`.

Question 5

> You want to upgrade a Windows 95 computer to Windows 2000 Professional. You need to ensure that applications on the Windows 95 computer will run after the upgrade has completed. What do you do?
>
> ○ a. You can't upgrade and run applications that run on Windows 95 under Windows 2000.
>
> ○ b. Use upgrade packs for the required applications during the upgrade process.
>
> ○ c. Use the **apcompat.exe** utility and select Windows 95 so that applications will run in Windows 2000.
>
> ○ d. Import the **comptwa.inf** security template to allow the applications to run in Windows 2000.

Answer b is correct. You can obtain upgrade packs (also called migration DLLs) from third-party vendors to ensure that the Windows 95 applications will run in Windows 2000 Professional after the upgrade. Answer a is incorrect because a Windows 95 computer can be upgraded, but some applications that run under Windows 95 may not be compatible with Windows 2000. Answer c is incorrect because `apcompat.exe` doesn't ensure that applications will be compatible; only upgrade packs can ensure this. `apcompat.exe` can be used as a last resort to try to run a noncompliant application in Windows 2000. Answer d is incorrect because the security settings found in `comptwa.inf` do not relate to application compatibility; they relate to security compatibility.

Question 6

> Before you upgrade 100 Windows 98 computers to Windows 2000 Professional, you want to see if there are any hardware or software incompatibility issues. What should you run before the upgrade to search for incompatibilities?
>
> ○ a. **winnt.exe /checkupgradeonly**
>
> ○ b. **apcompat.exe**
>
> ○ c. **winnt32.exe /cmdcons**
>
> ○ d. **winnt32.exe /checkupgradeonly**

Answer d is correct. You use `winnt32.exe /checkupgradeonly` to run the Readiness Analyzer, which searches for any hardware or software incompatibilities with Windows 2000. The Readiness Analyzer is a GUI tool, and you run it only within an operating system. `winnt.exe /checkupgradeonly` does not work; therefore, Answer a is incorrect. Answer b is incorrect because `apcompat.exe` is not used to test hardware and software compatibility. Answer c is incorrect because it would install the Recovery Console, which is used after Windows 2000 has been installed.

Question 7

You want to upgrade a Windows 98 computer that has 16MB of memory, a 1GB hard drive with 200MB of free space, and a Pentium 200MHz CPU. The installation of Windows 2000 fails due to insufficient hardware. What hardware do you have to upgrade before the installation can proceed?

- ○ a. Install an additional 16MB of memory.
- ○ b. Install an additional 16MB of memory and a 2GB hard drive.
- ○ c. Install a Pentium II 400MHz CPU.
- ○ d. Install an additional 32MB of memory.

Answer b is correct. The minimum requirements for Windows 2000 Professional are 32MB of memory, a 2GB drive with 650MB of free space, and a Pentium 133MHz or higher CPU.

Question 8

You've downloaded the most current SP and need to incorporate it into the distribution share. How do you accomplish this?

- ○ a. Run **setup.exe /s:\\server1\W2KSetup**.
- ○ b. Run **update.msi /slip:\\server1\W2KSetup**.
- ○ c. Run **update.exe**.
- ○ d. Run **update.exe /s:\\server1\W2KSetup**.

Answer d is correct. Slipstreaming, via running `update.exe /s`, is a new method of upgrading Windows 2000 to incorporate SPs into the operating system. This method replaces the current files with the files that are contained in the SP. Answer a is incorrect because `setup.exe` is used to install Windows 2000, not to update it. Answer b is incorrect because SPs don't have the `.msi` file extension. Answer c would apply the SP but it wouldn't slipstream the SP because the `/s` switch is not used.

Question 9

After the text phase of the installation of Windows 2000 Professional has finished, an error states that the master boot record is corrupted. How do you fix this problem?

○ a. Boot with the Windows 2000 CD-ROM, install the Recovery Console, and run the **fixmbr** command.

○ b. Turn off virus checking in the BIOS.

○ c. Run **winnt32.exe /checkupgradeonly**.

○ d. Run the **fixmbr.exe** utility from the Windows 2000 CD-ROM.

Answer b is correct. The error occurred because virus checking was enabled in the BIOS, so you need to turn off virus checking. Answer a is incorrect because the Recovery Console is only used after Windows 2000 has been installed; it cannot be used to troubleshoot a failed installation. winnt32.exe /checkupgradeonly can be used only to verify the compatibility of hardware and software with Windows 2000; it cannot be used to troubleshoot failed installations; therefore, Answer c is incorrect. fixmbr.exe is a command that runs inside the Recovery Console; therefore, Answer d is incorrect for the same reason Answer a is incorrect.

Question 10

How do you apply an SP after you have installed Windows 2000 Professional?

○ a. Run **setup.exe /s:\\server1\W2KSetup**.

○ b. Run **update.msi /s:\\server1\W2KSetup**.

○ c. Run **update.exe**.

○ d. Run **update.exe /s:\\server1\W2KSetup**.

Answer c is correct. You use update.exe to install SPs after you install Windows 2000. You apply update.exe /s:[path] to distribution files; therefore, Answer d is incorrect. Answer a is incorrect because setup.exe is used to install Windows 2000, not to apply an SP. Answer b is incorrect because SPs don't have the .msi file extension. Answer c would apply the SP but it would not slipstream the SP because the /s switch is not used.

Need to Know More?

 Boyce, Jim. *Microsoft Windows 2000 Professional Installation and Configuration Handbook.* Indianapolis: Que Publishing, 2000. This handbook focuses on installing and troubleshooting Windows 2000 Professional. It offers authoritative, easy-to-follow overviews and critical step-by-step processes for difficult tasks.

 You should read `unattend.doc` for more information regarding the unattended installation process. This document is located on every Windows 2000 CD-ROM, in `Support\Tools\deploy.cab\` `unattend.doc`.

 For more information regarding the installation and configuration of RIS, you can download Microsoft's white paper on this topic from `www.microsoft.com/windows2000/library/planning/management/` `remoteos.asp`.

Implementing, Managing, and Troubleshooting Hardware Devices and Drivers

Terms you'll need to understand:

✓ Universal serial bus (USB)
✓ Plug and Play versus non–Plug and Play
✓ Advanced Power Management (APM)
✓ Advanced Configuration and Power Interface (ACPI)
✓ Device Manager and Driver signing
✓ FireWire or Institute of Electrical and Electronics Engineers (IEEE) 1394
✓ Internet Printing Protocol (IPP)
✓ Smart cards and smart card readers
✓ Infrared Data Association (IrDA) devices
✓ Network adapter or network interface card (NIC)
✓ Multiple-display and processor support

Techniques you'll need to master:

✓ Installing and configuring hardware devices and drivers
✓ Managing and various types of input/output (I/O) devices
✓ Configuring and troubleshooting Multilink support for a dial-up connection

Hardware devices in conjunction with the proper combination of software comprise the very foundation of computer systems. On the hardware side, computers need at least one microprocessor each, memory, data storage, video display equipment, and mouse and keyboard input devices, among many other items. On the software side, computers require operating system software, software application programs, and software device drivers so that the various pieces of hardware can interface with each other and with the user. Properly functioning device drivers are vital to the successful operation of their hardware counterparts. This is why the proper installation, administration, and troubleshooting of device drivers is so critical to all operating systems, including Windows 2000 Professional.

Implementing, Managing, and Troubleshooting Hardware

Hardware includes any physical device that is connected to a computer and that the computer's processor controls, such as equipment that is connected to a computer when it is manufactured as well as equipment that is added later. Modems, disk drives, CD-ROM drives, printers, network cards, keyboards, display adapter cards, and USB cameras are all examples of hardware devices. Windows 2000 contains full support for Plug and Play devices and partial support for non–Plug and Play devices. "Partial" support means that some of these devices work, and some do not. Sometimes, testing a device may be the only sure way to determine whether it will work with Windows 2000. You should always consult the latest Windows 2000 hardware compatibility list (HCL) before you install a new device.

For a device to work properly with Windows 2000, software (called a *device driver*) must be installed on the computer. Each device has its own unique device driver(s), which the device manufacturer typically supplies. However, many device drivers are included with Windows 2000 and work even better with Windows 2000 than the manufacturer's own driver. You should look for Microsoft's drivers for a given device before you look for those of the manufacturer.

Because Windows 2000 controls a computer's resources and configuration, you can install Plug and Play hardware devices and many other devices without restarting the computer. Windows 2000 automatically identifies the new hardware and installs the drivers it needs. If you are using an older computer that does not support APM or the "newer APM," called ACPI, you must set up the device manually and restart the computer when you install new hardware devices. For now, you need ACPI-compliant hardware to make your Windows 2000 hardware setup experience smoothest. We discuss APM and ACPI in greater detail later in this chapter, in the sections "APM" and "ACPI."

Installing, Configuring, and Managing Hardware

You can configure devices on Windows 2000 machines by using the Add/Remove Hardware Wizard in the Control Panel or by using Device Manager. You need to keep in mind that in most cases, you need to be logged on to the local machine as a member of the Administrators group in order to add, configure, and remove devices.

 You can use the System Information snap-in to view (yes, view *only*!) configuration information about a computer.

Installing Plug and Play Devices

You need to connect a Plug and Play device to the appropriate port or slot on a computer, according to the device manufacturer's instructions. You might need to start or restart the computer while doing so, but this happens much less often with Windows 2000 than it does with previous versions of Windows NT and 9x. If you are prompted to restart the computer, you should do so. Windows 2000 should detect the device and then immediately start the Found New Hardware Wizard.

Installing Non–Plug and Play Devices

To install a device that is not a Plug and Play device, you need to follow these steps:

1. Open the Add/Remove Hardware Wizard in the Control Panel.

2. Click Next, click Add/Troubleshoot a Device, and then click Next. Windows 2000 attempts to detect new Plug and Play devices.

3. If the device is not in the device list, click Add a New Device.

4. Click Next, and then do one of the following:

   ➤ *Click Yes, Search for New Hardware*—Do this if you want Windows 2000 to try to detect the new non–Plug and Play device you want to install.

> ➤ *Click No, I Want to Select the Hardware from a List*—Do this if you know the type and model of the device you are installing and if you want to select it from a list of devices.

5. Click Next, and then follow the instructions onscreen. You might be prompted to restart the computer, depending on the type of non–Plug and Play device you have installed. If you are, restart the computer; otherwise, the new device should be ready to use.

Tips on Installing Devices

Using a Plug and Play driver to install a non–Plug and Play device might provide *some* Plug and Play support. (Don't get your hopes up.) Although the system cannot recognize the hardware and load the appropriate drivers on its own, the Plug and Play driver can oversee the installation by allocating resources, interacting with power options in the Control Panel, and recording any issues in the event log.

If the computer is connected to a network, network policy (group policy) settings might prevent you from installing any devices on the computer. To add and set up a non–Plug and Play device that is connected directly to the computer, you *must* be logged on as an administrator or as a member of the Administrators group.

 If an administrator has already loaded the drivers for the device, you can install the device without having administrator privileges.

Updating Drivers

Keeping drivers and system files updated ensures that the operating system performs at peak level. Microsoft recommends using Microsoft digitally signed drivers whenever possible. The `driver.cab` cabinet file on the Windows 2000 CD-ROM contains all the drivers that Windows 2000 ships with. This cabinet file is copied to the `%SystemRoot%` folder when Windows 2000 is installed. Whenever a driver is updated, Windows 2000 looks in the `driver.cab` file first. Windows 2000 remembers the location of the `driver.cab` file through the use of a registry key that you can modify with `Regedit.exe` or `Regedt32.exe`. The registry key is `HKLM\Software\Microsoft\Windows\ CurrentVersion\Setup\DriverCachePath`.

Updating Individual Drivers

To update individual drivers, you need to follow these steps:

1. In Device Manager, right-click the device you want to update and choose Properties. The Properties dialog box appears.

2. Choose the Drivers tab and then click the Update Driver button.

You can use Driver Verifier to troubleshoot and isolate driver problems. Driver Verifier is not enabled by default. To use it, you must enable it by changing a registry setting. The Driver Verifier Manager, `verifier.exe`, provides a command-line interface for working with Driver Verifier.

For the exam, you just need to know that the Driver Verifier tool does exist—it is not a figment of anyone's imagination. You do not need to learn the various parameters and switches that work with it.

Updating System Files by Using Windows Update

Windows Update is a Microsoft database of items such as drivers, patches, help files, and Internet products that you can download to keep your Windows 2000 installation up-to-date. By using the Product Updates section of Windows Update, you can scan a computer for outdated system files, drivers, and help files, and you can automatically replace them with the most recent versions.

To update the system files by using Windows Update, you need to follow these steps:

1. Go to Windows Update at `http://windowsupdate.microsoft.com`. You can also open Windows Update by clicking Start, Windows Update.

2. On the Windows Update home page, choose the option to have your computer system scanned for available updates.

You must be logged on as an administrator or as a member of the Administrators group to complete this procedure. If the computer is connected to a network, network policy settings may prevent you from updating any system files or drivers. The first time you have the computer system scanned for updates, you should click Yes when you are prompted to download or install any required software or controls.

Troubleshooting Device Conflicts

You can configure devices by using the Add/Remove Hardware Wizard in the Control Panel or by using Device Manager. Each resource—for example, a memory address range, an Interrupt Request (IRQ), an I/O port, a Direct Memory Access (DMA) channel—that is assigned to a device must be unique or else the device does not function properly. For Plug and Play devices, Windows 2000 attempts to ensure automatically that these resources are configured properly. For devices where there is a resource conflict or where the device is not working properly, you see next to the device name a yellow circle with an exclamation point inside it.

Occasionally, two devices require the same resources, but you should keep in mind that this does not always result in a device conflict—especially if the devices are Plug and Play compliant. If a conflict arises, you can manually change the resource settings to be sure that each setting is unique. Sometimes, two or more devices can share resources, such as interrupts on Peripheral Component Interconnect (PCI) devices, depending on the drivers and the computer. For example, you should get accustomed to seeing Windows 2000 share IRQ9 among multiple devices on many laptops.

When you install a non–Plug and Play device, the resource settings for the device are not automatically configured. Depending on the type of device you are installing, you might have to manually configure these settings, which should be supplied in the instruction manual for the device.

Generally, you should not change resource settings manually because when you do so, the settings become fixed, and Windows 2000 then has less flexibility when allocating resources to other devices. If too many resources become fixed, Windows 2000 may not be able to install new Plug and Play devices.

Managing and Troubleshooting Driver Signing

Microsoft is promoting driver signing for devices as a method to advance the quality of drivers and to reduce support costs for vendors and total cost of ownership (TCO) for customers. Windows 2000 uses a driver-signing process to make sure drivers have been certified to work correctly with the Windows Driver Model (WDM) in Windows 2000. After Microsoft successfully tests a device driver, it embeds a digital signature into the programming code of the driver itself to certify it. If you are having problems with a device, it might be because you are using a driver that is not correctly written for Windows 2000. To identify such drivers, you can use the Signature Verification tool. This utility, sigverif.exe, helps you quickly identify unsigned drivers if a device is not working or if you want to ensure that all drivers in use are signed.

Using the Signature Verification Tool

To use the Signature Verification tool, you perform the following steps:

1. Start sigverif.exe by selecting Start, Run, sigverif.exe.

2. Click Advanced.

3. Select Look for the Files That Are Not Digitally Signed.

4. Select the folder %SystemRoot%\system32\drivers.

Managing Driver-Signing Policy

Windows 2000 can provide a good degree of control over whether users can install signed or unsigned drivers for a chosen device. To view or modify the policy setting for Unsigned Driver Installation Behavior, open the Group Policy MMC snap-in for the local computer or for an Active Directory site, domain, or organizational unit. Select Computer Configuration, Windows Settings, Security Settings, Local Policies, Security Options. There you see three options when you double-click the Unsigned Driver Installation Behavior policy:

➤ *Silently Succeed*—Selecting this option simply ignores whether a driver is signed, allowing the user to proceed with the driver installation.

➤ *Warn But Allow Installation*—Selecting this option causes a dialog box warning to appear if an unsigned driver is encountered during a device installation. The dialog box gives the user the option of continuing with the installation or terminating the device's setup.

➤ *Do Not Allow Installation*—This is the most important of the three options. To prevent the installation of any unsigned device drivers, this is the setting you should select in the group policy or the local computer policy.

Managing and Troubleshooting I/O Devices

Windows 2000 supports a wide variety of I/O devices, including printers, scanners, and multimedia devices (such as cameras, keyboards, mice, smart card readers, modems, infrared devices, and network adapters). The following sections cover the specifics you need to know about supporting I/O devices on Windows 2000 Professional for the exam. You should think "big picture" when you are studying these hardware sections, and you should remember you do not need to know specifics about certain brands or models of hardware.

Using Printers

Windows 2000 Professional supports the following printer ports: line printer terminal (LPT), Component Object Model (COM), USB, FireWire (also called IEEE 1394), and network attached devices with universal naming convention (UNC) paths. Print services can be provided only for Windows and Unix clients on Windows 2000 Professional. Windows 2000 Professional automatically downloads the printer drivers for clients that are running Windows 2000, NT 4, NT 3.51, and 9x.

    Windows 2000 Server is required to support Macintosh and NetWare clients.

IPP

Internet printing using IPP is a feature in Windows 2000 that is also supported in Windows 98. Clients have the option of entering a URL to connect to network printers to manage their network print jobs. This is much easier for users than browsing aimlessly within My Network Places or Network Neighborhood to locate network printers. IPP's other advantage is that it can significantly help cut down browse traffic on a network.

The print server must be either a Windows 2000 Server running Internet Information Server (IIS) 5 or a Windows 2000 Professional system running Personal Web Server (PWS), which is the "junior" version of IIS. You can view all shared IPP printers at http://*servername*/printers (for example, http://Server2/printers).

Printer Property Settings

The following are some useful printer property settings:

➤ *Print Pooling*—This allows you to install two or more identical printers as one logical printer.

➤ *Print Priority*—You set this by creating multiple logical printers for one physical printer and assigning different priorities to each. Priority ranges from 1, the lowest (the default), through 99, the highest.

➤ *Availability*—Enabling this option allows administrators to specify the hours the printer is available. This option is good for large print jobs that should be printed in the middle of the night or in the early morning so they do not interfere with routine business.

➤ *Separator Pages*—This option allows you to separate print jobs at a shared printer. You can create and save a template with a .sep file extension for the design and appearance of the separator page in the %SystemRoot%\system32 directory.

➤ *Restart*—You can select this in the printer's menu to reprint a document. This option is useful when a document is printing and the printer jams. You can select Resume to start printing where you left off.

The Advanced Server Properties option allows you to change the directory that contains the print spooler for the printer. This feature is new to the Windows operating system with the release of Windows 2000.

Restarting the Spooler Service

You must restart the Spooler service if purging a print queue does not resolve a printing problem. To remedy a stalled spooler, you must stop and restart the Spooler service in the Services applet under Administrative Tools in the Control Panel. You need to be logged on as an administrator or as a member of the Administrators local group in order to successfully restart the Spooler service.

Using Keyboards and Mice

You install keyboards under Keyboards in Device Manager, and you install mice, graphics tablets, and other pointing devices under Mice and Other Pointing Devices in Device Manager. (See the "USB" section, later in this chapter, for more information on USB graphics tablets and pointing devices.) You troubleshoot I/O resource conflicts by using the System

Information console, which you reach by selecting Start, Programs, Accessories, System Tools. You can look under the Hardware Resources node and I/O subnode for a list of memory ranges in use.

Using Smart Cards and Smart Card Readers

Smart cards and smart card readers, which interpret the data on the cards, are fully supported in Windows 2000. Smart cards enable portability of user credentials and other private information among computers in many locations—such as at work, at home, and on the road. Smart card technology eliminates the need for you to transmit sensitive information, such as user authentication tickets and private keys, over networks. Smart cards also support certificate-based authentication. (See the "Authenticating Mobile Users" section, later in this chapter, for more information on certificate-based authentication.)

Installing Smart Card Readers

To install a smart card reader on a computer, you need to perform the following steps:

1. Shut down (power off) the computer.

2. Depending on the type of card reader you have, attach the reader to an available serial port or insert the PC card reader into an available PCMCIA Type II slot.

3. Restart the computer and log on as an administrator.

4. One of the following happens next:

   ➤ If the device driver software for the smart card reader is available in the `driver.cab` file, the driver is installed without any prompting. The installation could take a few minutes.

   ➤ If the device driver software for the smart card reader is not available in the `driver.cab` file, the Add/Remove Hardware Wizard starts. You need to follow the directions for installing the device driver software.

You know that installation has successfully taken place if you see the Unplug or Eject Hardware icon in the toolbar after it was not previously present; you should also see the just-installed reader in the list of hardware devices in the Unplug or Eject Hardware dialog box. You can display the Unplug or Eject Hardware dialog box by right-clicking the Unplug or Eject Hardware icon when it is displayed in the system tray. You can also locate this dialog box by clicking Start, Settings, Control Panel and then double-clicking System, selecting the Hardware tab, clicking the Hardware Wizard button, clicking Next, choosing Uninstall/Unplug a Device, clicking Next again, selecting Unplug/Eject a Device, and clicking Next.

If the smart card reader is not installed automatically, or if the Add/Remove Hardware Wizard does not start automatically, the smart card reader is probably not Plug and Play compliant. You should contact the smart card reader manufacturer for the device driver and instructions on how to install and configure the device for Windows 2000.

Logging on to a Computer with a Smart Card
To log on to a computer by using a smart card, you need to perform the following steps:

1. At the Windows logon screen, insert the smart card in the smart card reader.

2. Type the personal identification number (PIN) for the smart card when the computer prompts you to do so.

If the PIN you enter is recognized as being legitimate, you are logged on to the computer and to the Windows domain, based on the permissions that the domain administrator has assigned to the user account. If you enter the incorrect PIN for a smart card several times in a row, you cannot log on to the computer by using that smart card. The number of allowable invalid logon attempts before you are locked out varies according to the smart card manufacturer.

Authenticating Mobile Users
When you are configuring a computer for a *mobile user*, you need to enable the use of certificates on the user's mobile computer. Unless the system administrator preconfigures the computer with machine and user certificates, the user must connect to the corporate network by using conventional, password-based authentication methods to obtain the machine and user certificates. When the user connects, he or she needs to join the computer to the corporate domain, obtain certificates, and set certificates policy. The next time the user connects to the corporate network, the user can take advantage of certificate-based authentication methods such as Extensible Authentication Protocol (EAP), which is an extension to Point-to-Point Protocol (PPP).

EAP was developed in response to the increasing demand for remote access user authentication that uses security devices such as smart cards. EAP provides a standard mechanism for supporting authentication methods in addition to those in PPP. By using EAP, you can add support for a number of authentication schemes, including token cards, one-time passwords, public-key authentication using smart cards, and certificates. EAP, in conjunction with strong EAP authentication methods, is a critical technology component for secure virtual private network (VPN) connections because it offers more security against brute-force and dictionary attacks and password guessing than do other authentication methods, such as Challenge Handshake Authentication Protocol (CHAP).

A Windows 2000 Professional computer that needs to authenticate to a Remote Access Services (RAS) server by using a smart card and a certificate must have EAP, and Microsoft CHAP (MSCHAP) and/or MSCHAP version 2 enabled in the dial-up connection's properties settings.

Enabling the Use of Certificates

To enable the use of a certificate on a computer, you need to perform the following steps:

1. Connect to a network by using a dial-up or Point-to-Point Tunneling Protocol (PPTP) network connection, as well as authentication protocols such as MSCHAP or MSCHAP version 2. When you connect, your Windows 2000 computer joins the corporate domain and receives machine certificates.

2. Request a user certificate from one of the possible Certificate Authorities.

3. Create another connection that uses certificate-based authentication and then connect again by using a certificate-based authentication method such as EAP or IP Security (IPSec).

Using Cameras and Other Multimedia Hardware

Cameras and scanners appear in the Control Panel the first time you install a digital camera or scanner. If you have a Plug and Play camera or scanner, Windows 2000 detects it and installs it automatically. Then you can use the Scanners and Cameras applet from the Control Panel to install other scanners, digital still cameras, digital video cameras, and image-capturing devices.

After a device is installed, Scanners and Cameras can link it to a program on the computer. For example, you can set up your machine so that when you push Scan on the scanner, the scanned picture automatically opens in the program you want.

Installing Scanners and Digital Cameras

To install a scanner or digital camera, you need to perform the following steps:

1. Open Scanners and Cameras in the Control Panel.

2. Click Add and then follow the instructions onscreen.

You must be logged on as an administrator or as a member of the Administrators group in order to complete this procedure. If the computer is connected to a network, network policy settings might prevent you from installing devices.

Testing Scanners and Digital Cameras

To test whether a scanner or digital camera is installed properly, you need to perform the following steps:

1. Open Scanners and Cameras in the Control Panel.

2. Click the scanner or camera you want to test and then click Properties.

3. On the General tab, click Test Scanner or Camera.

An onscreen message indicates whether the camera or scanner completes the test successfully. You can also check the event log to see if the test is successful.

Using Modems

If you've used a computer, you have probably used a modem to connect to an office or to an Internet service provider (ISP) by using a dial-up connection. The following sections detail what you need to know about modem support and troubleshooting in Windows 2000 Professional.

Installing Modems

If Windows 2000 starts the Install New Modem Wizard as soon as the new modem is physically connected to the machine, you are in luck! You have nothing more to do than follow the prompts the wizard provides, if any, to complete the setup of the new modem.

If the Install New Modem Wizard does not detect the modem or you cannot find it listed in the Install New Modem section of the Add/Remove Hardware Wizard dialog box, you are faced with installing an unsupported modem. This can be a sometimes difficult challenge. Windows 2000 cannot automatically detect certain internal modems. You must install such a modem manually through the Add/Remove Hardware Wizard in the Control Panel or by following these instructions:

1. Open Phone and Modem Options in the Control Panel.

2. (Optional) If you are prompted for location information, enter dialing information for your location and click OK.

3. On the Modems tab, click Add.

4. Follow the instructions in the Install New Modem Wizard.

Using Multilink Support

Multilinking, or multiple-device dialing, allows you to combine two or more modems or Integrated Services Digital Network (ISDN) adapters into one logical link with increased bandwidth. The Network and Dial-up Connections feature performs PPP Multilink dialing over multiple ISDN, X.25, or modem lines. This feature combines multiple physical links into a logical bundle, and the resulting aggregate link increases the connection bandwidth. For example, you could use Multilink to combine the power of two 33.6Kbps modems to achieve approximately a 67.2Kbps dial-up connection. Although you do not see this frequently in the real world, Multilink is definitely a term to understand for the 70-210 exam.

To configure Multilink, you need to perform the following steps:

1. Select Start, Settings, Network and Dial-up Connections.

2. Right-click the connection where you want Multilink to be enabled, and then select Properties.

3. On the Options tab, in the Multiple Devices section, select one of the following from the drop-down list box:

   ➤ If you want Windows 2000 to dial only the first available device, click Dial Only First Available Device.

   ➤ If you want Windows 2000 to use all your devices, click Dial All Devices.

   ➤ If you want Windows 2000 to dynamically dial and hang up devices as needed, click Dial Devices Only as Needed. Click Configure to set up the parameters for automatic dialing and hanging up.

The following steps apply only to the Dial Devices Only as Needed option.

4. When you click Configure, the Automatic Dialing and Hanging Up dialog box appears. In the Automatic Dialing section, select the Activity at Least percentage and Duration at Least time that you want to set. Another phone line is dialed when connection activity reaches the specified level for the amount of time specified.

5. In the Automatic Hangup section, click the Activity No More Than percentage and Duration at Least time that you want to set. A device is hung up when connection activity decreases to the specified level for at least the amount of time specified.

If you use multiple devices to dial a server that requires callback, only one of the multilinked devices is called back. This is because only one phone number is stored in a user account. Therefore, only one device connects, all other devices fail to complete the connection, and the connection loses Multilink functionality. You can avoid this problem if the multilinked phonebook entry is to an ISDN line or to a modem with two channels that have the same phone number.

If you select Dial All Devices, links that get dropped in the multilinked bundle feature are not automatically reinitialized. You can force links to reinitialize by selecting Dial Devices Only as Needed and then clicking Configure; then you can set easily achieved automatic dialing conditions, which cause another line to be dialed. For example, you could set Activity at Least to 1% and Duration at Least to 3 seconds.

 To dial multiple devices, both the connection and the remote access server must support Multilink and have Multilink enabled.

Troubleshooting Modems

You can verify that a modem is working properly by using the diagnostic tool that is available through the Phone and Modem Options icon in the Control Panel or by using Device Manager. Another way to troubleshoot a modem problem is to use the Hardware Troubleshooter, which is available in the Add/Remove Hardware Wizard in the Control Panel. Unfortunately, the Hardware Troubleshooter is not all that useful because it offers only basic troubleshooting suggestions and it uses a similar format to Windows Help, which is often not very helpful. The troubleshooter is not an interactive tool.

Supporting Faxes

If a fax device or fax modem is installed, the Fax applet appears in the Control Panel. This applet does not appear if no fax device is installed. You use the Fax applet to set up rules for how a device receives faxes, the number of retries when it is sending, where to store retrieved and sent faxes, user security permissions, and so on. If the Advanced Options tab is not available in the Fax applet, you must log off and then log back on as an administrator. Configuring and administering the Fax service is covered in Chapter 5, "Configuring and Troubleshooting System Services and the Desktop Environment."

 You cannot share the fax printer in the Printers folder in Windows 2000 Professional or Windows 2000 Server. Shared faxing is available only in Small Business Server (SBS) 2000.

Using IrDA Devices and Wireless Devices

Windows 2000 supports IrDA protocols, which enable data transfer over infrared connections and provide an infrastructure that allows other devices and programs to communicate with Windows 2000 through the IrDA interface. Windows 2000 is installed with the Wireless Link program, which transfers files to and from another computer that runs Windows 2000, Windows XP, or Windows 98.

Windows 2000's Plug and Play architecture automatically detects and installs the infrared component for computers with built-in IrDA hardware. For computers without built-in IrDA hardware, a user can attach a serial port IrDA transceiver to a serial COM port and use the Add/Remove Hardware Wizard to install the device in Windows 2000. You can also install IrDA devices by using a USB connection for any device that is USB compatible.

After an infrared device is installed, the Wireless Link icon appears in the Control Panel. When another IrDA transceiver comes in range, the Wireless Link icon appears on the desktop and on the taskbar. You can then send a file over the infrared connection with any of the following actions:

➤ You can specify a location and one or more files by using the Wireless Link dialog box.

➤ You can use drag-and-drop operations to move files onto the Wireless Link icon on the desktop.

➤ You can right-click any selection of files on the desktop, in Windows Explorer, or in My Computer, and then click Send to Infrared Recipient.

➤ You can print to a printer that is configured to use an infrared port.

In addition to sending or printing files, you can create a network connection that connects two computers by using the infrared port. You can use this capability to map shared drives on a host computer and work with files and folders in Windows Explorer or My Computer. You can also use an infrared network connection to connect directly to another computer without modems, cables, or network hardware.

Enabling and Preventing Receiving Files

To enable or prevent receiving files, you need to perform the following steps:

1. Open the Wireless Link applet in the Control Panel.

2. On the File Transfer tab, do one of the following:

   ➤ Select the Allow Others to Send Files to Your Computer Using Infrared Communications check box to enable the computer to receive files from others.

   ➤ Select the Send Files to Your Computer Using Infrared Communications check box.

Remember that IrDA data transfer speeds are much slower than local area network (LAN) connections, especially if the IrDA device is connected via serial cable. You might want to limit file transfers between IrDA devices to just small files. You might also want to disable your computer from receiving files via IrDA connections most of the time to prevent just anyone from sending files to your PC. In a public area, an unscrupulous user could attempt to send virus-infected files to anyone's computer that is enabled to receive files.

Troubleshooting USB Hubs and Host Controllers

The introduction of USB devices ushered in the new Plug and Play standard that first appeared in Windows 95. Support for Plug and Play has improved with Windows 2000, but you sometimes still need to troubleshoot problems that can arise with USB devices, USB hubs, and USB host controllers. Power consumption of USB devices can pose problems, and bandwidth allocations can be a concern, especially for older USB 1.x devices.

Viewing Power Allocations for USB Hubs

If a computer has a USB hub with multiple ports or if a computer is connected to multiple USB hubs, the power consumed by the USB devices that
are connected to the USB hub(s) reduces the amount of power that is available to other USB devices. The reduced availability of power may indicate
that you need to use self-powered hubs for the more power-hungry devices.
To view power allocations for USB hubs, you need to perform the following
steps:

1. Open Device Manager.

2. Double-click Universal Serial Bus Controller.

3. Right-click USB Root Hub and then click Properties.

4. In the Devices on This Hub list on the Power tab, view the power
   consumed by each device.

Hubs for USB devices are self-powered or bus-powered. Self-powered
devices—that is, those that are plugged in to an electrical outlet—provide
maximum power to the device, whereas bus-powered devices—those that are
plugged in to another USB port—provides minimum power. Devices that
require a lot of power, such as cameras, should be plugged in to self-powered
hubs. The Universal Serial Bus Controller option appears in Device
Manager only if there is a USB port on the computer. The Power tab appears
only for USB hubs.

Viewing Bandwidth Allocations for USB Host Controllers

Device Manager can show you which USB controllers are consuming the
most bandwidth based on the USB devices that are connected to them. You
can view bandwidth only for a USB controller. By noticing which controllers
are maxed out, you can choose to add additional controllers to balance the
load for the USB devices. To view bandwidth allocation for a USB host controller, you need to perform the following steps:

1. Open Device Manager.

2. Double-click Universal Serial Bus Controllers.

3. Right-click Intel PCI to USB Universal Host Controller and then click
   Properties.

4. In the Bandwidth Consuming Devices list on the Advanced tab, view
   the bandwidth consumed by each device.

Certain ports are not listed in the Ports tab unless a printer that requires one of them is installed. USB and FireWire printers support Plug and Play, so when you plug a printer in to the correct physical port (USB or IEEE 1394), the correct port monitor is installed automatically. Windows 2000 detects the device and displays its settings onscreen, and then it prompts you to approve.

Dealing with USB Controllers That Do Not Install Properly

In Device Manager, USB controllers are listed under Human Interface Devices (when you are viewing in the Devices by Type view, which is the default view). If the controller you're looking for does not appear in Device Manager, USB may not be enabled in the system's basic input/output system (BIOS). When you are prompted to do so during system startup, you should enter the BIOS setup and enable USB.

If USB is enabled in the BIOS but the USB host controller does not appear in Device Manager under Universal Serial Bus Controllers or a yellow warning icon appears next to the host controller name, the version of BIOS on the machine might be outdated. In that case, you need to contact the computer's maker or vendor to obtain the current BIOS version.

If the controller appears in Device Manager, you can right-click the controller name and select Properties to verify whether the system considers the controller to be functioning normally. In the Device Status section, a message describes any problems and suggests what action to take. Each USB port has a separate entry in Device Manager. To check the device status, you can select Universal Serial Bus Controllers, right-click USB Root Hub, and then select Properties.

Configuring NICs

You can install NICs by using the Add/Remove Hardware Wizard in the Control Panel, although most NICs sold today are Plug and Play compliant. You can make changes to the binding order of protocols and the network provider order by using Advanced Settings under the Advanced menu of the Network and Dial-up Connections window (which you access by right-clicking the My Network Places icon or via the Control Panel). Each network adapter has its own separate icon in the Network and Dial-up Connections folder. You can right-click a network adapter icon to set its properties, install protocols, change addresses, or perform other configuration changes for the connection.

Managing and Troubleshooting Display Devices

You can manage desktop display properties (software settings) through the Display applet in the Control Panel. You can install, remove, and update the drivers of display adapters through the Display Adapters node in Device Manager. To do the same for monitors, you can use the Monitors node in Device Manager.

Changing Display Settings

For the most part, the display settings deal with aesthetics such as wallpaper, screen fonts, and screensavers. The 70-210 exam tests your knowledge of the technical aspects of display settings, not aesthetics. For example, if you receive an error about an unavailable overlay surface, you should reduce the display resolution or number of colors. The Display applet (located in the Control Panel) is also where you can update or change the video display driver. If you happen to install a new video display driver that is poorly designed, you may no longer be able to view your computer's display. If this occurs, you should restart the computer and press the F8 key to display the advanced startup options screen. You choose the Enable VGA Mode option and press Enter. Windows 2000 then boots, using a standard 16-color VGA display driver so that you can log on to the system and install the original (or a better) video display driver to bring the system's display back to normal.

Modifying Display Settings

To modify display settings, you need to perform the following steps:

1. Right-click the desktop and select Properties or open the Display applet in the Control Panel.

2. Select the Settings tab and make the appropriate changes.

Configuring Multiple-Display Support

Windows 2000 has a new multiple-monitor functionality that increases your work productivity by expanding the size of the desktop. Multiple displays have to use PCI or Accelerated Graphics Port (AGP) port devices in order to work properly with Windows 2000.

You can connect up to 10 individual monitors to create a desktop large enough to hold numerous programs or windows. The video graphics cards must be PCI- or AGP-compatible to use the multiple-monitor feature.

You can easily work on more than one task at a time by moving items from one monitor to another or by stretching items across multiple monitors. For example, you could edit images or text on one monitor while viewing Web activity on another. Or you could open multiple pages of a single, long document and drag them across several monitors to easily view the layout of text and graphics. You could also stretch a spreadsheet across two monitors in order to view numerous columns without scrolling.

One monitor serves as the primary display, on which you see the Logon dialog box when you start the computer. In addition, most programs display windows on the primary monitor when you initially open them. You can set different resolutions and different color depths for each monitor. You can also connect multiple monitors to individual graphics adapters or to a single adapter that supports multiple outputs.

Arranging Multiple Monitors

To arrange multiple monitors, you need to perform the following steps:

1. Open the Display applet in the Control Panel.

2. On the Settings tab, click Identify to display a large number on each of the monitors, to show which monitor corresponds with each icon.

3. Click the monitor icons and drag them to positions that represent how you want to move items from one monitor to another, and then click OK or Apply to view the changes.

The icon positions determine how you move items from one monitor to another. For example, if you are using two monitors and you want to move items from one monitor to the other by dragging left and right, you should place the icons side-by-side. To move items between monitors by dragging up and down, you should place the icons one above the other. The icon positions do not have to correspond to the physical positions of the monitors. You can place the icons one above the other even though the monitors are side-by-side.

Changing the Primary Monitor

To designate which monitor is the primary monitor, you need to perform the following steps:

1. Open the Display applet in the Control Panel.

2. On the Settings tab, click the monitor icon that represents the monitor you want to designate as the primary monitor.

3. Select the Use This Device as the Primary Monitor check box. This check box is unavailable when you select the monitor icon that is currently set as the primary monitor.

The monitor that is designated as the primary monitor displays the Logon dialog box when you start the computer. Most programs display their windows on the primary monitor when you first open them.

Working with Multiple Monitors

To move items between monitors or to view the same desktop on multiple monitors, you need to perform the following steps:

1. Open the Display applet in the Control Panel.

2. On the Settings tab, click the monitor icon that represents the monitor you want to use in addition to the primary monitor.

3. Select the Extend My Windows Desktop onto This Monitor check box. Selecting this check box allows you to drag items across the screen onto alternate monitors. You can also resize a window to stretch it across more than one monitor.

Troubleshooting Multiple Displays

The default monitor refresh frequency setting is typically 60Hz, although some monitors support higher settings. A higher refresh frequency might reduce flicker onscreen, but choosing a setting that is too high for the monitor can make the display unusable, and it might even damage the hardware.

 If the refresh frequency is set to anything higher than 60Hz and a monitor's display goes black when you start Windows 2000, you should restart the system in Safe Mode. Then you need to change the refresh frequency for all monitors to 60Hz. You might need to double-check this setting in your Unattended Installation script file, which is commonly called **unattend.txt**. Again, you should set it to 60Hz as a best practice.

Multiple-display support in Windows 2000 presents some challenges when you are dealing with some older applications and DOS applications. If you start a DOS application on a Windows 2000 machine with two (or more) monitors and then all the monitors flicker and completely go dark, you can fix the problem without much difficulty. Multiple-display support allows you to adjust the display settings so that your application runs and is viewable on all monitors. First, you might need to restart your system; then, you need to select Safe Mode at the F8 startup menu. Then, when you can see the contents of the desktop, you need to configure the DOS application to run in a window and change the Display settings from Default to Optimal.

Installing, Configuring, and Supporting a Video Adapter

When Windows 2000 is being installed, the system's BIOS selects the primary video/display adapter based on PCI slot order. You can install and configure any additional video adapters you want to use with your system by using the Display applet or the Add/Remove Hardware Wizard in the Control Panel.

Mobile Computer Hardware

PC Card (formerly known as PCMCIA) adapters, USB ports, FireWire, and infrared devices are supported in Windows 2000. You can manage them through Device Manager. Windows 2000 Professional also provides support for APM and ACPI, which are discussed shortly.

Hot (that is, the computer is fully powered) and warm (that is, the computer is in suspend mode) docking and undocking are fully supported in Windows 2000 Professional for computers with Plug and Play BIOS. Hibernation (that is, complete power-down while maintaining the state of open programs and connected hardware) and Suspend (that is, deep sleep with some power) modes, which extend battery life, are also supported in Windows 2000.

When you install a PC Card, USB, or infrared device, Windows 2000 automatically recognizes and configures it (if it meets Plug and Play specifications). If Windows does not have an entry in its driver.cab file for the new hardware, you are prompted to supply one.

Equipping mobile computers with smart cards and NT File System (NTFS) drive volumes that use the Encrypting File System decreases the likelihood of confidential data being compromised if the computer is stolen, lost, or simply placed in the wrong hands.

Managing Hardware Profiles

A *hardware profile* stores configuration settings for a collection of devices and services. Windows 2000 can store different hardware profiles so that users' needs can be met even though their computers may frequently require different device and service settings, depending on the circumstances. The best example is a laptop or portable computer that is used in an office while in a docking station that is then undocked so the user can travel with the laptop. The two situations require different power management settings, possibly different network settings, and various other configuration changes.

You can enable and disable devices in particular profiles through their properties in Device Manager. You can manage services by using the Services applet in the Control Panel. You can create and manage hardware profiles by using the System applet in the Control Panel or by right-clicking the My Computer icon on the desktop and choosing Properties. When you are in the System applet, you select the Hardware tab and then select Hardware Profiles.

At installation, Windows 2000 creates a single hardware profile called Profile 1 (Current). You are prompted to select a hardware profile at system startup only when two or more hardware profiles are stored on the machine. You can create and store as many hardware profiles on a machine as you like. You select the desired hardware profile at Windows 2000 startup to select which device and service configuration settings you need for the current session. If Windows 2000 detects that the computer is portable (a laptop), it tries to determine whether the system is docked or undocked; then it selects the appropriate hardware profile for the current conditions.

 You should not confuse hardware profiles with *user profiles*—the two are unrelated!

APM

Windows 2000 supports the APM 1.2 specification. APM helps to greatly reduce a computer's power consumption, which is particularly helpful for laptop users. You use the Power Options applet in the Control Panel to configure a computer to use APM. When you are in the Power Options applet, you should look for a tab labeled APM. On the APM tab, you select the Enable Advanced Power Management check box in order to enable APM. You do not need to then restart the system.

If the computer does not have an APM-compliant BIOS, Windows 2000 cannot install APM. This means there is no APM support for the machine, and there is no APM tab in the Power Options applet in the Control Panel. You should keep in mind, though, that the machine can still function as an ACPI computer if the BIOS is ACPI compliant. The ACPI-based BIOS takes over the system configuration and power management from the Plug and Play BIOS.

APM is available only in Windows 2000 Professional. It is not available in any of the Windows 2000 Server versions.

ACPI

ACPI is the next-generation replacement for the APM specification. ACPI is an open industry specification that defines a flexible and extensible hardware interface for the system board. Windows 2000 is a fully ACPI-compliant operating system. Software developers and designers use the ACPI specification to integrate power management features—including hardware, the operating system, and application software—throughout a computer system. This integration enables Windows 2000 to determine which applications are active and to handle all the power management resources for computer subsystems and peripherals.

ACPI enables the operating system to direct power management on a wide range of mobile, desktop, and server computers and peripherals. ACPI is the foundation for the OnNow industry initiative, which allows manufacturers to deliver computers that start at the touch of a key on a keyboard.

ACPI design is essential when you want to take full advantage of power management and Plug and Play in Windows 2000. If you are not sure whether the computer is ACPI compliant, you should check the manufacturer's documentation. To change power settings that take advantage of ACPI, you use the Power Options applet in the Control Panel.

Power Options Overview

By using Power Options in the Control Panel, you can reduce the power consumption of any number of the computer devices or of the entire system. You do this by choosing a *power scheme*, which is a collection of settings that manages the computer's power usage. You can create your own power schemes or use the ones provided with Windows 2000.

You can also adjust the individual settings in a power scheme. For example, depending on the hardware, you can do the following:

➤ Turn off the monitor and hard disks automatically to save power.

➤ Put the computer on standby, which puts the entire system in a low-power state (which you might want to do if you plan to be away from the computer for a while). While on standby, the entire computer switches to a low-power state; devices such as the monitor and hard disks turn off, and the computer uses less power. When you want to use the computer again, it comes out of standby quickly, and the desktop is restored exactly as you left it. Standby is useful for conserving battery power in portable computers.

> Standby does not save the desktop state to disk, so if there is a power failure while the computer is on standby, you can lose unsaved information. If there is an interruption in power, information in memory is lost. If this concerns you, hibernation or a complete power down might be choices you should consider.

➤ Put the computer in hibernation mode. When you restart the computer, the desktop is restored exactly as you left it. It takes longer to bring the computer out of hibernation than out of standby. You should put a computer in hibernation when you will be away from it for an extended time or overnight.

> The hibernation feature saves everything in memory on disk, turns off the monitor and hard disk, and then turns off the computer.

Managing Battery Power on a Portable Computer

By using the Power Options applet in the Control Panel, you can reduce consumption of battery power on a portable computer and still keep the computer available for immediate use. You can view multiple batteries separately or as a whole, and you can set alarms to sound during low battery conditions.

Managing Power When Installing a Plug and Play Device

Plug and Play works with Power Options in the Control Panel to be sure that a system runs efficiently while hardware devices are being installed or removed. Power Options controls the power supply to the devices attached to the computer, supplying power to those that you are using and conserving power for those you are not using. Windows 2000 automatically manages the power for devices. However, some devices have options that you can set in Device Manager.

To take full advantage of Plug and Play, you need to use Windows 2000 on an ACPI-compliant computer that is running in ACPI mode, and the hardware devices must be Plug and Play and/or ACPI compliant. In an ACPI computer, the operating system, not the hardware, configures and monitors the computer's devices.

Monitoring and Configuring Multiple Processors

Adding an additional processor to a Windows 2000 system to improve performance is called *scaling*. Windows 2000 Professional can support up to two processors. You might want to add a second processor due to the demands of central processing unit (CPU)-intensive applications, such as computer-aided design (CAD) and graphics rendering. Windows 2000 supports symmetric multiprocessing (SMP) as well as processor affinity. Asymmetric multiprocessing (ASMP) is not supported.

Windows 2000 provides support for single or multiple CPUs. However, if you originally installed Windows 2000 on a computer with a single CPU, you must update the Hardware Abstraction Layer (HAL) on the computer for it to recognize and use multiple CPUs.

 Windows 2000 Professional supports a maximum of two CPUs, without original equipment manufacturer (OEM) modifications. If you need more than two CPUs, you should consider using Windows 2000 Server (which supports up to four CPUs), Advanced Server (which supports up to eight CPUs), or Data Center Server (which supports maximum of 32 CPUs).

You should keep monitoring performance after you add an additional processor because upgrading to multiple CPUs can increase the load on other system resources.

In Windows NT 4, the `uptomp.exe` tool added support for multiple CPUs. However, that tool is no longer used in Windows 2000. Instead, you use Device Manager to make changes related to having multiple CPUs. Before changing the computer type, you should contact the computer manufacturer to determine whether there is a vendor-specific HAL you should use instead of the standard ones included in Windows 2000.

Installing Support for Multiple CPUs

To install support for multiple CPUs, you need to perform the following steps:

1. Click Start, Settings, Control Panel and then click System.

2. Click the Hardware tab and then click Device Manager.

3. Double-click the Computer branch to expand it. Note the type of support you currently have.

4. Double-click the computer type listed under the Computer branch, click the Drivers tab, click Update Driver, and then click Next.

5. Click Display a List of Known Drivers for This Device and then click Show All Hardware of This Device Class.

6. Click the appropriate computer type (one that matches the current type, except for multiple CPUs), click Next, and then click Finish.

You can use this procedure only to upgrade from a single-processor HAL to a multiple-processor HAL. If you use this procedure to change from a standard HAL to an ACPI HAL (for example, after a BIOS upgrade) or vice versa, unexpected results may occur—for example, you may be unable to boot the computer.

Practice Questions

Question 1

You have several Symmetric Multiprocessor (SMP)–compliant machines that you have upgraded from NT 4 Workstation to Windows 2000 Professional. Each machine has dual Pentium III 400MHz processors because the machines are used for high-end AutoCAD and CAD drawing applications. After the upgrade, users tell you that these machines are running drawing applications much more slowly than they did in NT 4. What should you do?

○ a. Use Device Manager to install ACPI-compliant drivers for the second processor in each machine.

○ b. During startup, press F8. Then install the SMP-compliant drivers for the second processor in each machine.

○ c. Use Device Manager to install the SMP-compliant drivers for the second processor in each machine.

○ d. Double the amount of memory in each machine.

○ e. Use Device Manager to enable the AGP bridge controller in each of the machines.

Answer c is correct. The SMP-compliant drivers for the second processor in each machine have not been installed. Drivers for a second processor are SMP compliant, not necessarily ACPI compliant; therefore, Answer a is incorrect. You do not need the F8 startup menu for this scenario, nor does this question have anything to do with adding memory or enabling AGP bridge controllers; therefore, Answers b, d, and e are incorrect.

Question 2

You have eight Windows 2000 Professional computers in your company's Art department. They all have built-in USB controllers. You install a USB tablet-pointing device on each machine. You also install the manufacturer's 32-bit tablet software on each machine. A tablet icon shows up in the Control Panel, but none of the tablets work. You examine Device Manager and see no device conflicts. What do you need to do to get the USB tablets to work?

○ a. Enable the USB ports in the system BIOS and then reinstall the USB tablet device drivers.

○ b. Enable the USB root hub controller and then reinstall the USB tablet device drivers.

○ c. Disable USB error detection for the USB root hub controller and then enable the USB tablet device in each machine's hardware profile.

○ d. Reinstall the USB tablet device drivers and then disable USB error detection.

Answer a is the correct answer. Answer b is incorrect because you do not need a USB root hub controller in order for these devices to work properly. Answer c is incorrect because disabling error detection for a USB root hub controller is also irrelevant to this question. Answer d is incorrect because reinstalling the device drivers and then disabling USB error detection makes no sense because you would always attempt to disable error detection prior to reinstalling the drivers.

Question 3

As your company's network administrator, you purchase a USB-based ISDN terminal adapter for a Windows 2000 Professional laptop. You plug it in to the USB port and are surprised when Plug and Play fails to detect the device. You test the adapter on a Windows 2000 desktop machine at your office, and Plug and Play detects the adapter with no difficulty. You have examined Device Manager on the laptop, and there are no device conflicts. You need this adapter to work with the laptop because you travel frequently. What should you do?

○ a. Turn off the laptop. Plug in the adapter and restart the machine.

○ b. Contact the hardware manufacturer to get an upgrade for the Plug and Play BIOS on the laptop.

○ c. Use Device Manager to enable the USB root hub in the current hardware profile.

○ d. Use Device Manager to enable the USB host controller in the current hardware profile.

Answer b is correct. Answer a is not a good choice because you have essentially already tried this, and it did not work. Answers c and d deal with a USB root hub and USB host controller, neither of which is needed to get this ISDN adapter to work properly. All that is really needed is a BIOS upgrade so that your USB support is current and can accommodate the new ISDN adapter.

Question 4

You have Windows 2000 Professional installed on six machines that are all equipped with network cards and static IP addresses. Setup detected and installed a 10/100Mbps unshielded twisted pair (UTP)-only NIC on Workstation 3 and Workstation 5, and it detected and installed a 10Mbps BNC/UTP combination NIC on the other four machines. You accepted the default settings for the network cards on all six machines. All six machines are connected to a 10/100Mbps switch that uses Category 5 UTP cable. Now only Workstation 3 and Workstation 5 can talk to each other on the network, but you need all the machines to be able to communicate with each other. What should you do?

- ❍ a. Configure the 10/100Mbps NICs to transmit at the 10Mbps rate.
- ❍ b. Configure the 10/100Mbps switch to transmit at only the 100Mbps rate.
- ❍ c. Change the BNC/UTP combination NICs so that they use the BNC transceiver setting only.
- ❍ d. Change the BNC/UTP combination NICs so that they use the UTP transceiver setting only.

Answer d is correct. All devices were detected, and the switch allows for cards at different speeds to communicate; therefore, the problem is most likely a transceiver setting—the BNC cards are using BNC. Changing the transmission rates would not help if the cards were still using different transceiver settings. Therefore Answers a, b, and c are incorrect.

Question 5

You install Windows 2000 Professional on a computer at home. You create a new dial-up connection to connect to your company's RAS server. You configure the connection to use both of your external modems and to use Multilink to bind the modems together. You start the dial-up connection and connect to the RAS server. You notice that only one of the modems is connected to the RAS server. What should you do to get both modems to successfully connect to the RAS server?

○ a. Configure the dial-up connection to use a Serial Line Internet Protocol (SLIP) connection instead of a PPP connection.

○ b. Replace your modems with new ones that support Multilink and ACPI.

○ c. Configure the company's RAS server to accept Multilink connections.

○ d. Grant your user account Multilink permission on the company's RAS server.

Answer c is correct. For Multilink to work, not only must the client have Multilink set up properly, but the RAS server must allow Multilink connections. Answer a is incorrect because SLIP connections are used to connect to Unix servers. Answer b is incorrect because the operating system, not the modems, needs to support Multilink. Answer d is incorrect because until the RAS server is configured to accept Multilink connections, it allows only one of the modems to connect at a time.

Question 6

Your Windows 2000 Professional computer has a 33.6Kbps built-in modem. You've just installed a new 56Kbps Industry Standard Architecture (ISA) modem. You want your computer to use only the 56Kbps modem. When you start up the computer, you notice in Device Manager that the two devices are in conflict with one another. What change should you make? (On the exam, a question like this could be multiple choice or drag and drop, so be prepared.)

○ a. Disable the 33.6Kbps modem in Device Manager and reinstall the 56Kbps modem.

○ b. Remove the 33.6Kbps modem in Device Manager and reinstall the 56Kbps modem.

○ c. No action is required; just reboot the computer, and Plug and Play will detect the device.

○ d. Remove both modems in Device Manager. Reboot into Safe Mode and then reinstall the 56Kbps modem.

Answer a is correct. Disabling the built-in 33.6Kbps modem prevents it from being re-enabled upon startup. Removing the 33.6Kbps modem in Device Manager produces an undesirable result: redetection of the device at system startup; therefore, Answer b is incorrect. You know that some action is required to fix this problem; therefore, Answer c is incorrect. Booting into Safe Mode is not going to help in this situation; therefore, Answer d is incorrect.

Question 7

You attach an IrDA transceiver to a serial port on a Windows 2000 machine. What step should you take to correctly install the device?

○ a. Use Device Manager.

○ b. Restart the computer and let Plug and Play detect the device.

○ c. Use the Add/Remove Hardware Wizard.

○ d. Use the Wireless Link icon in the Control Panel.

Answer c is correct. You must install an external IrDA device attached to a serial port by using the Add/Remove Hardware Wizard. You can use Device Manager to view port settings, but you must use the Add/Remove Hardware Wizard to add new hardware; therefore, Answer a is incorrect. Only internal IrDA devices are detected during Windows 2000 Setup or at the next system reboot; therefore, Answer b is incorrect. The Wireless Link icon is of use to you only *after* the device is correctly installed; therefore, Answer d is incorrect.

Question 8

You have replaced the network card on a computer running Windows 2000 Professional. The new card uses a different driver than the original network card. What utility should you use to ensure that the device driver for the original card is removed from the system's hard disk?

○ a. Device Manager

○ b. Add/Remove Programs

○ c. Network and Dial-up Connections

○ d. The Add/Remove Hardware Wizard

○ e. The network icon in the Control Panel

Answer d is correct. You must use the Add/Remove Hardware Wizard to make certain that the network card drivers that are no longer in use are completely removed from the hard disk. Answer a is incorrect because Device Manager would allow you to remove the device, but it would not remove the drivers from disk. Answer b is incorrect because Add/Remove Programs is not used to remove devices and their related drivers. Answer c is incorrect because Network and Dial-up Connections can be used to disable a network connection, but it has no functionality to allow you to remove a device and its drivers from disk. Answer e is incorrect because the Network icon in the Control Panel has the same limitation as the Network and Dial-Up Connections window.

Question 9

> You need to tell Windows 2000 users in your company how to connect to shared IPP printers on the network and how to manage their own print jobs by using a Web browser. The printers are all shared from a single Windows 2000 server named **PrintBoss** on the network. What is the correct syntax for the URL users should use in their browsers to make this type of connection?
>
> ○ a. ftp://PrintBoss/Printers
> ○ b. ipp://PrintBoss/Printers
> ○ c. http://PrintBoss/Printers
> ○ d. http://PrintBoss

Answer c is correct. The Windows 2000 Server machine that is the print server has IIS installed and a default virtual directory configured using the alias Printers. The clients and the print server use the Web service to communicate by using IPP, so the correct URL address to type in is http://servername/Printers. The server name is PrintBoss, and the virtual directory name is Printers. Answer a is incorrect because you cannot use FTP for IPP. Answer b is incorrect because IPP is not a network transport protocol and it cannot be used as such. Answer d is incorrect because the http://servername address alone only connects you to the default IIS Web site for that comp-uter.

Question 10

As your company's systems administrator, you want to set up multiple-monitor support for 10 Windows 2000 Professional computers. The computers are older Pentium II 366MHz machines with 256MB RAM each. You install an Extended Industry Standard Architecture (EISA) video display adapter card into each computer as the second video adapter. When you restart one of the computers and attempt to configure multiple-display support, Windows 2000 recognizes only one video adapter. What is the reason for this?

- ○ a. You must use a multiple-output video display adapter.
- ○ b. The multiple-monitor feature is supported only in Windows 2000 Server and Windows XP Professional.
- ○ c. The multiple-monitor feature supports only PCI and AGP video display adapters.
- ○ d. You must first install multiple-monitor support from the Add/Remove Programs applet in the Control Panel.

Answer c is correct because the multiple-monitor feature supports only PCI and AGP video display adapter cards. Answer a is incorrect because you do not have to use a multiple-output video display adapter, although that is an option. Answer b is incorrect because the multiple-monitor feature is supported by all editions of Windows 2000 and by Windows XP Professional. Answer d is incorrect because there is no software component to install for multiple-monitor support.

Need to Know More?

 Microsoft Corporation. *Microsoft Windows 2000 Professional Resource Kit*. Redmond, Washington: Microsoft Press, 2000. This book has invaluable information on installing, managing, and troubleshooting hardware devices.

 Boyce, Jim. *Microsoft Windows 2000 Professional Installation and Configuration Handbook*. Indianapolis: Que Publishing, 2000. This handbook focuses on installing and troubleshooting Windows 2000 Professional. It offers authoritative, easy-to-follow overviews and critical step-by-step processes for difficult tasks.

 Stinson, Craig, and Siechert, Carl. *Running Microsoft Windows 2000 Professional*. Redmond, Washington: Microsoft Press, 2000. This guidebook to Windows 2000 Professional is a good source for information on configuring devices and managing hardware devices.

 To find more information, search the TechNet CD (or its online version, through www.microsoft.com) and/or the *Windows 2000 Professional Resource Kit* CD, using the keywords device, hardware, driver update, driver signing, APM, ACPI, and Device Manager.

Implementing, Managing, and Troubleshooting Disk Drives and Volumes

Terms you'll need to understand:

✓ Basic versus dynamic disks
✓ Partitions and logical drives
✓ Simple, spanned, and striped volumes
✓ **diskperf.exe**
✓ File allocation table (FAT) and FAT16
✓ FAT32
✓ NT File System (NTFS) 5
✓ **convert.exe**
✓ Mounted drives or mount points
✓ Disk quotas and NTFS compression

Techniques you'll need to master:

✓ Using the Disk Management and Performance tools
✓ Using the Disk Cleanup Wizard and Disk Defragmenter
✓ Selecting a file system for Windows 2000
✓ Using **convert.exe** to convert a FAT partition to NTFS 5
✓ Establishing and managing disk quotas
✓ Managing NTFS compressed files and folders
✓ Using Device Manager to manage tape devices and DVD drives

Data storage is critical to any computer operating system, and Windows 2000 Professional is no exception. In this chapter, you will learn the differences between basic and dynamic disks and how dynamic disks support extended features, such as spanned volumes and striped volumes, that are not supported by basic disks. You'll learn about disk troubleshooting techniques, how to detect and repair disk problems, and how to use the Disk Defragmenter utility in Windows 2000. You will also learn about the file systems that Windows 2000 supports and how to modify local drive letters for disk volumes. You'll see how disk quotas enable you to set restrictions for disk storage on a per-user basis and how you can use NTFS data compression to save precious storage space by compressing files. This chapter also touches on managing tape backup devices and DVD devices.

Hard Disk Management

The following sections discuss how to manage and troubleshoot hard disks in Windows 2000 Professional. They look at options for creating partitions, formatting partitions, and disk administration that are available in Windows 2000. In addition, the following sections uncover features of the new disk storage types. Windows 2000 supports two new disk configuration types: basic storage and dynamic storage. The following sections also compare the basic and dynamic storage types and describe how to configure and manage disks that have been initialized with either type of storage.

Basic Disks

A Windows 2000 *basic disk*, which is similar to the disk configuration in NT, is a physical disk with primary and extended partitions. As long as you use the FAT file system (discussed in detail in the section "Files Systems Supported in Windows 2000," later in this chapter), Windows 2000, Windows NT, Windows 9x, and DOS can access basic disks. You can create up to three primary partitions and one extended partition on a basic disk, or you can create four primary partitions. You can create a single extended partition with logical drives on a basic disk. You *cannot* extend a basic disk.

Basic disks store their configuration information in the master boot record (MBR), which is stored on the first sector of the disk. The configuration of a basic disk consists of the partition information on the disk. Basic fault-tolerant sets inherited from Windows NT 4 are based on these simple partitions, but they extend the configuration with some extra partition relationship information, which is stored on the first track of the disk.

Basic disks may contain spanned volumes (volume sets), mirrored volumes (mirror sets), striped volumes (stripe sets), and Redundant Array of Independent Disks (RAID)-5 volumes (that is, stripe sets with parity) that are created by using Windows NT 4 or earlier. These kinds of volumes are covered in the section "Basic Volumes," later in this chapter.

Dynamic Disks

A Windows 2000 *dynamic disk* is a physical disk that does not use partitions or logical drives. Instead, a single partition is created that includes the entire disk, which can then be divided into separate volumes. Also, dynamic disks do not have the same constraints as basic disks. For example, a dynamic disk can be resized on-the-fly without requiring a reboot. Dynamic disks are associated with *disk groups*, which are disks that are managed as collections, which helps to organize dynamic disks. All dynamic disks in a computer are members of the same disk group. Each disk in a disk group stores replicas of the same configuration data. This configuration data is stored in a 1MB region at the end of each dynamic disk.

Dynamic disks can contain any of the types of volumes discussed later in this chapter, in the section "Dynamic Volumes." You can extend a volume on a dynamic disk. Dynamic disks can contain an unlimited number of volumes, so you are not restricted to four volumes per disk, as you are with basic disks. Regardless of the type of file system, only Windows 2000 computers can *directly* access dynamic volumes. However, computers that are not running Windows 2000 can access the dynamic volumes remotely when they are connected to shared folders over a network.

Comparing Basic Disks and Dynamic Disks

When you install Windows 2000, the system automatically configures the existing hard disks as basic disks. Windows 2000 does *not* support dynamic disks on laptops, and if you're using an older (non-laptop) machine that is not Advanced Configuration and Power Interface (ACPI) compliant, the Upgrade to Dynamic Disk option (discussed in the section "Dynamic Volumes," later in this chapter) is not available. Dynamic disks have some additional limitations. You can install Windows 2000 on a dynamic volume that you converted from a basic disk, but you can't extend either the system or the boot partition. (Volumes and upgrading are covered in the section "Upgrading Basic Disks to Dynamic Disks," later in this chapter.) Any troubleshooting tools that cannot read the dynamic Disk Management database work only on basic disks.

Basic and dynamic disks are Windows 2000's way of looking at hard disk configuration. If you're migrating to Windows 2000 from NT, the dynamic disk concept might seem odd in the beginning, but when you understand the differences between the two types of disks, you'll see that working with dynamic disks is not complicated. You can format partitions with FAT16, FAT32, or NTFS on a basic or a dynamic disk. FAT and NTFS are discussed in the section "File Systems Supported in Windows 2000," later in this chapter. Table 8.1 compares the terms used with basic and dynamic disks.

Table 8.1   Terms Used with Basic and Dynamic Disks

Basic Disks	Dynamic Disks
Active partition	Active volume
Extended partition	Volume and unallocated space
Logical drive	Simple volume
Mirror set	Mirrored volume (Windows 2000 Server and Windows Server 2003 only)
Primary partition	Simple volume
Stripe set	Striped volume
Stripe set with parity	RAID-5 volume (Windows 2000 Server and Windows Server 2003 only)
System and boot partitions	System and boot volumes
Volume set	Spanned volumes

Upgrading Disks

In Windows 2000 (Professional and Server Editions), all disks start out as basic disks. Only users who are members of the Administrators group have the authority to convert a basic disk to a dynamic disk. Dynamic disks support striped volumes and spanned volumes, which cannot be created by using basic disks under Windows 2000.

Upgrading Basic Disks to Dynamic Disks

You use Windows 2000's Disk Management tool to upgrade a basic disk to a dynamic disk. To access Disk Management, you select Start, Programs, Administrative Tools, Computer Management. Alternatively, you can simply right-click the My Computer icon on the desktop and then select Manage. You can find Disk Management under Storage.

For the upgrade to succeed, any disks to be upgraded must contain at least 1MB of unallocated space. Disk Management automatically reserves this space when creating partitions or volumes on a disk, but disks with partitions or volumes created by other operating systems may not have this space available. (This space can exist even if it is not visible in Disk Management.) Before you upgrade disks, you need to close any programs that are running on those disks.

To change or convert a basic disk to a dynamic disk, you perform the following steps:

1. Open the Disk Management tool.

2. Right-click the basic disk you want to change to a dynamic disk and then click Upgrade to Dynamic Disk.

When you upgrade a basic disk to a dynamic disk, you do not need to reboot. However, if you upgrade your startup disk or upgrade a volume or partition, you must restart the computer in order for the change to take effect. The good news is that you do not need to select a special command such as Commit Changes Now before you restart the computer or close the Disk Management tool.

When you upgrade a basic disk to a dynamic disk, any existing partitions on the basic disk become simple volumes on the dynamic disk. Any existing mirrored volumes, striped volumes, RAID-5 volumes, or spanned volumes become dynamic mirrored volumes, dynamic striped volumes, dynamic RAID-5 volumes, or dynamic spanned volumes, respectively.

You cannot dual-boot to another operating system if you upgrade a basic disk to a dynamic disk. This typically isn't an issue for servers. However, it's something to consider for Windows 2000 Professional machines. After you upgrade a basic disk to a dynamic disk, you cannot change the dynamic volumes back to partitions. Instead, you must delete all dynamic volumes on the disk and then use the Revert to Basic Disk command.

 NOTE Upgrading to a dynamic disk is a one-way process. Yes, you can convert a dynamic disk with volumes back to a basic disk, but when you do, you lose all your data. Major downside! If you find yourself needing to do this, you should first save your data, convert the disk to basic, and then restore your data.

Because the upgrade from basic to dynamic occurs per physical disk, all volumes on a physical disk must be either basic or dynamic. Again, you do not need to restart your computer when you upgrade from a basic to a dynamic disk. The only times you must restart your computer are when you upgrade a startup disk and when you upgrade a volume or partition. See Figure 8.1 for the Disk Management node.

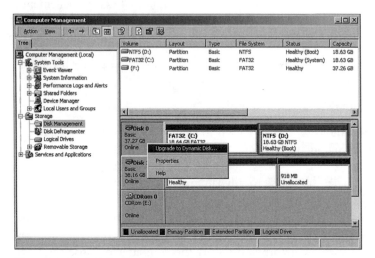

Figure 8.1 The Disk Management node of the Computer Management console.

Converting Dynamic Disks to Basic Disks

You must remove all volumes from a dynamic disk before you can change it back to a basic disk. After you change a dynamic disk back to a basic disk, you can create only partitions and logical drives on that disk. After a dynamic disk is upgraded, it cannot contain partitions or logical drives, nor can Microsoft operating systems prior to Windows 2000 access it.

To convert a dynamic disk to a basic disk, you perform the following steps:

1. Open Disk Management.

2. Right-click the dynamic disk you want to change back to a basic disk and then click Revert to Basic Disk.

Moving Disks to Another Computer

To move disks to another computer, you perform the following steps:

1. Before you disconnect the disks, look in Disk Management and make sure the status of the volumes on the disks is healthy. If the status is not healthy, repair the volumes before you move the disks.

2. Turn off the computer, remove the physical disks, and then install the physical disks on the other computer. Restart the computer that contains the disks you moved.

3. Open Disk Management.

4. Click Action and then click Rescan Disks.

5. Right-click any disk marked Foreign, click Import Foreign Disks, and then follow the instructions onscreen.

Guidelines for Relocating Disks

Every time you remove or import disks to a computer, you must click Action, click Rescan Disks, and then verify that the disk information is correct. Aside from following steps 1 through 5 in the section "Moving Disks to Another Computer," earlier in this chapter, you can choose which disks from the group you want to add by clicking Select Disk; you do not have to import all the new disks.

The Disk Management tool describes the condition of the volumes on the disks before you import them. You should review this information carefully. That way, if there are any problems, you will know what will happen to each volume on these disks after you have imported them. After you import a dynamic disk from another computer, you can see and use any existing volumes on that disk.

Reactivating a Missing or Offline Disk

A dynamic disk may become missing when it is corrupted, powered down, or disconnected. Only dynamic disks can be reactivated—basic disks cannot. Sorry!

To reactivate a missing or offline disk, you perform the following steps:

1. Open Disk Management.

2. Right-click the disk marked Missing or Offline, and then click Reactivate Disk. The disk should be marked Online after the disk is reactivated.

Basic Volumes

Basic volumes include partitions and logical drives, as well as volumes created using Windows NT 4 or earlier, such as volume sets, stripe sets, mirror sets, and stripe sets with parity. In Windows 2000, these volumes have been renamed spanned volumes, striped volumes, mirrored volumes, and RAID-5 volumes, respectively. You can create basic volumes on basic disks only.

Spanned Volumes on Basic Disks

Disk Management offers limited support of spanned volumes on basic disks. You can delete spanned volumes, but you cannot create new spanned volumes or extend spanned volumes on basic disks. You can create new spanned volumes only on dynamic disks. Deleting a spanned volume deletes all the data contained in the volume as well as the partitions that make up the spanned volume. You can delete only entire spanned volumes. Disk Management renames all existing volume sets to spanned volumes. These spanned volumes reside only on basic disks. In Windows 2000, you can delete spanned volumes created using Windows NT 4 or earlier.

Striped Volumes on Basic Disks

Disk Management offers limited support of striped volumes on basic disks. You can delete striped volumes, but you cannot create new striped volumes on basic disks. You can create new striped volumes on dynamic disks only. Deleting a striped volume deletes all the data contained in the volume as well as the partitions that make up the volume. You can delete only entire striped volumes. Disk Management renames all stripe sets to striped volumes. These striped volumes reside only on basic disks. In Windows 2000 you can delete striped volumes created using Windows NT 4 or earlier.

Partitions and Logical Drives on Basic Disks

You can create primary partitions, extended partitions, and logical drives only on basic disks. You should create partitions instead of dynamic volumes if your computer also runs a down-level Microsoft operating system.

Partitions and logical drives can reside only on basic disks. You can create up to four primary partitions on a basic disk or up to three primary partitions and one extended partition. You can use the free space in an extended partition to create multiple logical drives.

 You should create basic volumes, such as partitions or logical drives, on basic disks if you want computers running Windows NT 4 or earlier, Windows 98 or earlier, or MS-DOS to access these volumes.

Creating or Deleting a Partition or Logical Drive

To create or delete a partition or logical drive, you perform the following steps:

1. Open Disk Management.

2. Right-click an unallocated region of a basic disk and then click Create Partition. Alternatively, you can right-click free space in an extended partition and then click Create Logical Drive. (Delete Partition should be your selection if deleting a partition is your goal.)

3. In the Create Partition Wizard (see Figure 8.2), click Next. Click Primary Partition, Extended Partition, or Logical Drive, and then follow the instructions onscreen.

If you choose to delete a partition, all data on the deleted partition or logical drive is lost. You cannot recover deleted partitions or logical drives. You cannot delete a system partition, a boot partition, or any partition that contains the active paging file.

Windows 2000 requires that all the logical drives or other volumes in an extended partition be deleted before the extended partition can be deleted.

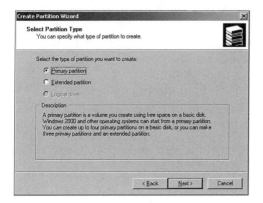

Figure 8.2 The Create Partition Wizard for a basic disk.

Dynamic Volumes

What are called *sets* (for example, mirrored sets and striped sets) in Windows NT 4 are called *volumes* (for example, mirrored volumes and striped volumes) in Windows 2000. Dynamic volumes are the only type of volume you can create on dynamic disks. With dynamic disks, unlike with basic disks, you are not limited to four volumes per disk. The only dynamic volumes on which you can install Windows 2000 are simple and mirrored volumes, and these volumes must contain partition tables (which means these volumes must be either basic or upgraded from basic to dynamic). Only computers running Windows 2000 can access dynamic volumes. The five types of dynamic volumes are simple, spanned, mirrored, striped, and RAID-5.

With Windows 2000 Professional, only three types of dynamic disk volumes are available:

➤ *Simple*—A simple volume contains disk space from one hard drive and is not considered fault tolerant in the event that it fails.

➤ *Spanned*—A spanned volume includes disk space from more than one hard drive (up to 32 physical hard drives), but it writes data to subsequent drives only as each drive fills up. Therefore, first it writes to Disk 0 until it fills up, then it writes to Disk 1 until its space is full, then it writes to Disk 2, and so on. If just *one* disk fails in the striped set, only the data contained on that failed drive is lost for the volume.

➤ *Striped*—A striped volume includes disk space from more than one hard drive (up to 32 physical hard drives), but this type of volume writes data across *all* the disks within the striped set. If just *one* disk fails in the striped set, all data is lost for the entire volume.

 Basic disks *can* contain mirrored volumes, RAID-5 volumes, and striped volumes created originally under Windows NT Server 4. However, "upgrading" from Windows NT Server 4 to Windows 2000 Professional is not supported by Microsoft. Fault-tolerant volumes are only officially supported under Windows 2000 Server products—whether they reside on basic or dynamic disks.

Simple Volumes

A *simple volume* is made up of disk space on a single physical disk. It can consist of a single area on a disk or multiple areas on a disk that are linked together.

To create a simple volume, you perform the following steps:

1. Open Disk Management.

2. Right-click the unallocated space on the dynamic disk where you want to create the simple volume and then click Create Volume.

3. In the Create Volume Wizard (see Figure 8.3), click Next, click Simple Volume, and then follow the instructions onscreen.

Here are some guidelines about simple volumes:

➤ You can create simple volumes on dynamic disks only.

➤ Simple volumes are not fault tolerant.

➤ Simple volumes cannot contain partitions or logical drives.

➤ Neither MS-DOS nor Windows operating systems other than Windows 2000 can access simple volumes.

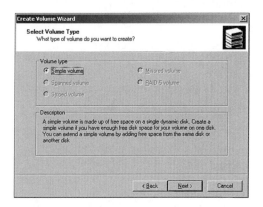

Figure 8.3   The Create Volume Wizard for a dynamic disk.

Spanned Volumes

A *spanned volume* is made up of disk space on more than one physical disk. You can add more space to a spanned volume by extending it at any time.

To create a spanned volume, you perform the following steps:

1. Open Disk Management.

2. Right-click the unallocated space on one of the dynamic disks where you want to create the spanned volume and then click Create Volume.

3. In the Create Volume Wizard, click Next, click Spanned Volume, and then follow the instructions onscreen.

Here are some guidelines about spanned volumes:

➤ You can create spanned volumes on dynamic disks only.

➤ You need at least two dynamic disks to create a spanned volume.

➤ You can extend a spanned volume onto a maximum of 32 dynamic disks.

➤ Spanned volumes cannot be mirrored or striped.

➤ Spanned volumes are not fault tolerant.

Extending a Simple or Spanned Volume

To extend a simple or spanned volume, you perform the following steps:

1. Open Disk Management.

2. Right-click the simple or spanned volume you want to extend, click Extend Volume, and then follow the instructions onscreen.

Here are some guidelines about extending a simple or spanned volume:

➤ You can extend a simple or spanned volume only if it contains *no* file system or if it is formatted using NTFS. You cannot extend simple or spanned volumes formatted using FAT or FAT32.

➤ You can extend a simple volume within its original disk or onto additional disks. If you extend a simple volume across multiple disks, it becomes a *spanned volume*.

➤ After a volume is extended onto multiple disks (that is, when it is spanned), you cannot mirror or stripe it.

➤ After a spanned volume is extended, no portion of it can be deleted without the entire spanned volume being deleted.

➤ You can extend a simple or extended volume only if the volume was created as a dynamic volume. You cannot extend a simple or extended volume that was upgraded from basic to dynamic.

➤ You can extend simple and spanned volumes on dynamic disks onto a maximum of 32 dynamic disks.

 You cannot extend a system volume or boot volume, nor can you extend striped, mirrored, or RAID-5 volumes.

Striped Volumes

A *striped volume* stores data in stripes on two or more physical disks. Data in a striped volume is allocated alternately and evenly (in stripes) to the disks of the striped volume. Striped volumes can substantially improve the speed of access to data on disk. In addition, you can create striped volumes on both Windows 2000 Professional and Windows 2000 Server machines.

To create a striped volume, you perform the following steps:

1. Open Disk Management.

2. Right-click unallocated space on one of the dynamic disks where you want to create the striped volume and then click Create Volume.

3. In the Create Volume Wizard, click Next, click Striped Volume, and then follow the instructions onscreen.

Here are some guidelines about striped volumes:

➤ You need at least two physical, dynamic disks to create a striped volume.

➤ You can create a striped volume onto a maximum of 32 disks.

➤ Striped volumes are not fault tolerant and cannot be extended or mirrored.

RAID-5 Volumes

You can create RAID-5 volumes only on Windows 2000 Server machines.

 NOTE Mirrored and RAID-5 volumes are available only on computers that are running Windows 2000 Server. Windows 2000 Professional computers can use basic and dynamic disks but cannot host software-based fault-tolerant disk configurations such as mirror sets and stripe sets with parity. You can, however, use a computer that is running Windows 2000 Professional to create mirrored and RAID-5 volumes on a remote computer that is running Windows 2000 Server.

When to Use Dynamic Disks and Dynamic Volumes

You can use dynamic disks and dynamic volumes in specific circumstances; you need to be familiar with when you can and cannot utilize them.

When You Are Installing Windows 2000

If you create a dynamic volume from unallocated space on a dynamic disk, you cannot install Windows 2000 on that volume. This setup limitation occurs because Windows 2000 Setup recognizes only dynamic volumes that contain partition tables. Partition tables appear in basic volumes and in dynamic volumes only when they have been upgraded from basic to dynamic. If you create a new dynamic volume on a dynamic disk, that new dynamic volume does not contain a partition table.

When You Are Extending a Volume

If you upgrade a basic volume to dynamic (by upgrading the basic disk to a dynamic one), you can install Windows 2000 on that volume, but you cannot extend the volume. The limitation on extending volumes occurs because the boot volume, which contains the Windows 2000 files, cannot be part of a spanned volume. If you extend a simple volume that contains a partition table (that is, a volume that was upgraded from basic to dynamic), Windows 2000 Setup recognizes the spanned volume but cannot install to it because the boot volume cannot be part of a spanned volume.

You can extend volumes that you created only after you convert the disk to a dynamic disk. You can extend volumes and make changes to disk configuration in most cases without rebooting the computer. If you want to take advantage of these features in Windows 2000—especially software fault-tolerant features—you must change or upgrade a disk from basic to dynamic status, as discussed earlier in this chapter, in the section "Upgrading Basic Disks to Dynamic Disks." You should use dynamic disks if the computer runs only Windows 2000. If you want to use more than four volumes per disk, you should create fault-tolerant volumes such as RAID-5 and mirrored volumes, or you should extend volumes onto one or more dynamic disks.

Troubleshooting Disks and Volumes

If a disk or volume fails, naturally you want to repair it as soon as possible to avoid losing data. The Disk Management console tool makes it easy to locate problems quickly. In the Status column of the list view, you can view the status of a disk or volume. The status also appears in the graphical view of each disk or volume.

Diagnosing Problems

To diagnose disk and/or volume problems, you perform the following steps:

1. Open Add/Remove Hardware in the Control Panel. Click Next.

2. Click Add/Troubleshoot a Device and then click Next. Windows 2000 tries to detect new Plug and Play devices.

3. Choose the device you want to diagnose and fix and then click Next.

4. Follow the instructions onscreen.

Monitoring Disk Performance

The *Windows 2000 Performance console* (which is called Performance Monitor in previous versions of Windows) has two parts: System Monitor and Performance Logs and Alerts. With System Monitor, you can collect and view real-time data about disk performance and activity in graph, histogram, or report form. Performance Logs and Alerts allows you to configure logs to record performance data and to set system alerts to notify you when a specified counter's value is above or below a defined threshold.

To open Performance, you perform the following steps:

1. Select Start, Settings, Control Panel.

2. In the Control Panel, double-click Administrative Tools and then double-click Performance. You can use System Monitor within Performance to monitor disk performance.

diskperf.exe

`diskperf.exe` controls the types of counters that you can view by using System Monitor. You must enable `diskperf.exe` before you can monitor logical disks. By default, the system is set to collect *physical* drive data. Logical drive data is *not* collected by default; you must enable it specifically with `diskperf.exe`. Table 8.2 lists the available `diskperf.exe` parameters.

Table 8.2 diskperf.exe Parameters	
Parameter	**Description**
-y	Sets the system to start both physical and logical disk performance counters when the system is restarted.

(continued)

Table 8.2   diskperf.exe Parameters *(continued)*

Parameter	Description
-yd	Enables disk performance counters that are used for measuring performance of physical drives when the system is restarted. This is the default setting.
-yv	Enables disk performance counters that are used for measuring performance of logical drives when the system is restarted.
-n	Sets the system to not use any disk performance counters when the system is restarted.
-nd	Disables disk performance counters for physical drives when the system is restarted.
-nv	Disables disk performance counters for logical drives when the system is restarted.
computername	Specifies the computer on which to set disk performance counter use. If a computer name is not specified, the local computer is assumed.

Detecting and Repairing Disk Errors

In pre-Windows 2000 operating systems ScanDisk detects and fixes disk errors. In Windows 2000 you can use the Error-Checking tool to check for file system errors and bad sectors on a hard disk.

To run the Error-Checking tool, you perform the following steps:

1. Open My Computer and right-click the local disk you want to check.
2. Select Properties.
3. Select the Tools tab.
4. Under Error-Checking, click Check Now.
5. Under Check Disk Options, select the Automatically Fix File System Errors check box if you want to enable this option. (See Figure 8.4 for the Check Disk dialog box.)
6. Under Check Disk Options, select the Scan for and Attempt Recovery of Bad Sectors check box if you want to enable this option.
7. Click the Start button to launch the error-checking process.

All files must be closed for the Error-Checking tool to run. The volume being checked cannot run any other tasks while the Error-Checking tool is running. If the volume is currently in use, a message asks if you want to reschedule the disk checking for the next time you restart the system. If you click Yes, the next time you restart the system, Error-Checking runs. If the volume is formatted as NTFS, Windows 2000 automatically logs all file transactions, replaces bad clusters, and stores copies of key information for all files on the NTFS volume.

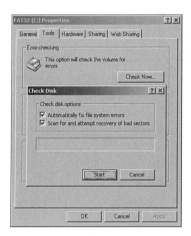

Figure 8.4 The Check Disk dialog box.

Using Disk Defragmenter

Disk Defragmenter rearranges files, programs, and unused space on a computer's hard disk(s), allowing programs to run faster and files to open more quickly. Putting the pieces of files and programs in a more contiguous space on disk reduces the time the operating system needs to open a requested item.

To run Disk Defragmenter, you perform the following steps:

1. Select Start, Programs, Accessories, System Tools and then click Disk Defragmenter.

2. Select which disk(s) you would like to defragment and any additional options you would like.

3. Click the Defragment button to begin the defragmentation process on the disk(s) that you selected.

Defragmentation and the NTFS Master File Table

Files are not moved to the beginning of NTFS volumes after defragmentation is complete. On NTFS volumes Windows 2000 reserves a portion of the free space for a system file called the *master file table* (MFT). The MFT is where Windows stores all the information it needs to retrieve files from the volume. Windows stores part of the MFT at the beginning of the volume. Windows reserves the MFT for exclusive use, so Disk Defragmenter cannot move files to the beginning of NTFS volumes.

Using the Disk Cleanup Wizard

The *Disk Cleanup Wizard* helps free up space on a hard drive by searching the drive(s) and then showing a list of temporary files, Internet cache files, and unnecessary program files that can safely be deleted. You can instruct Disk Cleanup to delete none, some, or all of those files.

To use the Disk Cleanup Wizard, you perform the following steps:

1. Select Start, Programs, Accessories, System Tools.

2. Click the Disk Cleanup icon.

3. Select the drive letter that you want to clean and click the OK button.

The Disk Cleanup Wizard calculates how much disk space can be made available by analyzing the drive for unneeded files and seldom-used programs. When the wizard completes its calculations, the Disk Cleanup for the `<drive_letter:>` dialog box appears. You can then accept, modify, or reject the list of files that the wizard thinks you no longer need. You also have the option of uninstalling programs and uninstalling Windows 2000 components. After you have reviewed and worked with all the files and programs to be deleted and/or uninstalled, you can click the OK button to have the wizard remove those items or click Cancel to leave all the existing files and programs as they are.

File Systems Supported in Windows 2000

The *Compact Disc File System* (CDFS) provides full support for CD-based media in Windows 2000. Although Windows 2000 does not support *High Performance File System* (HPFS), it fully supports the FAT, FAT32, and NTFS file systems.

FAT and FAT32

Windows 2000 provides full support for the FAT file system (also known as FAT16) and FAT32, with the following conditions or specifications:

➤ Preexisting FAT32 partitions up to 127GB mount and are supported in Windows 2000.

➤ Windows 2000 allows you to create new FAT32 volumes of only 32GB or less.

➤ You can install Windows 2000 onto a FAT, FAT32, or NTFS partition. Keep in mind, though, that you have *no* local security for Windows 2000 unless you place the operating system on an NTFS partition.

➤ If you initially install Windows 2000 to a FAT or FAT32 partition and then later used the convert.exe utility to convert the partition to NTFS, default security settings are not applied.

The New Flavor of NTFS: NTFS 5

Windows 2000 contains a new version of NTFS—NTFS 5—which is Windows 2000's native file system. This newest version of NTFS includes capabilities such as much more granular file permissions than with NTFS 4—including disk quotas, Encrypting File System (EFS), and a number of other useful features. (Disk quotas are covered in the section "Disk Quotas," later in this chapter.)

When you install Windows 2000, existing NTFS volumes are automatically upgraded to NTFS 5. No options are presented to choose NTFS 5 during the installation. The existing volumes are simply converted to NTFS 5, whether you want this to happen.

When you install Windows 2000 to an NTFS partition, part of the setup process is to apply default security settings to the system files and folders located on the boot partition (essentially the \WINNT and \Program Files folder structures).

All local NTFS volumes, including removable media, are upgraded to the new version of NTFS. This occurs after you restart the computer the first time after the graphical portion of Setup. Any NTFS volumes that are removed or powered off during the installation or upgrade process are upgraded automatically when those drives are mounted. If, during the installation, the system detects a version of Windows NT that is earlier than NT 4 Service Pack 4 (SP4), you see a warning message indicating that an earlier version of Windows NT was found; the message also states that Windows NT will not be accessible if you continue. Windows NT *can* be upgraded without SPs. However, if you want to create a new installation of Windows 2000 and dual-boot with Windows NT 4, you see the warning.

 If you want to configure a computer to run Windows NT 4 and Windows 2000, you need to upgrade the version of Windows NT 4.0 to SP4 or later. There is an updated **ntfs.sys** driver in Windows NT 4.0 SP4 and later SPs that allows Windows NT 4.0 to read from and write to NTFS 5 volumes in Windows 2000. If you expect to dual-boot Windows 98 and Windows 2000, you need to remember that Windows 98 can read only FAT and FAT32 file systems.

Converting from One File System to Another

Windows 2000 supports converting from one file system to another, with some special caveats and limitations that you need to be well aware of, as discussed in the following sections.

Reality: Converting a FAT Partition to an NTFS Partition

Let's say that you want to convert drive D: to NTFS, from either FAT or FAT32. No problem! From the command line (cmd.exe), you enter the command convert d: /fs:ntfs. This command is one-way and is not reversible. If the FAT or FAT32 partition is the system partition, the conversion takes place when the machine reboots next.

After the conversion, NTFS file permissions are set to Full Control for the Everyone group. However, if you install Windows 2000 directly to NTFS, the permissions for the \WINNT folder and \Program Files folder structures are secured by default.

Myth: Converting an NTFS Partition to a FAT Partition

You cannot convert an NTFS partition to a FAT partition. A simple conversion using the convert.exe command is not possible. The only course of action if you want to keep the data is to back up all the data on the drive. Then, you can use the Disk Management tool to reformat the disk to the flavor of FAT you prefer and restore your data backup to your newly formatted disk.

Reapplying Default NTFS Permissions

You might need or want to reapply the default NTFS permissions to the system boot partition if you have changed them or if you have never applied them to begin with (because you converted the boot partition to NTFS after installation). To reapply the default NTFS permissions, you use the seced-it.exe utility, which comes with Windows 2000, from the command prompt. The computer must still be bootable to Windows 2000 for this to work.

Assigning, Changing, and Removing Drive Letters

Changing local drive letters for disk volumes and CD-ROM drives is not easy under Windows 9x. Under Windows 2000, however, changing drive letters is a snap. You can even completely remove a drive letter designation from a volume if you wish. The Disk Management MMC snap-in is a very powerful tool for managing a computer's storage devices.

To assign, change, or remove a drive letter, you perform the following steps:

1. Open Disk Management.

2. Right-click a partition, logical drive, or volume, and then click Change Drive Letter and Path.

3. Do one of the following:

   ➤ *To assign a drive letter*—Right-click the target volume and select Add, click the drive letter you want to use, and then click OK.

   ➤ *To change a drive letter*—Right-click the target volume and select Edit, click the drive letter you want to use, and then click OK.

   ➤ *To remove a drive letter*—Right-click the target volume and then select Remove.

An old "gotcha" still applies: You need to be careful when assigning drive letters because many MS-DOS and Windows applications refer to a specific drive letter, especially at installation. For example, the path environment variable shows specific drive letters in conjunction with program names.

You can use up to 24 drive letters, from c: through z:. Drive letters A: and B: are reserved for floppy disk drives. However, if you do not have a floppy disk drive B:, you can use the B: for a network drive. You cannot change the drive letter of the system volume or the boot volume.

An error message may appear when you attempt to assign a letter to a volume, a CD-ROM drive, or another removable media device, possibly because a program in the system is using it. If this happens, you need to close the program that is accessing the volume or drive and then click Change Drive Letter and Path again.

Windows 2000 allows you to statically assign drive letters on volumes, partitions, and CD-ROM drives. This means that you permanently assign a drive letter to a specific partition, volume, or CD-ROM drive. When you add a new hard disk to an existing computer system, it does not affect statically assigned drive letters. You can also mount a local drive at an empty folder on an NTFS volume by using a drive path instead of a drive letter—this is accomplished through mount points, as discussed in the next section.

Mounted Drives

Mounted drives, also known as *mount points* or *mounted volumes*, are useful for increasing a drive's size without disturbing it. For example, you could create a mount point to drive E: as C:\CompanyData, thus seeming to increase the size available on the C: partition, which would specifically allow you to store more data in C:\CompanyData than you could otherwise. Drive paths are available only on empty folders on NTFS volumes. The NTFS volumes can be basic or dynamic.

Creating a Mounted Drive

To create a mounted drive, you perform the following steps:

1. Open Disk Management.

2. Right-click the partition or volume you want to mount and then click Change Drive Letter and Path.

3. Do one of the following:

   ➤ *To mount a volume*—Select Add. Click Mount in This NTFS Folder and type the path to an empty folder on an NTFS volume, or click Browse to locate an empty folder on an NTFS volume.

   ➤ *To unmount a volume*—Select the volume and then click Remove.

When you mount a local drive volume via an empty folder on an NTFS volume, Windows 2000 assigns a drive path rather than a drive letter to the volume. Mounted drives use the drive paths rather than individual drive letters as pointers to the actual drive volumes.

To modify a drive path, you remove it and then create a new drive path, using the new location. You cannot modify the drive path directly. If you are administering a local computer, you can browse NTFS folders on that computer. If you are administering a remote computer, browsing is disabled and you must type the path to an existing NTFS folder (see Figure 8.5).

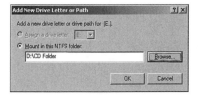

Figure 8.5 The Add New Drive Letter or Path dialog box.

The Logical Drives Tool

Logical Drives is a tool within the Computer Management snap-in that lets you manage mapped drives and local drives on a remote computer or local computer. You can change drive properties only on computers for which you are an administrator.

Viewing Drive Properties, Changing Drive Labels, and Changing Security Settings

To view drive properties, change drive labels, or change security settings, you perform the following steps:

1. Open Computer Management (Local). You can view drive properties on a remote computer as well if you want. To access a remote computer, right-click Computer Management (Local), click Connect to Another Computer, and then select the computer you want to manage.

2. In the console tree, expand the Storage node and then click Logical Drives.

3. Right-click the drive for which you want to view the properties and then click Properties.

The General tab shows the drive label, its type, the file system for which the drive is formatted, it's the drive's total capacity, how much space on the drive is used, and how much space on the drive is free (available). The Security tab shows the access permissions, audit entries, and ownership that have been set for the drive. The Security tab appears only on drives formatted to use NTFS.

Disk Quotas

Windows 2000 disk quotas track and control disk usage per user and per volume. You can apply disk quotas only to Windows 2000 NTFS volumes. Quotas are tracked for each volume, even if the volumes reside on the same physical disk. The per-user feature of quotas allows you to track every user's disk space usage, despite in which folder the user stores files. Disk quotas do not use compression to measure disk space usage, so users cannot obtain or use more space simply by compressing their own data. To enable disk quotas, you need to open the Properties dialog box for a disk, select the Quota tab, and configure the options.

When a user no longer stores data on a volume, you need to delete disk quota entries. The catch to this is that you can delete the user's quota entries only after you have removed from the volume all files that the user owns or after another user has taken ownership of the files. By default, only members of the Administrators group can view and change quota entries and settings.

You can set identical or individual disk quota limits for all user accounts that access a specific volume. Then you can use per-user disk quota entries to allow more (a fairly common scenario) or less (for those disk space hogs!) disk space to individual users when necessary.

NTFS File Compression

NTFS in Windows 2000 allows you to compress individual files and folders so that they occupy less space on the NTFS volume. Any Windows- or DOS-based program can read and write to compressed files without having to decompress them first. These files decompress when opened and recompress when closed, and NTFS handles the entire process. You can use Windows Explorer to have compressed items display in a different color than uncompressed items.

Setting the compression state (compressed or uncompressed) on a file or folder is as simple as setting a file or folder attribute. You simply right-click the object you'd like to compress/uncompress and select Properties. On the General tab, you select the Advanced button, and then you check or clear the Compress Contents to Save Disk Space check box. Finally, you click OK twice to exit both dialog boxes.

Moving and Copying Compressed Files and Folders

There is a simple method for remembering whether the original compression attribute of an object is retained or inherited when you are moving and/or copying files and folders: When you move a compressed or uncompressed file or folder from one location to another within the same NTFS volume, the original compression attribute is retained. That's it. That is the only piece of this puzzle you need to remember because in *all* other scenarios, the compression attribute is inherited from the new, or target, location.

NTFS Compression Guidelines

NTFS allocates disk space based on the *uncompressed* size of a file. If you try to copy a compressed file to an NTFS volume that has enough space for the compressed file but not the uncompressed file, you get an error message that tells you there is inadequate disk space to copy the file to the target. You need to plan ahead.

 If you attempt to copy or move a compressed file to a floppy disk, you should be prepared to get an **Insufficient disk space** error. If the uncompressed size of the file is larger than the capacity of the floppy disk, you cannot copy or move the file. You need to use a third-party compression tool, such as WinZip, before you attempt this operation.

You should make it a practice to compress only static data rather than data that frequently changes because applying or removing the compression attribute incurs system overhead. NTFS encryption and compression are mutually exclusive. You can encrypt or compress a file or folder—but you can't both encrypt and compress a file or folder. Windows 2000 does not support NTFS compression for volumes with cluster sizes larger than 4KB because of the performance degradation it would cause.

Managing Tape Backup and DVD Devices

Windows 2000 provides comprehensive control of tape devices. You can back up or restore from tape devices, enable or disable specific tapes in a library, insert and eject media, and mount and dismount media. The good news is that tape devices are no longer the exclusive media that the Windows Backup program utilizes. Backing up to tape is still very popular, though.

If a tape device is Plug and Play compliant, you can rely on Windows 2000 to detect the device and install the appropriate drivers and allocate system resources for the device. If you are using a tape device that is not Plug and Play compliant, you need to use the Add/Remove Hardware applet in the Control Panel to install the drivers and assign resources for the device. You can use Device Manager to enable, disable, or edit settings for any tape device.

Windows 2000 supports a variety of DVD drives and formats. You should check with the most recent Microsoft Hardware Compatibility List (HCL) or your hardware vendor to see if your DVD device will work with Windows 2000. (For more details on managing hardware in Windows 2000, see Chapter 7, "Implementing, Managing, and Troubleshooting Hardware Devices and Drivers.")

If the DVD device is Plug and Play compliant, you can rely on Windows 2000 to detect the device and install the appropriate drivers and allocate system resources for the device. If you are using a DVD drive that is not Plug and Play compliant, you need to use the Add/Remove Hardware applet in the Control Panel to install the drivers and assign resources for the device.

 You can control whether unsigned drivers for DVD drives and other hardware are permitted. You can make this decision in two places. If you are performing unattended installations of Windows 2000, you can add to the **Unattend.txt** file in the **[Unattended]** section the entry **DriverSigningPolicy=Ignore**. The other location where you can control whether drivers must be signed is within policy settings—either a group policy object applied to a site, domain, or OU (SDOU) or simply the local computer policy. With policy settings, you have three choices for how unsigned drivers are handled when they are encountered: ignore them, warn about them but allow their installation, and block their installation completely.

Your DVD drive needs either a hardware or software decoder to play movies, as well as Windows 2000–compatible sound and video cards with their respective drivers. Your decoder must be Windows 2000 compliant to play movies after you install Windows 2000. Most hardware decoders are Windows 2000 compliant. Most software decoders, however, need to be updated. You do not need a decoder for reading data DVDs. If no update is available, you can buy a new decoder that is Windows 2000 compliant.

Practice Questions

Question 1

You upgrade a computer that is running Windows NT 4 Workstation to Windows 2000 Professional. The computer has a single disk drive with three primary partitions and one extended partition. The extended partition is configured with four logical drives. One of the primary partitions is configured as drive **F:** and is formatted as NTFS. You convert the disk to a dynamic disk. You add a second hard disk, convert it to a dynamic disk, and then attempt to extend drive **F:** to include 2GB of the unallocated space on the new disk; however, you cannot extend drive **F:**. What is the most likely reason for this?

- ○ a. Drive **F:** is formatted with a pre–Windows 2000 version of NTFS.
- ○ b. You do not have enough free space (you need at least 1MB) on the original hard disk.
- ○ c. A volume can be extended only on its original hard disk.
- ○ d. You cannot extend a volume that was originally created on a basic disk.

Answer d is correct. When Windows 2000 is installed on a machine running Windows NT Workstation 4, any existing NTFS partitions and logical drives are updated to the Windows 2000 version of NTFS (NTFS 5). If a primary partition or a logical drive is created on a basic disk and the disk is then converted to a dynamic disk, the partitions and logical drives on the disk are converted to simple volumes. You cannot extend these simple volumes that were originally created on a basic disk. It is true that 1MB of free space must be available on a basic disk before it can be converted to a dynamic disk. It is also true that a volume can be extended to include available space on another fixed disk. After this is done, the extended volume becomes, in Windows 2000 terms, a spanned volume instead of a simple volume. Answer a is incorrect because it does not matter that drive F: is formatted with a version of NTFS prior to Windows 2000. Answer b is incorrect because the disk was able to be converted to dynamic. Answer c is incorrect because a dynamic volume can be extended onto other hard disks.

Question 2

> You want to run Windows 98 and Windows 2000 Professional on a computer.
> The computer has three disks that are each configured as a single partition. Disk
> 0 is where you have Windows 98 installed. Disk 1 is where Windows 2000 is
> installed. You need file security for Windows 2000. Disk 2 is where you are stor-
> ing Graphics Department files and projects. You need to be able to access the
> data on Disk 2 regardless of which operating system you are using. Write the
> best file system choice for each drive in the appropriate space.
>
> Disk 0 _____   FAT16
>
> Disk 1 _____   FAT32
>
> Disk 2 _____   NTFS

The correct answer should show Disk 0 as FAT32, Disk 1 as NTFS, and Disk
2 as FAT32. FAT32 is needed on Disk 2 so that both operating systems can
access files stored on this disk, plus it is the most efficient file system. NTFS
is needed on Disk 1 because file security is needed.

Question 3

> You create two primary partitions and one extended partition on a basic disk of
> a computer that is running Windows 2000 Professional. The disk has 8GB of
> unallocated space. You create three logical drives in the extended partition. You
> format one of the logical drives (let's call it drive **G:**) as NTFS and use it for stor-
> ing Engineering Department data. You decide that you need more space allocat-
> ed to this logical drive. You have 4GB of unallocated space available on a sec-
> ond disk drive on the same machine. What can you do to increase the amount
> of storage available on that logical drive?
>
> ○ a. Convert both disk drives to dynamic disks. Extend the simple volume
>   that was the original logical drive by using that volume and unallocated
>   space from the second disk drive.
>
> ○ b. Extend drive **G:** by creating a volume set, using the logical drive and
>   unallocated space from the second disk drive.
>
> ○ c. Create a new partition or volume on the second disk drive. Create a
>   new folder on drive **G:**. Mount the new partition or volume to that
>   folder.
>
> ○ d. Create a new partition or volume on the second disk drive and mount it
>   to the folder in which the Engineering Department data resides.

Answer c is correct. You need to create a new partition (basic disk) or volume (dynamic disk) and mount it to an empty folder on drive G:. A partition or folder can be mounted only to an empty NTFS folder. Only a volume you initially create on a dynamic disk can be extended. Because the logical drive in this case was created on a basic disk, it cannot be extended; therefore, Answers a and b are incorrect. Answer d is incorrect because it would make the problem worse: Mounting the folder to this partition would decrease the amount of space available.

Question 4

For a new DVD drive, you have decided to use a vendor-supplied hardware driver that is not digitally signed. You are preparing for the unattended installation of 150 Windows 2000 Professional machines that will have identical hardware, including the new DVD drive. How do you prepare for using nonsigned drivers in an unattended installation to avoid interactive warnings?

- ○ a. In the driver subdirectory of the distribution folder, change the vendor-supplied driver's **.INF** file where it references the driver catalog file.
- ○ b. In the **[Unattended]** section of the unattended installation answer file, add this entry: **DriverSigningPolicy=Ignore**.
- ○ c. On the server where the distribution source resides, go to the System Properties Hardware tab. Select the Driver Signing button and then choose the Ignore radio button. After you complete the unattended installations, change this setting back to the default.
- ○ d. Flag this specific driver in the **txtsetup.oem** file specified in the **[OEMBootFiles]** section of the answer file.

Answer b is correct. You must use the answer file to indicate that there is a nonsigned driver so that Setup will continue without requiring user intervention. Any manual settings in this case, other than within the answer file, are incorrect and cause Setup to halt and require intervention; therefore, Answers a and c are incorrect. The [OEMBootFiles] section is the wrong place to make the setting change in the answer file; therefore, Answer d is incorrect. The txtsetup.oem file cannot be used for assigning an unsigned driver parameter, which makes Answer d incorrect.

Question 5

> You install Windows 2000 Professional on a computer in your office on which Windows NT 4 Workstation was installed. During the installation, you create a new 3.5GB partition and indicate that the partition should be formatted as FAT. You want to be able to boot back to Windows NT 4, so you indicate that the Windows 2000 system files should be installed on this new 3.5GB partition. When the installation is finished and you boot the computer back to Windows NT 4, you discover that you cannot access the new partition from Windows NT 4. What's the most likely reason?
>
> ○ a. Setup converted the partition to FAT32.
>
> ○ b. Windows NT 4 cannot access a partition that is larger than 2.5GB.
>
> ○ c. Setup converted the partition to Windows 2000 NTFS when you indicated that the partition should be used for the system files.
>
> ○ d. The Windows NT logon account you are using does not have permission to access the new partition.

Answer a is correct. When you use Setup to create and format a partition, Setup formats a partition larger than 2GB as FAT32, even if you indicate that it is to be formatted as FAT. The FAT file system does not support partitions larger than 2GB. Windows 2000 system files do not have to be on an NTFS partition, so Setup does not convert the partition to NTFS 5; therefore, Answer c is incorrect. If you have at least SP4 for NT 4 installed, you can access NTFS 5 partitions from your Windows NT 4 installations. Windows NT can access partitions larger than 2GB—in fact, it can access partitions as large as 16GB; therefore, Answer b is false. Permissions for your NT account are a potential problem only if you formatted the new partition as NTFS. For both NT 4 and Windows 2000, the default NTFS permissions for a new partition give Full Control to the Everyone group; therefore, Answer d is incorrect.

Question 6

You are teaching people in your office how to manage NTFS permissions and compression attributes because they are unfamiliar with NTFS. You want to give them a simple system to help them remember what happens to the original NTFS file and folder permissions and attributes when you move and/or copy data. Write the correct result—either RETAINED or INHERITED—on the line next to each action on the left. You can use each selection more than once if needed.

Files and folders moved among different NTFS volumes _____

Files and folders moved within the same NTFS volume _____

Files and folders copied to a different NTFS volume _____

Files and folders copied within the same NTFS volume _____

The correct answer should be INHERITED, RETAINED, INHERITED, INHERITED, from top to bottom. There is only one instance when file permissions are retained: when a file has been moved to a new location on the same partition. In all other instances file permissions are inherited.

Question 7

You want to delete a quota entry defined for a user's account on drive **E:** of a computer that is running Windows 2000 Professional. What utility or command should you use to locate the files owned by the user and move the files to a shared folder on another Windows 2000 machine on the network?

○ a. The System applet in Control Panel

○ b. Windows Explorer

○ c. Disk Management

○ d. Active Directory Users and Computers

Answer c is correct. You use the properties sheet for a particular drive within Disk Management. You click the Quota tab and then you click the Quota Entries button. From the dialog box where Quota Entries for drive E: are listed, you delete the user's quota entry. Doing so causes the Disk Quota dialog box to appear and allows you to move, delete, or take ownership of the files that the user owns on drive E:. Therefore, Answer a is incorrect because the System applet can be used to open the Disk Management console, but it cannot be used to edit quota entries. Windows Explorer does have a search feature, but a file's owner is not an available search criterion; therefore, Answer b is incorrect. Information about individual files that a user owns is not available in Active Directory Users and Computers, and Active Directory

Users and Computers is not installed by default on Windows 2000 Professional; therefore, Answer d is incorrect.

Question 8

You install a new 10GB hard drive in your Windows 2000 Professional computer, and you want to divide it into five equal 2GB sections. How can you accomplish this? (Select all the correct answers.)

❏ a. Leave the disk as a basic disk. Create three primary partitions of 2GB each. Create one extended partition and make two logical drives of 2GB each within the extended partition.

❏ b. Leave the disk as a basic disk. Create four primary partitions of 2GB each. Create one extended partition of 2GB for the fifth partition.

❏ c. Upgrade the disk to a dynamic disk and create five 2GB simple volumes on it.

❏ d. Upgrade the disk to a dynamic disk. Create five primary partitions of 2GB each on the disk.

Answers a and c are correct. You cannot have more than four partitions on a basic disk, but you can overcome this limitation by converting a disk from basic to dynamic. Dynamic disks do not contain partitions or logical disks; they contain volumes. Answer d is incorrect because a dynamic disk cannot contain primary partitions; it just contains volumes. A basic disk can have the maximum of four primary partitions or three primary partitions and one extended partition; therefore, Answer b is incorrect.

Question 9

You are trying to create a striped volume on a Windows 2000 Professional computer to improve performance. You confirm that you have plenty of unallocated free space on two disks in the computer. When you right-click an area of free space on a disk, your only option is to create a partition. Explain the problem and the best way to resolve it.

- a. You can create striped volumes only when you have at least one dynamic disk. You need to upgrade one of the disks from basic to dynamic, and then you can create the striped volume.
- b. You can create striped volumes only if the disks involved are dynamic, not basic. You need to upgrade the disks that will be participating in the striped volume from basic to dynamic. After the disks are dynamic, you can create the striped volume.
- c. In order to create a striped set, you need a second controller in the computer so that there is a single controller for each disk. Upgrading the disks from basic to dynamic is also required.
- d. Windows 2000 Professional does not support striped volumes. To create a striped volume, you need to first install Windows 2000 Server or Advanced Server on your computer.

Answer b is correct. You can create striped volumes only on dynamic disks, but you do not need multiple controllers. The option to create a partition rather than a (striped) volume indicates that the disk you are trying to use is a basic disk. If you upgrade all the disks to dynamic, they can be part of a striped volume. Answer a is incorrect because a minimum of two dynamic disks, not one, are required to create a striped volume. Answer c is incorrect because a second controller is not needed. Windows 2000 Professional does support striped volumes, but it does not support RAID-5 volumes; therefore, Answer d is incorrect.

Question 10

You add a new disk to a computer. Next, you try to extend an existing volume to include the unallocated space on the new disk, but the option to extend the volume is not available. What is the most likely cause of the problem?

- a. The existing volume is part of a striped volume on a dynamic disk.
- b. The existing volume is part of a spanned volume on a basic disk.
- c. You cannot extend the volume because the disk is basic instead of dynamic.
- d. The existing volume is not formatted with NTFS. Only NTFS volumes can be extended.

Answer d is correct because the volume is not formatted with NTFS—a volume can be extended regardless of whether it is on a basic or dynamic disk, provided that it is formatted with NTFS. Answer c is incorrect because a basic disk can be extended. Answers a and b are incorrect because the option to extend the disk is only related to the fact the drive had not been formatted with NTFS; it has nothing to do with the existing volume being part of a striped or spanned volume.

Need to Know More?

 Microsoft Corporation. *Microsoft Windows 2000 Professional Resource Kit.* Redmond, Washington: Microsoft Press, 2000. Chapter 1 of this book provides invaluable information on file systems and disk concepts. Chapter 6 offers valuable details on file system considerations and multiple-boot configurations.

 Barker, Gord, and Harrison, Doug. *MCSE Training Guide Windows 2000 Professional.* Indianapolis: Que Publishing 2002. This book is the perfect complement to this *Exam Cram 2* book because it provides more in-depth information on all aspects of working with Windows 2000 Professional, including details about NTFS 5, Windows 2000 disks, volumes, and file systems.

 Stinson, Craig, and Siechert, Carl. *Running Microsoft Windows 2000 Professional.* Redmond, Washington: Microsoft Press, 2000. This book is a good source for information on NTFS 5 and disk management.

 To find more information, search the TechNet CD (or its online version, through www.microsoft.com) and/or the *Windows 2000 Professional Resource Kit* CD, using the keywords disk, volume, basic and dynamic, NTFS 5, file system, disk quota, and disk management.

Implementing, Managing, and Troubleshooting Network Protocols and Services

Terms you'll need to understand:

✓ Transmission Control Protocol/Internet Protocol (TCP/IP)
✓ Dynamic Host Configuration Protocol (DHCP)
✓ Domain Name System (DNS)
✓ Windows Internet Name Service (WINS)
✓ Internet Information Services (IIS) 5
✓ File Transfer Protocol (FTP)
✓ Simple Mail Transfer Protocol (SMTP)
✓ Remote Access Service (RAS)
✓ Virtual private network (VPN)
✓ Internet Connection Sharing (ICS)

Techniques you'll need to master:

✓ Configuring and troubleshooting TCP/IP and ICS
✓ Setting up dial-up connections
✓ Establishing VPN connections
✓ Use the **hostname**, **ipconfig**, **ping**, **route**, and **tracert** commands

You can think of computer networking protocols as languages. Just as two people must speak the same language in order to communicate well, two or more computers on a network must share the same protocol in order to communicate. Imagine that we could build a bridge to China from the United States. Think of the bridge as the physical cabling of a network that allows traffic to pass over it. But even though traffic can be physically transported over the bridge, if the people going across the bridge can't speak a common language (for example, English or Chinese), very little communication can take place. The popularity of the Internet has made TCP/IP a de facto standard for networking today, and Windows 2000 makes extensive use of TCP/IP.

The importance of TCP/IP in Windows 2000 makes this protocol the underlying foundation for all the other topics covered in this chapter. Dial-up connections enable users to connect to remote computers via modems and common telephone lines. ICS allows users on the same LAN segment to share a single connection to the Internet, whether the connection is a dial-up or a high-speed connection, such as a Digital Subscriber Line (DSL) or T1 circuit. A VPN provides an encrypted tunnel connection for secure communications via the public Internet. All these features rely on TCP/IP as the communications protocol that makes connecting to similar and dissimilar computer systems possible.

Configuring and Troubleshooting TCP/IP

TCP/IP is a time-proven and robust set of computer networking tools and services. Born in the 1960s out of the Advanced Research Projects Agency Network (ARPANET) project for the U.S. Department of Defense (DoD), TCP/IP encompasses a vast array of utilities and network services. This suite of services has evolved to become a de facto standard for both the Internet and for local area networks (LANs) using personal computer network operating systems such as Novell NetWare 5 and Windows 2000.

TCP/IP is the default protocol when you install Windows 2000 Professional. It provides a means for connecting dissimilar computer systems. TCP/IP scales well—that is, it works well for small, medium-sized, and large organizations. TCP/IP and its name resolution partner, DNS, are both required components for implementing Active Directory in the Windows 2000 Server family of products.

Deciphering the TCP/IP Protocol Suite for Windows 2000

TCP/IP is more than just a standardized specification for data transport over a network. It is a sophisticated toolbox of data transport services, name resolution services, and troubleshooting utilities. Microsoft's implementation of TCP/IP for Windows 2000 includes the following network services and components:

➤ *DHCP*—This service is based on an industry-standard specification for automatically assigning (or leasing) IP addresses to computers connected to a network. The addresses are assigned from a predefined pool (or *scope*) of IP addresses that an administrator must specify. DHCP makes the chore of assigning and maintaining TCP/IP addresses on hundreds or thousands of computers much easier than having to maintain an exhaustive list of IP addresses and computer names by hand. However, administrators should manually assign static IP addresses for server computers. For current Microsoft products, the DHCP Server service can be installed only on the Windows 2000 Server and the Windows Server 2003 product lines. DHCP can assign addresses to both servers and workstations. Any operating system that can make DHCP-compliant requests for IP addresses can utilize a DHCP server. DHCP client-compatible operating systems include Windows 3.x, 9x, Me, NT, 2000, XP, and Windows Server 2003.

➤ *DNS servers*—Computers understand and work well with numbers, but humans have more of an affinity for names. TCP/IP requires that each network device be assigned a numeric IP address. DNS, in conjunction with DNS servers, maps numeric IP addresses to computer names (host-names) and vice versa. DNS employs a hierarchical system of domains and subdomains that helps make this name resolution service very scalable. DNS servers mitigate the need for a manually maintained HOSTS file to be stored on each computer. Windows 2000 DNS servers offer added functionality such as Active Directory integrated zones, incremental zone transfers, and dynamic updates. DNS is a requirement for implementing Active Directory.

➤ *WINS*—This service is Microsoft's implementation of a name resolution mechanism to match IP addresses to Network Basic Input/Output System (NetBIOS) computer names and vice versa. WINS servers can greatly reduce NetBIOS traffic on networks by decreasing the amount of broadcast traffic that occurs when computers attempt to resolve unknown IP addresses to NetBIOS computer names. For an Active

Directory–based network in Windows 2000 native mode with no applications that require NetBIOS, WINS is unnecessary.

➤ *APIPA*—Microsoft first introduced this feature in Windows 98. For computers that are configured to obtain IP addresses automatically, APIPA kicks in if no DHCP server is available on the network to lease out IP addresses. APIPA automatically queries the other computers on the network and then assigns a unique IP address to the local computer, using the IP address scheme 169.254.x.y, with the subnet mask 255.255.0.0. The Internet Assigned Numbers Authority (IANA) reserves the IP address range 169.254.0.0 through 169.254.255.255 for APIPA. This ensures that any IP address that APIPA generates does not conflict with any public, routable addresses. This feature is turned on by default in Windows 2000 Professional.

➤ *SLIP*—This specification is an older Unix standard for serial communications. Windows 2000 supports SLIP primarily for backward-compatibility purposes. You can use SLIP only for outbound connections on Windows 2000 Professional.

➤ *PPP*—PPP has effectively replaced SLIP. PPP is a remote access/dial-up protocol that supports industry-standard network protocols such as TCP/IP, NWLink, NetBIOS Extended User Interface (NetBEUI), and AppleTalk. PPP is optimized for low-bandwidth connections, so it is the preferred remote access protocol for dial-up/modem connections.

➤ *PPTP*—The only VPN protocol that shipped with Windows NT 4, PPTP encapsulates TCP/IP, Internetwork Packet Exchange (IPX), or NetBEUI data packets and encrypts the data being transmitted as it travels (that is, tunnels) through the Internet. PPTP clients can connect to any Microsoft-compatible PPTP servers via the Internet if they have proper security credentials. This service, which is shipped with Windows 2000 Professional, allows users to connect to the Internet using local (non–long distance) connections and offers them a way to connect to PPTP computers in remote locations without incurring toll charges or requiring dedicated data lines.

➤ *L2TP*—An alternative to PPTP, L2TP is new to Windows 2000 and offers similar functionality. However, L2TP is an industry-standard VPN protocol and is shipped with Windows 2000 Professional. L2TP also encapsulates TCP/IP, IPX, or NetBEUI data packets and encrypts the data being transmitted as it travels (that is, tunnels) through the Internet. You can also use L2TP in conjunction with Microsoft IP Security (IPSec) for enhanced security. L2TP is covered in the section "New Authentication Protocols," later in this chapter.

➤ *IPSec*—This is a relatively new Internet security protocol, also referred to as Secure IP. It provides computer-level authentication in addition to data encryption for VPN connections that use L2TP. IPSec negotiates between the client computer and the remote tunnel server before an L2TP connection is established; this secures both passwords and data. L2TP uses standard PPP-based authentication protocols, such as Extensible Authentication Protocol (EAP), Challenge Handshake Authentication Protocol (CHAP), Microsoft CHAP (MS-CHAP), Shiva Password Authentication Protocol (SPAP), and Password Authentication Protocol (PAP) with IPSec. IPSec and EAP are covered in more detail in the section "New Authentication Protocols," later in this chapter.

➤ *WWW publishing service*—This is a major component of IIS 5, which ships with Windows 2000 Professional. Although they are not installed by default in Windows 2000 Professional, IIS 5 and the WWW publishing service provide Web page hosting for HTML-based and Active Server Pages (ASP)–based documents.

➤ *FTP*—This is another major component of IIS 5. FTP is an industry standard protocol for transferring files between computers over TCP/IP-based networks, such as the Internet.

➤ *SMTP*—The Microsoft SMTP service implements the industry-standard SMTP to transport and deliver email messages. The SMTP service for Windows 2000 is also a component of IIS 5.

Understanding TCP/IP Computer Addresses

TCP/IP assigns a unique set of numbers to each computer that is connected to a TCP/IP-based network or internetwork. This set of numbers consists of four separate numbers, each delimited by a period, called a dot (.). For example, the IP address 192.168.1.20 illustrates this concept, which is known as *dotted-decimal notation*. Each device on a TCP/IP-based network must be assigned a *unique* IP address so that it can send and receive data with the other devices on the network. A network device can be a computer, a printer, a router, a firewall, and so on.

We write IP addresses in dotted-decimal format for ease and convenience. However, TCP/IP addresses are actually 32-bit *binary* numbers. By converting these binary numbers into decimal, most of us can work with these addresses much more easily than if we had to work with them in their native binary format. The address 192.168.1.20, mentioned previously, translates into binary 11000000.10101000.1.10100.

If you're not sure how to convert decimal numbers into binary or vice versa, you can use the Windows Calculator by selecting Start, Run, typing **calc**, and clicking OK. Then you click View, Scientific from the menu bar, and you can easily perform these conversions.

Certain IP addresses are reserved for specific functions:

➤ The address 255.255.255.255 (11111111.11111111.11111111.11111111 in binary) is reserved for network broadcasts.

➤ The IP address 127.0.0.1 (1111111.0.0.1 in binary) is reserved as a loopback address for testing proper configuration of the IP address(es) for the local host computer.

➤ The address schemes 10.0.0.0/8 through 10.255.255.255/8 (class A), 172.16.0.0/16 through 172.31.255.255/16 (class B), and 192.168.0.0/24 through 192.168.255.255/24 (class C) are reserved as private and non-routable by the bodies that govern the Internet.

Therefore, IP addresses such as 10.0.0.7, 192.168.1.20, and 172.16.109.84 are restricted to being used only for the internal addressing of LANs. By definition, you cannot route such addressing schemes onto the Internet. *Routers* (devices that route network data packets) do not forward any data packets that originate with nonroutable addressing schemes.

Configuring TCP/IP

TCP/IP is installed by default when you install Windows 2000 Professional, unless you override this default setting. In addition, the protocol's default configuration is to *obtain an IP address automatically*. This means that the computer automatically requests a unique TCP/IP address for the network from a DHCP server. If no DHCP server is available, the operating system invokes APIPA to query the other computers that are currently powered on and connected to the network so that it can assign itself a unique IP address.

If you work with TCP/IP, you need to become familiar with the following terms:

➤ *Subnet mask*—This is essentially an IP address filter that is applied to each unique IP address. The subnet mask (or filter) determines which part of the IP address for a computer specifies the network segment where the computer is located versus which part of the IP address specifies the unique node (or host) address for that individual computer. For example, an IP address of 192.168.1.20 with a subnet mask of 255.255.255.0 is determined to have the network segment address of 192.168.1. The node or host address for the computer, therefore, is 20.

This is analogous to the street name of a postal address versus the actual house number of the address: There may be many houses on the same street, but only one house has the house number 20.

➤ *Default gateway*—This IP address specifies the router for the local network segment (or subnet). If this address is absent, the computer cannot communicate with other computers that are located outside the local network segment (also known as a *subnet* or *subnetwork*). Default gateway information is often obtained through DHCP if the computer is configured to obtain an IP address automatically.

➤ *Preferred and alternate DNS servers*—Having more than one DNS server on a network helps provide load balancing and fault tolerance for client computers that need to perform IP address-to-hostname lookups as well as hostname-to-IP address lookups. Name resolution is a critical issue in TCP/IP. DNS server information is often obtained through DHCP if the computer is configured to obtain an IP address automatically.

➤ *WINS addresses*—WINS provides name resolution between IP addresses and NetBIOS computer names. WINS server addresses are often obtained through DHCP if the computer is configured to obtain an IP address automatically.

To manually set up a Windows 2000 Professional computer with a static IP address for TCP/IP, you select Start, Settings, Network and Dial-up Connections. Then you right-click the icon for the LAN connection that you want to configure and select Properties.

If TCP/IP is not currently installed, you need to follow these steps:

1. Click Install from the LAN connection's properties sheet.

2. Click Protocol and then click Add.

3. Click Internet Protocol (TCP/IP) and then click OK.

4. Restart the computer.

To configure the necessary settings so that TCP/IP can communicate with other computers and devices over the network, you need to follow these steps:

1. Click Internet Protocol (TCP/IP) and then click Properties.

2. Click Use the Following IP Address.

3. Enter the IP address, subnet mask, and default gateway.

4. Enter the proper IP address for a preferred DNS server and an alternate DNS server (if any).

5. Click the Advanced button to add additional IP addresses and default gateways. You can also add, edit, or remove DNS server address information, and you can change other DNS settings. You can specify IP addresses for any WINS servers on the network, you can enable NetBIOS name resolution using an LMHOSTS file, and you can enable or disable NetBIOS over TCP/IP. You can also set up IPSec and TCP/IP filtering as optional settings from the Advanced TCP/IP Settings properties sheet.

6. Click OK to close the Advanced TCP/IP Settings Properties dialog box.

7. Click OK to close the Internet Protocol (TCP/IP) Properties dialog box.

8. Click OK to close the Local Area Connection Properties dialog box.

Troubleshooting TCP/IP

Windows 2000 Professional comes with several software tools and utilities to help isolate and resolve TCP/IP-related issues. You must run all these utilities from the command line. Connectivity tools include the following:

➤ *finger*—Displays information about a user for a particular computer. The target computer must be running the *finger* service.

➤ *ftp*—Copies files to and from FTP servers over a TCP/IP connection.

➤ *lpr*—Sends one or more files to be printed via a line printer daemon (*lpd*) printer.

➤ *rcp*—Copies files between a Windows 2000 Professional computer and a computer system running the remote shell daemon (*rshd*).

➤ *rexec*—Executes commands on remote computer systems that are running the *rexec* service.

➤ *rsh*—Executes commands on remote computer systems that are running the *rsh* service.

➤ *telnet*—Establishes a terminal emulation session for working on remote systems, including environments such as Unix, mainframe, and mini computers.

➤ *tftp*—Copies files to and from remote computers that are running the Trivial File Transfer Protocol (TFTP) service.

Diagnostic tools include the following:

➤ *arp*—Lists and edits the IP-to-ethernet (or token ring) physical translation tables that ARP uses.

➤ *hostname*—Lists the name of the local host (computer).

➤ *ipconfig*—Shows all the current TCP/IP configuration settings for the local computer, such as its IP address, subnet mask, and any WINS servers and DNS servers assigned to the computer.

➤ *lpq*—Shows the current status of the print queue on a computer that is running the lpd service.

➤ *nbstat*—Delineates network protocol statistics and lists the current connections that are using NetBIOS over TCP/IP.

➤ *netstat*—Delineates network protocol statistics and lists the current TCP/IP connections.

➤ *ping*—Tests TCP/IP-related connectivity to remote computers. This command also verifies the proper TCP/IP configuration of the local host computer by attempting to ping the loopback address for the local host (for example, ping 127.0.0.1).

➤ *route*—Edits the local computer's routing tables.

➤ *tracert*—Displays the route (path) that data packets follow as they travel from the local computer to a remote destination computer.

Troubleshooting TCP/IP Configuration and Connectivity

When you initially set up TCP/IP, you should test to verify that the protocol is working properly. Here are the steps you can take to check a computer's TCP/IP configuration and test its connectivity:

1. Open a command prompt window; ipconfig and ping are strictly command-line utilities.

2. Run ipconfig to display the computer's current IP configuration. Use ipconfig /all to display more detailed information (see Figure 9.1).

3. Use the ping command to ping the computer's loopback address:

   ```
   ping 127.0.0.1
   ```

   This tests whether TCP/IP is correctly installed and bound to the network adapter card (see Figure 9.2).

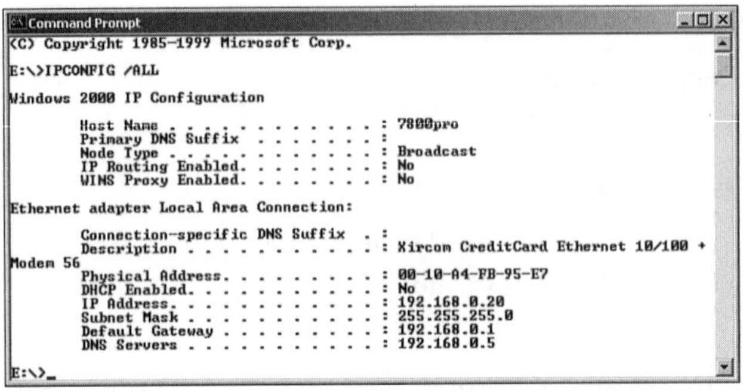

```
Command Prompt
(C) Copyright 1985-1999 Microsoft Corp.

E:\>IPCONFIG /ALL

Windows 2000 IP Configuration

        Host Name . . . . . . . . . . . . : 7800pro
        Primary DNS Suffix  . . . . . . . :
        Node Type . . . . . . . . . . . . : Broadcast
        IP Routing Enabled. . . . . . . . : No
        WINS Proxy Enabled. . . . . . . . : No

Ethernet adapter Local Area Connection:

        Connection-specific DNS Suffix  . :
        Description . . . . . . . . . . . : Xircom CreditCard Ethernet 10/100 +
Modem 56
        Physical Address. . . . . . . . . : 00-10-A4-FB-95-E7
        DHCP Enabled. . . . . . . . . . . : No
        IP Address. . . . . . . . . . . . : 192.168.0.20
        Subnet Mask . . . . . . . . . . . : 255.255.255.0
        Default Gateway . . . . . . . . . : 192.168.0.1
        DNS Servers . . . . . . . . . . . : 192.168.0.5

E:\>_
```

Figure 9.1 An example of running the **ipconfig** command.

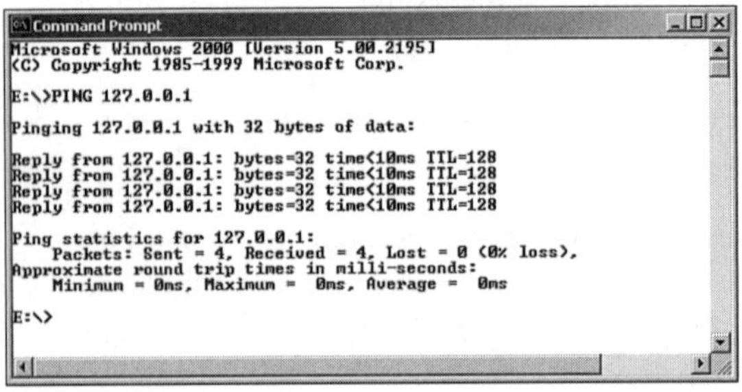

```
Command Prompt
Microsoft Windows 2000 [Version 5.00.2195]
(C) Copyright 1985-1999 Microsoft Corp.

E:\>PING 127.0.0.1

Pinging 127.0.0.1 with 32 bytes of data:

Reply from 127.0.0.1: bytes=32 time<10ms TTL=128
Reply from 127.0.0.1: bytes=32 time<10ms TTL=128
Reply from 127.0.0.1: bytes=32 time<10ms TTL=128
Reply from 127.0.0.1: bytes=32 time<10ms TTL=128

Ping statistics for 127.0.0.1:
    Packets: Sent = 4, Received = 4, Lost = 0 (0% loss),
Approximate round trip times in milli-seconds:
    Minimum = 0ms, Maximum =  0ms, Average =  0ms

E:\>
```

Figure 9.2 An example of pinging a computer's loopback address.

4. `ping` the IP address of the local computer to verify the uniqueness of the IP address on the network.

5. `ping` the IP address of the default gateway for the local subnet to ensure that the default gateway is up and running. This step also demonstrates whether the computer can successfully communicate over the local network segment.

6. `ping` the IP address of a computer that is located on a different network segment (subnet). This step indicates whether the computer can send and receive network data packets through a router.

Using APIPA

If a computer is set up to obtain an IP address automatically from a DHCP server but no DHCP servers are available, APIPA temporarily assigns an IP address to the local computer while it searches the network to make sure no other network devices have been assigned the same IP address. By running `ipconfig`, you can view the current TCP/IP information for the local computer. An address such as 169.254.x.y generally indicates that APIPA is currently in effect.

Connecting to Remote Computers Using Dial-Up Connections

Dial-up connectivity maintains an important role for connecting remote computers. In Microsoft terms, *dial-up connections* generally refer to client computers dialing out to server computers. RAS generally refers to server computers that accept inbound remote connections from dial-up clients. Dial-up connections usually involve regular phones using analog modems and/or dial-up Integrated Services Digital Network (ISDN) lines.

New Authentication Protocols

Windows 2000 Professional provides advanced support for remote access authentication protocols, which offer enhanced security and dynamic bandwidth allocation for remote access. These authentication protocols, such as IPSec, validate the logon credentials for all users who attempt to connect to a Windows 2000–based network. Windows 2000 Professional supports all the authentication protocols that Windows NT 4 offers, including PAP, CHAP, MS-CHAP, SPAP, and PPTP (which is used for VPN support).

Windows 2000 Professional also supports several new authentication protocols that greatly enhance its dial-up and remote access capabilities for data encryption, user authentication, and bandwidth allocation. These newly supported standards include IPSec, L2TP, EAP, Remote Authentication Dial-in User Service (RADIUS), and Bandwidth Allocation Protocol (BAP).

IPSec

IPSec is a suite of security-related protocols and cryptographic functions for establishing and maintaining private and secure IP connections. IPSec is easy to implement and offers vigilant security for potential network attacks. IPSec-enabled clients establish a security association (SA) that serves as a private key for encrypting data. IPSec uses policies for configuring its security services. IPSec policies support different gradations of security levels for different types of network traffic. Administrators can set IPSec policies at the User, Group, Application, Domain, Site, and Global Enterprise levels. You configure IPSec policies with the IP Security Policy Management snap-in of the Microsoft Management Console (MMC).

L2TP

You can compare *L2TP* to PPTP in that it provides an encrypted tunnel for data to pass through an untrusted (public) network such as the Internet.

However, although L2TP provides a tunnel for data to pass through, it does not provide encryption for the data. L2TP works in conjunction with other encryption services and security protocols, such as IPSec, to provide secure VPN connections. Both L2TP and PPTP use PPP to establish initial communications. The following are some of the major differences between L2TP and PPTP:

➤ L2TP requires IPSec for encryption services. PPTP uses the encryption functions of PPP.

➤ L2TP provides header compression support. When you enable header compression, L2TP uses only 4 bytes for its overhead. PPTP requires 6 bytes for its overhead and does not support header compression.

➤ L2TP offers support for tunnel authentication; PPTP does not support tunnel authentication. If you implement IPSec with L2TP or PPTP, IPSec provides its own tunnel authentication, rendering L2TP's tunnel authentication unnecessary.

➤ Unlike PPTP, L2TP does not have to run over an IP-based network transport. L2TP needs only a packet-oriented, point-to-point connection. L2TP can function using User Datagram Protocol (UDP), Frame Relay permanent virtual circuits (PVCs), X.25 virtual circuits (VCs), or Asynchronous Transfer Mode (ATM) VCs over TCP/IP.

EAP

EAP is an extension of PPP for dial-up connections, L2TP, and PPTP clients. EAP supports a negotiated authentication model in which the actual authentication mechanism is determined between the dial-up connection client and the remote access server. EAP provides support for several authentication protocols, including the following:

➤ *Message Digest 5 CHAP (MD5-CHAP)*—This encrypts usernames and passwords, using its own MD5 algorithm.

➤ *Generic token cards*—These cards provide passwords for users and can support multiple authentication methods.

➤ *Transport Level Security (TLS)*—The TLS protocol works with smart cards and other types of security certificates. A *smart card* stores a user's security certificate and private key electronically. Smart card technology requires physical cards and card readers.

By using EAP application programming interfaces (APIs), software developers can design and implement new authentication methods for smart cards, generic token cards, and even biometric devices such as fingerprint identification scanners. In this way, EAP can support authentication technologies that will be developed in the future. To add EAP authentication methods, you can go to the Security tab of the remote access server's properties sheet.

RADIUS

RADIUS offers accounting services and authentication functions for distributed dial-up connections. Windows 2000 Professional can take on the role of a RADIUS server or a RADIUS client, or it can assume the roles of both. A RADIUS client is often used as a remote access server for an Internet service provider (ISP). The RADIUS client forwards authentication requests to a RADIUS server. A Windows 2000 RADIUS client can also forward remote access accounting information to a RADIUS server. You configure RADIUS client settings from the Security tab of the remote access server's properties sheet.

RADIUS servers validate requests from RADIUS clients. For authentication, Windows 2000 provides Internet Authentication Services (IAS) as an optional Windows component that you can add during installation or through Add/Remove Programs in the Control Panel. RADIUS servers maintain RADIUS accounting data from RADIUS clients in associated log files.

BAP

BAP works in conjunction with Bandwidth Allocation Control Protocol (BACP) as an enhancement to the Multilink feature found in Windows NT 4. Multilink enables you to bind together two or more modem or ISDN lines, allowing you to achieve higher throughput (that is, more bandwidth) than you would if you used the lines individually. BAP and BACP work together to dynamically add or drop lines for multilinked devices on an on-demand basis. Both protocols serve as PPP control protocols, which provide a means for optimizing bandwidth while holding down connection costs by responding to network bandwidth needs on demand. For organizations that incur line-usage charges based on bandwidth use (such as for ISDN lines), BAP and BACP can significantly cut costs.

As an administrator, you can turn on the Multilink feature as well as BAP and BACP from the PPP tab of each remote access server's properties sheet. You configure BAP settings by using remote access policies. By implementing a remote access policy using BAP, you can specify that an extra line should be dropped if the connection for that line falls below 65% usage, for example, for a particular group. You can additionally specify that an extra line should be dropped only if usage falls below 35% for a different group of users.

Connecting to Remote Access Servers

You create new connections to remote access servers in the Network and Dial-up Connections window. You can make new connections as well as modify or delete existing dial-up connections in this window. To create a new dial-up connection for connecting to remote access servers, you need to follow these steps:

1. Select Start, Settings, Network and Dial-up Connections.

2. Click Make New Connection to display the Network Connection Wizard.

3. Click Next.

4. At the Network Connection Type dialog box, you can accept the default choice—Dial-up to Private Network—as shown in Figure 9.3.

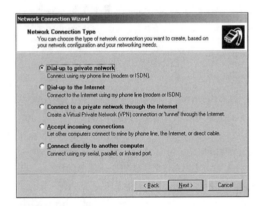

Figure 9.3 The Network Connection Type dialog box of the Network Connection Wizard.

5. Click Next.

6. Select the check box for the device(s) that you want to use for this connection.

7. Click Next.

8. Specify the phone number for the remote access server to which you want to connect. Select the Use Dialing Rules check box if you want the system's dialing rules to automatically determine how to dial from different locations.

9. Click Next.

10. Specify the Connection Availability for This Dial-up entry. Click For All Users or Only for Myself.

11. Click Next.

12. Complete the Network Connection Wizard by entering the name that you want to assign to this connection. Select the Add a Shortcut to My Desktop check box if you would like a shortcut to be added.

13. Click Finish.

As soon as you complete the Network Connection Wizard, a Connect dialog box appears. It prompts you for a username and a password and offers a Dial drop-down list for the phone number to be dialed (see Figure 9.4). You can type the proper username and password as well as verify the phone number to be dialed for connecting to the remote access server. You click the Dial button to initiate the connection. You click the Properties button to modify some of the dial-up connection's properties.

Figure 9.4 The Connect dialog box for connecting to remote access servers.

You can modify the properties of any dial-up connection or network connection listed in the Network and Dial-up Connections window by right-clicking the connection's icon and selecting Properties, as shown in Figure 9.5. From the dial-up connection's properties sheet, you can configure connection devices (modems and so on), list alternate phone numbers, and configure dialing options and redialing options. You can specify security options, configure dial-up server settings, and modify network connection components. You can also set up ICS from the Sharing tab, if this connection connects to the Internet. ICS is covered in more detail in the section "Configuring and Troubleshooting ICS," later in this chapter.

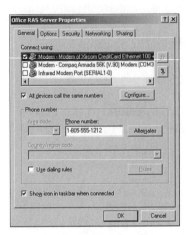

Figure 9.5 The Properties sheet for a dial-up connection.

The Networking tab of a dial-up connection's properties sheet allows you to configure several essential components for successful connections (see Figure 9.6). You need to be sure your connection has at least one dial-up network protocol in common with the remote access server to which it will be attempting to connect. You can install and uninstall networking components, such as protocols, on the Networking tab. You can also enable or disable any listed component by selecting or clearing its check box.

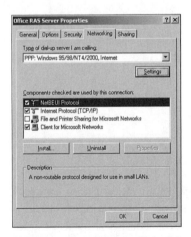

Figure 9.6 The Networking tab of a dial-up connection's properties sheet.

You should be sure to specify the proper dial-up server type to which you will be connecting (either PPP or SLIP). You can change PPP settings by clicking the Settings button located just below the Type of Dial-up Server I Am Calling drop-down list box. The PPP Settings dialog box is shown in Figure 9.7.

Figure 9.7 The PPP Settings dialog box.

Setting Up and Configuring VPN Connections

Setting up and configuring VPN connections is similar to establishing dial-up connections. VPN connections allow you to connect to remote computers anywhere in the world by tunneling through the Internet, using a VPN protocol such as PPTP or L2TP. VPN protocols encapsulate TCP/IP, NetBEUI, or NWLink data packets for transport over TCP/IP via the Internet. PPTP and L2TP utilize encryption to secure all the data that they encapsulate as it travels to the destination VPN server.

To create a new VPN connection, you need to follow these steps:

1. Select Start, Settings, Network and Dial-up Connections.

2. Click Make New Connection to display the Network Connection Wizard.

3. Click Next.

4. At the Network Connection Type dialog box, click Connect to a Private Network Through the Internet.

5. Click Next.

6. At the Public Network dialog box, select Do Not Dial the Initial Connection if This Computer Does Not Need to Dial Up to Connect with the Internet. Click the Automatically Dial This Initial Connection drop-down list to select an existing dial-up connection for connecting to the Internet.

7. Click Next.

8. Type the hostname or IP address of the computer or network to which the machine will be connecting.

9. Click Next.

10. Specify the connection availability for this dial-up entry. Click For All Users or Only for Myself.

11. Click Next.

12. Complete the Network Connection Wizard by entering the name that you want to assign to this connection. Select the Add a Shortcut to My Desktop check box if you would like a shortcut to be added.

13. Click Finish.

When you double-click the Virtual Private Connection icon to access a VPN server, you are prompted to connect to the Internet by using the dial-up connection you specified. After you have established a connection to the Internet, Windows 2000 Professional attempts to connect to the remote VPN server.

Connecting to the Internet Using Dial-Up Connections

Creating a dial-up connection to the Internet is similar to adding a connection for a remote access server. To set up a new dial-up connection to connect to an ISP, you need to perform the following steps:

1. Select Start, Settings, Network and Dial-up Connections.

2. Click Make New Connection to display the Network Connection Wizard.

3. Click Next.

4. At the Network Connection Type dialog box, click Dial-up to the Internet.

5. Click Next. The Internet Connection Wizard appears.

6. Select the type of Internet connection that you want to use. Unless you want to establish a new Internet access account with an ISP through the Microsoft Internet Referral Service, you can select one of the other two options: I Want to Set Up My Internet Connection Manually or I Want to Connect Through a Local Area Network.

7. Click Next.

8. Specify how this computer will connect to the Internet: I Connect Through a Phone Line and a Modem or I Connect Through a Local Area Network. To use a dial-up connection, choose the first option.

9. Click Next.

10. From the drop-down list select the communications device (modem) to use for this dial-up connection to the Internet.

11. Click Next.

12. Enter the area code and telephone number for the ISP connection you will be using. Clear the Use Area Code and Dialing Rules check box if you do not want to use those features.

13. Click the Advanced button to specify settings for the ISP's connection. You can modify the connection type and logon procedure settings on the Connection tab, if necessary.

14. Click the Addresses tab to open the Advanced Connection Properties dialog box. On this page you can click Always Use the Following and type the IP address required by the ISP if the ISP requires that you use a static IP address.

15. In the DNS Server Address section, click Always Use the Following and enter a primary IP address and an alternate IP address for the ISP's DNS servers (unless the ISP provides this information automatically).

16. Click OK to close the Advanced Connection Properties dialog box.

17. Click Next.

18. Type the username and password for the ISP account to which the machine will be connecting.

19. Click Next.

20. Type a connection name for this dial-up Internet connection.

21. Click Next.

22. Click No when you are prompted to set up an Internet mail account. You can always set up Internet email accounts later.

23. Click Next.

24. Complete the Network Connection Wizard by clearing the To Connect to the Internet Immediately, Select This Box check box.

25. Click Finish.

26. Right-click the Internet connection you just created and select Properties. Click the Security tab. Verify that Typical is selected and that The Validate My Identity as Follows drop-down list has Allow Unsecured Password selected.

27. Click OK.

After you complete the preceding steps, you should be able to connect to the Internet via a dial-up connection. If you double-click the icon for the Internet connection that you just configured, you should see a Connect dialog box that displays the username and password that you specified. You should clear the Save Password check box if you do not want the password saved for future connection attempts. You can click the Dial button to have the connection established.

Configuring and Troubleshooting ICS

Windows 2000 Professional allows you to have one IP address from an ISP and share that connection (through the Windows 2000 Professional computer) with other computers on the network. This feature is known as ICS. Microsoft accomplishes this feat by enabling a feature that is new to Windows 2000: network address translation (NAT). NAT translates (or maps) a set of nonroutable IP addresses (such as 192.168.x.y) to an external (public) IP address that exists on the Internet. Computers on the LAN can then access external resources on the Internet, such as Web sites and FTP sites, but they are somewhat sheltered from outside intrusions because the LAN computers are using nonroutable IP addresses.

 Although turning on NAT can be a good idea, you should never use it as a substitute for a high-quality firewall product that can provide a much higher level of security between the LAN and the public Internet. Generally speaking, you should always place a firewall product between your internal local network and the external public network. With more and more people gaining access to the Internet, you need to keep security concerns at the forefront to ensure the integrity of all your internal systems and your users' valuable, private, and confidential data.

Configuring ICS

To set up ICS, you need to follow these steps:

1. Select Start, Settings, Network and Dial-up Connections.

2. Right-click a connection icon for an Internet connection and select Properties.

3. Click the Sharing tab.

4. Click the Enable Internet Connection Sharing for This Connection check box. After you have selected this check box, the other settings for ICS become available.

5. Select the Enable On-Demand Dialing check box if you want this Internet connection to automatically dial and establish a connection to

the Internet when another computer on the LAN attempts to access Internet resources through this computer.

6. Click the Settings button. On the Applications tab, you can specify individual application programs that you want to enable for other computers that will be sharing this connection over the LAN.

7. Click the Services tab. Select the check box for each Internet-related service you want to enable for this shared connection. You can also add services that are not currently listed by clicking the Add button.

8. Click OK to close the Internet Connection Sharing Settings dialog box.

9. Click OK to close the properties sheet for the Internet connection. As soon as you close the properties sheet, you see the message box shown in Figure 9.8.

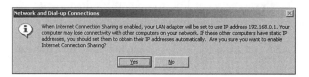

Figure 9.8   The Network and Dial-up Connections message box for ICS.

10. Click Yes in this message box if you are sure you want to enable this feature.

After you have set up ICS, you should verify that the computer's IP address is set to 192.168.0.1, with a subnet mask of 255.255.255.0. You should test the local Internet connection to verify that the computer can connect to the Internet successfully. For each computer on the LAN that wants to take advantage of the shared Internet connection, you need to perform the following steps:

1. Select Start, Settings, Network and Dial-up Connections.

2. Right-click the LAN connection and select Properties.

3. Click Internet Protocol and then click Properties.

4. Configure TCP/IP to obtain an IP address automatically. This is the preferred method to use with ICS (as opposed to obtaining the address manually, which is covered next). When you enable ICS, the Windows 2000 Professional DHCP allocator uses the default IP addressing range 192.168.0.1 through 192.168.0.254, and the DNS proxy service becomes enabled so that clients on the network can connect to the shared Internet resource.

As an alternative, you can manually set up workstations to work with ICS; however, this is not the recommended method, according to Microsoft. To manually set up workstations to work with ICS, you follow these steps:

1. Select Start, Settings, Network and Dial-up Connections.

2. Right-click the LAN connection and select Properties.

3. Click Internet Protocol and then click Properties.

4. Click Use the Following IP Address and type a unique IP address in the range 192.168.0.2 through 192.168.0.254.

5. Type `255.255.255.0` for the subnet mask.

6. Type `192.168.0.1` for the default gateway (the IP address for the Windows 2000 Professional computer that is hosting the shared Internet connection).

7. Enter the preferred DNS server according to your ISP's documentation (if your ISP does not provide this information automatically).

8. Enter the alternate DNS server according to your ISP's documentation (if your ISP does not provide this information automatically).

9. Click OK in the Internet Protocol (TCP/IP) properties sheet.

10. Click OK in the LAN connection Properties window.

Troubleshooting ICS

Here are some tips for troubleshooting ICS:

➤ If you encounter problems with computers on the network not being able to connect to Web sites through the shared Internet connection, you should verify the DNS server IP addresses with the ISP.

➤ To verify that the new IP settings have taken effect, you can type `ipconfig` at a command prompt. Sometimes you might need to restart the computer in order for all the settings to become active.

➤ You should check the subnet mask; it must read 255.255.255.0, or else the computer that is attempting to connect to the ICS computer cannot connect.

➤ You need to make sure that each IP address that you assign to the other computers on the network falls within the range 192.168.0.2 through 192.168.0.254, with no duplicate addresses on any computer.

➤ If computers on the network can connect to the Internet only after you manually initiate the Internet connection from the ICS host computer, you should make sure Enable On-Demand Dialing is checked on the Sharing tab of the Internet connection's properties sheet.

Practice Questions

Question 1

A computer named **Station01** is configured with TCP/IP and is set up to obtain
an IP address automatically. There is a DHCP server on the network. When Mary
turns on the workstation, she cannot access any network resources. As the
administrator, you run **ipconfig** on the workstation and discover that the computer has the IP address 169.254.0.2. What is the most likely cause of this
problem?

- ○ a. Someone has entered for this workstation a static IP address for a different subnet.
- ○ b. The DHCP server is currently down, or the network cable for the workstation has become disconnected.
- ○ c. DHCP has been configured with an incorrect scope.
- ○ d. The WINS server is currently unavailable.

Answer b is correct. If a computer that is configured with TCP/IP to obtain
an IP address automatically cannot contact a DHCP server, Windows 2000
Professional invokes APIPA to assign a unique, nonroutable IP address in the
range 169.254.0.1 through 169.254.255.254. The computer's IP address
169.254.0.2 would indicate that it obtained its IP address from APIPA.
Answer a is incorrect because the question states that the computer is configured to obtain an IP address automatically. Answer c is incorrect because
if the DHCP server had been configured with an incorrect scope, all the
workstations would still have obtained IP addresses within the same subnet.
Answer d is incorrect because a WINS server does not assign IP addresses to
clients; it maps NetBIOS names to IP addresses and vice versa.

Question 2

As the administrator, you need to set up a dial-up connection by using TCP/IP on a Windows 2000 remote access server computer. Which settings do you need to configure for the Windows 2000 Professional dial-up client to create the dial-up connection and enable it to connect to the remote access server?

- ○ a. The type of connection, the server's phone number, and which EAP the server is using

- ○ b. The DNS server IP addresses for the dial-up server and whether DHCP is enabled

- ○ c. The phone number for the server, how IP addresses are allocated to dial-up clients, and which authentication options have been enabled on the server

- ○ d. The phone number for the server, whether to use PPTP or L2TP, and the scope of IP addresses for the subnet

Answer c is correct. A dial-up connection must know the server's phone number. In addition, the connection must either have a static IP address that is compatible with the remote access server's addressing scheme or obtain a dynamic IP address from the remote access server when it connects. The dial-up client must also be compatible with at least one of the authentication methods for which the server is configured. Answer a is incorrect because EAP is not by default required as part of a dial-up connection. Answer b is incorrect because the DNS server addresses are not required for a dial-up connection. Answer d is incorrect because PPTP and L2TP are used for VPN connections and are not required for dial-up connections between two Windows 2000 computers.

Question 3

What additional settings must you configure to enable smart card support with custom settings for dial-up connections?

○ a. From the dial-up connection's properties sheet, go to the Advanced Security Settings dialog box, select Use Extensible Authentication Protocol (EAP), and choose Smart Card or Other Certificate (Encryption Enabled) from the drop-down list.

○ b. From the dial-up connection's properties sheet, go to the Advanced Security Settings dialog box, select Use Extensible Authentication Protocol (EAP), and choose MD5-Challenge from the drop-down list.

○ c. From the dial-up connection's properties sheet, go to the Advanced Security Settings dialog box, select Allow These Protocols, and choose Shiva Password Authentication Protocol (SPAP) from the drop-down list.

○ d. From the dial-up connection's properties sheet, go to the Advanced Security Settings dialog box, select Allow These Protocols, and choose Challenge Handshake Authentication Protocol (CHAP) from the drop-down list.

Answer a is correct. EAP provides smart card support. The Advanced Security Settings dialog box allows you to specify custom settings for smart card support. Answer b is incorrect because MD5-Challenge does not support smart card devices. SPAP and CHAP do not support smart cards; therefore, Answers c and d are incorrect.

Question 4

You are the administrator for a LAN that has four different subnets. TCP/IP is the only network protocol used on the LAN. The network has 110 Windows 2000 Professional workstations, 4 Windows 2000 servers, and 3 Windows NT 4 servers. Currently, the network uses NetBIOS computer names for name resolution on the network. The workstations are all set up using static IP addresses. What do you need to configure on a new Windows 2000 Professional computer to get it up and running on the network without incurring increased network broadcast traffic?

○ a. A unique IP address, the subnet mask, and the DNS server address

○ b. A unique IP address, the subnet mask, the DHCP server address, and the default gateway address

○ c. A unique IP address, the subnet mask, the default gateway address, and a properly configured **HOSTS** file

○ d. A unique IP address, the subnet mask, the default gateway address, and a WINS server address

Answer d is correct. WINS resolves NetBIOS computer names to IP addresses and vice versa. Answer a is incorrect because it does not specify a means for resolving NetBIOS names and therefore NetBIOS broadcasts have to be used. Answer b is incorrect because it does not specify a means for resolving NetBIOS names and therefore NetBIOS broadcasts have to be used as well. Answer c is incorrect because a HOSTS file resolves hostnames to IP addresses, but it does not resolve NetBIOS names; that is the job of an LMHOSTS file.

Question 5

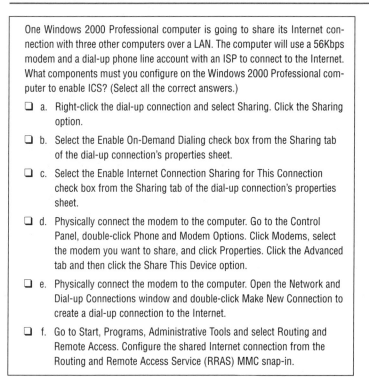

One Windows 2000 Professional computer is going to share its Internet connection with three other computers over a LAN. The computer will use a 56Kbps modem and a dial-up phone line account with an ISP to connect to the Internet. What components must you configure on the Windows 2000 Professional computer to enable ICS? (Select all the correct answers.)

❑ a. Right-click the dial-up connection and select Sharing. Click the Sharing option.

❑ b. Select the Enable On-Demand Dialing check box from the Sharing tab of the dial-up connection's properties sheet.

❑ c. Select the Enable Internet Connection Sharing for This Connection check box from the Sharing tab of the dial-up connection's properties sheet.

❑ d. Physically connect the modem to the computer. Go to the Control Panel, double-click Phone and Modem Options. Click Modems, select the modem you want to share, and click Properties. Click the Advanced tab and then click the Share This Device option.

❑ e. Physically connect the modem to the computer. Open the Network and Dial-up Connections window and double-click Make New Connection to create a dial-up connection to the Internet.

❑ f. Go to Start, Programs, Administrative Tools and select Routing and Remote Access. Configure the shared Internet connection from the Routing and Remote Access Service (RRAS) MMC snap-in.

Answers b, c, and e are correct. To enable ICS, you need a LAN connection or a dial-up connection to the Internet. You also need to select the Enable Internet Connection Sharing check box for this connection. For a dial-up Internet connection, you should select the Enable On-Demand Dialing check box. Answer a is incorrect because the context menu for a dial-up connection does not have a Sharing option. Answer d is incorrect because modems cannot be shared in Windows 2000 Professional. Answer f is incorrect because ICS cannot be configured from the RRAS MMC snap-in.

Question 6

Robert wants to be able to use a VPN connection via dial-up to connect to his company's headquarters in New York. He already uses a dial-up connection to access the Internet from his notebook PC. At times, he wants to have the option of logging on to the corporate Windows 2000 network domain from the Log on to Windows dialog box by selecting the Log on Using Dial-up Connection check box. He wants to use the corporate VPN connection for this purpose. What must Robert configure to accomplish this?

○ a. When creating the VPN connection, he must select For All Users in the Connection Availability dialog box of the Network Connection Wizard.

○ b. He must select the Include Windows Logon Domain check box from the Options tab of the VPN connection's properties sheet.

○ c. He must make sure that the Netlogon service startup type is set to Automatic. He needs to use the Services console in the MMC.

○ d. No special settings are necessary after the VPN connection has been created.

Answer a is correct. To display the VPN option for logging on to a Windows 2000 Professional computer, you cannot select the Only for Myself option in the Connection Availability dialog box of the Network Connection Wizard. Answer b is incorrect because Robert must select the For All Users option first when creating the VPN connection. Answer c is incorrect because the Netlogon service startup type is set to Automatic by default. Answer d is incorrect because the For All Users option must be selected when the VPN connection is being created.

Question 7

Heidi uses a Windows 2000 Professional computer at her company's branch office in San Mateo, California. Her computer is connected to the LAN for the branch office. Heidi's computer uses a public IP address for Internet access over the LAN. What is the best method for her to connect to a remote access server computer in Toronto, Canada (the company's headquarters), which has the public Internet IP address 197.41.146.12?

○ a. Heidi can use a dial-up connection to the Internet to use a VPN connection to the remote access server.

○ b. Heidi can use a dial-up connection to connect directly to the remote access server, using a modem and a phone line.

○ c. Heidi can use her computer's public IP address for Internet access to establish a VPN connection to the remote access server over the existing LAN.

○ d. Heidi can take advantage of an infrared connection to the remote access server.

○ e. Heidi can connect directly to the remote access server by using SLIP and the remote access server's IP address, 197.41.146.12.

Answer c is correct. A VPN connection works well over a LAN connection to the Internet. Answer a is incorrect because VPN connections via LANs are always preferable to VPN connections over dial-up links. Answer b is incorrect because Heidi would incur long-distance phone charges to connect directly to the remote access server in Toronto, and the RAS server might not accept direct dial-up connections. Answer d is incorrect because infrared connections are based on limited line-of-sight distances. Answer e is incorrect because Windows 2000 RAS servers use PPP; SLIP is a legacy protocol that is used mostly by Unix computers.

Question 8

> Alexis is the administrator for a LAN with 2 Windows 2000 servers and 17 Windows 2000 Professional computers. TCP/IP is the only network protocol that is used on the LAN. One of the server computers is also a DHCP server for the network, and all 17 workstations are configured to obtain their IP addresses automatically. Alexis decides to give her users access to the Internet by connecting a 56Kbps modem with a phone line to one of the Windows 2000 Professional computers and enabling ICS. After Alexis sets up the computer to dial up to the Internet successfully, she turns on ICS. However, none of the other computers on the LAN can access the shared connection. What is the most likely cause of this problem?
>
> ○ a. Alexis needs to add the ISP's DNS server addresses as DHCP options.
>
> ○ b. Alexis must remove the DHCP server service from the network.
>
> ○ c. Alexis must assign static IP addresses to all the computers on the LAN.
>
> ○ d. Alexis needs to configure ICS for the LAN connection instead of for the dial-up connection to the Internet.

Answer b is correct. When ICS is enabled, it becomes the DHCP allocator as long as no active DHCP server is on the network. A DHCP server on the same network inhibits ICS from operating as the DHCP allocator. DNS server settings are by proxy in ICS as long as the ISP is acting as the external DNS host. Answer a is incorrect because adding the ISP's DNS server addresses as a DHCP option does not change the default gateway nor IP subnet to properly correspond with the ICS settings. Answer c is incorrect because Microsoft does not recommend assigning static IP addresses for use with ICS. Answer d is incorrect because ICS is sharing the dial-up connection to the Internet, not a LAN connection.

Question 9

What is APIPA?

○ a. It's DHCP for Windows 2000 Professional.

○ b. It's used only in conjunction with ICS to assign IP addresses to other computers on the network so that they can share an Internet connection.

○ c. It's a scope of IP addresses assigned to Windows 2000 Professional computers by default.

○ d. It's a feature of Windows 2000 Professional for computers using the TCP/IP protocol that are configured to obtain IP addresses automatically. APIPA becomes active only if no DHCP server is available on the network. APIPA assigns nonroutable IP addresses to computers on a LAN.

Answer d is correct. APIPA becomes active only if the Windows 2000 Professional computers connected to the LAN cannot contact any DHCP servers. APIPA uses the reserved IP address range 169.254.0.0 through 169.254.255.254, which is nonroutable, with the subnet mask 255.255.0.0. Answer a is incorrect because APIPA was not designed to be used instead of DHCP. Answer b is incorrect because APIPA does not work only with ICS. Answer c is incorrect because APIPA is not just a static scope of IP addresses; the IP addresses allocated by APIPA vary depending on which IP addresses are already in use on the network.

Question 10

You are the administrator for a Windows 2000 Server network, complete with DNS servers, WINS servers, and DHCP servers, that are all up and running. You will be installing 30 new Windows 2000 Professional computers with all the default installation settings. You want to ensure that all these new workstations will obtain their IP addresses automatically. What do you need to do?

○ a. Open the Network and Dial-up Connections window. Right-click the LAN and select Properties. Click Client for Microsoft Networks and then click Properties to configure automatic IP addressing.

○ b. Open a command prompt window and run the command **ipconfig /configure** to allow the computer to obtain an IP address automatically.

○ c. Open the Network and Dial-up Connections window. Right-click the LAN and select Properties. Select Internet Protocol (TCP/IP) and click Properties. Click the Advanced button and enable automatic IP addressing on the IP Settings tab.

○ d. Nothing. Life is good.

Answer d is correct. The TCP/IP network protocol is the default protocol when you install Windows 2000 Professional. Obtaining an IP address automatically is the default selection for TCP/IP. Therefore, you do not need to make any adjustments in order for the new computers to be automatically assigned IP addresses from the DHCP servers on the existing LAN. Answer a is incorrect because you do not need to configure the Client for Microsoft Networks to obtain an IP address automatically. Answer b is incorrect because /configure is not a valid command-line option for the ipconfig command. Answer c is incorrect because the Advanced TCP/IP Settings dialog box does not provide any options for enabling automatic IP addressing.

Need to Know More?

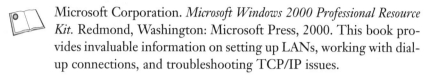 Microsoft Corporation. *Microsoft Windows 2000 Professional Resource Kit.* Redmond, Washington: Microsoft Press, 2000. This book provides invaluable information on setting up LANs, working with dial-up connections, and troubleshooting TCP/IP issues.

Stinson, Craig, and Siechert, Carl. *Running Microsoft Windows 2000 Professional.* Redmond, Washington: Microsoft Press, 2000. This book contains good information on administering and troubleshooting LAN configurations and dial-up connections.

Barker, Gord, and Harrison, Doug. *MCSE Training Guide: Windows 2000 Professional.* Indianapolis: Que Publishing, 2002. This book is the perfect complement to this *Exam Cram 2* book; it provides in-depth information on all aspects of working with Windows 2000 Professional, including details on NTFS 5, Windows 2000 disks, volumes, and file systems.

To find more information, search the TechNet CD-ROM (or its online version, through www.microsoft.com) and/or the *Windows 2000 Professional Resource Kit* CD-ROM, using the keywords APIPA, dial-up connection, TCP/IP, PPTP, L2TP, DNS, and ICS.

Monitoring and Optimizing Performance and Reliability

. . . .

Terms you'll need to understand:

✓ Windows 2000 Backup
✓ Normal backup
✓ Differential and Incremental backup
✓ System state
✓ Safe Mode startup options
✓ Last Known Good Configuration
✓ Recovery Console
✓ Emergency repair disk (ERD)
✓ **makeboot.exe** and **makebt32.exe**
✓ Optimization, Counters, and Objects
✓ Sample (or update) interval
✓ Baselining
✓ Paging file

Techniques you'll need to master:

✓ Backing up and restoring data
✓ Backing up and restoring the system state
✓ Using System Monitor
✓ Setting performance alerts

After a Windows 2000 system has been installed, configured, and secured, an administrator's goal is to ensure reliable and optimal performance. This chapter explores the skills required to prepare for and recover from system failures, and it provides a foundation for performance monitoring and optimization.

Backing Up and Restoring Data

In Windows 2000 Windows Backup helps you plan for and recover from data loss by allowing you to back up and restore files, folders, and system state data (including the registry) manually, or on a schedule. The new-and-improved Backup tool supports all kinds of storage devices and media, including tape drives, logical drives, removable disks, and recordable CD-ROMs. The Backup tool also has wizards to help administrators, especially those who are new to Windows 2000, implement backup and recovery processes.

Using Windows Backup

To open Windows Backup, you need to perform one of the following steps:

➤ Select Start, Run. Type `ntbackup` and then click OK.

➤ Select Start, Programs, Accessories, System Tools, Backup.

Windows Backup provides the Backup Wizard, which steps you through the choices and configurations related to the backup. Rather than use the wizard, you can manually configure a backup by clicking the Backup tab of the Windows Backup program.

Permissions and Rights

To successfully back up or restore data on a Windows 2000 system, users must have appropriate *permissions* and *user rights*. Users can back up all their own files and folders, plus files for which they have Read permission. To restore files and folders, users must have Write permission.

Each system has two user rights: Backup Files and Directories and Restore Files and Directories. Users with these rights can back up or restore all files, regardless of the permissions assigned to them. By default, the Administrators, Backup Operators, and (on a server) Server Operators groups have these two user rights. You can assign one or both of these rights to any other security principal (user, group, or computer), although the best practice is to assign rights to a domain local group in a Windows 2000 native-mode domain.

Backup Types

With the several kinds of backup jobs available in Windows 2000, you can create a backup strategy that maximizes efficiency, minimizes media utilized, and minimizes performance impact. Each file has an archive attribute, also called a *backup marker*. When a file is changed, the archive attribute is set, indicating that the file has been modified since the last backup. This marker is the focus of the different backup types because some types look for the marker, and others do not. Some types clear the marker, and others do not. Table 10.1 describes the different backup types.

Table 10.1	The Different Backup Types		
Backup Type	**Looks for Marker**	**Clears Marker**	**Resulting Backup Set**
Normal	No	Yes	Backup of all selected files and folders. This is the most complete backup and the most straightforward to recover, but it is also the lengthiest to create.
Copy	No	No	Copy of all selected files and folders.
Differential	Yes	No	Backup of selected files that have changed since the last normal backup. If you create a normal backup, one week later you create a differential backup, and another week later you create another differential backup, you could restore all data by using the normal backup and the second differential backup, which contains all files that have changed since the normal backup. You could, in this example, discard the first differential backup.

(continued)

Table 10.1	The Different Backup Types *(continued)*		
Backup Type	Looks for Marker	Clears Marker	Resulting Backup Set
Incremental	Yes	Yes	Backup of all data that has changed since the most recent (normal or incremental) backup. If you create a normal backup, one week later you create an incremental backup, and another week later you create a second incremental backup, you would need all three backups to recover data.
Daily	Yes	No	Backup of all files and folders that have changed during the day.

Backup Strategies

Backup strategies generally combine different backup types. Some backup types require more time than others to create the backup. A normal backup takes the most time to create because it is backing up all selected files; however, it creates a *baseline*, or complete backup. The second backup could be incremental or differential—the result would be the same. The third and subsequent backups are where the difference in strategy starts to be significant. If the second and third backups are differential, the third backup includes all files changed since the normal backup. If the second and third backups are incremental, the third backup includes only files changed since the second backup, which was an incremental backup.

So why wouldn't you just do a normal backup and then do incremental backups until the end of time period you determine? Incremental backups take longer than a differential backup to *recover*. Imagine recovering a machine that had a normal backup one year ago and that has had an incremental backup every week since. To recover that system after a catastrophe, you would have to restore the normal backup and then restore 51 incremental backups. If you had used differential backups, you would have to restore only the normal backup and the most recent differential backup.

Therefore, you should balance the cost of backup time against the cost of recovery time. You also need to factor in the media required to support your backup plan. You must save incremental backups until the next normal backup. You need to keep only the most recent differential backup, along with the most recent normal backup.

Configuring File and Folder Backups

When you create a backup job by using the Backup Wizard or the Backup tab of the Windows Backup utility, you can specify the following:

➤ Drives, files, or folders to back up. You can place a checkmark next to a drive, file, or folder, and selected items are backed up according to the backup type. Cleared items are not backed up. A grayed-out checkmark indicates a container (disk or folder) in which some, but not all, contents are selected.

➤ A backup destination. You can back up to a file or to any other storage device configured on a system.

➤ A pathname and filename for the backup file, or a tape to use.

➤ Backup options, such as backup type and log file type.

➤ A description of the job, to help you identify the job.

➤ Whether the backup medium already contains existing backup jobs.

➤ Advanced backup options, including compression and data verification.

Backing Up the System State

The Backup utility can back up what is called *system state* data, which includes critical operating system files that you can use to rebuild the system. You can reinstall a failed system with the Windows 2000 CD-ROM. Then, you can restore the system state data, bringing the system back to its original condition as of the time of the system state backup.

 You need to be familiar with backing up the system state. You should know that the backup program *can* provide you with a backup of the system's registry as a whole, but it cannot back up individual components of system state data.

System state data includes the following:

➤ The registry

➤ The component services class registration database—that is, Component Object Model + (COM+) objects

➤ System startup files

➤ The Certificate Services database—that is, domain controllers (DCs) and member servers running Certificate Services only

➤ Active Directory—that is, DCs only

➤ The sysvol folder—that is, DCs only

Configuring a System State Backup

To configure a system state backup, you need to perform the following steps:

1. In the Backup Wizard, on the What to Back Up page, select Only Back Up the System State Data.

2. In the Backup Wizard, on the Items to Back Up page, expand My Computer and select the System State Data check box.

Scheduling Backup Jobs

You can use the Backup utility in conjunction with Task Scheduler to schedule backups to occur at regular intervals or during periods of relative inactivity on a network.

Scheduling a Backup by Using the Backup Wizard

To schedule a backup by using the Backup Wizard, you need to perform the following steps:

1. In the Backup Wizard, on the Completing the Backup Wizard page, click Advanced.

2. On the When to Back Up page, click Later.

3. Enter a job name.

4. Click Set Schedule.

5. In the Schedule Job dialog box, configure start time and frequency.

6. Click OK.

Configuring a Job by Using the Scheduled Jobs Tab

To configure a job by using the Scheduled Jobs tab, you need to perform the following steps:

1. In the Backup utility, select the Scheduled Jobs tab.

2. Double-click the day on which you want to start scheduled backups.

3. Complete the information in the Backup Wizard.

Restoring Files and Folders

You can restore files and folders by using the Backup utility, using the Restore Wizard, or manually restoring them (without the wizard). When you restore files and folders, you specify which ones to restore, a restore location (original location, alternate location, or a single folder), and options (such as replace existing files with backup files).

If you backed up data from an NT File System (NTFS) volume, you must restore data to an NTFS volume to avoid data loss and preserve permissions, Encrypting File System (EFS) settings (that is, encryption), disk quota settings, mounted drive configuration, and remote storage information.

Troubleshooting and Repairing a Windows 2000 System

Windows 2000 has several features that allow you to repair a system that will not start or will not load Windows 2000: Safe Mode (and other advanced startup options), the Recovery Console, and the ERD. These features are useful if some system files become corrupted or are accidentally erased, or if software or device drivers that have been installed cause the system to not work properly.

Safe Mode and Other Advanced Startup Options

The Safe Mode option, which was first introduced in Windows 95, allows you to launch Windows 2000 Professional with only a subset of drivers and services loaded into memory. You can usually run the system under Safe Mode when the system won't run in normal mode. You also have the option of turning on Boot Logging so that you can better determine which services or drivers may not be loading. Windows 2000 still offers you the ability to boot under VGA mode in case of a video driver problem, and you can also roll back the system to the Last Known Good Configuration, just like in Windows NT 4.0.

Safe Mode

Safe Mode lets you start a system with a minimal set of device drivers and services. For example, if newly installed device drivers or software are preventing a computer from starting, you may be able to start the computer in Safe Mode and then remove the software or device drivers from the system. Safe Mode does not work in all situations, especially if system files are corrupted or missing or if the hard disk is damaged or has failed. All Safe Mode states start using standard VGA and create a boot log, which is useful when you are determining the exact cause of system startup problems.

To view the Advanced Startup options, press the F8 key when the operating system is booting. When you see the operating system selection screen, press the F8 key as well. Three different Safe Mode states are available as advanced startup options under Windows 2000 Professional:

> *Safe Mode*—This basic Safe Mode state launches Windows 2000 using default settings, including the VGA monitor, Microsoft mouse driver, no network connections, and the minimal device drivers required to start Windows. If a computer does not start successfully using Safe Mode, you might need to use the Recovery Console feature or an ERD, as discussed later in this chapter, in the "ERDs and the Emergency Repair Process" section, to repair the system.

> *Safe Mode with Networking*—This Safe Mode state starts Windows 2000 using only Safe Mode drivers and services and drivers required to enable network connections. If you are confident that network issues are not the cause of a problem, it can be useful to boot to a mode that allows you to connect to a remote system, access installation files and service packs (SPs), or back up data.

> *Safe Mode with the Command Prompt*—This option uses the Safe Mode configuration but displays the command prompt instead of the Windows graphical user interface (GUI) after you log on successfully. This is useful if you believe a process spawned by the Explorer shell is causing the problem.

Advanced Startup Options

Windows 2000 provides several startup modes to help you troubleshoot and repair Windows 2000 systems as well as to recover from various types of disaster. Understanding each option allows you to make informed decisions about the best startup method to use in a particular crisis situation. Just as with Safe Mode, to select an advanced startup option, you press F8 during the operating system selection phase of the Windows 2000 startup process.

The following startup options provide extra troubleshooting capabilities for Windows 2000 machines:

> *Enable Boot Logging*—This option starts Windows 2000 and logs all drivers and services that the system loads (or fails to load) to a log file called

`ntbtlog.txt`, located in the `%SystemRoot%` directory. Safe Mode, Safe Mode with Networking, and Safe Mode with Command Prompt also create a boot log file. The boot log is useful when you are determining the exact cause of system startup problems.

➤ *Enable VGA Mode*—This option employs the extremely stable and well-debugged standard VGA driver for Windows 2000. This mode is useful when you have installed a new video card or have configured the wrong driver or a faulty driver. Video is a common troubleshooting issue in the Windows environment. The VGA driver is used in the various Safe Mode states.

➤ *Last Known Good Configuration*—Windows 2000 starts using the registry configuration (`ControlSet`) that was saved at the last successful logon to Windows 2000. The Last Known Good Configuration option helps you recover from incorrect configuration of hardware device drivers and services. However, it does not solve problems caused by corrupted or missing drivers or files. Any changes made to the `ControlSet` key of the registry since the last successful startup and logon are lost when you select to start up with the Last Known Good Configuration option. You should try this option before resorting to the emergency repair process, which is discussed later in this chapter.

➤ *Directory Services Restore Mode*—This option applies only to Windows 2000 Server DCs and is used to restore Active Directory and the `sysvol` folder.

➤ *Debugging Mode*—In this mode, Windows 2000 starts and sends debugging information through a serial cable to another computer.

➤ *Remote Installation Options*—If you are using or have used Remote Installation Service (RIS) to install Windows 2000 on a computer, you might see additional options related to restoring or recovering a system using RIS. RIS is covered in detail in Chapter 6, "Installing Windows 2000 Professional."

Windows 2000 Recovery Options

To specify Windows 2000 behavior if a system stops unexpectedly, you need to follow these steps:

1. Right-click My Computer and then select Properties.

2. On the Advanced tab, click Startup and Recovery, and under Recovery, select the actions that Windows 2000 should perform if a `stop` error occurs.

Available Recovery Actions

The following are the available recovery actions:

➤ If you select Write an Event to the System Log or Send an Administrative Alert, you must have a paging file that is at least 2MB on the computer's boot volume.

➤ The Write an Event to the System Log option is available only on Windows 2000 Professional. On Windows 2000 Server, this action occurs by default every time a Stop error occurs.

➤ The Write Debugging Information To option requires a paging file on the boot volume that is large enough to hold all the computer's physical RAM, plus 1MB. If you also select the Write Kernel Information Only check box, Windows 2000 writes only kernel information to the listed file instead of writing the entire contents of system memory.

➤ You can save some memory if you clear the Write Debugging Information To, Write an Event to the System Log, or Send an Administrative Alert options. How much memory is saved depends on the computer, but the drivers that enable these features typically require about 60KB to 70KB.

➤ If you contact Microsoft Product Support Services about a Stop error, the person you contact might ask for the system-memory dump file generated by the Write Debugging Information To option. For each dump file generated, Windows always writes to the same filename. To save successive dump files, you need to change the filename after each Stop error.

Setting Up Recovery Actions to Take Place When a Service Fails

To set up recovery actions to take place when a service fails, you need to perform the following steps:

1. Open Services.

2. Right-click the service for which you want to set recovery actions and then click Properties.

3. On the Recovery tab, select the actions you want under First Attempt, Second Attempt, and Subsequent Attempts.

If you select Run a File, you should not specify programs or scripts that require user input. If you select Reboot the Computer, you can specify how long to wait before restarting the computer by clicking Reboot Computer

Information. You can also create a message to display to remote users before the computer restarts.

The Recovery Console

The *Recovery Console* is a startup option that provides a command-line interface that lets you repair system problems by using a limited set of command-line commands. By using the Recovery Console, you can start and stop services, read and write data on local drives (including drives formatted to use NTFS), format drives, repair corrupted master boot records (MBRs), and perform many other administrative tasks. This feature gives you maximum control over the repair process; only advanced users and administrators should use it.

The Recovery Console is particularly useful if you need to repair a system by copying a file from a floppy disk or CD-ROM to the hard drive. It can also help you when you need to reconfigure a service that is preventing a computer from starting properly. You should try this option before resorting to the emergency repair process, which is discussed later in this chapter, in the "ERDs and the Emergency Repair Process" section.

Running the Recovery Console on a System That Will Not Start

To run the Recovery Console on a system that will not start, you need to perform the following steps:

1. Insert the Windows 2000 Professional Setup Disk 1 (3.5-inch floppy) into the disk drive; or, if you have a bootable CD-ROM drive, insert the Windows 2000 Professional CD-ROM into the CD-ROM drive.

2. Restart the computer.

3. Follow the directions onscreen. If you are using the Setup disks, you are prompted to insert the others into the disk drive. It might take several minutes to load files. Choose the options to repair the Windows 2000 installation and, finally, to start the Recovery Console.

 Before a system fails, you should open a command prompt in Windows 2000, and, from the **i386** folder on the Windows 2000 CD-ROM or an equivalent distribution, enter the command **winnt32 /cmdcons**. Doing so installs the command console on the local hard drive (this requires 7MB of disk space) and configures it as a valid startup option. Then, if you want to start the system to the Recovery Console, you do not need the Windows 2000 CD-ROM or Setup disks. You can simply boot the machine and press F8 for startup options.

Launching the Recovery Console

The Recovery Console is quite powerful, and only advanced users who have a thorough knowledge of Windows 2000 should use it. Also, it is recommended that you install the Recovery Console on each Windows 2000 machine so it is always an available startup option.

After you start the Recovery Console, you must choose which drive you want to log on to (if you have a dual-boot or multiboot system), and you must log on with a local Administrator account and password. The Recovery Console grants the administrator access to the root of the hard drives, the \cmdcons directory if it exists, and the \winnt directory and all directories below it. An administrator has full access to the CD-ROM and to floppy drives. These limitations are in place for security concerns, and access to other devices or systems is functionally beyond the scope and purpose of the Recovery Console. The Recovery Console only allows you to repair the existing installation and to successfully boot Windows 2000.

Recovery Console Commands

The easiest way to work in the Recovery Console—as in any unfamiliar environment—is to type help at the command prompt and then press the Enter key. The commands that are available in the Recovery Console are listed in Table 10.2.

Table 10.2 Recovery Console Commands	
Command	**Description**
chdir (cd)	Displays the name of the current folder or changes the current folder.
chkdsk	Checks a disk and displays a status report.
cls	Clears the screen.
copy	Copies a single file to another location.
delete (del)	Deletes one or more files.
dir	Displays a list of files and subfolders in a folder.
disable	Disables a system service or a device driver.
enable	Starts or enables a system service or a device driver.
exit	Exits the Recovery Console and restarts the computer.
fdisk	Manages partitions on hard disks.
fixboot	Writes a new partition boot sector onto the system partition.
fixmbr	Repairs the MBR of the partition boot sector.
format	Formats a disk.
help	Displays a list of the commands that you can use in the Recovery Console.

Table 10.2 Recovery Console Commands *(continued)*	
Command	**Description**
logon	Logs on to a Windows 2000 installation.
map	Displays the drive letter mappings.
mkdir (md)	Creates a folder.
more	Displays a text file.
rename (ren)	Renames a single file.
rmdir (rd)	Deletes a folder.
systemroot	Sets the current folder to the **SystemRoot** folder of the system that you are currently logged on to.
type	Displays a text file.

ERDs and the Emergency Repair Process

The *ERD* feature helps you repair problems with system files, the startup environment (if you have a dual-boot or multiboot system), and the partition boot sector on the boot volume. Before you use the emergency repair process feature to repair a system, you must create an ERD. You should periodically create new ERDs to keep the ERD as up-to-date as possible. Without a recent ERD, you may not be able to leverage the full functionality of the repair process.

An ERD is quite different in Windows 2000 than it is in Windows NT 4, and you create an ERD in Windows 2000 by using a different method than in NT 4. An ERD does not contain a complete, or even partial, copy of the registry—it simply contains system and disk configuration information. But the ERD remains a very important tool.

 The **rdisk.exe** tool, which in Windows NT allows you to create an ERD, does not exist in Windows 2000.

To create an ERD, you need to perform the following steps:

1. Start the Windows Backup program.

2. Click Emergency Repair Disk on the Welcome tab.

3. Insert a blank 1.44MB floppy disk into the floppy disk drive and click OK.

You can also specify to back up the registry to the Repair folder (for example, c:\Winnt\Repair) to help recover from a damaged registry. When you back up the registry in this way, the registry files are copied from their default location (for example, c:\Winnt\Config) to the repair folder. When the process is complete, click OK and then remove and label the floppy disk.

 No, you cannot boot a Windows 2000 machine with an ERD. The ERD never has been and is not now a bootable disk. You always need to read the exam questions and answers carefully, or you may get tripped up!

The *emergency repair process* enables you to restore corrupted system files and configuration. Even if you have not created an ERD, you can still try to use the emergency repair process; however, you might lose any changes you have made to the system, such as installation of SPs and updates, and you might need to reinstall them.

You can also use the emergency repair process to reinstall Windows 2000 over a damaged Windows 2000 system. This might be time-consuming, but is useful if the emergency repair process does not solve a problem. To have a chance at making the emergency repair process work properly, you must closely follow the five steps described in the following sections.

Step 1: Starting with the Windows 2000 Setup Disks or CD-ROM

You start the emergency repair process by booting the computer, using the Windows 2000 CD-ROM (you might need to configure the system's BIOS to enable booting to the CD-ROM if the system supports bootable CDs). You can, alternatively, boot with the first of the four Windows 2000 Setup disks (the process prompts you for subsequent disks). If you don't have a bootable CD-ROM and don't have the boot disks handy, you can run the batch file in the CD-ROM's bootdisk folder.

 makeboot.exe and **makebt32.exe** in Windows 2000 replace the **winnt /ox** and **winnt32 /ox** commands in Windows NT. You can produce boot disks on any system—it does not have to be a Windows 2000 system. You simply execute **makeboot.exe** on a 16-bit operating system or **makebt32.exe** on a 32-bit platform.

Step 2: Choosing the Repair Options During Setup

As the computer starts, Windows 2000 Setup launches. During Setup, you are prompted about whether you want to continue installing Windows 2000. You should press Enter to confirm and start the process. You are then asked whether you want to install a new installation of Windows 2000 or repair an existing installation. To repair a damaged or corrupt system, you press R. You are then prompted about whether you want to use the Recovery Console or the emergency repair process. To select the emergency repair process, you press R again.

Step 3: Choosing the Type of Repair

There are only two types of repair to choose from in the emergency repair process. You are asked to select either of the following:

➤ *Fast Repair*—This type of repair requires no further interaction or choices. It checks the system and attempts to repair any problems related to the registry, system files, the partition boot sector on the boot volume, and the startup environment (in a multiboot environment). The Fast Repair option restores the registry from the repair directory, so it is important to have updated that directory recently. You can back up the registry to the Repair directory as part of the ERD creation procedure. If the Repair directory is quite outdated, Fast Repair is not the best choice because you might lose any recent changes to hardware, software, drivers, services, or other settings.

➤ *Manual Repair*—This requires user interaction and prompts you to select whether to repair system files, boot sector problems, or startup environment problems.

 The Manual Repair option does not allow you to repair the registry. To select that option, you must choose the Fast Repair option.

Step 4: Starting the Repair Process

To start the repair process, you should have the ERD for the system. It is *not* advisable to repair a system with another system's ERD because each system is unique; therefore, each system's ERD is also unique. You should also have the Windows 2000 installation CD handy. If you do not have the ERD, the emergency repair process attempts to locate the Windows 2000 installation on the system and begin the repair process, but it might fail.

Step 5: Restarting the Computer

If the repair was successful, you should be able to restart into a functional Windows 2000 system. If it was not successful, you should consider other recovery options or, perhaps, the option of recovering by re-installing the system and restoring data from backup sets.

Optimizing and Troubleshooting Performance

Although Windows 2000 Professional performs extremely well as a general workstation platform, with the right tools, techniques, and knowledge, you can further optimize the operating system for particular roles as well as troubleshoot performance challenges. The following sections look at System Monitor, Performance Logs and Alerts, Task Manager, and other tools you can use to improve Windows 2000's performance.

Using System Monitor

The *System Monitor snap-in* is a node of the Performance console (which you access by selecting Start, Settings, Control Panel, Administrative Tools, Performance) and is available for inclusion in custom Microsoft Management Console (MMC) consoles. This tool allows you to visually inspect the activity of system components such as the memory, processor, disk subsystem, network cards, paging file, and applications. The plethora of performance metrics, or *counters*, available for monitoring can make the task a daunting one indeed. You will examine the most useful counters later in this section.

System Monitor, like all MMC snap-ins, is best controlled by right-clicking. If you right-click the main portion of the Details pane, you can select Add Counters. *Counters* show the granular statistics related to specific aspects of system performance. But counters are just one aspect of the entire system monitoring scheme. The available performance monitoring components are hierarchically organized into the following groups:

➤ *Computer*—With this performance option you can monitor performance on the local (default) or a remote system.

➤ *Object*—This component is composed of a computer system's core elements, such as processor, memory, physical disk, or network interface. You must first select one of these objects before you can select any counters to monitor system performance.

➤ *Counter*—Counters are performance metrics that measure various aspects of System Monitor objects. For example, you would select the Memory object along with the Available Mbytes counter if you wanted to measure how much free memory was available on a system at any given point in time. There can literally be thousands of counters available for monitoring, so you should take advantage of the Explain button in the Add Counters dialog box; clicking it produces a description of the selected counter.

➤ *Instance*—When an object occurs more than once on a computer, you see instances. For example, a multiprocessor machine has instances for each processor when you select the processor object. When you select the logical disk object, you see instances for each drive volume on a system. Often, instances are numbered, with the first instance being 0, the second instance 1, and so on. Many times, an additional instance provides the total for all instances. For example, a dual-processor system has a _Total instance, which reflects the combination of processors 0 and 1.

After you select a computer, object, counter, and (if necessary) instance, you need to click Add to add the counter to the System Monitor view. By right-clicking the view and choosing Properties, you can alter all the properties of the monitor, including the display colors of counters, the scale and sample rate, and the format of the monitor's display—which can be in graph (default), histogram (bar chart), or report (numeric display) format.

Using Performance Logs and Alerts

The *Performance Logs and Alerts snap-in*, which is part of the Performance console, allows you to collect and save performance data as well as proactively configure a system to generate a notification based on a performance threshold.

Configuring Alerts

Alerts allow you to generate actions based on a counter reaching a particular threshold. For example, you might want to be notified when a disk's capacity reaches 90% so that you can try to increase the disk's capacity before the disk fills up. By specifying a counter (such as %Free Space for a logical disk) and a threshold (under 10%), you can cause an event to be logged, a program to be run, a log to be started, or a network message to be sent.

To configure alerts, you select the Alerts node in the Performance Logs and Alerts snap-in. Then you right-click in the Details pane and choose New Alert Settings. You need to enter a name for the alert settings; this name is for your use only. Then in the Properties dialog box, you add the appropriate counter(s) for the alert you are configuring. For each counter, you must specify a threshold (over or under a particular amount) on the General tab. You can then configure, on the Action tab, what will happen when those alerts are generated. On the Schedule tab, you can specify when the selected counters should be scanned. If you specify no schedule, scanning begins as soon as you click OK. The alert settings you have specified appear in the Alerts node of the snap-in. You can right-click an alert setting to change its configuration, delete it, or stop or start scanning.

Configuring Logs

Logs collect and store performance counters. You can view them by using System Monitor, retrieve them in a spreadsheet such as Excel, or import them into a database. There are two types of logs:

➤ *Counter logs*—These logs record data captured over a span of time and are useful for detecting trends, setting baselines of performance, and spotting performance bottlenecks. Baselines are discussed later in this chapter.

➤ *Trace logs*—These logs collect performance data when an event such as a process creation, disk input/output (I/O), or page fault occurs. Trace logs are useful for debugging.

To create a counter log, you select the Counter Logs node of the snap-in and then right-click the Details pane and choose New Log Settings. You need to give the log a name that will help you identify it in the future and then click OK. In the Log dialog box, you need to add one or more counters to be recorded and then specify the *sample rate*—the interval at which counter data will be collected. Obviously, a shorter sample rate provides more data but also fills up the log more quickly than a longer sample rate.

By default, logs are stored in the %SystemDrive%\Perflogs folder, and the default format is binary (.blg extension). You can stop and start logs as desired and view them in System Monitor. To view a log with System Monitor, you need to right-click the Details pane (where the monitoring graph is displayed) and choose Properties. Then, on the Source tab, click Log File and enter or browse to the log file filename.

To analyze a log with Excel, Access, or another database and with reporting tools, you need to save the log as a comma- or tab-delimited file (with a .csv or .tsv extension). When you stop these logs, you cannot restart or append them as you can with binary logs.

Managing Performance

Monitoring, troubleshooting, and optimizing performance are some of the most important tasks an administrator performs on Windows 2000 Professional systems. Managing performance involves several steps:

1. Creating a baseline

2. Proactively monitoring

3. Evaluating performance

4. Identifying potential bottlenecks

5. Taking corrective action

6. Monitoring the effectiveness and stability of the change

7. Returning to step 2

Being proactive as a network and systems administrator is key to avoiding lots of system downtime. By establishing baselines for important system components, you can compare how the system is currently running (in terms of processor, memory, disk usage, and so on) to unbiased historical data. Because there are so many different objects and counters that you can monitor, you should become familiar with some of the most important ones.

Creating a Baseline

A *baseline* is a range of acceptable performance of a system component under normal working conditions. One of the most important, and most often overlooked, steps of managing performance is creating a baseline. Baselining, or establishing a baseline, requires that you capture key counters while a system performs with normal loads and all services running. Then, you can compare future performance against the baseline to identify potential bottlenecks, troubleshoot sudden changes in performance, and justify system improvements.

A baseline should cover a relatively large timeframe so that it captures a range of data reflecting acceptable performance. The sample interval for the log should be somewhat large as well so that the baseline log does not become enormous. You should generate baselines regularly—perhaps even once a month—so that you can identify performance trends and evaluate bottlenecks to system and network performance. If you follow these guidelines, you will produce a baseline that gives an accurate overview of system performance.

The most useful objects to understand and monitor are the following:

➤ *Cache*—This is the physical memory used to store recently accessed disk data.

➤ *Memory*—This is the RAM used to store code and data.

➤ *Paging file*—This file is used to extend physical RAM and create virtual memory.

➤ *Physical disk*—This is the disk drive or Redundant Array of Independent Disks (RAID) device. A physical disk may contain multiple logical disks.

➤ *Logical disk*—This is the disk volume, including simple, logical, spanned, striped, mirrored, or RAID-5 volumes. A logical disk may span multiple physical disks.

➤ *Process*—This is executable code that represents a running program.

➤ *Processor*—The processor is the central processing unit (CPU).

➤ *Server*—This is the server service, which offers data and print services, even on a Windows 2000 Professional system.

➤ *System*—System counters apply to all system hardware and software.

➤ *Thread*—This is the code that the processor is processing.

Baselines should include these critical objects as well as the other counters discussed in this chapter.

Managing Memory Performance

The counters in the Memory object represent the memory available through the system's physical RAM and virtual memory or paging file. The most important counters in the Memory object are the Pages/sec counters and the Available Bytes counter:

➤ *Memory:Pages/sec, Threshold over 20 pages/sec*—This counter, and all related counters (including Page Reads/sec, Page Writes/sec, Page Faults/sec, Page Inputs/sec, and Page Outputs/sec) reflect the transfer of data and code from physical RAM to the virtual paging file, and they reflect paging-related events. When any one of these counters is high, it indicates a potential memory shortage because when a system does not have enough RAM to satisfy its needs, inactive data and code are moved from physical RAM to the virtual paging file to make room for active data and code.

➤ *Memory:Available Bytes, Threshold under 4MB*—Available Bytes reflects the amount of physical RAM available after the working sets of applications and the cache have been served. Windows 2000 Professional trims working sets and page memory to the disk to maintain at least 4MB of available RAM. If this counter is consistently lower than 4MB, it generally indicates a memory shortage.

Memory is often the first performance bottleneck in the real world. The counters related to processor and hard drive utilization might be well beyond their thresholds simply because inadequate memory is causing paging, which affects processor and hard drive utilization. So you should always check the memory counters to make sure that they are not the root performance bottleneck.

To correct a memory shortage, your first reaction might be to add more RAM, which is certainly one solution. However, it is often equally helpful to optimize memory usage by stopping unnecessary services, drivers, and background applications or by moving services or applications to systems with excess capacity.

Managing the Paging File

When physical RAM is not sufficient to support active processes, the *Virtual Memory Manager* (VMM) moves less active data or code from physical RAM to virtual memory stored in the paging file. When a process later attempts to address data or code that is currently in the paging file, the VMM transfers that memory space into physical RAM. The paging file thus provides for efficient utilization of a system's physical RAM and allows a system to support more activity than its physical RAM alone would allow. Transfer of *pages*, which are 4KB blocks of memory, to and from the paging file is normal on any system, but excessive paging, called *thrashing*, indicates a memory shortage. In addition, the paging file itself can impede performance if it is not properly optimized.

You configure the paging file by using the System applet in the Control Panel. You click the Advanced tab, the Performance Options button, and then, in the Virtual Memory section, Change. The paging file, called `pagefile.sys`, is created on the `%SystemRoot%` volume by default, and its default initial size is 1.5 times physical RAM. You can configure the paging file to be placed on other volumes or to be split across multiple volumes, in which case there is a `pagefile.sys` on selected volumes, and the total size of the paging file is the sum of all the paging files. You can also configure the initial size—the space created initially by the VMM and reserved for paging activity—and the maximum size—a setting that can permit the VMM to expand the paging file to a size greater than the initial size.

You can optimize paging in a number of ways:

➤ *Remove the paging file from the system and boot partitions.* The system partition is technically the partition that is used to start the system—it contains the NTLDR boot file and the boot sector. To make things confusing, the boot partition contains the operating system and is indicated by the variable %SystemRoot%. Luckily, most computers are configured with Windows 2000 on the c: drive (the first partition), making the boot partition, the system partition, and %SystemRoot% all pointing to the c: drive. To remove the paging file from a partition, go to the Control Panel and open the System applet. Select the Advanced tab and click the Performance Options button. Click Change and select the existing paging file drive. Set both its initial size and maximum size to 0 and then click the Set button. Click OK for each of the three dialog boxes that you've navigated through, and you are prompted to restart the computer for your changes to take affect.

➤ *Configure the paging file to reside on multiple physical disks and configure the initial size and maximum size identically on all drives.* When you do this, the paging subsystem spreads written pages evenly across all available pagefile.sys files.

➤ *Configure the paging file to reside on fast, less active drives.* If you have drives of various speeds, you should put the paging file on the fastest one. If you have drives that are less active than others, you should put the paging file on those so the paging system doesn't have to compete as often with other read and write requests.

➤ *Before moving the paging file, defragment the volumes on which you will put the paging file.* Doing this helps prevent the paging file from becoming fragmented.

➤ *Set the initial size to be sufficient for the system's paging requirements, and then set the maximum size to the same size.* When the maximum size is greater than the initial size and the system must expand the paging file, the expansion puts an additional burden on both the processor and disk subsystems. In addition, the paging file is likely to become fragmented, further hitting the performance of paging.

The ideal paging file configuration is to split the paging file evenly over multiple *physical* disks, except for the disk with the system and boot partitions.

Managing Disk Performance

The PhysicalDisk and LogicalDisk performance objects collect metrics related to individual disk drives and logical disk volumes, respectively. PhysicalDisk counters focus on storage devices, so you should use them to analyze hardware performance. You use LogicalDisk counters, which focus on specific volumes, to analyze read and write performance.

In Windows 2000 PhysicalDisk counters are available in System Monitor and Performance Logs and Alerts, but LogicalDisk counters are not gathered until you run the diskperf -yv command. The switches for the diskperf command include -yd (enables PhysicalDisk counters, which is the default); -y (enables both PhysicalDisk and LogicalDisk counters); and -nv, -nd, and -n (disable LogicalDisk counters, disable PhysicalDisk counters, and disable both sets of counters, respectively).

Until you enable the counters with the appropriate **diskperf** switch, the counters are not visible in System Monitor or Performance Logs and Alerts.

These disk performance objects and counters help you to monitor and manage disk performance:

➤ *PhysicalDisk/LogicalDisk: %DiskTime*—This counter reports the amount of time that a disk is busy servicing read or write requests. When this counter consistently approaches the 100% level, its threshold level is being met, and you might need to add more RAM or try to balance this computer's load with another computer.

➤ *PhysicalDisk/LogicalDisk: Average and Current Disk Queue Length*—These counters reflect the read/write requests that are pending and being serviced. If the queue is long, processes are being delayed. The threshold for these counters is 2; if this threshold is being met, you might need to add more RAM, balance the load with another computer, or run fewer programs simultaneously.

When disk performance is a bottleneck, you can add capacity; replace disks with faster hardware; move applications, services, or data to underutilized disks; or implement spanned or striped, volumes (RAID-5 volumes on servers).

Managing Network Performance

Windows 2000 Server can support Network Monitor for relatively sophisticated network traffic analysis, but Windows 2000 Professional has limited network performance tools. Counters are available for the number of bytes and packets received and sent over a particular network interface. However, you cannot analyze the contents or properties of packets by using Windows 2000 Professional tools alone.

To conduct detailed network analysis for a Windows 2000 Professional system, you need to install Network Monitor Driver. From the Network and Dialup Connections folder, you need to right-click a connection, choose Properties, and then click Install, Protocol, Network Monitor Driver. Network Monitor Driver can collect packets that the Windows 2000 Professional network interfaces send or receive. You can then analyze those packets by using the version of Network Monitor that ships with Systems Management Server (SMS) 2, SP1, or later.

Managing Processor Performance

A system's processor is one of the most difficult system components to optimize because every other component affects it. Low memory leads to paging, which increases processor usage; fragmented disk drives increase processor usage; hardware interrupts keep the processor busy; and, of course, applications and services place demands on the processor. Therefore, to optimize a processor, you need to look at Processor counters as well as counters for other objects. The following are some of the most useful Processor counters:

➤ *Processor:%ProcessorTime*—This counter's threshold occurs when it approaches 100% utilization. A processor being fully used (100%) is not necessarily a sign of a performance bottleneck. In fact, one would hope that you would be utilizing this expensive system component at its full capacity. Therefore, although the %ProcessorTime counter is a flag that indicates a potential bottleneck, it is not in itself enough to prescribe a solution. You should check Memory:Pages/sec to examine paging and determine whether low memory is causing excessive paging.

➤ *Processor:Interrupts/sec*—A malfunctioning hardware device may send excessive interrupts to the processor. You should compare this counter with a baseline; a significant rise in this counter without a corresponding increase in system activity may indicate a bad device. Network cards are particularly infamous for generating bogus interrupts.

➤ *System:Processor Queue Length*—A queue length that is regularly above 2 indicates that threads are backing up as they wait for processor attention.

➤ *Process:%ProcessorTime (Instance—Each Service or Application)*—This counter enumerates the activity of individual application and service, allowing you to identify processes that are placing demands on the processor.

If the Processor Queue Length counter value is low and the %ProcessorTime counter is averaging above 85% for extended periods of time, a single-threaded application or service is keeping the processor busy. A faster processor might improve performance of such a system. However, if the Processor Queue Length counter value is high, adding a second processor would be a better solution, or you might consider moving processes to underutilized systems.

Using Task Manager

Task Manager enables you to view applications and processes and a number of other common performance counters. To open Task Manager, you right-click the taskbar and choose Task Manager, or you can press Ctrl+Shift+Esc. The Applications tab enumerates active applications. The Performance tab displays useful performance metrics, beginning when Task Manager is opened. The Processes tab can display a number of process-related counters. You should click View, Select Columns to indicate which counters you want to view.

Managing Application Performance

Windows 2000 preemptively multitasks active processes, ensuring that all threads gain access to the processor. Processes run at different priorities, however. Priority levels of 0 to 31 are assigned to a process, and higher-level processes are executed before lower-level processes. As a user, you can specify process priority by using Task Manager. Right-clicking a process on the Processes tab enables you to set a process's priority. A process is assigned a priority of Normal by default. Choosing Above Normal or High increases the priority of a process and thereby increases the frequency with which its threads are serviced. Choosing Below Normal or Low diminishes the servicing of a process.

 You should not use the Realtime priority. This priority should be reserved for real-time data-gathering applications and operating system functions. Setting an application to Realtime priority can cause instability and can be difficult to reverse without restarting the system.

Process priority can also be controlled when an application is launched, using the `start` command with the `/low`, `/belownormal`, `/normal`, `/abovenormal`, `/high`, and `/realtime` switches.

Practice Questions

Question 1

> You have just installed a new tape drive in a Windows 2000 Professional computer. You want to create a reliable backup of the machine's entire registry, all system settings, and the COM+ objects. How would you accomplish this?
>
> ○ a. Use Windows Backup to back up the system state to tape.
>
> ○ b. Use Windows Backup to perform an incremental backup of the system to tape.
>
> ○ c. Use Windows Backup to perform a full backup of the system to tape.
>
> ○ d. Copy the contents of **\WINNT\SYSTEM32\CONFIG** to a secure network share on a server.

Answer a is correct. Backing up the system state in Windows 2000 allows you to obtain a backup of the registry and system settings, as well as COM+ objects. Backing up data does not back up these settings, so Answers b and c are incorrect. The `config` directory's files are locked during operation, so they cannot be copied; therefore, Answer d is incorrect.

Question 2

> You are attempting to install a Plug and Play modem in a Windows 2000 Professional computer. The modem appears to be working when you install it, but later it stops working entirely. You try several more times to reinstall the modem, but it keeps failing. What should you do?
>
> ○ a. Use the Add/Remove Hardware Wizard to remove the modem driver. Power down the computer, and then power up the computer again and let Windows 2000 locate the device driver of its choice.
>
> ○ b. Start the computer in Safe Mode. Remove the device driver for the modem. Restart the computer normally and let Windows 2000 find the device driver of its choice.
>
> ○ c. Use the Add/Remove Hardware Wizard to troubleshoot the device. Select the modem from the list that appears. The Hardware Troubleshooter starts.
>
> ○ d. Install the modem in another computer to see if it fails there as well. If it does not fail there, reinstall it in the first computer and use the manufacturer's most current driver when Windows 2000 prompts for the file location of the driver files.

Answer b is correct. To fix a device installation "gone wrong" when reinstallation doesn't work, you should use Safe Mode to remove the device driver and then let Windows 2000 select a device driver. Remember that the manufacturer's driver may not work as well as a driver from Windows 2000, which is similar. Answers a, c, and d do not enable the modem to function.

Question 3

You have been editing the Windows 2000 registry with **regedt32.exe** to try to get a device to work. Now, as punishment for your attempted good deed, the Windows 2000 computer does not boot. What should you try first for a quick system restoration?

○ a. Power on the computer and press the F8 key to get into Safe Mode.

○ b. Power on the computer and press the F8 key; then select Last Known Good Configuration.

○ c. Use the ERD to boot and restore system files.

○ d. In the Recovery Console, set the path to a floppy drive or a CD drive where you have a backup of the system files. Copy the files from the floppy disk or CD to the hard drive.

Answer b is correct. Powering on the computer, pressing the F8 key, and selecting Last Known Good Configuration should be your first choice because you know that the registry was just changed—by you! Safe Mode is best for situations where a new device or software was just added and now the system won't start up; therefore, Answer a is incorrect. You cannot boot using the ERD; therefore, Answer c is incorrect. The Recovery Console is an option, but you would resort to it only if selecting Last Known Good Configuration did not work; therefore, Answer d is incorrect.

Question 4

You perform a normal backup of the Windows 2000 Professional computer on Sunday. For the remaining days of the week, you want to back up only the files and folders that have changed since the previous day. What is the best backup type for you to select?

○ a. Daily

○ b. Differential

○ c. Incremental

○ d. Normal

Answer c is correct. An incremental backup backs up the changes since the last markers were set and then clears the markers. Therefore, for Monday through Saturday, you back up only the changes since the previous day. Differential, normal, and daily backups do not perform the same function, and therefore, Answers a, b, and d are incorrect.

Question 5

> You install a new device driver for a SCSI adapter in a Windows 2000 machine. When you restart the computer, though, trouble is on the horizon. Windows 2000 stops responding after the kernel load phase. How can you get Windows 2000 to restart successfully?
>
> ○ a. Boot the computer with the ERD and then remove the new device driver.
>
> ○ b. Boot the computer with the Windows 2000 CD-ROM and then select Restore to restore the system state.
>
> ○ c. Restore the system from the most recent backup.
>
> ○ d. Select the Last Known Good Configuration option to start Windows 2000.

Answer d is correct. The Last Known Good Configuration option is the best, and quickest, choice because it does not contain any reference to the new (and possibly noncompliant) device driver for the SCSI adapter. The ERD is not bootable, and there is no Restore startup option; therefore, Answers a and b are incorrect. Answer c might produce something like the desired result, but it is not the best answer.

Question 6

> You want to monitor **PhysicalDisk** performance counters of a logical drive. With a standard installation of Windows 2000 Professional, what additional operation must you perform to enable the monitoring of the **PhysicalDisk** counters?
>
> ○ a. Install Network Monitor Driver.
>
> ○ b. Run the **diskperf** command with the **–y** switch.
>
> ○ c. Install Network Monitor Driver and run **diskperf –yv**.
>
> ○ d. No additional operations are required. The **PhysicalDisk** counters are accessible by default.

Answer d is correct. `PhysicalDisk` counters are enabled in Windows 2000 Professional, unlike in Windows NT 4. Network Monitor Driver is used for collecting network traffic counters and for capturing packets. It is not used for any physical disk monitoring. Therefore, Answers a and c are incorrect. The `diskperf -y` command does enable the `PhysicalDisk` counters if they have been disabled, as does `diskperf -yd` in Answer c, but it is not necessary to run these commands because the counters are enabled by default; therefore, Answer b is incorrect.

Question 7

A user runs the CADDraw application several times a day to produce renderings of technical drawings. While CADDraw is running, the user catches up on email and writes memos and reports. You want to teach the user how to maximize the responsiveness of CADDraw so that the renderings don't take so long to complete. What do you teach the user?

- ○ a. Configure Performance Options in the System applet to optimize for applications.
- ○ b. Use Task Manager to change the priority of all applications to Above Normal.
- ○ c. Use Task Manager to set the CADDraw process priority to Realtime.
- ○ d. Use Task Manager to set the CADDraw process priority to High.

Answer d is correct. By setting the CADDraw process priority to High, CADDraw will be relatively higher than all other applications, including email and word processors, which launch at a default priority of Normal. Using Task Manager to set the CADDraw process priority to High increases the amount of attention CADDraw receives from the processor and improves its performance. Answer a is incorrect because Performance Options changes the performance for *all* applications, not just CADDraw, and that does not maximize CADDraw. Answer b is incorrect because raising all applications to Above Normal does not maximize CADDraw; CADDraw would still be at the same priority level as the other applications. Answer c, although it might maximize CADDraw, would likely cause system instability and would not be the best choice.

Question 8

> A Windows 2000 Professional system is experiencing decreased performance, and you suspect excessive paging. Which counter provides you with the best measure with which to confirm your suspicion?
>
> ○ a. Paging File:%Usage
> ○ b. Paging File:%Usage Peak
> ○ c. Memory:Pages/sec
> ○ d. PhysicalDisk:Disk Writes/sec

Answer c is correct. The Pages/sec counters (of which there are many) all relate to paging activity—the transfer of memory from physical RAM to the virtual memory of the paging file. The paging file counters are useful to determine whether you need a larger paging file but do not really tell you what is excessive. For example, you might have a %Usage counter of 90%, but if the paging file is only 20MB, there might not be too much paging; you might just have a paging file that's too small. Therefore, Answers a and b are incorrect. PhysicalDisk counters increase when there is paging, but they do not tell you specifically that paging is causing the disk activity. Therefore, Answer d is incorrect.

Question 9

> A Windows 2000 Professional system is not performing to specifications. You want to determine what course of action to take, and you examine a performance log, which reveals the following:
>
> Processor: %ProcessorTime: 95
>
> System: Processor Queue Length: 3
>
> Memory: Pages/sec: 10
>
> PhysicalDisk: Avg Disk Queue Length: 1
>
> Paging File: %Usage: 25
>
> What should you do to improve performance?
>
> ○ a. Add a second processor.
> ○ b. Add memory.
> ○ c. Replace the hard disk with a faster disk drive.
> ○ d. Enlarge the paging file.

Answer a is correct. The processor is overworked, and the processor queue indicates that threads are backed up and are not being serviced. Answer b would often be correct because memory is often the primary bottleneck, but in this instance, paging is well within the acceptable range. Therefore, Answer b is incorrect. The disk subsystem and paging file are not beyond thresholds either. Therefore, Answers c and d are incorrect.

Question 10

> Which of the following tools is best suited for creating a baseline of system performance?
>
> ○ a. System Monitor
>
> ○ b. Performance Logs and Alerts
>
> ○ c. Task Manager
>
> ○ d. System Information
>
> ○ e. NTBackup

Answer b is correct. Performance Logs and Alerts captures counters during a representative period of normal activity to create the baseline. You can use System Monitor to *view* the baseline, but that tool is not appropriate for creating the baseline in the first place; therefore, Answer a is incorrect. Task Manager, System Information, and NTBackup are not suited for baselining either; therefore, Answers c, d, and e are incorrect.

Need to Know More?

 Microsoft Corporation. *Microsoft Windows 2000 Professional Resource Kit.* Redmond, Washington: Microsoft Press, 2000. This book provides invaluable information on backing up and recovering data, as well as on using the Recovery Console and the emergency repair process.

 Boyce, Jim. *Microsoft Windows 2000 Professional Installation and Configuration Handbook.* Indianapolis: Que Publishing, 2000. This handbook focuses on installing and troubleshooting Windows 2000 Professional. It offers authoritative, easy-to-follow overviews and critical step-by-step processes for difficult tasks.

 Stinson, Craig, and Siechert, Carl. *Running Microsoft Windows 2000 Professional.* Redmond, Washington: Microsoft Press, 2000. This book is a good source for information on optimizing and troubleshooting Windows 2000 systems and on using the Recovery Console.

 To find more information, search the TechNet CD (or its online version, through www.microsoft.com) and/or the *Windows 2000 Professional Resource Kit* CD, using the keywords backup, restore, Recovery Console, emergency repair, system state, taskman, performance, optimizing, counter, and last known good.

Sample Test

Now it's time to put the knowledge that you've learned from reading this book to the test! Write down your answers to the following questions on a separate sheet of paper. That way, you will be able to take this sample test multiple times. After you have answered all the questions, compare your answers with the correct answers listed in Chapter 12, "Sample Test Answer Key." When you can correctly answer at least 45 of the 50 sample test questions (90%), you are ready to start using the *PrepLogic Practice Tests* CD-ROM that is included with this book. By using this sample test along with the *PrepLogic Practice Tests*, you can prepare yourself quite well for the actual Microsoft certification exam. Good luck!

Question 1

You want to secure a Windows 2000 Professional system beyond the default
security level, with as little guesswork as possible. Which tool should you use?

○ a. Local policy

○ b. Group policy

○ c. Security Configuration and Analysis

○ d. Domain security policy

Question 2

You have a domain policy that clears from the logon dialog box the name of the
last user who logged on. However, you want your Windows 2000 laptop to display your name each time you log on, to save time logging on. What must you
do to achieve this?

○ a. Change the **DontDisplayLastUser** registry entry.

○ b. Configure a local security policy that disables the Do Not Display Last
User Name in Logon Screen policy.

○ c. Configure a security database with the Do Not Display Last User Name
in Logon Screen option cleared.

○ d. Configure for the OU of your laptop a group policy that disables the Do
Not Display Last User Name in Logon Screen policy.

Question 3

What can you use to configure user rights in Windows 2000? (Select all the correct answers.)

❏ a. Local security policy

❏ b. Group policy

❏ c. User Manager

❏ d. The Users and Passwords applet

Question 4

You want Cory to be able to format partitions on the hard drive of her Windows 2000 Professional system. Which tool would you use to give her that privilege?

○ a. The Users and Passwords applet

○ b. The Disk Management snap-in

○ c. Local security policy

○ d. The Registry Editor

Question 5

You have a template account created for all new salespeople. It specifies group membership, logon script, profile location, dial-up permission, and other attributes that are common to sales users. Immediately after you create individual user accounts based on the template, users report that they cannot log on. Which setting is causing the problem?

○ a. Account Is Locked Out

○ b. Account Is Disabled

○ c. User Must Change Password at Next Logon

○ d. Enforce Password Complexity

Question 6

You back up **PRO1** each morning, using the following backup strategy:

Monday: Incremental

Tuesday: Incremental

Wednesday: Incremental

Thursday: Incremental

Friday: Normal

On Wednesday afternoon, **PRO1** crashes, and you must recover the hard drive. Which backup sets must you restore, and in which order?

Monday

Tuesday

Wednesday

Thursday

Friday

Question 7

You want to back up service and software settings on a Windows 2000 Professional system. What must you do?

- ○ a. Create an ERD.
- ○ b. Back up the system state.
- ○ c. Copy the **WINNT** folder to a server.
- ○ d. Back up the user profile folder.

Question 8

You are monitoring performance of a Windows 2000 Professional system that seems to be performing below expectations. You note the following results from these Performance Monitor counters:

Memory: Pages/sec = 80

Processor: % Utilization = 90

Physical Disk: % Disk Time = 85

System: Processor Queue Length = 3

Which of the following would be most likely to overcome the performance bottleneck on this system?

- ○ a. Additional memory
- ○ b. A faster processor
- ○ c. A second processor
- ○ d. A faster hard drive
- ○ e. A larger hard drive

Question 9

You are monitoring performance of a Windows 2000 Professional system that seems to be performing below expectations. You note the following results from these Performance Monitor counters:

Memory: Pages/sec = 10

Processor: % Utilization = 99

Physical Disk: % Disk Time = 20

System: Processor Queue Length = 2.5

Which of the following would be most likely to overcome the performance bottleneck on this system?

○ a. Additional memory

○ b. A faster processor

○ c. A second processor

○ d. A faster hard drive

○ e. A larger hard drive

○ f. A larger paging file

Question 10

You have noticed steadily decreasing performance of your system and suspect drive fragmentation. From what tool can you initiate disk defragmentation?

○ a. The properties sheet of a drive volume

○ b. The Disk Management snap-in

○ c. The Add/Remove Hardware Wizard

○ d. The System applet in the Control Panel

Question 11

Which of the following tools allows you to monitor an application's priority?

○ a. Computer Management

○ b. The System applet in the Control Panel

○ c. Task Manager

○ d. Add/Remove Programs

Question 12

What folder contains local profiles on a clean installation of a Windows 2000
Professional computer?

- ○ a. **%SystemRoot%\Winnt\system32\profiles**
- ○ b. **%SystemRoot%\profiles**
- ○ c. **%SystemRoot%\documents and settings**
- ○ d. **%SystemDrive%\documents and settings**

Question 13

Your sales staff needs to keep a locally cached copied of the **presentations**
share on **server1**, which is a Windows 2000 server. When members of the sales
staff select the **presentations** share on **\\server1**, they report there is no option
to make files available offline. How do you resolve this problem?

- ○ a   Configure the caching properties to allow caching of files for the
     presentation share on the sales staff members' computers.
- ○ b. Configure the caching properties to allow caching of files for the
     presentation share on **\\server1**.
- ○ c. Configure the caching properties to manual caching for documents for
     the **presentation** share on the sales staff members' computers.
- ○ d. Configure the caching properties to manual caching for documents for
     the **presentation** share on **\\server1**.

Question 14

As the administrator for a Windows 2000 domain called **corp.com**, you create a
group policy to deploy a Windows Installer Service package service release (SR)
to update the clients' word processing application. The update applies successfully to all but one client computer. What should you do to apply the SR to the
remaining client?

- ○ a. Redeploy the SP with a **.zap** file.
- ○ b. Redeploy the SP with an **.mst** file.
- ○ c. Restart Windows Installer Service on the DC.
- ○ d. Restart Windows Installer Service on the failed client computer.

Question 15

A user, Jerry, has enabled files located on the network to be available for offline usage. Jerry has configured synchronization to occur every day at 4:30 p.m. and has disabled synchronization during logon or logoff. Today, Jerry needs to leave at 3:00 p.m. and must synchronize the changes that have been made before he logs off. How can he synchronize the offline files before he logs off from the network?

- ○ a. Configure Synchronization Manager to synchronize during an idle period.
- ○ b. Use Synchronization Manager to force synchronization before leaving.
- ○ c. Configure Synchronization Manager to synchronize during logon.
- ○ d. Copy the files that have been changed to the network file server share point.

Question 16

You need to enable Windows 2000 Professional to read text from all dialog boxes and all applications to visually impaired users. What must you configure to allow for this functionality?

- ○ a. SoundSentry
- ○ b. ShowSounds
- ○ c. Narrator
- ○ d. Windows Media Player captioning

Question 17

What is the function of the **sysprep.inf** file?

- ○ a. It is used for remote installations.
- ○ b. It is the answer file for **sysprep** installations.
- ○ c. It is used to configure custom parameters for **sysprep.exe**.
- ○ d. It is the settings file for custom keyboard layouts.

Question 18

You want to deploy Windows 2000 Professional to network clients by using a remote installation server. However, when a client attempts to boot her computer from their network adapter, the client cannot connect to the remote installation server. How else can the client connect to the service?

○ a. Use Network Client Administrator to create a network boot disk to connect to the remote installation server.

○ b. Use **rbfg.exe** to create a network boot disk to connect to the remote installation server.

○ c. Use **dcpromo.exe** to create a network boot disk to connect to the remote installation server.

○ d. Use Recovery Console to create a network boot disk to connect to the remote installation server.

Question 19

A computer on which you want to install Windows 2000 Professional has 96MB of memory, a Pentium II 400MHz CPU, and a 4GB hard drive with 500MB of free space. You attempt the installation, but it fails before the graphic phase of the process. What must you do to install Windows 2000 Professional on this computer?

○ a. Install a Pentium III 500MHz CPU.

○ b. Install 128MB of memory.

○ c. Configure the hard drive with at least 650MB of free space.

○ d. Install an AGP video adapter.

Question 20

You have eight Windows 2000 Professional computers in your company's Art Department. They all have built-in USB controllers. You install a USB tablet-pointing device, as well as the manufacturer's 32-bit tablet software, on each machine. A Tablet icon shows up in the Control Panel, but none of the tablets work. You examine Device Manager and notice no device conflicts. What should you do to get the USB tablets to work?

  ○ a. Enable the USB ports in the system BIOS and then reinstall the USB tablet device drivers.

  ○ b. Enable the USB root hub controller and then reinstall the USB tablet device drivers.

  ○ c. Disable USB error detection for the USB root hub controller and then enable the USB tablet device in each machine's hardware profile.

  ○ d. Reinstall the USB tablet device drivers and then disable the USB error detection.

Question 21

You plan to install Windows 2000 Professional on a new computer that has two monitors. All the hardware is Windows 2000 compatible. You want to accomplish the following:

➤ Allow the user to place items on either monitor.

➤ Configure the display adapter that is built in to the motherboard as the secondary display.

➤ Provide the user with the ability to start applications from the primary display.

➤ Allow the resolution for each display to be configured separately.

You perform the following tasks:

  1. Install the additional display adapter in an available slot.

  2. Attach the cable from each monitor to the appropriate display adapter.

  3. Run Setup to install Windows 2000 and allow Setup to detect and configure the display adapters.

Which result or results do these actions produce? (Select all the correct answers.)

  ❑ a. Gives the user the ability to start applications from the primary display.

  ❑ b. Gives the user the ability to place items on either monitor.

  ❑ c. Configures the display adapter that is built in to the motherboard as the secondary display.

  ❑ d. Allows the resolution for each display to be configured separately.

Question 22

You back up **PRO1** each morning, using the following backup strategy:

Monday: Incremental

Tuesday: Differential

Wednesday: Differential

Thursday: Incremental

Friday: Normal

On Wednesday afternoon, **PRO1** crashes, and you must recover the hard drive. Which backup sets must you restore, and in which order?

Monday

Tuesday

Wednesday

Thursday

Friday

Question 23

You are deciding on specifications for 50 new computers your company will purchase for the Engineering Department. These machines will run Windows 2000 Professional. You want Windows 2000 to be able to use all the hardware that comes in the computers. What is the maximum amount of memory you could have in your new Windows 2000 computers?

○ a. 2GB

○ b. 4GB

○ c. 8GB

○ d. 16GB

Question 24

Your original network adapter card fails. You replace the network adapter card on your computer, which is running Windows 2000 Professional. What utility should you use to make sure that the device driver for the original network card is removed from your machine?

○ a. Device Manager

○ b. Add/Remove Programs

○ c. Network and Dial-up Connections

○ d. The System applet in the Control Panel

○ e. The Add/Remove Hardware Wizard

Question 25

You are dual-booting Windows 98 and Windows 2000 Professional on your computer. You upgraded the second hard drive in the machine from basic to dynamic, and you are using it to store business records. The next time you boot the machine to Windows 98 and try to access your business records, you cannot read the files at all. What is the most likely cause of this problem?

○ a. You formatted the partition(s) on the second drive to NTFS 5, so now Windows 98 cannot read the data on that drive.

○ b. You forgot to convert the second disk from dynamic back to basic before booting to Windows 98.

○ c. The data on the second drive is either encrypted or corrupt.

○ d. Only Windows 2000 can read data stored on dynamic disks.

Question 26

Your Windows 2000 Professional machine has a shared compressed folder on drive **D:** called **Sales**. The **D:** drive is formatted as NTFS. You move the **Sales** folder into an uncompressed folder called **CompanyData** on drive **D:**. Which of the following statements most accurately describes the **Sales** folder now?

○ a. The **Sales** folder is uncompressed because it resides in an uncompressed folder.

○ b. The **Sales** folder is uncompressed because it was removed from its original location.

○ c. The **Sales** folder is still compressed because it was moved within the same NTFS volume.

○ d. The **Sales** folder is still compressed because it was moved between two NTFS volumes.

Question 27

You want to dual-boot your computer, using Windows 98 and Windows 2000 Professional. You are going to be using resource-intensive CAD applications while you're booted to both of the operating systems, and you need to be able to access all files on the machine, regardless of which operating system you are using. What file system should you select for this single-partition, single-disk, machine?

○ a. FAT16

○ b. FAT32

○ c. NTFS

○ d. HPFS

Question 28

You are viewing the status of all disks and volumes by using Disk Management on your Windows 2000 machine. You notice that all the disks and respective volumes have their status listed as Healthy, except for one. One disk shows the status of each of its volumes listed as Healthy (At Risk). What does this mean, and what step(s) should you take, if any?

○ a. The volume is initializing and is displayed as Healthy after initialization is finished. You do not need to take any action.

○ b. The volume is accessible, but errors have been detected on this disk. You can return the disk to Healthy and Online status by reactivating the disk. To do so, you right-click the disk and select Reactivate Disk. You must make sure you have a recent backup of the data on the disk.

○ c. This status indicator has appeared because the disk is on the verge of failure. You need to make sure you have a recent backup of the data on the disk, and you should replace the disk before failure occurs.

○ d. This status indicator appears when the underlying disk is no longer online. You need to right-click the disk and select Bring Online.

Question 29

On a Windows 2000 Professional computer, which type of volume includes areas of equal size on multiple physical disks to which data is written at the same time?

- ○ a. Mirrored volume
- ○ b. Spanned volume
- ○ c. Simple volume
- ○ d. Striped volume
- ○ e. RAID-5 volume

Question 30

In Windows 2000, how do you change or convert a hard disk from dynamic to basic?

- ○ a. In Disk Management, right-click the disk and select Revert to Basic Disk.
- ○ b. In the Storage snap-in, right-click the disk and select Revert to Basic Disk After Rescan.
- ○ c. Remove all the volumes from the disk. Then use Disk Management to right-click the disk and select Revert to Basic Disk.
- ○ d. You cannot do this in Windows 2000; you can convert only from basic to dynamic.

Question 31

You need to delete a quota entry defined for a user's account on drive **F:** of a computer running Windows 2000. What utility should you use to locate the files owned by the user and move the files to a shared folder on another server?

- ○ a. **ntdsutil**
- ○ b. Windows Explorer
- ○ c. Active Directory Users and Computers
- ○ d. Disk Management

Question 32

What happens to encrypted files that are made available offline?

- ○ a. Nothing happens; the files are available and are still encrypted.
- ○ b. Encrypted files can't be made available offline.
- ○ c. The user who encrypted the file must decrypt the file for offline usage.
- ○ d. Encrypted files are not encrypted in the offline cache.

Question 33

Users report that when they access the **Presentations** share on a Windows 2000 server named **\\server1**, they can select from this share files that will be available while the users are offline. However, when users select files located in the **Finance** share on **\\server1**, the Make Available Offline option does not appear. What do you need to do to allow files in the **Finance** share to be available while users are offline?

- ○ a. Configure the caching properties for the **Finance** share to allow caching of files.
- ○ b. Ensure that the users have the share permission to the **Finance** share on **\\server1**.
- ○ c. Enable offline files on the users' computers.
- ○ d. Create a logon script that maps **\\server1\finance** for all users.

Question 34

Users in the **corp.com** domain require that the settings and configurations that have been established on their computers be available on any computer they may log on to. How do you accomplish this task? (Select all the correct answers.)

- ❑ a. Configure the local user account to use the local profile on every client computer.
- ❑ b. Change the name of **ntuser.dat** to **ntuser.man**.
- ❑ c. Create a profile share point.
- ❑ d. Configure each user's Profile option with the UNC path for his or her profile.

Question 35

You have created a group policy software package to assign an office suite package to all domain users. You want to prevent the office suite from appearing in the Add/Remove Programs applet. How do you configure this?

- ○ a. Configure a group policy to hide the Add/Remove Programs applet.
- ○ b. Configure the properties of the software installation group policy to display the office suite in a category.
- ○ c. Enable the Uninstall This Application When It Falls out of the Scope of Management feature.
- ○ d. Configure the properties of the office package in the group policy.

Question 36

Alice has enabled files located on the network to be available for offline usage. She wants to configure synchronization to occur every day at 4:30 p.m. How should Alice configure synchronization to occur each day at a specific time?

- ○ a. Configure Synchronization Manager to synchronize during an idle period.
- ○ b. Use Synchronization Manager to force synchronization before leaving.
- ○ c. Use the Scheduled Task Wizard to configure when synchronization should occur.
- ○ d. Use Scheduled Synchronization Manager to configure when synchronization should occur.

Question 37

A user requires that the Narrator accessibility tool be launched automatically when Windows 2000 starts. How do you configure this option?

- ○ a. Use the Accessibility Options applet to configure the Narrator settings to start when Windows starts.
- ○ b. Select the Start Narrator Minimized option.
- ○ c. Add a registry entry to enable Narrator to run when Windows starts.
- ○ d. Use Accessibility Utility Manager to enable the option to start automatically when Windows starts.

Question 38

A user needs to move the mouse pointer by using the numeric keypad on her keyboard. What feature of Windows 2000 Professional do you need to enable to provide this functionality?

○ a. ToggleKeys

○ b. FilterKeys

○ c. MouseKeys

○ d. StickyKeys

Question 39

You need to configure a user's Windows 2000 Professional computer to display a virtual keyboard to allow the user to type data by using the mouse pointer. What utility must you enable?

○ a. ToggleKeys

○ b. FilterKeys

○ c. StickyKeys

○ d. On-Screen Keyboard

Question 40

You are using a 32-bit Windows word processing application. You have added the French input locale. You have been typing documents in English and now want to start typing in French. How do you do this?

○ a. Change to the French input locale within the word processor.

○ b. Close the application and select the French user locale from the Regional Options applet and restart the application.

○ c. Close the application and log off the computer and then log back on and choose the French input locale.

○ d. Select the French input locale by using the Language icon in the system tray.

Question 41

You work for a large multinational company that has offices in Europe and the United States. Users in Europe regularly need to read and write documents in several different languages and work with the interface of the required language. You need to deploy Windows 2000 to support a multilanguage configuration while keeping to a minimum the administrative overhead of the deployment and ongoing administration of these computers. How should you deploy Windows 2000 to achieve these goals?

○ a. Deploy a separate version of Windows 2000 for each needed language.

○ b. Deploy the Multilanguage edition of Windows 2000 and install language user interfaces as needed.

○ c. Deploy Windows 2000 with all the required language groups.

○ d. Deploy Windows 2000 with all the required input locales.

Question 42

A user accidentally presses the Shift key five times. The computer makes a high-pitched sound when this occurred. Why does the computer make this sound?

○ a. MouseKeys is enabled.

○ b. FilterKeys is enabled.

○ c. StickyKeys is enabled.

○ d. ToggleKeys is enabled.

Question 43

You have lost the setup diskettes that come with Windows 2000 Professional, and you need to re-create them. You boot a Windows 2000 Professional computer and put the Windows 2000 Professional installation CD-ROM in the computer. What command do you use to create the setup disks?

○ a. **winnt32.exe /ox**

○ b. **makebt32.exe**

○ c. **makeboot.exe**

○ d. **winnt.exe /ox**

Question 44

You want to create a remote installation image of a Windows 2000 Professional computer and its installed applications. What utility is required for this task?

○ a. **risetup.exe**

○ b. **rbfg.exe**

○ c. **sysprep.exe**

○ d. **riprep.exe**

Question 45

A computer on which you want to install Windows 2000 Professional has 28MB of memory, a Pentium II 400MHz CPU, and a 500MB hard drive with 50MB of free space. You attempt the installation but it fails. What must you do to install Windows 2000 Professional on this computer? (Select all the correct answers.)

❑ a. Install a Pentium III 500MHz CPU.

❑ b. Install 32MB or more of memory.

❑ c. Configure the hard drive with at least 650MB of free space.

❑ d. Install a 2GB hard drive or greater.

Question 46

You want to deploy Windows 2000 Professional with an RIS server. The client computers have PXE-compliant network adapters. You have installed a Windows 2000 DC as well as DNS and DHCP on a Windows 2000 server. You have installed and configured RIS. However, when clients boot from their network adapters, they fail to connect to the RIS server. What do you need to do?

○ a. Verify that DHCP has been authorized in Active Directory.

○ b. Create reserved TCP/IP addresses for all RIS clients in the RIS scope.

○ c. Configure the clients with static TCP/IP addresses.

○ d. Create a host record in DNS for the RIS server.

Question 47

Which of the following operating systems can you directly upgrade to Windows 2000 Professional? (Select all the correct answers.)

❑ a. Windows 95

❑ b. Windows 98

❑ c. Windows 3

❑ d. Windows NT 4

❑ e. Windows NT 3.51

❑ f. Windows 3.11

Question 48

Which two protocols work with the Multilink feature to dynamically add or remove dial-up connections as needed? (Select all the correct answers.)

❑ a. BACP

❑ b. EAP

❑ c. BAP

❑ d. RADIUS

Question 49

How do you configure encryption settings for both passwords and data for a dial-up connection?

○ a. Open the Network and Dial-up Connections window. Right-click the dial-up connection and choose Properties. Select the Networking tab. Select Client for Microsoft Networks and choose Properties.

○ b. Configure a remote access policy.

○ c. Open the Network and Dial-up Connections window. Right-click the dial-up connection and choose Properties. Select the Options tab.

○ d. Open the Network and Dial-up Connections window. Right-click the dial-up connection and choose Properties. Select the Security tab.

Question 50

What IP address range does ICS use by default?

○ a. 10.0.0.2 through 10.0.0.254

○ b. 169.254.0.1 through 169.254.255.254

○ c. 192.168.1.2 through 192.168.1.254

○ d. 192.168.0.2 through 192.168.0.254

Sample Test Answer Key

1. C
2. D
3. A, B
4. A
5. B
6. Friday, Monday, Tuesday, and Wednesday
7. B
8. A
9. C
10. A
11. C
12. D
13. B
14. D
15. B
16. C
17. B
18. B
19. C
20. A
21. A, D
22. Friday, Monday, and Wednesday
23. B
24. E
25. D
26. C
27. B
28. B
29. D

30. C

31. D

32. D

33. A

34. C, D

35. D

36. D

37. D

38. C

39. D

40. D

41. B

42. C

43. B

44. D

45. B, D

46. A

47. A, B, D, E

48. A, C

49. D

50. D

This is the answer key to the sample test presented in Chapter 11, "Sample Test."

Question 1

Answer C is correct. Security Configuration and Analysis allows you to apply
security templates, including the High Security Workstation template created by Microsoft. Local policy and group policy would require more
guesswork, and domain security policy applies only to domain controllers;
therefore, Answers A, B, and D are incorrect.

Question 2

Answer D is correct. A group policy for the organizational unit (OU) of your
laptop overrides a domain policy. The registry entry and local security policy are overridden by the domain policy, so Answers A and B are incorrect.
A security database is used to evaluate security settings, so Answer C is
incorrect.

Question 3

Answers A and B are correct. You can use local security policy to configure
user rights on any Windows 2000 Professional system. You can use group
policy to configure user rights for Windows 2000 Professional systems that
are members of a domain. You cannot use User Manager (which is a
Windows NT 4 tool) or the Users and Passwords applet to manage user
rights; therefore, Answers C and D are incorrect.

Question 4

Answer A is correct. The right to format a hard drive partition is given to
administrators only. Therefore, you would have to put Cory into the
Administrators group, which you can do with the Users and Passwords
applet. The other tools do not let you manage the Administrators group.
Therefore, Answers B, C, and D are incorrect.

Question 5

Answer B is correct. Template accounts are generally disabled so that they
are not active accounts. When you copy the account, you should ensure that

the Disabled attribute is cleared for the new user. Answer A is not a setting of a template account, and Answers C and D would not be causing the logon problem; therefore, those answers are incorrect.

Question 6

The correct order is Friday, Monday, Tuesday, and Wednesday. Normal backups are complete backups, so you can begin with Friday's backup. Incremental backups back up only what has changed since the last incremental or normal backup, so you must restore each incremental backup since the normal backup.

Question 7

Answer B is correct. You must back up the system state so that you can back up the registry in Windows 2000. The emergency repair disk (ERD) no longer contains a backup of the registry; therefore, Answer A is incorrect. You cannot copy the registry while the system is running, and the user profile does not contain machine-specific registry settings; therefore, Answers A, C, and D are incorrect.

Question 8

Answer A is correct. A Memory: Pages/sec value higher than 20 indicates too much paging activity, which itself contributes to processor and disk usage. Lack of memory is therefore the bottleneck on this system. Enhancing the processor or disk subsystem would not address this bottleneck, so Answers B, C, D, and E are incorrect.

Question 9

Answer C is correct. This system's processor is at capacity, and the queue length is higher than 2, indicating that threads are waiting to be processed and a second processor could alleviate the bottleneck. Answers A, B, D, E, and F would not be the best solutions to address this bottleneck.

Question 10

Answer A is correct. From the properties sheet of a drive volume, you can launch defragmentation from the Tools tab. You cannot perform defragmentation by using the tools in Answers B, C, and D.

Question 11

Answer C is correct. Task Manager allows you to monitor at what priority an application is running. Computer Management, System, and Add/Remove Programs do not allow you to change an application's priority, so Answers A, B, and D are incorrect.

Question 12

Answer D is correct. The local profiles on a Windows 2000 Professional computer are found in `%SystemDrive%\documents and settings` (for example, `C:\Documents and Settings`). However, if the computer was upgraded from Windows NT to Windows 2000, the profiles would be found in `%SystemRoot%\profiles` (for example, `C:\Winnt\Profiles`).

Question 13

Answer B is correct. If a share point is not configured to allow caching of files, you cannot cache files from that share point. Also, the option to make files available offline is not available until this option is selected, so Answer A is incorrect. Answer D is not an available option until the share point has been configured to allow for caching of files; therefore, Answer D is incorrect. Answer C is incorrect because it is the wrong computer; the problem is on `\\server1`, not on one of the sales staff's computers.

Question 14

Answer D is correct. If you restart the Windows Installer Service, the service release (SR) is installed the next time the client logs on to his or her computer. If there had been a problem with the SR `.msi` file, the SR would not have installed on any computers. However, it did install on all but one of the client computers. This indicates that the failed installation of the SR is an issue with the client computer. Therefore, Answers A and B are incorrect. Restarting the Windows Installer Service would be an appropriate answer only if the application couldn't be installed on the DC. The DC is simply being used to deploy applications; therefore, Answer C is incorrect.

Question 15

Answer B is correct. Jerry can use Synchronization Manager to synchronize on-the-fly by clicking the Synchronize button. Doing so forces a synchronization of all files that have been changed. Copying the file to the share point could potentially overwrite the existing files. Therefore, Answer d is incorrect. Answer A would require the user to wait until an idle period before the files were synchronized. The user must disconnect the computer from the network before the idle period sets in; therefore, Answer A is incorrect. If Answer C were chosen, the user might not have synchronized files before removing the computer from the network. The user must synchronize files before logging off the network. Answer C doesn't synchronize files until the user logs back on to the network, which is too late; therefore, Answer C is incorrect.

Question 16

Answer C is correct. You use the Narrator accessibility option to read aloud onscreen text, dialog boxes, menus, and buttons that are selected in Windows 2000 Professional. SoundSentry generates visual warnings when the computer generates sound alerts, and ShowSounds tells applications to display captions for sounds the application may make; therefore, Answers A and B are incorrect. Windows Media Player cannot speak aloud written text, but it can display text in closed captioning; therefore, Answer D is incorrect.

Question 17

Answer B is correct. The sysprep.inf file is the answer file for sysprep installations of Windows 2000. It is not used for remote installations, but it could be used for remote installations if it were renamed and placed in the correct location; therefore, Answer A is incorrect. This file is not used to configure sysprep.exe, nor could it ever be used to adjust settings for keyboard layouts; therefore, Answers C and D are incorrect.

Question 18

Answer B is correct. The only utility that you can use to create network boot disks to connect to a remote installation server is `rbfg.exe`. Network Client Administrator is a Windows NT 4 server utility that creates generic network boot disks, and you can't use it to find and connect to a remote installation server; therefore, Answer a is incorrect. You use `dcpromo.exe` to promote a member server to a DC, and the Recovery Console is a Windows 2000 troubleshooting tool; therefore, Answers C and D are incorrect.

Question 19

Answer C is correct. Windows 2000 Professional requires at least 650MB of free hard disk space to complete a successful installation. You can install Windows 2000 Professional on a computer that has only 32MB of memory and a Pentium 166MHz CPU, so this system meets the minimum requirements, which makes Answers A and B incorrect The installation fails before Plug and Play would attempt to find the video adapter, so that is not the issue; therefore, Answer D is incorrect. By process of elimination, you should determine that an incorrect configuration of the hard drive is the best answer.

Question 20

Answer A is correct. The operating system is recognizing the tablets, but they do not work. You need to enable the USB ports in the system's BIOS and then reinstall the drivers for the tablets. Having the single USB tablet device on each machine does not necessitate having a USB root hub controller, nor would Answers B and C solve the problem unless the USB ports were enabled in the BIOS. Therefore, Answers b and c are incorrect. Answer D is a distracter, and it is incorrect.

Question 21

Answers A and D are correct. You have to install Windows 2000 before you install a display adapter other than the one that is built in. Otherwise, Setup disables the built-in adapter when it detects that another one is present. The order in which you completed the tasks results in only one display adapter and monitor being enabled. Therefore, the user can start applications from the primary display and configure each display's settings separately—but that's it. Answers B and C are incorrect.

Question 22

The correct order is Friday, Monday, and Wednesday. Normal backups are complete backups, so you can begin with Friday's backup. Incremental backups back up only what has changed since the last incremental or normal backup, so you must restore each incremental backup since the normal backup (Monday). Differential backups back up all files that have changed since the last normal or incremental backup, so Wednesday's backup includes all files that have changed since Monday morning.

Question 23

Answer B is correct. Windows 2000 Professional can address up to 4GB of RAM.

Question 24

Answer E is correct. You must use the Add/Remove Hardware Wizard to ensure that drivers are removed from your hard disk. You can use Device Manager to uninstall drivers, but it does not remove drivers from your machine—it just makes sure the drivers are not loaded during system startup; therefore, Answer A is incorrect. From Network and Dial-up Connections, you can disable a local area connection for a network adapter card, but the drivers are not removed from the hard disk; therefore, Answer C is incorrect.

Question 25

Answer D is correct. Down-level operating systems (that is, Windows versions before Windows 2000) cannot read the Windows 2000 or Windows XP/Windows Server 2003 dynamic disks. Answer A is incorrect because you have no information about the file systems in use in this scenario. You do not convert dynamic disks back to basic disks solely for the purpose of reading them after you've rebooted to a down-level operating system; therefore, Answer B is incorrect. You have no evidence to support the assertion that data on the second drive is missing or corrupt, so Answer C is incorrect.

Question 26

Answer C is correct. When you move an object within the same NTFS volume, it retains its compression attribute. This is a golden rule to remember.

Question 27

Answer B is correct. Windows 98 cannot read NTFS (Windows 2000's NT File System)or HPFS (IBM OS/2's High Performance File System). FAT32 (File Allocation Table 32-bit file system) uses smaller cluster sizes and is more efficient than FAT16, and both Windows 98 and Windows 2000 can use FAT32. FAT16 would work, but it is not the best choice because it uses larger cluster sizes, and it makes less efficient use of disk space; therefore, Answer A is incorrect. Answers c and d are incorrect because Windows 98 cannot read NTFS or HPFS.

Question 28

Answer B is correct. When the disk is Healthy (At Risk), it is not simply offline. *At Risk* means errors have been detected on the disk. Healthy (At Risk) does not display when a volume is initializing, so Answer A is incorrect. There is not enough information to conclude that this disk is on the verge of failure, so Answer C is incorrect.

Question 29

Answer D is correct. This questions deals with the straight definition of a striped volume. A striped volume has areas of equal size on multiple disks to which data is written at the same time. Windows 2000 Professional does not support mirrored volumes or RAID-5 volumes; therefore, Answers A and E are incorrect.

Question 30

Answer C is correct. You *must* remove all the volumes from the disk before you convert or revert a dynamic disk to basic. You do not use the Storage snap-in for this. Therefore, Answer B is incorrect. Answer D is preposterous; of course you can convert a disk from dynamic to basic.

Question 31

Answer D is correct. You use the disk quota management system within Disk Management. When you delete the user's quota entry, a dialog box that allows you to move, delete, or take ownership of files owned by the user on drive F: appears. ntdsutil is a command-line utility that manages the Active Directory database, so Answer A is incorrect. Windows Explorer has no feature to expose files owned by a specific user; therefore, Answer B is incorrect. Information about individual files owned by a user is not available in Active Directory Users and Computers; therefore, Answer C is incorrect.

Question 32

Answer D is correct. Files that have been encrypted can be made available while a user is offline, so Answer B is incorrect. However, the encrypted files are not encrypted in the offline cache, so Answer D is correct. Answer C is not a required action. Files are encrypted and decrypted in the same manner, whether they are tagged for offline usage. No user action is necessary to decrypt a file that has been encrypted; this action is performed automatically by the security subsystem.

Question 33

Answer A is correct. The caching properties for the Finance share have been disabled, and you need to enable them before the clients can cache files contained in that share. Because the users can get to the files in the Finance share, we know that there is nothing wrong with the permissions. Therefore, Answer B is incorrect. We know that the users' computers have the Offline Files option enabled because they can make files in the Presentations share available for offline usage; therefore Answer C is incorrect. Answer D wouldn't correct the problem. A drive mapping would be created, but the files would not be cached; therefore, Answer D is incorrect.

Question 34

Answers C and D are correct. To allow a user profile that has been created on a user's computer to be available on any computer the user logs on to, there must be a central profile share to which the user's profile is uploaded. In addition, you must enter the UNC path to the share for each user account that needs roaming profiles. Answer A would not use a central profile that would be available on every computer a user might log on to. Instead, the local profile would be used; thus, Answer A is incorrect. Answer B would simply make a profile mandatory, but it does not enable a profile to roam; therefore, Answer B is incorrect.

Question 35

Answer D is correct. You can configure assigned applications not to appear in the Add/Remove Programs applet. This configuration is simply a software policy option that you can use for either assigned or published applications. However, you should use it just for assigned applications. You don't want to hide the entire Add/Remove Programs applet; you just want to hide the presence of the office suite within the applet. Therefore, Answer A is incorrect. Answer B doesn't solve anything because the Category option is found within the Add/Remove Programs applet. The policy had instructed the package not to appear in the Add/Remove Programs applet, so placing the software within a category won't make the application appear; therefore, Answer B is incorrect. Answer C does not control whether a software package will appear in the Add/Remove Programs applet; it is used to remove the entire application from a computer when a user account is moved from one OU to another.

Question 36

Answer D is correct. You can use Synchronization Manager to control synchronization and cause it to occur during an idle period or at a scheduled interval. In this case, the user Alice needed to schedule synchronization to occur at 4:30 each day. Answer D provides this capability. You can use Synchronization Manager to synchronize on-the-fly by clicking the Synchronize button. Doing so forces a synchronization of all files that have been changed but requires the users to be present to manually push a button. This option doesn't allow for synchronization to be configuration at a specific time; therefore, Answer B is incorrect. The Scheduled Task Wizard doesn't control when offline files can be synchronized; therefore, Answer C is incorrect.

Question 37

Answer D is correct. You can use Accessibility Utility Manager to configure the Narrator tool to start automatically when Windows starts. The other options do not provide this capability; therefore, Answers A, B, and C are incorrect.

Question 38

Answer C is correct. You use the MouseKeys accessibility option to control the mouse pointer with the numeric keypad. The other options do not allow for this functionality; therefore, Answers A, B, and D are incorrect.

Question 39

Answer D is correct. On-Screen Keyboard is a virtual keyboard that is displayed on a user's desktop. Users can use a pointing device such as a mouse to enter data with this keyboard. ToggleKeys plays a high-pitched sound when the Caps Lock key is pressed; therefore, Answer A is incorrect. FilterKeys adjusts the keyboard repeat delay; therefore, Answer B is incorrect. StickyKeys allows users to select keystrokes such as the strokes in the combination Ctrl+Alt+Delete individually; therefore, Answer C is incorrect.

Question 40

Answer D is correct. You can select an input locale by using a keyboard shortcut or by selecting the Language icon in the system tray. Changing the user locale to French would not affect the input locale. French characters do not appear until the input locale is selected; therefore, Answer b is incorrect. Answer A is not even possible. The input locale has to be switched by using either hotkeys or the system tray. At that point, an application could type characters from different languages. Therefore, Answer A is incorrect. It is not necessary to log off the computer to invoke different input locales. They can be changed on-the-fly; therefore, Answer C is incorrect.

Question 41

Answer B is correct. If you use the Multilanguage edition of Windows 2000, you don't need to use separate SPs, hot fixes, and upgrades. If you deploy a separate version of Windows, you increase the administrative burden because these computers do require separate SPs, hot fixes, and upgrades. Therefore, Answer A is incorrect. Although the Multilanguage edition can use the same service packs, Answers C and D do not provide enough options for the user.

Question 42

Answer C is correct. By default, pressing the Shift key five times enables StickyKeys. Pressing left Alt+left Shift+Num Lock enables MouseKeys; thus, Answer A is incorrect. Holding down the right Shift key for eight seconds enables FilterKeys; thus, Answer B is incorrect. ToggleKeys can be invoked by holding down the Num Lock key for five seconds, which makes Answer D incorrect.

Question 43

Answer B is correct. The user booted into a Windows 2000 computer, so makebt32.exe is the correct executable. Answer A is incorrect because Winnt32.exe /ox is not a supported command. This switch provides no functionality at all with this executable. If the user had booted to a DOS prompt, makeboot.exe would have been the right executable to use. Therefore, Answer C is incorrect. You can use winnt.exe /ox to create setup floppy disks for Windows NT 4, but the /ox switch does not create the setup disks for Windows 2000; therefore, Answer D is incorrect.

Question 44

Answer D is correct. riprep.exe creates remote installation images of Windows 2000 Professional computers. These images are automatically placed on an RIS server. In contrast, risetup.exe is used to configure a server to become a remote installation server; thus, Answer A is incorrect. The rbfg.exe utility is used to create remote boot disks for RIS clients to connect to an RIS server; thus, Answer B is incorrect. Sysprep.exe is used to prepare a computer to be imaged with third-party imaging software by removing unique parameters from the computer; therefore, Answer C is incorrect.

Question 45

Answers B and D are correct. The minimum requirements for Windows 2000 Professional are 32MB of memory, a 2GB drive with 650MB of free space, and a Pentium 133MHz or higher CPU.

Question 46

Answer A is correct. Active Directory needs to authorize a Windows 2000 DHCP (Dynamic Host Configuration Protocol) server to lease out TCP/IP addresses. If the server has not been authorized, it does not give out IP addresses, and the Remote Installation Services (RIS) clients cannot connect to the RIS server. Unless the DHCP server has been authorized, any reserved TCP/IP addresses for the RIS clients will still not be assigned to those computers; thus, Answer b is incorrect. Answer c is incorrect because the client must obtain a TCP/IP address from a DHCP server. A static TCP/IP address can't be used; therefore, Answer C is incorrect. Answer D is not related to the problem. Unless the DHCP server has been activated, clients cannot get TCP/IP addresses and cannot connect to the RIS server. RIS cannot be completely configured unless there is a host record for the RIS server on the appropriate Domain Name System (DNS) server(s); therefore, Answer D is incorrect.

Question 47

Answers A, B, D, and E are correct. You can upgrade only Window 95, 98, NT 4, and NT 3.51 to Windows 2000 Professional. You cannot upgrade Windows 3 or 3.11; therefore, Answers C and F are incorrect.

Question 48

Answers A and C are correct. BAP and BACP work together in conjunction with Multilink to combine multiple communications devices (such as modems and ISDN terminal adapters) in order to achieve higher throughput. BAP and BACP can dynamically drop or add lines based on predetermined usage rates, as specified in remote access policies. EAP is an authentication protocol, not a bandwidth protocol. RADIUS is a set of remote access accounting services, and such services do not concern bandwidth.

Question 49

Answer D is correct. The Security tab displays the settings that are necessary for configuring password and data encryption. Encryption settings are not configured on the Networking tab or on the Options tab, nor are they configured in remote access policies; therefore, Answers A, B, and C are incorrect.

Question 50

Answer D is correct. By default, Internet Connection Sharing (ICS) uses the IP address range 192.168.0.2 through 192.168.0.254 for clients, with 192.168.0.1 reserved for the Windows 2000 computer that is sharing its Internet connection. Although the IP scheme 10.x.y.z is a private nonroutable set of addresses, ICS does not use it, so Answer A is incorrect. The range 169.254.x.y is used by Automatic Private IP Addressing (APIPA), not by ICS; therefore, Answer B is incorrect. The range 192.168.1.x is also private and nonroutable, and it is not the default IP scheme that ICS uses; therefore, Answer C is incorrect.

Glossary

. . . .

A (address) resource record
A resource record that is used to map a Domain Name System (DNS) domain name to a host Internet Protocol (IP) address on the network.

ACE (access control entry)
An element in an object's discretionary access control list (DACL). Each ACE controls or monitors access to an object by a specified trustee. An ACE is also an entry in an object's system access control list (SACL) that specifies the security events to be audited for a user or group.

account lockout
A Windows 2000 security feature that locks a user's account if a certain number of failed logon attempts occur within a specified amount of time, based on security policy lockout settings. Locked accounts cannot log on.

ACPI (Advanced Configuration and Power Interface)
A power management specification developed by Intel, Microsoft, and Toshiba that enables Windows 2000 to control the amount of power given to each device attached to the computer. With ACPI, the operating system can turn off peripheral devices, such as CD-ROM players, when they are not in use. As another example, ACPI enables manufacturers to produce computers that automatically power up as soon as you touch the keyboard.

Active Directory

The directory service that is included with Windows 2000 Server. Active Directory is based on the X.500 standards and those of its predecessor, Lightweight Directory Access Protocol (LDAP). It stores information about objects on a network and makes this information available to users and network administrators. Active Directory gives network users access to permitted resources anywhere on the network, using a single log-on process. It provides network administrators a hierarchical view of the network and a single point of administration for all network objects.

Active Directory Users and Computers snap-in

An administrative tool designed to perform daily Active Directory administration tasks, including creating, deleting, modifying, moving, and setting permissions on objects stored in the Active Directory database. These objects include organizational units (OUs), users, contacts, groups, computers, printers, and shared file objects.

AGP (Accelerated Graphics Port)

An interface specification developed by Intel that was released in August 1997. AGP is based on peripheral connection interface (PCI) but is designed especially for the throughput demands of 3D graphics. Rather than use the PCI bus for graphics data, AGP introduces a dedicated point-to-point channel so that the graphics controller can directly access main memory. The AGP channel is 32 bits wide and runs at 66MHz. This translates into a total bandwidth of 266Mbps, as opposed to the PCI bandwidth of 133Mbps. AGP also supports two optional faster modes, with throughputs of 533Mbps and 1.07Gbps. In addition, AGP allows 3D textures to be stored in main memory rather than in video memory. AGP has a couple important system requirements: The chipset must support AGP, and the motherboard must be equipped with an AGP bus slot or must have an integrated AGP graphics system.

APIPA (Auto Private IP Addressing)

A client-side feature of Windows 98 and 2000 Dynamic Host Configuration Protocol (DHCP) clients. If the client's attempt to negotiate with a DHCP server fails, the client automatically receives an Internet Protocol (IP) address from the 169.254.0.0 Class B range.

APM (Advanced Power Management)

An application programming interface (API) developed by Intel and Microsoft that allows developers to include power management in basic input/output systems (BIOSs). APM defines a layer between the hardware and the operating system that effectively shields programmers from hardware details. Advanced

Configuration and Power Interface (ACPI) has replaced APM.

ARP (Address Resolution Protocol)

A Transmission Control Protocol/Internet Protocol (TCP/IP) protocol that translates an IP address into a physical address, such as a media access control (MAC) address (hardware address). A computer that wants to obtain a physical address sends an ARP broadcast request onto the TCP/IP network. The computer on the network that has the IP address in the request then replies with its physical hardware address.

ARPANET

A large wide area network (WAN) that was created in the 1960s by the U.S. Department of Defense (DoD) Advanced Research Projects Agency for the free exchange of information between universities and research organizations.

ATM (Asynchronous Transfer Mode)

A networking technology that transfers data in cells (that is, data packets of a fixed size). Cells used with ATM are small compared to packets used with older technologies. The relatively small, constant cell size allows ATM hardware to transmit video images, audio, and computer data over the same network as well as ensures that no single type of data consumes all of the connection's available bandwidth. Current implementations of ATM support data transfer rates from

25Mbps to 622Mbps. Most Ethernet-based networks run at 100Mbps or below.

attribute

A single property that describes an object; for example, the make, model, or color that describes a car. In the context of directories, an attribute is the main component of an entry in a directory, such as an email address.

auditing

The process that tracks the activities of users by recording selected types of events in the security log of a server or workstation.

authentication ticket

A permission to indirectly access resources that a Kerberos Key Distribution Center (KDC) grants to clients and applications.

authorize

To register the Remote Installation Service (RIS) server or the Dynamic Host Configuration Protocol (DHCP) server with Active Directory.

BAP (Bandwidth Allocation Protocol)

A protocol that dynamically controls the use of multilinked lines. BAP eliminates excess bandwidth by allocating lines only when they are required. You can control dynamic links with remote access policies, which are based on the percentage of line utilization and the length of time the bandwidth is reduced.

baselining

The process of measuring system performance so that you can ascertain a standard or expected level of performance.

basic disk

A Windows 2000 term that indicates a physical disk, which can have primary and extended partitions. A basic disk can contain up to three primary partitions and one extended partition, or it can have four primary partitions. A basic disk can also have a single extended partition with logical drives. You *cannot* extend a basic disk.

BDC (backup domain controller)

In Windows NT Server 4, a server that receives a copy of the domain's directory database (which contains all the account and security policy information for the domain). BDCs can continue to participate in a Windows 2000 domain when the domain is configured in mixed mode.

BIOS (basic input/output system)

Built-in software that determines what a computer can do without accessing programs from a disk. On PCs, the BIOS contains all the code required to control the keyboard, display screen, disk drives, serial communications, and a number of miscellaneous functions. A BIOS that can handle Plug and Play devices is known as a Plug and Play BIOS. A Plug and Play BIOS is always implemented with flash memory rather than read-only

memory (ROM). Windows 2000 benefits if a machine has the latest Advanced Configuration and Power Interface (ACPI)-compliant BIOS.

boot partition

The partition that contains the Windows 2000 operating system and its support files.

CHAP (Challenge Handshake Authentication Protocol)

An authentication protocol used by Microsoft remote access as well as network and dial-up connections. By using CHAP, a remote access client can send its authentication credentials to a remote access server in a secure form. Microsoft has created several variations of CHAP that are Windows specific, such as Microsoft CHAP (MS-CHAP) and MS-CHAP 2.

compression

The process of making individual files and folders occupy less physical disk space. Data compression can be accomplished using NT File System (NTFS) compression or through third-party utilities. See also *data compression* and *NTFS compression*.

computer account

An account that a domain administrator creates and that uniquely identifies the computer on the domain. The Windows 2000 computer account matches the name of the computer that joins the domain.

container
An object in a directory that contains other objects.

convert.exe
A Windows 2000 command-line utility that turns a file allocation table (FAT) or FAT32 drive volume into an NT File System (NTFS) drive volume without having to reformat or delete any data that is stored on the drive. The command-line syntax is `convert.exe x: /FS:NTFS`, where `x:` represents the drive letter that you want to convert to NTFS. There is no equivalent command to convert from NTFS to FAT or FAT32.

counter
A metric that provides information about particular aspects of system performance.

CSC (client-side caching)
See *offline files*.

DACL (discretionary access control list)
A list of access control entries (ACEs) that lets administrators set permissions for users and groups at the object and attribute levels. This list represents part of an object's security descriptor that allows or denies permissions to specific users and groups.

daily backup
A backup of files that have changed today but that does not mark them as being backed up.

data compression
The process of making individual files and folders occupy less physical disk space. Data compression can be accomplished by using NT File System (NTFS) compression or through third-party utilities. See also *NTFS compression*.

default gateway
An address that serves an important role in Transmission Control Protocol/Internet Protocol (TCP/IP) networking by providing a default route for TCP/IP hosts to use when communicating with other hosts on remote networks. A router (either a dedicated router or a computer that connects two or more network segments) generally acts as the default gateway for TCP/IP hosts. The router maintains its own routing table of other networks within an internetwork. The routing table maps the routes required to reach the remote hosts that reside on those other networks.

Device Manager
The primary tool that is used in Windows 2000 to configure and manage hardware devices and their settings.

DHCP (Dynamic Host Configuration Protocol) server

A Windows 2000 server that dynamically assigns Internet Protocol (IP) addresses to clients. The DHCP server can also provide direction toward routers, Windows Internet Name Service (WINS) servers, and Domain Name System (DNS) servers.

dial-up access

A type of access in which a remote client uses the public telephone line or Integrated Services Digital Network (ISDN) line to create a connection to a Windows 2000 remote access server.

differential backup

A backup in which files created or changed since the last normal or incremental backup are copied. A differential backup does *not* mark files as having been backed up (in other words, the archive attribute is not cleared). If you are performing a combination of normal and differential backups, when you restore files and folders, you need to have the last normal backup as well as the last differential backup.

digital signature

Public key cryptography that authenticates the integrity and originator of a communication.

disk group

In Windows 2000, a collection of multiple dynamic disks that are managed together. All dynamic disks in a computer are members of the same disk group. Each disk in a disk group stores replicas of the same configuration data, and this configuration data is stored in a 1MB region at the end of each dynamic disk.

Disk Management

A Windows 2000 MMC snap-in that you use to perform all disk maintenance tasks, such as formatting, creating partitions, deleting partitions, and converting a basic disk to a dynamic disk.

disk quota

A control that is used in Windows 2000 to limit the amount of hard disk space available for all users or an individual user. You can apply a quota on a per-user, per-volume basis only.

diskperf.exe

A command-line utility that enables or disables physical and logical disk counters for use with the System Monitor tool within the Performance console.

DMA (Direct Memory Access)

A technique for transferring data from main memory to a device without passing it through the CPU. Computers that have DMA channels can transfer data to and from devices much more quickly than can computers without DMA channels. This is useful for making quick backups and for real-time applications. Some expansion boards, such as CD-ROM cards, can access the computer's DMA channel. When you install the board, you must specify the DMA

channel to be used, which sometimes involves setting a jumper or
dual in-line package (DIP) switch.

DNS (Domain Name System)
The standard by which hosts on
the Internet have both domain
name addresses (for example,
rapport.com) and numeric Internet
Protocol (IP) addresses (for example, 192.33.2.8). DNS is used primarily for resolving fully qualified
domain names (FQDNs) to IP
addresses.

domain
The fundamental administrative
unit of Active Directory. A domain
stores information about objects in
the domain's partition of Active
Directory. You can give user and
group accounts in a domain privileges and permissions to resources
on any system that belongs to the
domain.

domain controller
A computer running Windows
2000 Server that hosts Active
Directory and manages user access
to a network, including logons,
authentication, and access to the
directory and shared resources.

domain forest
A collection of one or more
Windows 2000 domains in a non-
contiguous DNS namespace that
share a common schema, configuration, and global catalog and that
are linked with two-way transitive
trusts.

domain tree
A set of domains that form a contiguous DNS namespace through a
set of hierarchical relationships.

DRA (data recovery agent)
A Windows 2000 administrator
who has been issued a public key
certificate for the express purpose
of recovering user-encrypted data
files that have been encrypted with
Encrypting File System (EFS).
Data recovery refers to the process
of decrypting a file without having
the private key of the user who
encrypted the file. A DRA may
become necessary if a user loses his
or her private key for decrypting
files or if a user leaves an organization without decrypting important
files that other users need.

driver signing
A method for marking or identifying driver files that meet certain
specifications or standards.
Windows 2000 uses a driver-
signing process to make sure drivers have been certified to work
correctly with the Windows Driver
Model (WDM) in Windows 2000.

DVD (digital versatile disc or digital video disc)

A type of CD-ROM that holds a minimum of 4.7GB, enough for a full-length movie. The DVD specification supports disks with capacities from 4.7 to 17GB and access rates of 600Kbps to 1.3Mbps. One of the best features of DVD drives is that they are backward compatible with CD-ROMs. This means that DVD players can play old CD-ROMs, CD-I disks, video CDs, and new DVD-ROMs. Newer DVD players can also read CD-R disks. DVD uses Moving Picture Experts Group (MPEG)-2 to compress video data.

dynamic disk

A physical disk in a Windows 2000 computer that does not use partitions or logical drives. It has dynamic volumes that you create by using the Disk Management console. A dynamic disk can contain any of five types of volumes. In addition, you can extend a volume on a dynamic disk. A dynamic disk can contain an unlimited number of volumes, so you are not restricted to four volumes per disk as you are with a basic disk.

dynamic volume

The only type of volume you can create on dynamic disks. There are five types of dynamic volumes: simple, spanned, mirrored, striped, and Redundant Array of Independent Disks (RAID)-5. Only computers running Windows 2000 can directly access dynamic volumes. Windows 2000 Professional machines *cannot* host but *can* access mirrored and RAID-5 dynamic volumes that are on remote Windows 2000 servers.

EAP (Extensible Authentication Protocol)

An extension of Point-to-Point Protocol (PPP) that provides remote access user authentication by means of other security devices. You can add support for a number of authentication schemes, including token cards; dial-up; the Kerberos version 5 protocol; one-time passwords; and public key authentication using smart cards, certificates, and other methods. EAP works with dial-up, Point-to-Point Tunneling Protocol (PPTP), and Layer 2 Tunneling Protocol (L2TP) clients. EAP is a critical technology component for secure virtual private networks (VPNs) because it offers more security against brute-force or dictionary attacks (where all possible combinations of characters are attempted) and password guessing than other authentication methods, such as Challenge Handshake Authentication Protocol (CHAP).

EFS (Encrypting File System)

A subsystem of NT File System (NTFS) that uses public keys and private keys to provide encryption for files and folders on computers using Windows 2000. Only the user who initially encrypted the file and a data recovery agent (DRA) can decrypt encrypted files and folders.

emergency repair process

A process that helps you repair problems with system files, the startup environment (in a dual-boot or multiple-boot system), and the partition boot sector on a boot volume. Before you use the emergency repair process to repair a system, you must create an emergency repair disk (ERD). You can do this by using the Windows Backup utility. Even if you have not created an ERD, you can still try to use the emergency repair process; however, any changes you have made to the system—for example, service pack updates—may be lost and might need to be reinstalled. Also known simply as the repair process.

ERD (emergency repair disk)

A disk created by the Windows Backup utility that contains information about the current Windows system settings. You can use this disk to attempt to repair a computer if it will not start or if the system files are damaged or erased.

Fax Service Management console

A Microsoft Management Console (MMC) snap-in that allows you to administer the settings for sending and receiving faxes by using the Fax service.

FAT (file allocation table)

Also known as FAT16, a 16-bit table that many operating systems use to locate files on disk. The FAT keeps track of all the pieces of a file. The FAT file system for older

versions of Windows 95 is called virtual file allocation table (VFAT); the one for Windows 95 (OEM Service Release [OSR] 2) and Windows 98 is called FAT32. Windows 2000 can use the FAT file system; however, it is often not used on Windows 2000 and NT machines (which use NT File System [NTFS]) because of its larger cluster sizes and inability to scale to larger volume sizes. The FAT file system has no local security.

FAT32

A 32-bit version of FAT that is available in Windows 95 OEM Service Release (OSR) 2 and Windows 98. FAT32 increases the number of bits used to address clusters and reduces the size of each cluster. The result is that FAT32 can support larger disks (up to 2TB) and better storage efficiency (less slack space) than the earlier version of FAT. The FAT32 file system has no local security. Windows 2000 can use and format partitions as FAT, FAT32, or NT File System (NTFS).

fault tolerance

The capability of a computer or an operating system to ensure data integrity when hardware failures occur. Within the Windows 2000 Server product line and within the Windows Server 2003 product line, mirrored volumes and Redundant Array of Independent Disks (RAID)-5 volumes are fault tolerant.

FireWire

Also known as Institute of Electrical and Electronics Engineers (IEEE) 1394, a relatively new, very fast external bus standard that supports data transfer rates of up to 400Mbps. Products that support the IEEE 1394 standard have different names, depending on the company. Apple originally developed the technology and uses the trademarked name FireWire. Other companies use other names, such as i.link and Lynx, to describe their 1394 products. You can use a single 1394 port to connect up to 63 external devices. In addition to its high speed, 1394 supports time-dependent data, delivering data at a guaranteed rate. This makes it ideal for devices, such as video devices, that need to transfer high levels of data in real-time. Although it is extremely fast and flexible, 1394 is expensive. Like universal serial bus (USB), 1394 supports both Plug and Play and hot plugging, and it provides power to peripheral devices. The main difference between 1394 and USB is that 1394 supports faster data transfer rates and is more expensive. For these reasons, it is used mostly for devices that require large throughputs, such as video cameras, whereas USB is used to connect most other peripheral devices.

forward lookup

In Domain Name System (DNS), a query process in which the friendly DNS domain name of a host computer is searched to find its Internet Protocol (IP) address.

forward lookup zone

A Domain Name System (DNS) zone that provides host name–to–Transmission Control Protocol/Internet Protocol (TCP/IP) address resolution. In DNS Manager, forward lookup zones are based on DNS domain names and typically hold host (A) address resource records.

Frame Relay PVC (permanent virtual circuit)

A protocol in which messages are divided into packets before they are sent. Each packet is then transmitted individually, and the packets can even follow different routes to their destinations. When all the packets that form a message arrive at the destination, they are recompiled into the original message. Several wide area network (WAN) protocols, including Frame Relay, are based on packet-switching technologies. Ordinary telephone service is based on circuit-switching technology, in which a dedicated line is allocated for transmission between two parties. Circuit switching is best suited for data that must be transmitted quickly and must arrive in the same order in which it is sent. Most real-time data, such as live audio and video, requires circuit-switching technology. Packet switching is more efficient and robust for data that can withstand some delays (latency) in transmission, such as email messages and Web content.

global group

A group that can be granted rights and permissions and can become a member of local groups in its own domain and trusting domains. However, a global group can contain user accounts from its own domain only. Global groups provide a way to create sets of users from inside the domain that are available for use both in and out of the domain.

GPE (Group Policy Editor)

A Windows 2000 snap-in that allows customers to create custom profiles for groups of users and computers.

GPO (group policy object)

An object that is created by the Group Policy Editor (GPE) snap-in to hold information about a specific group's association with selected directory objects, such as sites, domains, or organizational units (OUs).

group policy

A mechanism for managing change and configuration of systems, security, applications, and user environments in an Active Directory domain.

HAL (Hardware Abstraction Layer)

A component of an operating system that functions something like an application programming interface (API). In strict technical architecture, HALs reside at the device level, a layer below the standard API level. HAL allows programmers to write applications and game titles with all the device-independent advantages of writing to an API, but without the large processing overhead that APIs normally demand.

hardware profile

A profile that stores configuration settings for a collection of devices and services. Windows 2000 can store different hardware profiles so that users' needs can be met even though their computer may frequently require different device and service settings, depending on circumstances. The best example is a laptop or portable computer used in an office while in a docking station and then undocked so that the user can travel with it. The two environments require different power-management settings, possibly different network settings, and various other configuration changes.

hibernation

A power option in Windows 2000 Professional portable computers that helps to conserve battery power. Hibernation is a complete power-down while maintaining the state of open programs and connected hardware. When you bring the computer out of hibernation, the desktop is restored exactly as you left it, in less time than it takes for a complete system restart. However, it does take longer to bring the computer out of hibernation than out of standby. It's a good idea to put a computer in hibernation when you will be away from the computer for an extended time or overnight.

HMAC (Hash Message Authentication Code) MD5 (Message Digest 5)

A hash algorithm that produces a 128-bit hash of the authenticated payload.

hidden share

A shared folder that has a dollar sign ($) appended to its share names, such as admin$, c$, and d$. Windows 2000 creates certain hidden shares by default. Administrators can create their own hidden shares. Hidden shares do not show up in the network browse list.

home directory

A location for a user or group of users to store files on a network server. The home directory provides a central location for files that users can access and back up.

HOSTS file

A local text file in the same format as the 4.3 Berkeley Software Distribution (BSD) Unix /etc/hosts file. This file maps hostnames to Internet Protocol (IP) addresses. In Windows 2000, this file is stored in the \%SystemRoot%\System32\Drivers\ Etc folder.

IEEE (Institute of Electrical and Electronics Engineers) 1394

See *FireWire*.

ICS (Internet Connection Sharing)

A feature that is intended for use in a small office or home office in which the network configuration and the Internet connection are managed by the computer running Windows 2000 where the shared connection resides. ICS can use a dial-up connection, such as a modem or an Integrated Services Digital Network (ISDN) connection to the Internet, or it can use a dedicated connection such as a cable modem or Digital Subscriber Line (DSL) connection. It is assumed that the ICS computer is the only Internet connection—the only gateway to the Internet—and that it sets up all internal network addresses.

incremental backup

A backup that backs up only files created or changed since the last normal or incremental backup. It marks files as having been backed up (in other words, the archive attribute is cleared). If you use a combination of normal and incremental backups, you need to have the last normal backup set as well as all incremental backup sets in order to restore data.

input locale
The specification of the language in which you want to type.

integrated zone storage
Storage of zone information in an Active Directory database rather than in a text file.

I/O (input/output) port
Any socket in the back, front, or side of a computer that you use to connect to another piece of hardware.

IP (Internet Protocol)
One of the protocols of the Transmission Control Protocol/Internet Protocol (TCP/IP) suite. IP is responsible for determining whether a packet is for the local network or a remote network. If the packet is for a remote network, IP finds a route for it.

IP (Internet Protocol) address
A 32-bit binary address that is used to identify a host's network and host ID. The network portion can contain either a network ID or a network ID and a subnet ID.

ipconfig
A command that allows you to view, renegotiate, and configure Internet Protocol (IP) address information for a Windows NT or 2000 computer.

IPP (Internet Printing Protocol)
A standard that allows network clients the option of entering a uniform resource locator (URL) to connect to network printers and manage their network print jobs, using a Hypertext Transfer Protocol (HTTP) connection in a Web browser. In Windows 2000 IPP is fully supported. The print server is either a Windows 2000 server running Internet Information Services (IIS) 5 or a Windows 2000 Professional system running Personal Web Server (PWS). PWS is the "junior" version of IIS. All shared IPP printers can be viewed at `http://servername/ printers` (for example, `http:// Server2/printers`).

IPSec (Internet Protocol Security)
A Transmission Control Protocol/Internet Protocol (TCP/IP) security mechanism that provides machine-level authentication, as well as data encryption, for virtual private network (VPN) connections that use Layer 2 Tunneling Protocol (L2TP). IPSec negotiates between a computer and its remote tunnel server before an L2TP connection is established, which secures both passwords and data.

IrDA (Infrared Data Association) device

A device that exchanges data over infrared waves. Infrared technology lets devices "beam" information to each other in the same way that a remote control tells a TV to change the channel. You could, for example, beam a document to a printer or another computer instead of having to connect a cable. The IrDA standard has been widely adopted by PC and consumer electronics manufacturers. Windows 2000 supports the IrDA standard.

IRQ (Interrupt Request)

A hardware line over which a device or devices can send interrupt signals to the microprocessor. When you add a new device to a PC, you sometimes need to set its IRQ number. IRQ conflicts used to be a common problem when you were adding expansion boards, but the Plug and Play and Advanced Configuration and Power Interface (ACPI) specifications have helped to remove this headache in many cases.

ISDN (Integrated Services Digital Network)

An international communications standard for sending voice, video, and data over digital telephone lines or normal telephone wires. ISDN supports data transfer rates of 64Kbps. Most ISDN lines offered by telephone companies provide two lines at once, called B channels. You can use one line for voice and the other for data, or you can use both lines for data, giving you data rates of 128Kbps.

Kerberos version 5

A distributed authentication and privacy protocol that protects information on a network between devices and enables single sign-on (SSO). Kerberos version 5 is used in the Windows 2000 security model.

L2TP (Layer 2 Tunneling Protocol)

An industry-standard Internet tunneling protocol that provides the same functionality as Point-to-Point Tunneling Protocol (PPTP). Unlike PPTP, L2TP does not require Internet Protocol (IP) connectivity between the client workstation and the server. L2TP requires only that the tunnel medium provide packet-oriented point-to-point connectivity. You can use L2TP over media such as Asynchronous Transfer Mode (ATM), Frame Relay, and X.25.

language group

A Regional Options configuration that allows you to type and read documents composed in languages of that group (for example, Western Europe and United States, Japanese, and Hebrew).

Last Known Good Configuration

A setting that starts Windows 2000 by using the registry information that Windows saved at the last shutdown. You should use this setting only in cases when you have incorrectly configured a device or driver. Last Known Good Configuration does not solve problems caused by corrupted or missing drivers or files. Also, when you use this setting, you lose any changes made since the last successful startup.

local group

A group account that is stored in the Security Accounts Manager (SAM) of a single system. You can give a local group access to resources only on that system.

local user

A user account that is stored in the Security Accounts Manager (SAM) of a single system. A local user can belong only to local groups on the same system and can be given access to resources only on that system.

logical drive

A simple volume or partition indicated by a drive letter that resides on a Windows 2000 basic disk.

logon script

A file that you can assign to one or more user accounts. Typically a batch file, a logon script runs automatically every time the user logs on. You can use it to configure a user's working environment at every logon, and it allows an administrator to influence a user's environment without managing all aspects of it.

makeboot.exe or makebt32.exe

The command that you use to create a set of four setup boot disks for Windows 2000. You use `makeboot.exe` on 16-bit operating systems and `makebt32.exe` on 32-bit operating systems. To create the setup disks, you need four 3.5-inch floppy disks, which are formatted before they are created.

mirrored volume

A fault-tolerant set of two physical disks that contain an exact replica of each other's data within the mirrored portion of each disk. Mirrored volumes are supported only on Windows 2000 Server versions.

mixed-mode domain

A migration concept that provides maximum backward compatibility with earlier versions of Windows NT. In mixed-mode domain, domain controllers that have been upgraded to Active Directory services allow servers running Windows NT versions 4 and earlier to exist within the domain.

MMC (Microsoft Management Console)

A set of Windows 2000 utilities that allow authorized administrators to manage the directory remotely. The MMC provides a framework for hosting administrative tools, called consoles.

mounted drive

A pointer from one partition to another. Mounted drives are useful for increasing a drive's size without disturbing it. For example, you could create a mount point to drive E: as C:\CompanyData. Doing so makes it seem that you have increased the size available on the c: partition, specifically allowing you to store more data in C:\CompanyData than you would otherwise be able to. Also known as a mount point or a mounted volume.

MPEG (Moving Picture Experts Group)

A family of digital video compression standards and file formats. MPEG generally produces better-quality video than competing formats. MPEG files can be decoded by special hardware or by software. MPEG achieves a high compression rate by storing only the changes from one frame to another, instead of storing each entire frame. There are two major MPEG standards: MPEG-1 and MPEG-2. The MPEG-1 standard provides a video resolution of 352×240 at 30 frames per second (fps), which is video quality slightly below that of conventional VCR tapes. A newer standard, MPEG-2, offers resolutions of 720×480 and 1,280×720 at 60fps, with full CD-quality audio. This is sufficient for all the major TV standards, including National Television Standards Committee (NTSC) and even high-definition television (HDTV).

DVD-ROMs use MPEG-2. MPEG-2 can compress a two-hour video into a few gigabytes. Currently, work is being done on a new version of MPEG called MPEG-4 (there is no MPEG-3), which will be based on the QuickTime file format.

MPS (Multiple Processor Support) compliant

Compatible with Windows 2000 symmetric multiprocessing (SMP). Windows 2000 provides support for single or multiple CPUs. If you originally installed Windows 2000 on a computer with a single CPU, you must update the Hardware Abstraction Layer (HAL) on the computer so that it can recognize and use multiple CPUs. Windows 2000 Professional supports a maximum of two processors.

MS-CHAP (Microsoft Challenge Handshake Authentication Protocol)

A special version of Challenge Handshake Authentication Protocol (CHAP) that Microsoft uses. The encryption in MS-CHAP is two-way and consists of a challenge from the server to the client that is made up of a session ID. The client uses a Message Digest 4 (MD4) hash to return the username to the server.

Multilink

An extension to Point-to-Point Protocol (PPP) that allows you to combine multiple physical connections between two points into a single logical connection. For example, you can combine two 33.6Kbps modems into one logical 67.2Kbps connection. The combined connections, called *bundles*, provide greater bandwidth than a single connection.

name resolution

The process of mapping a computer name—either a fully qualified domain name (FQDN) or a NetBIOS name—to an Internet Protocol (IP) address.

namespace

The hierarchical structure of objects in a group of cooperating directories or databases.

native-mode domain

A migration concept in which all domain controllers are running Windows 2000. A native-mode domain uses only Active Directory services multimaster replication between domain controllers, and no Windows NT domain controllers can participate in the domain through single-master replication.

network directory

A file or database where users or applications can get reference information about objects on the network.

NIC (network interface card)

A piece of computer hardware that physically connects a computer to a network cable. Also known as a network adapter or an adapter card.

normal backup

A backup that copies all files and marks those files as having been backed up (in other words, clears the archive attribute). A normal backup is the most complete form of backup.

NTFS (NT File System) 5

An advanced file system that is designed for use specifically within the Windows 2000 operating system. It supports file system recovery, extremely large storage media, and long filenames.

NTFS (NT File System) compression

The process of making individual files and folders occupy less disk space with the NTFS version 5.0 file system in Windows 2000. Compressed files can be read and written to over a network by any Windows- or DOS-based program without having to be decompressed first. Files decompress when opened and recompress when closed. The NTFS 5 file system handles this entire process. Compression is simply a file attribute that you can apply to any file or folder stored on an NTFS 5 drive volume.

NTFS (NT File System) permission

A rule associated with a folder, file, or printer that regulates which users can gain access to the object and in what manner. The object's owner allows or denies permissions. The most restrictive permissions take precedence if conflicting permissions exist between share permissions and NTFS permissions on an object.

object

In the context of performance monitoring and optimization, a system component that has numerous counters associated with it. For example, objects include processor, memory, system, logical disk, and paging file objects.

offline files

A new feature in Windows 2000 that allows users to continue to work with network files and programs even when they are not connected to the network. When a network connection is restored or when users dock their mobile computers, any changes that were made while users were working offline are updated to the network. When more than one user on the network has made changes to the same file, users are given the option of saving their specific version of the file to the network, keeping the other version, or saving both. Also known as *client-side caching* (*CSC*).

optimization

The process of tuning performance for a particular system component.

OSI (Open Systems Interconnect) model

A layer architecture developed by the International Organization for Standardization (ISO) that standardizes levels of service and types of interaction for computers that are exchanging information through a communications network. The OSI model separates computer-to-computer communications into seven layers, or levels, each of which builds on the standards contained in the levels below it.

OU (organizational unit)

A type of container object that is used within the Lightweight Directory Access Protocol (LDAP)/X.500 information model to group other objects and classes together for easier administration.

pagefile

See *paging file*.

paging file

A system file that is an extension of random access memory that is stored on the disk drive as a kind of virtual memory. Also called a pagefile. Under Windows 9x, a paging file is referred to as a *swap file* or *virtual memory file*.

PAP (Password Authentication Protocol)

A protocol that allows clear-text authentication.

partition

The information area that begins at a branch of a directory tree and continues to the bottom of that tree and/or to the edges of new partitions controlled by subordinate Directory System Agents (DSAs).

PC card

See *PCMCIA (Personal Computer Memory Card International Association)*.

PCI (Peripheral Component Interconnect)

A local bus standard developed by Intel. Most modern PCs include a PCI bus in addition to a more general Industry Standard Architecture (ISA) expansion bus. Many analysts believe that PCI will eventually replace ISA entirely. PCI is a 64-bit bus, although it is usually implemented as a 32-bit bus. It can run at clock speeds of 33MHz or 66MHz. Although Intel developed it, PCI is not tied to any particular family of microprocessors.

PCMCIA (Personal Computer Memory Card International Association)

An organization of some 500 companies that developed a standard for small, credit card–sized devices called PC cards. Originally designed for adding memory to portable computers, the PCMCIA standard has been expanded several times and is suitable for many types of devices. There are in fact three types of PCMCIA cards, along with three types of PC slots the cards fit into: Type I, II, and III. Also known as *PC card*.

PDC (primary domain controller)

In a Windows NT Server 4 or earlier domain, the computer running Windows NT Server that authenticates domain logons and maintains the directory database for a domain. The PDC tracks changes made to accounts of all computers on a domain. It is the only computer to receive these changes directly. A domain has only one PDC.

ping (packet internet groper) utility

A utility that determines whether a specific Internet Protocol (IP) address for a network device is reachable from an individual computer. ping works by sending a data packet to the specified address and waiting for a reply. You can use ping to troubleshoot network connections in the Transmission Control Protocol/Internet Protocol (TCP/IP) network protocol.

Plug and Play

A standard developed by Microsoft, Intel, and other industry leaders to simplify the process of adding hardware to PCs by having the operating system automatically detect devices. The intent of the standard is to conceal unpleasant details, such as Interrupt Requests (IRQs) and Direct Memory Access (DMA) channels, from people who want to add new hardware devices to their systems. A Plug and Play monitor, for example, can communicate with both Windows 2000 and the graphics adapter to automatically set itself at the maximum refresh rate supported for a chosen resolution. Plug and Play compliance also ensures that devices will not be driven beyond their capabilities.

policy

A configuration or setting that is specified for one or more systems or users. Policies are refreshed at startup, logon, and after a refresh interval, so if a setting is manually changed, the policy refreshes the setting automatically. Policies provide for centralized management of change and configuration.

PPP (Point-to-Point Protocol)

A method of connecting a computer to a network or to the Internet. PPP is more stable than the older Serial Line Internet Protocol (SLIP) and provides error-checking features. Windows 2000 Professional is a PPP client when dialing in to any network.

PPTP (Point-to-Point Tunneling Protocol)

A communication protocol that tunnels through another connection, encapsulating PPP packets. The encapsulated packets are Internet Protocol (IP) datagrams that can be transmitted over IP-based networks, such as the Internet.

primary master

An authoritative Domain Name System (DNS) server for a zone that you can use as a point of update for the zone. Only primary masters can be updated directly to process zone updates, which include adding, removing, and modifying resource records that are stored as zone data. Primary masters are also used as the first sources for replicating the zone to other DNS servers.

primary monitor

The monitor designated as the one that displays the logon dialog box when you start a computer. Most programs display their window on the primary monitor when you first open them. A Windows 2000 computer can support multiple monitors, or displays.

privilege

The capability to perform a system behavior, such as changing the system time, backing up or restoring files, or formatting the hard drive. A privilege used to be, and often still is, referred to as a user right.

public key cryptography

An asymmetric encryption scheme that uses a pair of keys to code data. The public key encrypts data, and a corresponding secret key decrypts it. For digital signatures, the sender uses the private key to create a unique electronic number that can be read by anyone who has the corresponding public key, thus verifying that the message is truly from the sender.

RADIUS (Remote Authentication Dial-in User Service)

A protocol used by Internet Authentication Services (IAS) to enable the communication of authentication, authorization, and accounting to the homogeneous and heterogeneous dial-up or virtual private network (VPN) equipment in the enterprise.

RAID (Redundant Array of Independent Disks)-5 volume

A fault-tolerant collection of equal-sized partitions on at least three physical disks, in which the data is striped and includes parity data. The parity data is used to help recover a member of the striped set if the member fails. Windows 2000 Professional cannot host a RAID-5 volume, but Windows 2000 Server versions can. Also known as a *striped set with parity volume.*

Recovery Console

A command-line interface (CLI) that provides a limited set of administrative commands that are useful for repairing a computer. For example, you can use the Recovery Console to start and stop services, read and write data on a local drive (including drives formatted to use NT File System [NTFS]), repair a master boot record (MBR), and format drives. You can start the Recovery Console from the Windows 2000 Setup disks or by using the winnt32.exe command with the /cmdcons switch.

reverse lookup zone

A Domain Name System (DNS) zone that provides Transmission Control Protocol/Internet Protocol (TCP/IP) address-to-hostname resolution.

RIS (Remote Installation Service)

A server that provides Windows 2000 Professional operating system images that can be downloaded and installed by network clients using network adapters that comply with the pre-boot execution environment (PXE) boot read-only memory (ROM) specifications. RIS requires Active Directory, Dynamic Host Configuration Protocol (DHCP), and Domain Name System (DNS) to serve clients.

route

A Windows 2000 command-line utility that manipulates Transmission Control Protocol/Internet Protocol (TCP/IP) routing tables for the local computer.

SACL (system access control list)

An access control list that specifies the security events to be audited for a user or group.

Safe Mode startup options

The options you get at startup when you press the F8 function key while in Safe Mode. Safe Mode helps you diagnose problems. When started in Safe Mode, Windows 2000 uses only basic files and drivers (mouse, monitor, keyboard, mass storage, base video, and default system services, but no network connections). You can choose the Safe Mode with Networking option, which loads all the above files and drivers plus the essential services and drivers to start networking. Or you can choose the Safe Mode with Command Prompt option, which is exactly the same as Safe Mode except that a command prompt is started instead of Windows 2000. You can also choose Last Known Good Configuration, which starts the computer by using the registry information that Windows 2000 saved at the last shutdown. If a symptom does not reappear when you start in Safe Mode, you can eliminate the default settings and minimum device drivers as possible causes. If a newly added device or a changed driver is causing problems, you can use Safe Mode to remove the device or reverse the change. In some circumstances, such as when Windows system files required to start the system are corrupted or damaged, Safe Mode cannot help you. In such a case, an emergency repair disk (ERD) may be of use.

SAM (Security Accounts Manager)

The database of local user and local group accounts on a Windows 2000 member server or Windows 2000 Professional system.

sampling interval

The frequency with which a performance counter is logged. A shorter interval provides more detailed information but generates a larger log. Also known as the update interval.

scalability

A measure of how well a computer, a service, or an application can grow to meet increasing performance demands.

Scheduled Tasks

A system folder that stores scheduled jobs that run at predefined times. Administrators can create scheduled jobs.

Scheduled Tasks Wizard

A series of dialog boxes that simplifies the process of creating scheduled task jobs.

Setup Manager

A program that ships on the Windows 2000 Professional CD-ROM that is used to create answer files for Windows 2000 unattended installations. Setup Manager can create answer files for unattended, `sysprep`, or RIS installations.

shared folder
A folder that is shared for use by remote users over a network.

share permission
A rule that is associated with a folder to regulate which users can gain access to the object over the network and in what manner.

SID (security identifier)
A unique number that represents a security principal such as a user or group. You can change the name of a user or group account without affecting the account's permissions and privileges because the SID is what is granted user rights and resource access.

simple volume
In Windows 2000, the disk space on a single physical disk. A simple volume can consist of a single area on a disk or multiple areas on the same disk that are linked together. You can extend a simple volume within the same disk or among multiple disks. If you extend a simple volume across multiple disks, it becomes a spanned volume.

SLIP (Serial Line Internet Protocol)
An older remote access communication protocol that is used in Windows 2000 for outbound communication only. SLIP is commonly used for connecting to Unix servers.

slipstreaming
The process of integrating a Windows 2000 service pack (SP) into an existing Windows 2000 installation share. Subsequent installations of Windows 2000 then include the SP that you have slipstreamed into the installation share.

smart card
A credit card–sized device that is used to securely store public and private keys, passwords, and other types of personal information. To use a smart card, you need a smart card reader attached to the computer and a personal identification number (PIN) for the smart card. In Windows 2000 you can use smart cards to enable certificate-based authentication and single sign-on (SSO) to the enterprise.

smart card reader
A small external or internal device, or even a built-in slot, into which you insert a smart card so that it can be read.

SMP (symmetric multiprocessing)

A computer architecture that provides fast performance by making multiple CPUs available to complete individual processes simultaneously (that is, multiprocessing). Unlike with asymmetric processing, with SMP you can assign any idle processor any task as well as add additional CPUs to improve performance and handle increased loads. A variety of specialized operating systems and hardware arrangements support SMP. Specific applications can benefit from SMP if their code allows multithreading. SMP uses a single operating system and shares common memory and disk input/output (I/O) resources. Windows 2000 supports SMP.

spanned volume

In Windows 2000, the disk space on more than one physical disk. You can add more space to a spanned volume by extending it at any time. In NT 4 and earlier operating systems, a spanned volume is called a volume set.

SPAP (Shiva Password Authentication Protocol)

A protocol that third-party clients and server typically use. The encryption for SPAP is two-way, but it is not as good as that for Challenge Handshake Authentication Protocol (CHAP).

spooler service

The primary Windows 2000 service that controls printing functionality.

SRV (service) record

A resource record that is used in a zone to register and locate well-known Transmission Control Protocol/Internet Protocol (TCP/IP) services. The SRV resource record is specified in Request for Comments (RFC) 2052 and is used in Windows 2000 or later to locate domain controllers for Active Directory service.

standard zone storage

Storage of zone information in a text file rather than in an Active Directory database.

standby mode

A power-saving option in Windows 2000 in which a computer switches to a low-power state where devices, such as the monitor and hard disks, turn off and the computer uses less power. When you want to use the computer again, it comes out of standby quickly, and the desktop is restored exactly as you left it. Standby is useful for conserving battery power in portable computers. Standby does not save the desktop state to disk; if you experience a power failure while in standby mode, you can lose unsaved information. If there is an interruption in power, information in memory is lost.

static pool

A range of Internet Protocol (IP) addresses configured on the remote access server that allows the server to allocate IP addresses to the remote access clients.

striped volume

A volume that stores data in stripes on two or more physical disks. Data in a striped volume is allocated alternately and evenly (in stripes) to the disks of the striped volume. Striped volumes are not fault tolerant. Striped volumes can substantially improve the speed of access to the data on disk. You can create them on both Windows 2000 Professional and Server machines. Striped volumes with parity, also known as RAID-5 volumes, can be created only on Windows 2000 Server machines. In Windows NT 4 and earlier, a striped volume is called a striped set.

subnet mask

A filter that is used to determine which network segment, or subnet, an Internet Protocol (IP) address belongs to. An IP address has two components: the network address and the host (computer name) address. For example, if the IP address 209.15.17.8 is part of a Class C network; the first three numbers (209.15.17) represent the Class C network address, and the last number (8) identifies a specific host (computer) on that network.

By implementing subnetting, network administrators can further divide the host part of the address into two or more subnets.

suspend mode

A deep-sleep power-saving option that does use some power.

sysprep

A tool that prepares a Windows 2000 computer to be imaged by using third-party disk image software. It does this by removing unique identifiers such as computer name and security identifiers (SIDs). sysprep adds to the image a service that generates a unique local domain SID after the image has been applied.

system state

In the Windows Backup utility, a collection of system-specific data that you can back up and restore. For all Windows 2000 operating systems, the system state data includes the registry, the Component Object Model (COM)+ Class Registration database, and the system boot files. For Windows 2000 Server, the system state data also includes the Certificate Services database (if the server is operating as a certificate server). If the server is a domain controller, the system state data also includes the Active Directory database and the sysvol directory.

sysvol

A shared directory that stores the server copy of the domain's public files, which are replicated among all domain controllers in the domain.

ticket

A feature of the Kerberos security model by which clients are granted access to objects and resources only indirectly, through services. Application servers use the service ticket to impersonate the client and look up its user or group security identifiers (SIDs).

tracert

A Windows 2000 command-line utility that follows that path of a data packet from a local computer to a host (computer) somewhere on the network (or internetwork). It shows how many hops the packet requires to reach the host and how long each hop takes. You can use tracert to figure out where the longest delays are occurring for connecting to various computers.

UDP (User Datagram Protocol)

A connectionless protocol that runs on top of Internet Protocol (IP) networks. Unlike Transmission Control Protocol/Internet Protocol (TCP/IP), UDP provides very few error-recovery services and does not guarantee delivery of data. UDP is a direct way to send and receive datagrams over an IP network. It's used primarily for sending broadcast messages over an IP network.

universal group

A security or distribution group that you can use anywhere in a domain tree or forest. A universal group can have members from any Windows 2000 domain in the domain tree or forest. It can also include other universal groups, global groups, and accounts from any domain in the domain tree or forest. Universal groups can be members of domain local groups and other universal groups but cannot be members of global groups. Universal groups appear in the global catalog and should contain primarily global groups.

update interval

See *sampling interval*.

USB (universal serial bus)

An external bus standard (released in 1996) that supports data transfer rates of 12Mbps. You can use a single USB port to connect up to 127 peripheral devices, such as mice, modems, and keyboards. USB also supports Plug and Play installation and hot plugging. It is expected to completely replace serial and parallel ports.

user locale

A group of settings that control the date, time, currency, and numbers on a per-user basis. These settings are used by all applications and can be configured via the Regional Options applet in the Control Panel.

user profile
A collection of desktop and environmental settings that define the work area of a local computer.

user right
See *privilege*.

video adapter
The electronic component that generates the video signal that is sent through a cable to a video display. The video adapter is usually located on the computer's main system board or on an expansion board.

VPN (virtual private network)
A private network of computers that is at least partially connected using public channels or lines, such as the Internet. A good example of a VPN is a private-office local area network (LAN) that allows users to log in remotely over the Internet (an open, public system). VPNs use encryption and secure protocols such as Point-to-Point Tunneling Protocol (PPTP) and Layer 2 Tunneling Protocol (L2TP) to ensure that unauthorized parties do not intercept data transmissions.

WDM (Windows or Win32 Driver Model)
A 32-bit layered architecture for device drivers that allows for drivers that Windows 2000, NT, and 98 can use. It provides common input/output (I/O) services that all operating systems understand. It also supports Plug and Play; universal serial bus (USB); Institute of Electrical and Electronics Engineers (IEEE) 1394; and various devices, including input, communication, imaging, and DVD.

Windows Backup
A Windows 2000 utility that helps you plan for and recover from data loss by allowing you to create backup copies of data as well as restore files, folders, and system state data (which includes the registry) manually or on a schedule. The Windows 2000 Backup program allows you to back up data to a variety of media types besides tape.

Windows Installer Service package
A file with the .msi extension that installs applications. Such files contain summary and installation instructions as well as the actual installation files. You can install Windows Installer Service packages locally or remotely through Windows 2000 group policies.

winnt32 /cmdcons
The command and switch used to install the Recovery Console on a Windows 2000 computer. This command uses winnt32 on the installation media or in the distribution source.

WINS (Windows Internet Name Service)
A service that dynamically maps NetBIOS names to Internet Protocol (IP) addresses.

WMI (Windows Management Instrumentation)

An initiative that is supported in Windows 2000 that establishes architecture to support the management of an enterprise across the Internet. WMI offers universal access to management information for enterprises by providing a consistent view of the managed environment. This management uniformity allows you to manage the entire business rather than just its components. You can obtain more detailed information regarding the WMI Software Development Kit (SDK) from the Microsoft Developer Network (MSDN).

workgroup

A peer-to-peer network in which user accounts are decentralized and stored on each individual system.

X.25 VC (virtual circuit)

A connection between two devices that acts as though it's a direct connection although the data packets on the connection may take different physical routes. X.25 connections involve at least two hosts in a packet-switching network. With X.25 VCs, two hosts can communicate as though they have a dedicated connection, although the data packets might actually travel very different routes before arriving at their destinations. VCs can be either permanent or temporary.

ZAP file

A file that you use to allow applications without an .msi file to be deployed via Windows 2000 Group Policy.

zone

In Domain Name System (DNS) standards, the namespace partition formed by each domain within the global namespace or within an enterprise namespace. Each zone is controlled by an authoritative DNS server, or in the case of Active Directory services, by a group of domain controllers.

zone transfer

Copying of Domain Name System (DNS) database information from one DNS server to another.

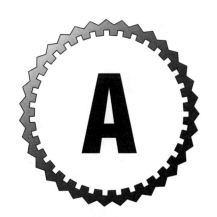

What's on the CD-ROM

This appendix is a brief rundown of what you'll find on the CD-ROM that comes with this book. For a more detailed description of the *PrepLogic Practice Tests, Preview Edition* exam simulation software, see Appendix B, "Using *PrepLogic Practice Tests, Preview Edition* Software." In addition to the *PrepLogic Practice Tests, Preview Edition*, the CD-ROM includes the electronic version of the book in Portable Document Format (PDF), several utility and application programs, and a complete listing of test objectives and where they are covered in the book. Finally, a pointer list to online pointers and references are added to this CD. You will need a computer with Internet access and a relatively recent browser installed to use this feature.

PrepLogic Practice Tests, Preview Edition

PrepLogic is a leading provider of certification training tools. Trusted by certification students worldwide, we believe PrepLogic is the best practice exam software available. In addition to providing a means of evaluating your knowledge of the Exam Cram material, *PrepLogic Practice Tests, Preview Edition* features several innovations that help you to improve your mastery of the subject matter.

For example, the practice tests allow you to check your score by exam area or domain to determine which topics you need to study more. Another feature allows you to obtain immediate feedback on your responses in the form of explanations for the correct and incorrect answers.

PrepLogic Practice Tests, Preview Edition exhibits most of the full functionality of the *Premium Edition* but offers only a fraction of the total questions. To get the complete set of practice questions and exam functionality, visit PrepLogic.com and order the *Premium Edition* for this and other challenging exam titles.

Again, for a more detailed description of the *PrepLogic Practice Tests, Preview Edition* features, see Appendix B.

Exclusive Electronic Version of Text

The CD-ROM also contains the electronic version of this book in Portable Document Format (PDF). The electronic version comes complete with all figures as they appear in the book. You will find that the search capabilities of the reader comes in handy for study and review purposes.

Easy Access to Online Pointers and References

The Suggested Reading section at the end of each chapter in this Exam Cram contains numerous pointers to Web sites, newsgroups, mailing lists, and other online resources. To make this material as easy to use as possible, we include all this information in an HTML document entitled "Online Pointers" on the CD. Open this document in your favorite Web browser to find links you can follow through any Internet connection to access these resources directly.

Using the *PrepLogic*
Practice Tests,
Preview Edition Software

This Exam Cram includes a special version of PrepLogic Practice Tests—a revolutionary test engine designed to give you the best in certification exam preparation. PrepLogic offers sample and practice exams for many of today's most in-demand and challenging technical certifications. This special *Preview Edition* is included with this book as a tool to use in assessing your knowledge of the Exam Cram material, while also providing you with the experience of taking an electronic exam.

This appendix describes in detail what *PrepLogic Practice Tests, Preview Edition* is, how it works, and what it can do to help you prepare for the exam. Note that although the *Preview Edition* includes all the test simulation functions of the complete, retail version, it contains only a single practice test. The *Premium Edition*, available at PrepLogic.com, contains the complete set of challenging practice exams designed to optimize your learning experience.

Exam Simulation

One of the main functions of *PrepLogic Practice Tests, Preview Edition* is exam simulation. To prepare you to take the actual vendor certification exam, PrepLogic is designed to offer the most effective exam simulation available.

Question Quality

The questions provided in the *PrepLogic Practice Tests, Preview Edition* are written to the highest standards of technical accuracy. The questions tap the content of the Exam Cram chapters and help you to review and assess your knowledge before you take the actual exam.

Interface Design

The *PrepLogic Practice Tests, Preview Edition* exam simulation interface provides you with the experience of taking an electronic exam. This enables you to effectively prepare yourself for taking the actual exam by making the test experience a familiar one. Using this test simulation can help to eliminate the sense of surprise or anxiety you might experience in the testing center because you will already be acquainted with computerized testing.

Effective Learning Environment

The *PrepLogic Practice Tests, Preview Edition* interface provides a learning environment that not only tests you through the computer, but also teaches the material you need to know to pass the certification exam. Each question comes with a detailed explanation of the correct answer and often provides reasons the other options are incorrect. This information helps to reinforce the knowledge you already have and also provides practical information you can use on the job.

Software Requirements

PrepLogic Practice Tests requires a computer with the following:

➤ Microsoft Windows 98, Windows Me, Windows NT 4.0, Windows 2000, or Windows XP

➤ A 166MHz or faster processor is recommended

➤ A minimum of 32MB of RAM

➤ As with any Windows application, the more memory, the better your performance

➤ 10MB of hard drive space

Installing *PrepLogic Practice Tests, Preview Edition*

Install *PrepLogic Practice Tests, Preview Edition* by running the setup program on the *PrepLogic Practice Tests, Preview Edition* CD. Follow these instructions to install the software on your computer:

1. Insert the CD into your CD-ROM drive. The Autorun feature of Windows should launch the software. If you have Autorun disabled, click the Start button and select Run. Go to the root directory of the CD and select setup.exe. Click Open, and then click OK.

2. The Installation Wizard copies the *PrepLogic Practice Tests, Preview Edition* files to your hard drive; adds *PrepLogic Practice Tests, Preview Edition* to your Desktop and Program menu; and installs test engine components to the appropriate system folders.

Removing *PrepLogic Practice Tests, Preview Edition* from Your Computer

If you elect to remove the *PrepLogic Practice Tests, Preview Edition* product from your computer, an uninstall process has been included to ensure that it is removed from your system safely and completely. Follow these instructions to remove PrepLogic Practice Tests, Preview Edition from your computer:

1. Select Start, Settings, Control Panel.

2. Double-click the Add/Remove Programs icon.

3. You are presented with a list of software currently installed on your computer. Select the appropriate *PrepLogic Practice Tests, Preview Edition* title you wish to remove. Click the Add/Remove button. The software is then removed from you computer.

Using *PrepLogic Practice Tests, Preview Edition*

PrepLogic is designed to be user friendly and intuitive. Because the software has a smooth learning curve, your time is maximized, as you will start practicing almost immediately. *PrepLogic Practice Tests, Preview Edition* has two major modes of study: Practice Test and Flash Review.

Using Practice Test mode, you can develop your test-taking abilities, as well as your knowledge through the use of the Show Answer option. While you are taking the test, you can reveal the answers along with a detailed explanation of why the given answers are right or wrong. This gives you the ability to better understand the material presented.

Flash Review is designed to reinforce exam topics rather than quiz you. In this mode, you will be shown a series of questions, but no answer choices. Instead, you will be given a button that reveals the correct answer to the question and a full explanation for that answer.

Starting a Practice Test Mode Session

Practice Test mode enables you to control the exam experience in ways that actual certification exams do not allow:

➤ **Enable Show Answer Button**—Activates the Show Answer button, allowing you to view the correct answer(s) and a full explanation for each question during the exam. When not enabled, you must wait until after your exam has been graded to view the correct answer(s) and explanation(s).

➤ **Enable Item Review Button**—Activates the Item Review button, allowing you to view your answer choices, marked questions, and facilitating navigation between questions.

➤ **Randomize Choices**—Randomize answer choices from one exam session to the next; makes memorizing question choices more difficult, therefore keeping questions fresh and challenging longer.

To begin studying in Practice Test mode, click the Practice Test radio button from the main exam customization screen. This will enable the options detailed above.

To your left, you are presented with the options of selecting the pre-configured Practice Test or creating your own Custom Test. The pre-configured test has a fixed time limit and number of questions. Custom Tests allow you to configure the time limit and the number of questions in your exam.

The *Preview Edition* included with this book includes a single pre-configured Practice Test. Get the compete set of challenging PrepLogic Practice Tests at PrepLogic.com and make certain you're ready for the big exam.

Click the Begin Exam button to begin your exam.

Starting a Flash Review Mode Session

Flash Review mode provides you with an easy way to reinforce topics covered in the practice questions. To begin studying in Flash Review mode, click the Flash Review radio button from the main exam customization screen. Select either the pre-configured Practice Test or create your own Custom Test.

Click the Best Exam button to begin your Flash Review of the exam questions.

Standard *PrepLogic Practice Tests, Preview Edition* Options

The following list describes the function of each of the buttons you see. Depending on the options, some of the buttons will be grayed out and inaccessible or missing completely. Buttons that are accessible are active. The buttons are as follows:

➤ **Exhibit**—This button is visible if an exhibit is provided to support the question. An exhibit is an image that provides supplemental information necessary to answer the question.

➤ **Item Review**—This button leaves the question window and opens the Item Review screen. From this screen you will see all questions, your answers, and your marked items. You will also see correct answers listed here when appropriate.

➤ **Show Answer**—This option displays the correct answer with an explanation of why it is correct. If you select this option, the current question is not scored.

➤ **Mark Item**—Check this box to tag a question you need to review further. You can view and navigate your Marked Items by clicking the Item Review button (if enabled). When grading your exam, you will be notified if you have marked items remaining.

➤ **Previous Item**—This option allows you to view the previous question.

➤ **Next Item**—This option allows you to view the next question.

➤ **Grade Exam**—When you have completed your exam, click this button to end your exam and view your detailed score report. If you have unanswered or marked items remaining you will be asked if you would like to continue taking your exam or view your exam report.

Time Remaining

If the test is timed, the time remaining is displayed on the upper right corner of the application screen. It counts down the minutes and seconds remaining to complete the test. If you run out of time, you will be asked if you want to continue taking the test or if you want to end your exam.

Your Examination Score Report

The Examination Score Report screen appears when the Practice Test mode ends—as the result of time expiration, completion of all questions, or your decision to terminate early.

This screen provides you with a graphical display of your test score with a breakdown of scores by topic domain. The graphical display at the top of the screen compares your overall score with the PrepLogic Exam Competency Score.

The PrepLogic Exam Competency Score reflects the level of subject competency required to pass this vendor's exam. While this score does not directly translate to a passing score, consistently matching or exceeding this score does suggest you possess the knowledge to pass the actual vendor exam.

Review Your Exam

From Your Score Report screen, you can review the exam that you just completed by clicking on the View Items button. Navigate through the items viewing the questions, your answers, the correct answers, and the explanations for those answers. You can return to your score report by clicking the View Items button.

Get More Exams

Each *PrepLogic Practice Tests, Preview Edition* that accompanies your Exam Cram contains a single PrepLogic Practice Test. Certification students worldwide trust PrepLogic Practice Tests to help them pass their IT certification exams the first time. Purchase the *Premium Edition* of PrepLogic Practice Tests and get the entire set of all new challenging Practice Tests for this exam. PrepLogic Practice Tests—Because You Want to Pass the First Time.

Contacting PrepLogic

If you would like to contact PrepLogic for any reason, including information about our extensive line of certification practice tests, we invite you to do so. Please contact us online at `http://www.preplogic.com`.

Customer Service

If you have a damaged product and need a replacement or refund, please call the following phone number:

800-858-7674

Product Suggestions and Comments

We value your input! Please email your suggestions and comments to the following address:

`feedback@preplogic.com`

License Agreement

YOU MUST AGREE TO THE TERMS AND CONDITIONS OUT-
LINED IN THE END USER LICENSE AGREEMENT ("EULA")
PRESENTED TO YOU DURING THE INSTALLATION PROCESS.
IF YOU DO NOT AGREE TO THESE TERMS DO NOT INSTALL
THE SOFTWARE.

Index

B

backing up data, 288
  backup strategies, 290
  backup types, 289
  configuring file and folder backups, 291
  permissions, 288-289
  user rights, 288-289
  Windows Backup, 288
backing up system state, 291-292
  configuring, 292
backup markers, 289
Backup Operators, 31
  local group accounts, 83
backup strategies, 290
Backup Wizard, 291
  scheduling backups, 292
backups
  configuring
    file and folder backups, 291
    with Scheduled Jobs tab, 292
  copy backups, 289
  daily backups, 290
  differential backups, 289
  incremental backups, 290
  normal backups, 289
  scheduling with Backup Wizard, 292
BACP (Bandwidth Allocation Control Protocol), 265
band allocations, viewing for USB host controllers, 198
Bandwidth Allocation Control Protocol (BACP), 265
BAP, authentication protocols, 265-266
baselines, creating, 305-306
basic disks, 218-219, 226
  converting from dynamic, 222
  logical drives, 224
  partitions, 224
  spanned volumes, 224
  striped volumes, 224
  upgrading to dynamic, 220-222
  versus dynamic disks, 219-220
basic permissions, NTFS, 37-38
basic volumes, 223
  spanned volumes on basic disks, 224
  striped volumes on basic disks, 224

batteries, mobile computer hardware, 206
behaviors, Unsigned Driver Installation, 187
binary numbers, 257
BIOS, USH controllers, 199
Boot Logging, 293-294
Bootdisk, 159
build-list-and-reorder questions, 7-8
built-in system groups, installed by default, 32

C

C$, 27
Cachemov.exe tool, 29
caching
  client-side caching, shared folders, 28-29
  files with certain extensions, 114
  offline files, 114
Caching Settings dialog box, 28
CACLS.exe, 36-37
cameras, 192-193
case studies, 4-5, 13
  strategies for taking, 16
CD-ROM installation, attended installation of Windows 2000 Professional, 159
CDFS (Compact Disc File System), 234
central processing unit (CPU), 207
certificates, enabling, 192
Challenge Handshake Authentication Protocol (CHAP), 192
Change Permissions, advanced NTFS permissions, 42
changes on the Web, 22
changing
  default security settings for system root folder, 43
  display settings on display devices, 200
  drive labels, 239
  drive letters, 237-238
  NTFS permissions, 40
  primary monitors, 201
  resource settings, 186
  security settings, 239
CHAP (Challenge Handshake Authentication Protocol), 192
choosing repair options during setup, 300

How can we make this index more useful? Email us at indexes@quepublishing.com

Multilink, configuring, 194-195
multilinking modems, 194-195
multimaster replication model, Active
Directory, 93
multiple processors, configuring, 207-208
multiple-answer multiple-choice questions,
5-7
multiple-choice questions, 5-7
multiple-device dialing, 194-195
multiple-display support, configuring,
200-201
My Documents, storing data, 112
My Network Places window, connecting to
shared network resources, 26

N

naming user accounts, 85
Narrator, 142
NAT (network address translation), 272
nbstat, diagnostic tools, 261
net use command, connecting to shared network resources, 26
netstat, diagnostic tools, 261
Network, built-in system groups, 32, 84
network address translation (NAT), 272
Network and Dial-up Connections, 194-195
Network Connection Wizard, 266-267
network installation, attended installation of
Windows 2000 Professional, 159
network interface cards (NICs), 199
network logon, 91
network performance, 309-310
network servers, configuring RIS, 167
network share permissions, 29-30
networks
connecting to printers, 63-65
via command line, 66
removing shares, 25
sharing folders, 24-25
NICs (network interface cards), 199
nodes, Disk Management node, 222
non-Plug and Play devices, installing,
183-184
normal backups, 289

NT File System (NTFS), 203
NTFS (NT File System), 30, 203
ACLs, 36-37
built-in system groups, installed
by default in Windows 2000
Professional, 32
compression, 44
for files, 44-45
for folders, 46
moving and copying compressed files
and folders, 47
controlling access with permissions, 48
converting from FAT partitions, 236
denying access to resources, 49-50
domains, 33
EFS (Encyrpting File System), 56-57
file compression, 240
guidelines for, 241
local accounts versus domain accounts,
33-34
local groups, installed by default in
Windows 2000 Professional, 31
logon processes, 34-35
master file table, 233
moving compressed files, 241
permissions
advanced permissions, 39-42
basic permissions, 37-38
changing, 40
conflicts, 43
controlling access to files and folders,
48
moving files and folders, 50-51
setting security permissions, 32-33
users and groups, 30-31
reapplying default permissions, 237
security permissions, 42
default security permissions, 42-43
optimizing access to files and folders,
50
setting, 32-33
uncompressing files, 45
workgroups, 33
NTFS 5, 235-236
NTFS permissions, 30
NTFS volume, roaming user profiles, 113

power scheme, 205
Power Users, 31
  local group accounts, 83
PPP (Point-to-Point protocol), 256
PPTP (Point-to-Point Tunneling protocol), 256
practice exams, 20-21
preboot execution (PXE), 166
preboot execution (PXE) ROM chip, 166
preferred DNS servers, 259
PrepLogic, 386
  contacting, 395
PrepLogic Exam Competency Score, 395
PrepLogic Practice Tests, 390
  exam simulation interface, 390
  Examination Score Report, 394
  Flash Remove mode, starting, 393
  Flash Review mode, 392
    buttons, 393
    options, 393
  Practice Test mode
    Enable Item Review Button, 393
    Enable Show Answer Button, 392
    Randomize Choices, 393
    starting, 392
    studying in, 393
    PrepLogic Exam Competency Score, 395
  question quality, 390
  removing from your computer, 391
  reviewing exams, 395
  software requirements, 391
  study modes, 392
PrepLogic Practice Tests, Preview Edition, 386
preventing files to wireless devices, 197
print devices, 62
print jobs, 63
  managing, 68-69
print queues, 63
print resolution, 63
print servers, 62
print spoolers, 63
printer drivers, 63
printer ports, 62
printers, 62, 188
  configuring properties, 66
    Advanced tab, 67-68
    Device Settings tab, 68

    General tab, 66
    Ports tab, 67
    Security tab, 68
    Sharing tab, 67
  connecting to local and network printers, 63-65
  IPP, 188
  managing, 68-69
  property settings, 189
  restarting Spooler service, 189
printing IPP, 69
priorities, Realtime, 311
privileges. *See* user rights
process performance, 310-311
processors, configuring multiple processors, 207-208
profiles
  local profiles, 110
  roaming user profiles, 110-112
    configuring, 112-113
  user profiles. *See* user profiles
properties. *See also* attributes
  configuring account properties, 86
  drive properties, viewing, 239
  modifying domain user account properties, 89
  printers. *See* printers, configuring properties
  WWW service master, 60
property settings, printers, 189
protecting local and roaming profiles, 113
protocols
  authentication protocols, 263
    BAP, 265-266
    EAP, 264-265
    IPSec, 263
    L2TP, 263-264
    RADIUS, 265
  BACP, 265
  CHAP, 192
  DHCP, 255
  FTP, 257
  IPP, 69
  IPP (Internet Printing Protocol), 188
  L2TP, 256
  PPP, 256
  PPTP, 256
  SLIP, 256

restoring
  data, 288. *See also* backing up data
  files, 293
  folders, 293
rexec, connectivity tools, 260
rights
  access control settings, 35
  user rights. *See* user rights
riprep.exe, 169-170
RIS (Remote Installation Service), 295
  automatic installation of Windows 2000, 166
  configuring
    clients, 166
    network servers, 167
  downloading images to clients, 170
  images
    creating, 169-170
    disk partitions, 167
  installing and configuring
    servers, 167-169
roaming user profiles, 110-112
  configuring, 112-113
  NTFS volume, 113
route, diagnostic tools, 261
rsh, connectivity tools, 260
running
  Error-Checking tool, 232
  Recovery Console on systems that will not start, 297

S

/s:sourcepath, 163
Safe mode, 293-294
Safe Mode with Command Prompt, 294
Safe Mode with Networking, 294
SAM (Security Accounts Manager), 81, 92
SBS (Small Business Server), 196
scaling, 207
scanners, 192-193
Scheduled Jobs tab, configuring backups, 292
Scheduled Task Wizard, 146
scheduling backups with Backup Wizard, 292
SDOU (site, domain or OU), 99

security
  authentication. *See* authentication
  NTFS. *See* NTFS
  passwords, 85, 91
Security Accounts Manager (SAM), 81, 92
Security Configuration and Analysis
  snap-in, 99
security dialog box, authentication, 91-92
security identifiers (SIDs), 87, 164
Security Options node, 98
security permissions, 50
  NTFS. *See* NTFS
security settings
  changing, 239
  changing system root default security settings, 43
Security tab, configuring printer properties, 68
select-and-place questions, 11-12
selecting user locales, 137
Send an Administrative Alert, 296
Send Fax Wizard, 143
sending faxes via Send Fax Wizard, 143
Serial Internet Line Protocol (SLIP), 256
SerialKey, 142
servers
  DHCP, 167
  distribution servers, 159
  domain controllers, 93
  network servers, configuring RIS, 167
  remote access servers, connecting to, 266-268
  RIS, installing and configuring, 167-169
service packs. *See* SPs
sets. *See* volumes
setup disks installation, attended installation of Windows 2000 Professional, 159
Setup Manager
  automatic installation of Windows 2000 Professional, 160-164
  extracting, 160
setupcl.exe, 165
setupmgr.exe, 161
share points, configuring for offline files, 113-114

How can we make this index more useful? Email us at indexes@quepublishing.com

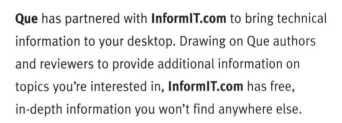